The Qur'ãnic Foundations and Structure of Muslim Society

The Qur'ãnic Foundations and Structure of Muslim Society

By

Dr. Muhammad Fazl-ur-Rahman Ansari

B. Th., M.A., Ph.D.

President

World Federation of Islamic Missions

Volume II

KITAB BHAVAN

NEW DELHI-110002

Kitab Bhavan
Publishers, Distributors, Exporters & Importers
1784, Kalan Mahal, Darya Ganj
New Delhi-110002 (India)

Phone : (91-11) 3277392/93, 3274686
Web Site: www.kitabbhavan.com
E-mail : nasri@vsnl.com
Fax : (91-11) 3263383

Edition ... 2002

ISBN : 81-7151-319-0
Book Code :

Laser Typesetting at:
Laser Track
Darya Ganj, New Delhi-2

Published in India by:
Nusrat Ali Nasri for Kitab Bhavan
1784, Kalan Mahal, Darya Ganj
New Delhi-110002 [India]

Printed in India at:
Nice Printing Press
Khureji Khas, Delhi-110051

CONTENTS

Volume II

Preamble

Book I
DUTIES TO SELF

Part I. Duties as Spiritual Being

Part II. Duties as Physical Being

Part III. Duties as Rational Being

Part IV. Duties as Aesthetical Being

Part V. Duties as Moral Being

Book II
DUTIES TO OTHER INDIVIDUALS

Part I. Fundamental Duties Towards All Human Beings

Part II. Duties of Condition Towards Other Individuals

Part III. The Penal Code

PREAMBLE

Chapter I

THE MORAL CODE: WHY AND HOW?

Chapter II

CLASSIFICATION OF DUTIES

Chapter I

THE MORAL CODE: WHY AND HOW?

I. Need for a Comprehensive Code of Life

Human life moves under the impact of different types of conflicts. To start with: there exists a conflict between the individual's theoretical yearnings, and that to an extent that the fulfilment of one implies the frustration of another. For instance, in the field of Ethics, the yearning for Knowledge implies 'causality' and 'necessity', while the yearning for Morality affirms 'freedom'; and, in the domain of Metaphysics, the yearning for Knowledge demands the affirmation of the principles of 'unfolding' and 'immanence', while the yearning for Religion insists on accepting the validity of the principles of 'creation' and 'transcendence'. Secondly, there is the problem of the emergence of conflicts in the life of the individual at the instinctive level. For instance, the parental instinct which forces the parents to behave tenderly and affectionately towards the offspring stands in direct conflict with the instinct of self-assertion which requires the adoption of a stern attitude when the offspring commits an act of disobedience. Thirdly, the instinctive nature of the individual comes into conflict with his rational nature. Fourthly, the ideals embedded in the individual's rational nature may—and, in fact, do—come into conflict with one another. Fifthly, every individual is unique in respect of his or her past experiences and environmental factors, and this uniqueness becomes the breeding ground of conflicts between individual and individual. Then, beyond the individual level, existence of conflicts between the individual and the society is a fact of human life. Lastly, the narrow racial, territorial and ideological loyalties and economic interests of different communities and nations become sources of conflicts which threaten the very existence of humanity, as they are doing nowadays,—not to speak of the realisation of the spiritual and moral ideals.

In such a situation of manifold conflicts and of the dangers involved in respect of realisation of the highest human ideals, the question emerges in the mind of every thoughtful and conscientious person: "How ought I to behave to realise my ideals?" In other words: "What should be the Code for determining my conduct?"

The Holy Qur'ãn provides the answer to that all-important question by imparting sure[1] and complete[2] guidance in all the different problems of

1. XVI:9.

2. XVI:89.

human life, including the metaphysical and ethical problems with which philosophy deals, and a comprehensive and genuine Moral Code.

Viewing the problem of the need for a Code from another angle: It is the Code which imparts *uniform pattern of behaviour* and the *bond of community* to the group. It also creates optimistic outlook on life and forms the sure ground for progress. Because, if the individuals who constitute a group have a Code to govern their modes of behaviour, they will always have a genuine and firm basis for reciprocal social responses.[3] On the contrary, if a human group is devoid of a Code with social reference, as we find in respect of the Christian and the Greek pagan outlooks, the consequence shall be the emergence of a pessimistic view of life along with all its resultant evils.

II. Basis of Systematisation of the Qur'ãnic Moral Code—the Qur'ãnic Ideal

The effort to systematise the Moral Code has passed through several stages in the history of human thought. Among the ancients, it was Aristotle who gave a classification that is based on the main psychological aspects of human nature *viz.*, Knowing, Feeling and Willing. The highest virtue pertaining to Knowing is Wisdom, pertaining to Feeling is Temperance, and pertaining to Willing is Courage, while Justice governs them all. But the Greek mind does not seem to have developed its moral consciousness properly[4], and that because of the

---

3. It may be remarked here in passing that it is the radical conflict in outlooks because of which Islam does not permit marriage between a Believer and a *mushrikah* (pagan woman), while it allows marriage between a Believer and a *Kitãbiyah* (i.e., a woman professing faith in some revealed religion), because the *Kitãbiyah* has an avenue, however imperfect, through which an appeal can be made to her personality. (See: The Holy Qur'ãn, II:221; V:6).

4. Speaking of that period in the life of humanity as a whole, Illingworth observes: ".....as a rule it is beyond dispute that neither the *universality* nor the *unity* of personality, its two most important features were adequately understood...." (*Personality: Human and Divine*, p. 8).

Commenting on the deficiencies in Greek moral thought, D. M. Donaldson says: "As evidence of Aristotle's unwillingness to grant the benefits of his conception of personality universally we may instance the facts that he was ready to rule out some men on the ground that they were of barbarous origin, others because they were of slave origin, and women he regarded 'as nature's failures in the attempt to produce men.' That he was likewise unable to unify

fact that, as the historical account of Greek civilisation available today shows, it was pagan in character and possessed no proper conception of 'personality'; whereas morality is inseparably related to 'personality' and seems to have developed under the impact of the teachings of revealed religions and not otherwise[5].

Among the philosophers of the modern age, it is Kant who has made an important contribution. But his emphasis on the form of the Moral Law as the standard of morality and his attitude of leaving the contents of that Law to be traced from the established morality and the moral situation did not provide much lead in respect of the Moral Code, though the importance of his contribution to Moral Philosophy cannot be denied without injustice. Kant did furnish us with a classification of duties in order to complete his ethical system. But, the Code prescribed by him is through and through ideational and individualistic in character, because it does not attach importance to the duties of the moral agent towards the societal whole, nor is there any reference to the duties of the societal whole to its parts. This appears to be due to his limitation that he was born and lived in Christian environment,—the Christian point of view being that man's socio-cultural yearnings are inherently incompatible with his spirituo-moral yearnings.

What, then is the basis of systematisation of the Qur'ãnic Moral Code? Answer to this question necessitates the statement of the Qur'ãnic Ideal, which emerges in the following terms:

The Qur'ãn places equal emphasis on the sensate and the transcendental yearnings of man[6] and harmonises them; and thus it lays down for humanity a comprehensive Ideal, which consists in the cultivation of: (i) Holiness based on a dynamic, vibrant and living faith in

---

human nature is clear from his 'unsolved dualism between the soul and its organism', and from the fact that he had 'no clear conception of the will, and hardly any of the conscience'." (*Studies in Muslim Ethics*, p. 274).

5. *Cf.* The role of religions which claim to be revealed, i.e., Judaism, Christianity and Islam; as also of other and earlier religions of the world, including those of primitive peoples, in which the idea of personality with reference to the Supreme Being has found emphasis,—their monotheism providing the clue to their revealed origin. (*Ref.*: among other works, Wilhelm Schmidt's book, entitled: *Der Ursprung der Gottesidee*: *Eine historisch - Kritische und positive Studie.* 12 vols. Munster in Westfalen, Germany, 1912—1955).

6. *Cf.* Along with other references, the prayer taught by the Qur'ãn in II : 201.

God, an earnest and courageous pursuit of Truth, and an ever-present consciousness of Final Accountability; (ii) sound and comprehensive Morality; (iii) social, economic and political Justice; (iv) Knowledge in all its dimensions; and (v) Aesthetic Grace,—all of these resulting in the conquest of harmful propensities within the individual, the conquest of evil within the society, and the conquest of the physical environment, or, Nature. In the pursuit of this Ideal, Holiness, Love for Humanity, Truth, Justice, Beauty, Discipline and Progress are the watchwords, while the concept of Unity[7] permeates the entire movement towards the Ideal, and the motto of 'simple living, hard labour and high thinking' forms the wheel of progress.

7. *Ref:* Vol. I, Book I, Part IV, Chapter VI: "The Philosophy of Unity".

Chapter II

CLASSIFICATION OF DUTIES

I. Preliminary Observations

The function of the Code should be the realisation of the Ideal and the actualisation of the norms that it implies.

Before we proceed to the structural constituents of systematisation, however, it is necessary to establish the Qur'ãnic point of view with respect to the concepts of 'Duty' and 'Right'.

Duty and Right:

The Qur'ãnic moral code is based on the emphasis on 'obligation' or 'duty' in contrast to the emphasis on 'right' (v:44; etc.). Now, the implications of the emphasis respectively on duty and right are:

Right is a right *against* someone. Duty is a duty *towards* someone. Right means that someone else owes something to us. For, when we say: 'it is our right', it means that someone has to perform a duty to us. On the contrary, when we say: 'it is our duty', it means that someone has a right against us.

The emphasis on duty creates *harmony* in social life, because if everyone were to concentrate on his or her duty, the emphasis on grumbling for rights will naturally vanish. On the contrary, the emphasis on rights creates *strife*, because if everyone were to think about his rights on others, he would hardly have the mind to think of his duties towards others. The immense increase in quarrels and strifes between the different classes of human beings, as for instance, between labourers and capitalists, and between races and nations, which we find in the world today, is the direct outcome of the emphasis on rights. As regards the political life in different countries, the subjects or citizens clamour for their rights more than taking pains for fulfilling their duties towards their fellow-beings, the state and the country. Everyone tries thus to transfer blame to the shoulders of others, and the confusion gets worse confounded. This state of affairs will not improve unless the world adopts the Qur'ãnic emphasis on duty.

Then, the emphasis on duty creates *unity* among human beings, because it is built up on the idea and the sentiment of sympathy,— sympathy in the sense that in fulfilling our duty we have always to do some positive good to someone in the world. On the contrary, the emphasis on rights is conducive to disintegration and *disunity* among human beings, because it is based on the idea of demanding something from others. We all know that we feel happy when anyone *gives* something to us, and most people feel unhappy and miserably when anyone *demands* anything from them.

The Empire of Duties:

As to the classification of Duties: Since, according to the Holy Qur'ãn, man is not merely being but also a spiritual, physical, rational and aesthetical being, as we shall shortly see, the fulfilment of duties relating to all those aspects of the human personality is necessary for the realisation of the Qur'ãnic moral Ideal.

Now, since morality originates in the attitude that man takes towards personality in his own being or in the being of others, the moral duties should be classified basically as: (*i*) *Duties to Self,* and (*ii*) *Duties to Others*. And since the person who is nearest to the moral agent in his own person, Duties to Self should come first and the Duties to Others thereafter.

The question may now be raised: What is the relation between Duties to Self and Duties to Others?

If the problem is viewed in the light of the ideational cultural philosophy, the two duties remain unconnected; because the point of view there is individualistic. Their relationship can be affirmed only on the basis of the Qur'ãnic philosophy of idealistic, or integralistic, culture which is based on the synthesis of the ideational and the sensate, and which, consequently, stands for interdependent relationship between morality and social life. Thus moral perfection of the moral agent is conceived there with reference to the happiness of others, which, in its turn, is possible only in terms of social welfare.

II. Duties to Self

Human Personality and its Functions:

According to the Holy Qur'ãn, humanity emerged in Creation primarily in the transcendental dimension of existence:

"We (God) said: 'O Adam! dwell thou and thy wife in the Garden; and eat of the bountiful things therein as ye wish; but approach not this tree, or else ye run into harm and transgression." (II:35).[1]

1. That the "Garden" did not belong to the earth is borne out by the next verse which tells us unambiguously that the Divine decree in respect of "getting down" and "dwelling on the earth" was pronounced afterwards, i.e., after Adam's and Eve's Deception.

At that stage of existence itself, they possessed not only the spiritual but also the rational and the aesthetical dimensions of personality.

The spiritual dimension was there because of the very fact of the transcendental nature of their existence.

The existence of the rational dimension has been affirmed thus:

"And He (i.e., God) taught Adam the nature of all things." (II:31).

The existence of the aesthetical dimension is established in the very concept of the "Garden" where Adam and Eve lived in innocent enjoyment.

Subsequently they fell victim to the Devil's Deception. After that they appeared in the physical world, which is spatio-temporal, as physical and moral beings:

"Then Satan caused them both (i.e., Adam and Eve) to deflect therefrom and expelled them from that in which they had been. We (God) said: 'Get ye down *all* (i.e., let entire humanity commence its descent from the then transcendental stage towards the spatio-temporal, or, the physical, stage of existence[1]), with the spirit of clash between yourselves (that being the condition of all struggle, including the moral). On earth (where you will stay with physical qualities required for a physical environment) will be your dwelling place and provision for a time (i.e., for the duration of each individual's earthly sojourn)". (II:36).

Hence, the human personality and its functions are to be understood in the following terms:

1. The Real Human Personality is Spiritual in Nature

Besides the above reference (II:35), this fact is also corroborated by the following verse, which speaks, not only of the existence of all human beings—from the first to the last—at the dawn of Creation, but also of the possession of Consciousness—self-consciousness as well as consciousness of the Personality of God—and hence of personality, which is based and built up on conscious, appreciative and non-mechanical response to other personality or personalities:

"And recall what time (at the dawn of Creation and in the 'world of spirits') thy Lord took from the children of Adam[2] their

---

1. The emergence of individual human beings on the earth seems to have been designed to take place through a process of evolution covering countless stages of transformation and in the form of a series spread over a vast span of time, as different Qur'ãnic verses and the verdict of Muslim thinkers like Rumi affirms. (See: Iqbal's *Reconstruction of Religious Thought in Islam*, p. 115).
2. Adam and Eve have not been mentioned here, because they had already experienced intimate relation with God (II:31 ff).

posterity from their backs[3], and made them testify as to themselves, saying: 'Am I not your Lord?' They said: 'Yea we testify'[4]. (Thus was the Covenant of Monotheism inscribed on every human Soul). That was lest ye should say on the Day of Resurrection: verily of this we have been unaware." (VII:172).

Thus, because this event relates to the transcendental world and conditions of transcendental existence, the transcendental, or spiritual, nature of the original, *i.e.*, the real, human personality is thereby established.

This fact is further affirmed by the following verses:

"And they ask thee regarding the (human) Soul. Say thou: the Soul proceeds from my Lord's *Amr*, (or Command, Created by Him, like other things); and of knowledge ye have been vouchsafed but little. (Therefore, in spite of its intangibility, or non-physical character, do not doubt its reality)". (XVII:85).

"Surely there came over Man a period of Time when he was not a *thing that could be spoken of* (i.e., a thing tangible)". (LXXVI:1).

2. The earthly existence of every human being commences when the human Soul, whose original abode is the transcendental world, projects itself into spatio-temporal dimensions and takes on the physical form, even as the personalities of Adam and Eve were projected into the material world (II:36).[5]

The assumption, under the Command of God, of tangibility, *i.e.*, physical form and function, after passing through different stages of evolution, has been directly referred to thus:

"O Man! what hath made thee careless concerning thy Lord, the Bountiful?—Him Who created thee, then fashioned thee in due proportion, then wrought thee in symmetry: (then) into whatever *form* (*or, figure*) He willed, He constituted thee."[6] (LXXXII:6-8).

---

3. The world 'backs' should be understood in terms of transcendental existence.

4. Here, the fact should be kept in mind that in Qur'ãnic view of life, it is the Soul, and not any physiological mechanism, which is the real repository of Consciousness and they dynamo for Activity. Hence in respect of the verse under reference, the postulation of anything beside the Soul stands ruled out.

5. Quoted already.

6. There is a Qur'ãnic statement: "When I have made him and have breathed into him of My spirit...." (XV:29). It should be noted that the spirit mentioned here

3. Then, the human Soul, while retaining its transcendental dimension, *viz.*, function and activity, and centred in devotion to its Source of Existence and Capabilities, namely God, of Whom it is the vicegerent (II:30), functions in four other dimensions also: namely, physical, rational, moral and aesthetical.

4. Thus: the spiritual, the physical, the rational, the moral and the aesthetical constitute the *five* dimensions of human personality, and activity relating to all these five *should be pursued in a balanced and integrated manner*, in order that the human personality may evolve and function in a healthy form on the basis of healthy activity (*al-'amal al-sãleh*):

"O ye who believe! enter into Submission *wholly* (*i.e.*, adopt the Way of Life consisting of total submission to the Will of God with the totality of your life)." (II:208).

"For those who believe and practise *al-sãlihãt* (*i.e.*, engage in healthy activity according to God's Law and with comprehensiveness and integration) is a reward that will never fail." (XLI:8).

"....and healthy (or, righteous) activity doth He exalt (thereby raising the practiser of healthy activity, or, righteousness, to higher and higher levels of his personality)". (XXXV:10)[7].

5. Moral activity being thus a part of an empire of Activity, which forms an organic Whole, it cannot be taken up with genuine and rational enthusiasm, and cannot be pursued consequentially—namely, cannot lead to the proper enrichment of the human personality—, unless it is grounded in the very foundation of human personality, which is spiritual in nature and transcendental in its reach and scope, and also unless all the other aspects of human activity are properly co-ordinated with it.

Such being the Qur'ãnic view, it is necessary that the Qur'ãnic Moral Code should be viewed not only in the essentially moral perspective but also in the background of those spiritual, physical, intellectual and aesthetical duties that have a direct or indirect bearing on the moral life of

---

is 'God's spirit', and not the human soul; and consequently this verse should not be understood as saying that God perfected first a soulless physical structure and then placed the soul in it. And 'the breathing of God's spirit' seems to stand for the bestowal of those extraordinary qualities that relate to the earthly and the cosmic mission of the human being in terms of the vicegerency of God.

7. *Cf.* Other Qur'ãnic verses relating to the importance of *healthy* activity.

a human being—moral life as it is conceived in the strict sense.

The above discussion leads us to the following five categories of Duties to Self:

A. Duties as Spiritual Being

1. *Duties with reference to God:*

(i) Duties of Commission; (ii) Duties of Omission.

2. *Duties with reference to the Holy Prophet (in whom God's Blessing and Peace abide!)*

(i) Duties of Commission; (ii) Duties of Omission.

3. *Duties with reference to the Angels:*

(i) Duties of Commission; (ii) Duties of Omission.

B. Duties as Physical Being

(a) Duties of Commission; (b) Duties of Omission.

C. Duties as Rational Being

(a) Duties of Commission; (b) Duties of Omission.

D. Duties as Aesthetical Being

(a) Duties of Commission; (b) Duties of Omission.

E. Duties as Moral Being

(a) Duties of Commission; (b) Duties of Omission.

The Spirituo-Moral Duties—Some Vital Facts

Among the Duties to Self, besides the duties based on the earthly environment of Man, the Holy Qur'ān has explicitly prescribed certain duties which bear reference to the transcendental dimension of his personality and may, therefore, be termed as spirituo-moral, or, ethico-religious duties. It says, for instance:

"Virtue does not consist in turning your faces towards the east and the west (in direction-worship, which has formed part of the practices of superstitious nations, including the Greeks, the Hindus and the Christians), but virtue is of him who believes in Allah and the Last Day and the Angels and the Book (*i.e.*, the Divine Scriptures) and the Prophets; and gives of his wealth, for love of Him (*i.e.*, from the purest selfless motive), unto kindred and orphans and the needy and the wayfarer and those who ask and for the emancipation of slaves; and establishes Prayer; and pays the Poor-rate; and is of those who perform their covenants when they have covenanted; and is of the patient in adversity and affliction and time of violence. Such are those who have proved themselves true (in their Faith). Such are the god-fearing". (II:177).

Besides the essentially moral duties, this verse bears reference to the spirituo-moral duties also; which, though they appear to stand in the category of duties to Others, are actually duties to Self—as we shall shortly observe.

The function of such duties is to nourish the faith that the world is a Moral Order, thereby continuously reinforcing the moral fibre of human beings and furnishing the ground for moral struggle—indeed, *the sure* ground; and they are to three types of personalities, *viz.,* (i) God, (ii) the Holy Prophet Muhammad (Peace be on him!)[8], and (iii) the Angels. With them may also be mentioned the duties of belief in Divine Guidance and in the Life Hereafter.

Now, since the Holy Qur'ãn affirms the existence of the personal God, Who is the Possessor of all Perfection and Who undertakes to lead His creatures to perfection adequate to them, duties to Him become the foremost duties. However, those duties are, in the final analysis, duties to Self, because God being *al-samad* (CXII:2), He dose not stand in need of anything from anyone while the entire Creation depends on Him for everything. Moreover, God being the ultimate condition of the realisation of Man's moral ideal, every duty to God is really duty to Self.

Duties to the Holy Prophet Muhammad (the Divinely-Blessed) originate, like the duties to God, in the Islamic Article of Faith itself, and they have been laid down by the Qur'ãn in the interest of the Muslims themselves, because:

---

8. The Holy Qur'ãn has ordained that Muslim should *affirm* the Blessings of God on the Holy Prophet and should salute him (XXXIII:56). Hence, while mentioning his sacred name, a Muslim may proclaim the affirmation as, for instance, has been done on page xi, or may salute him—the standard form of Islamic salutation being in terms of the prayerful expression: 'Peace be on you', or, 'Peace be on him!' etc.

Firstly, he *alone* is the Leader who is to be followed *unconditionally*. Thus *the bond of loyalty to him is the bond of integrity of the Islamic world-community.*

[In that connection, it is necessary to emphasise that the 'bond of loyalty' to the Holy Prophet Muhammad (Peace be on him!) resides in *absolute allegiance* to him, which means that the association of anyone else in that allegiance as a condition of faith in Islam—in terms of conferring upon anyone, or accepting anyone's claim to, divinely bestowed Authority, on the basis of prophetic status or any status akin to it, in any sense whatsoever, so that disbelief in that person's status is regarded as disbelief in Islam itself, and that in spite of otherwise absolute allegiance to the Holy Prophet Muhammad (Peace be on him!)—expels a person from the fold of Islam in the same way as when he associates anyone in any manner in the Godhood of Allah.]

Secondly, he is the Model of Perfection whom every Muslim is under obligation to imitate for advancement in his spiritual and moral life. But to imitate him consequentially is not possible without practising love and respect for him, which has been prescribed as duty.

Thirdly, he is the Medium through whom Divine Grace flows to his followers[9] in respect of their spiritual and moral purification. (LXII:3-4).

9. In fact, as "Mercy unto the worlds" (XXI:107), he has been exalted by God to be the Medium of His Blessings in an immeasurably wider perspective. The unique position which he holds among all creatures has been unambiguously affirmed also in *hadîth* reported by the Holy Prophet's Companions Jãbir and upheld as authentic in Islamic history by eminent authorities, among whom may be mentioned, by way of example, one of the classical Qur'ãnic commentators, Allãma Alusi (*vide* his classical *Tafsîr*, the *Rûh al-Ma'ãnî*, vol. I, p. 51). It is to the effect: "Jãbir (Allah be pleased with him!) reports: I said: 'O Messenger of Allah! Inform me about the thing which Allah created before all (other) things. He replied: 'Verily, Allah, the Almighty, created before all (other) things the Light of thine Prophet through His Light....." [Quoted on the authority of *muhaddith* 'Abd al-Razzãq, (the eminent forerunner of Imam Bukhari and author of *Al-Musannaf*) by Allãma Yusuf b. Ismã'il al-Nabhãni, in *Al-Anwãr al-Muhammadiyyah min Mawãhib al-Ludunniyah*, p., 12 Beirut, 1310 A.H.]. The *hadîth* then proceeds to inform that the entire universe was created by God from the original created Light, which the luminaries of Islam have named as the '*Light of Muhammad*'. It may be pointed out that the statement made on the basis of the Qur'ãn on p. 289 (footnote) of the present volume, is corroborated by this *hadîth* (Relevant discussions in volume I in respect of the Holy Prophet's personality may also be referred to).

These facts necessitate the maintenance of a constant dutiful attitude in terms of love and respect for him.

However, just as duties to God are really duties to Sefl, because they involve the self-perfection of the moral agent, in the same manner duties to the Holy Prophet (Peace be on him!) are really duties to Self, because of the benefits that accrue to the person who fulfils them.

As regards the Angels, they are, according to the Holy Qur'ãn, possessors of the attribute of personality[10] (III:39; etc.). Also, they are sinless (=holy) beings and function as executors of Divine Will in the universe (LXVI:6). Thus, duties towards them[11] appear to stand under three categories, *viz.*, (i) duty of belief in their existence; (ii) duty of love for their sinlessness; and (iii) duty of respect for them as functionaries of the Divine Order.

The duty of belief in the existence of the angels forms a part of the Islamic Creed, which means that it has a basic significance in the Islamic system. The question might arise here, however, that moral duty is duty of action and not of belief, and hence the duty of belief should not be included here. But the fact is that the duty of belief in the angels is a duty of attitude and is actually a necessary prerequisite to the cultivation of purity in moral outlook on the basis of which alone moral life can be Islamically pursued. Thus it comes under the duty of the Moral Perfection of the Self. Also, this duty has a reference to Divine Control in the life of humanity, which highlights God's function as the Moral Ruler of the world.

We learn from the Holy Qur'ãn about two functions of the angels which bear a direct reference to our *moral* life, *viz.*, bringing the Revelations to the Prophets from God for the guidance of man—archangel Jibreel (Peace be on him!) being the chief functionary in this respect (XXII:75; II:97); and recording the deeds of human beings for presentation to them on the Day of Judgment (LXXXII:10-12), when virtue and vice shall be finally and comprehensively recompensed by God.

---

10. Mark that this bears reference to moral relationship, because morality consists in the attitude of one personality towards another. Also, it should be noted that the affirmation of personality in the angels does not imply anthropomorphism.

11. It may be emphasised that they are basically duties of attitude, and are not meant to be institutionalised.

It may be observed here in passing that belief in the Divine Messengers and the Divine Scriptures, mentioned in the above-quoted verse (II:177), and forming part of the Islamic Creed, bears reference to the existence of the Law concerning the Guidance of Man as a spiritual and moral being. Similarly, belief in the Life Hereafter has a bearing on the moral life of man, as also on his spiritual life, being the prerequisite to the performance of the moral action with the purest motive wherein all earthly considerations are transcended.

Before closing the discussion on the spirituo-moral duties, we might discuss the question, which can possibly arise in certain minds: Are those duties real and meaningful?

At the. very outset, the answer is: They are, because, in the Qur'ãnic view of the cosmos, the transcendental plane of existence, or, the Spiritual Realm of the Cosmos, is not a fantasy, or jus a regulative Idea, but a fact—and, for that matter, *the basic fact.*

The materialists hold to a naturalistic view of the universe. The idealists affirm what might be termed as a psychicalistic view. The Holy Qur'ãn, in harmony with its integralistic approach and its philosophy of *Unity*, affirms the reality of both the realms of the cosmos, namely: (i) the realm governed by the Natural Law, or, the Spatio-Temporal level of Reality;—we may also call it the phenomenological level; (ii) the realm governed by the Metaphysical Law, or, the Spaceless-Timeless level of Reality. And it integrates both through the bond of the Unitary Divine Plan and Purpose, which has brought into existence both of them and maintains them within the framework of *Unity*.

Without going into the details of Qur'ãnic cosmology: God's relationship with the cosmos as its Creator emerges in the Qur'ãn at two levels, i.e., the levels of *al-Amr* and *al-Khalaq*,—both established and united under that Attribute of God which relates to cherishing, nourishing, evolving and perfecting, i.e., *al-Rubb*: ".....Lo! His is *al-Khalq* and *al-Amr*. Blessed is Allah the *Rabb* of the worlds (i.e., the entire cosmos.)". (VII:54).

Thus, the Creation began with God's *Amr*: "The Originator of the heavens and the earth; and whensoever He decrees an affair (*Amr*), He only says to it 'Be' and it *becomes*. (Hence the origination of the cosmos also took place as a result of Allah's Command 'Be')". (II:117). "His *Amr* (i.e., law of bringing something into existence is that when He intends a thing , He only says to it (by way of Command, or, *Amr*): 'Be'; and it *becomes*." (XXXVI:82).

Hence, the first stage in the creation of the cosmos should be affirmed in terms of 'Becoming'. We may also call it the stage of subtle existence, intangibility (as opposed to the tangibility of Matter), and spacelessness-cum-timelessness.

Looking at the process of creation in the background of the concept of evolution projected explicitly in the Qur'ãn, we arrive at the view of evolutionary creation, wherein—like the evolutionary hypothesis in modern Science—we are led to the affirmation of the '*Primeva Atom*' as the starting point, which functioned as the *nucleus* and out of which grew the entire cosmos through an evolutionary process;—even as we find it mentioned in the *hadîth* quoted in the foregoing page xx, wherein the concept of the 'First Created Light functioning as Nucleus' has been projected.

As for the nature of the evolutionary process, it should be conceived, in the very nature of the case, in terms of progressive decrease in subtlety, refinement, intangibility and qualitativeness, and progressive increase in respect of concreteness, crystallisation, tangibility and quantitativeness; on the basis of a progressive crystallisation of the process of *al-Khalaq*, which implies the creation of new objects from the existing materials. In other words, it must have been a progress towards more and more profound 'expression'. This is what we understand from the Qur'ãn as well as from Science.

Indeed, different things appear in the Qur'ãn to have emerged into dynamic existence at different stages of the evolutionary process. Thus, there existed the angels, the *jinns* and the human beings in that pre-physical, or, transcendental, dimension of existence; and, among them, the angels and the *jinns* were there prior to the existence of the human beings, as the Holy Qur'ãn testifies (II:30-34). Then, according to what we read in the holy book in plain terms, humanity was made to appear before God in her transcendental, or, pre-earthly, dimension of existence, to proclaim the Covenant of Monotheism (VII:172),—which means that human beings existed at that stage of Creation. Similarly, the event of the 'Covenant of the Prophets' has been mentioned therein to have occurred in that stage of Creation (III:81),—which proves the existence of the Prophets at that stage.

All this means that a Realm of Created Beings and Things became gradually established in respect of their essential or ideal nature, even in the first stage of creation. But evolution was to continue, and has continued, according to God's Plan. However, because "Allah has set a measure (or, a scale of growth and maturity—which enshrines its destiny) for every thing," (LXV:3), certain things that had emerged from potentiality into actuality, had to stay in the state they had acquired:— the angels, for instance; while others had to continue their evolutionary journey, finally emerging in the Spatio-Temporal Order of Existence:— the human beings, for instance.

However, we are not actually concerned here with the elaboration of the Qur'ãnic cosmology. Rather, the above discussion has been undertaken to emphasise the following facts:

(i) For the *formalistic* religious outlook, the world-view consists of certain dogmas, which are there to be believed in dogmatically, rather than to provide a dynamic, meaningful and comprehensive approach to the Spiritual Reality. Such an outlook is barren, and the Qur'ãn does not endorse it.

(ii) The *naturalistic* outlook confines itself to the Physical Reality, and it leads, even in the case of a believer in religion, to a materialistic approach to life and its problems—at least, for all practical purposes. The Qur'ãn also affirms the Physical Reality, giving a coherent and illuminating view of it—a view which is receiving increasing support from the world of Science as knowledge is advancing. However, it is conjoined therein to a clear-cut view of the Transcendental Reality—both the views forming thus one organic Whole.

(iii) The Qur'ãnic view that emerges thereby is an *Integralistic Spiritual View of the Universe*, wherein the spiritual, or, the transcendental, has primacy over the physical, or, the spatio-temporal, and which provides not merely a formal ground for religious life but a sound vision as well as philosophy for meaningfully *cultivating* a life dedicated to God and directed to the realisation of the ultimate human destiny, which is essentially spiritual,—that being the mission of Islam.

(iv) The essential human personality (*al-Rûh*), called 'the Soul' in common usage, belongs originally and basically to the Transcendental Realm of Existence.

The human being is, therefore, essentially a spiritual being, and should behave as such for his success.

(v) Not only God, but the entire spiritual world created by Him, is *responsive* to human spiritual quest. The spiritual quest, in its turn, is of vital importance for the human being because of the fact that he is *essentially* a spiritual being and, as such, *can build up his essential personality only through exercise in that response.*

(vi) The spiritual world plays the same role in the preservation and development of the essential human personality (which has been already emphasised time and again to be spiritual) as the physical world plays in respect of the physical aspect of human existence.

There are numerous things in the physical environment of the human being which contribute to his physical preservation and development,—they being of *different grades*, with the planet sun fulfilling the most basic role, and the others standing next in importance in a descending order of merit. Human beings have to remain in a state of contact and communication with them in order to benefit from them, or, in other words, to obtain the physical blessings placed in them by God.

Similarly, there are things of *different grades* in the spiritual world, on the Transcendental Realm, out of which the physical world has emerged and through which it is controlled by God. Those things contribute to the spiritual preservation and development of the human being,—and, because the spiritual is the essential, to his *essential* preservation and development. Among them, the role of the Holy Prophet's personality is most basic in respect of a Muslim's spiritual preservation and development; while the roles of the angels and the other spiritual things in Creation stand thereafter. Contact with the spiritual Blessings placed by God in the Holy Prophet's personality is obtained through the imitation of his *Sunnah*, with the ideal of acquiring greater and greater spiritual and moral purity, and the exercise in *Salãt* and *Salãm* with intense devotion; while contact with the Spiritual Blessings placed by God in the angels is obtained through leading a life of spiritual and moral purity and recitation of the Qur'ãn.

Then, just as in the physical world there are forces of physical destruction, or, forces of physical evil, similarly there are forces of spiritual destruction, or, forces of spiritual evil, that influence the spiritual life of human beings. The Qur'ãn has commanded the Muslims to avoid the former in the interest of their physical preservation, and to shun the latter for ensuring their spiritual preservation.

It is to be vehemently emphasised that Allah—and *none else*—is the Creator and the Bestower of all Blessings, whether physical or spiritual. But, *His Blessings flow to the human beings, not in a vacuum, but through the physical and the spiritual objects that He has created for that purpose.*

To confer divinity on any of those objects, even indirectly, is the worst form of infidelity to God; while to refuse to benefit from them is the worst form of ungratefulness to Him.

(vii) Communion with God, and communication, in terms of the establishment of spiritual contact, with the Holy Prophet (Peace be on him!), with the angels and with the spiritual verities in general, emerge, in the final analysis, as active sources of light and energy for the meaningful pursuit of Religion, in contrast to adherence to religious verities in lifeless formalism. In consequence, 'Duties to the Holy Prophet' and 'Duties to the Angels' assume vital importance for the spiritual development of a Muslim's personality.

Finally, we may recall what Dr. Sir Muhammad Iqbal, the Rumi of the modern age and the greatest Islamic thinker of the present century of Islamic era, said more than four decades ago: "Humanity needs three things today—a spiritual interpretation of the universe, spiritual emancipation of the individual, and basic principles of a universal import directing the evolution of human society on a spiritual basis. Modern Europe has, no doubt, built idealistic systems on these lines; but experience shows that truth revealed through pure reason is incapable of bringing that fire of living conviction which personal revelation alone can bring. This is the reason why pure thought has so little influenced men while religion has always elevated individuals, and transformed whole societies. The idealism of Europe never became a living factor in her life, and the result is a perverted ego seeking itself through mutually intolerant democracies whose sole function is to exploit the poor in the interests of the rich. Believe me, Europe today is the greatest hindrance in the way of man's ethical development."

Unfortunately, the formalistic religious outlook that has emerged among the Muslims in the present age of their spiritual, moral and over-all degeneration, has been progressively leading to the unconscious acceptance of the naturalistic and, for all practical purposes, materialistic, view of the human being as a mere 'superior animal', to the forgetfulness of the fact that he is essentially—namely, in his origin, being and destiny—a 'spiritual being, whose nature was created by God, according to the explicit and unambiguous verdict of the Qur'ãn, in terms of His vicegerency through the infusion of what He names as 'My spirit' (*rûh*) (XV:29; etc.), and to the view of the angels as mere "forces of Nature"—in the sense of naturalistic forces. In such a view of the human being and of the angels, very naturally the Holy Prophet is also regarded as nothing more than a 'good man', a 'great leader' and a 'divine postman'; and any description of the transcendental dimension of his august personality appears to the upholders of that view as nothing less than superstition, even though they overthrow in this process of thinking the spiritual foundations of the Qur'ãnic world-view which the profoundest Islamic theological thinkers down to Shah Waliullah took the greatest pains to preserve during the ages that have elapsed since the Qur'ãnic Revelation.

Duties to Animals, Plants and Things—as Duties to Self:

We may also refer here to duties towards animals, plants, and things, to which the Holy Qur'ãn has referred implicitly while in the *Hadith* they have been mentioned explicitly. They seem to fall under the category of duties to Others. But they are basically duties to Self in so far as they relate to the maintenance of the purity of our moral tone. They have, therefore, been dealt with in the Appendix to the 'Duties to Self'.

III. Duties to Others

The obligatoriness of duties to Others is to be conceived in their two-fold origin: (i) in human shortcomings at the different stages of life, which necessitate assistance by other human beings; and (ii) in the inherent social nature of human life[12]. Indeed, the individual and the society are

12. Says Aristotle: "He who is unable to live in society, or who has no need because he is sufficient for himself, must be either a beast or a god." (*Politics*, Bk. 1, Ch. 2).

mutually related and interdependent, and the individual's realisation of moral good is not conceivable, according to the Qur'ãnic view, without reference to the societal whole.

Now, viewing the human personality in its two basic aspects, *i.e.*, the empirical and the rational, duties to Others split up into two categories *with regards to the ends that they should serve*,—namely: (i) Duties relating to 'Happiness', or, Material Well-being; (ii) Duties relating to 'Moral Perfection'—meant actually to ensure Spiritual and Moral Preservation and Advancement.

Viewed with reference to those who are to be served by these duties, two basic categories emerge, namely: (i) Individualistic duties, or, duties to other individuals as individuals; (ii) Collectivistic duties, or, duties relating to the Societal Whole.

As regards 'Duties to Other Individuals', they may be viewed basically in two perspectives: (i) other individuals in general, and (ii) other individuals as related to the moral agent through specified functional relationships. Then, the other individuals may be Muslims—and that would form the primary reference—, and as such they have to be treated as members of the Islamic social order. Also, there may be—in fact, there are—the non-Muslims who, in the first instance, cannot be regarded properly as members of the Islamic social order, even though they may be living in an Islamic state; and, secondly, there may be among them persons belonging to different categories: for example: (i) non-Muslims who are friendly towards Muslims and tolerent towards Islam; (ii) non-Muslims who are simply indifferent to Muslims and Islam; and (iii) non-Muslims who are hostile to Muslims and Islam.

Islam prescribes duties towards all the above categories of other individuals, laying down certain duties that are based on the concept that all human beings have ertain inviolable rights as human beings and that absolute justice must be practised towards all; and giving another set of duties, in addition, relating to the specified areas of relationships.

IV. Duties Relating to the Societal Whole

Duties relating to the Societal Whole split up into two categories, namely: (i) Duties *to* the Societal Whole; and (ii) Duties *of* the Societal Whole.

With reference to *Duties to the Societal Whole*, the Holy Qur'ãn has commanded thus:

"And hold fast, all together, by the Convenant of Allah (*habl-Allah*), and be not split up among yourselves". (III:103).

The word *habl*, translated here as Covenant, means primarily a rope or a cord, and hence a cause of union or a Covenant which renders one responsible for the safety of a person or a thing. (Lane's *Lexicon*).

The *habl-Allah* (Covenant with God) is, abstractly, allegiance to the objectives of *al-Din*, or, the Way of Collective Obedience to God, and, concretely, loyalty to the Islamic Society through loyalty and devotion to its Founder and Leader, the Holy Prophet Muhammad (Peace be on him!), which loyalty should manifest itself basically in doing utmost to preserve the unity, the solidarity and the social, moral and spiritual health of the Islamic society. Hence the *Duties to the Societal Whole*.

Similarly, the *Duties of the Societal Whole* towards the Individual have been emphasised in the Holy Qur'ãn; for instance, in the following verse which bears comprehensive reference to the spiritual, economic, moral and social welfare of the individuals:

"(Mulsims are) those who, if We establish them in the land, set up regular Prayer and give regular charity, enjoin what is right and forbid what is wrong...." (XXII:41).

Now, every organised Societal Whole takes, whenever and wherever possible, the form of the State, which, as an institution, is an indispensable means for the realisation of the social ideal. As regards its structural ethics, the following observations may be made.

Organisation of the Societal Whole as a state gives rise to subordination and superordination, wherein the foremost duty of the subordinate becomes obedience to the superordinate (IV:59) and of the superordinate to administer the state through coercive authority, or, *al-Amãrah* (mentioned in IV:59),—and that in the interest of the subordinate.[13] Also, besides the multifarious dimensions of positive administration, the duty of punishing offenders for all cognisable

---

13. It may be emphasised here that the greater the selflessness and sacrifice which the super-ordinate imposes on itself, the stronger will it be in wielding its authority; and the more the vested interests it creates, the weaker will be its authority. The Holy Prophet (Peace be on him!) set a perfect example of selflessness and the elimination of all forms of vested interests by: (1) banning the payment of *Zakãt* to his progeny; (ii) avoiding the giving of key posts to his kith and kin during his regime as head of the Islamic state; and (iii) keeping open to all Muslims the office of the head of the state for all time after his demise.

offences against life, honour, property, and ensuring the spiritual, moral and economic well-being of the people, also devolves on the superordinate. Then, a further duty of the superordinate is that of preserving or reclaiming, as the case may be, the autonomy of the state against internal turmoil and external aggression, and for that purpose to wage war against all hostile forces.

An important fact should be noted here with respect to the State Authority. The Holy Prophet Muhammad (Peace be on him!) is the founder of the Islamic society, as also of the Islamic state. As such, and as the Medium of Obediecne to God—indeed, as the representative *par excellence* of the Authority of God on earth, he is the Super-Leader of the Islamic state *for all time* (IV:80; etc.). Hence no State Authority can claim Islamically the right of obedience to itself except as the *representative* of the Holy Prophet (Peace be on him!)[14]

Note on Penal Code:

In the perspective of the superordinate's duty of punishing offenders of the Law, mentioned in the foregoing, emerges the *Penal Code*, to which we have devoted a separate section. As to the Qur'ãnic *Philosophy of Punishment*, readers should refer to Volume I, Book II, Chapter IV, of the present book, where we have come to the following conclusion:

"Viewing the Qur'ãnic punishments in the light of ethics, the punishments relating to fornication, adultery and homosexuality are reformative in the sense that they imply the spiritual purification of the offenders; the punishments prescribed for theft, dacoity and treason are of deterrent character; and the punishment in respect of murder is based on retribution which is tempered with mercy (II:178). The guiding light in all cases, however, is the procurement of spiritual good of the individuals concerned and of the society."

Note on Tabligh[15]:

The word *tabligh* means 'to reach out the Message' As a term it means 'propagation of the Message of Islam'.

The Holy Qur'ãn has given to it the status of an institution (III:104; etc.) and has ordained it as an important *societal duty*.

---

14. This truth is borne out by the fact that the first Caliph, Abu Bakr, and all other Caliphs after him, have called themselves *Khalîfatur-Rasûlillãh* (Vicegerent of the Messenger of God) and not *Khalifatillãh* (Vicegerent of God).

15. Also written as '*tableegh*'.

This duty has been conceived to function at two levels, *i.e.*, within the Islamic social order, and outside the Islamic social order, where entire humanity comes under its purview.

The ends it serves are: (i) preservation, (ii) development, and (iii) perpetuation of the Islamic Community—and that in service to the cause of humanity (III:110).

The dimension of this duty are:

(i) education of new generations of Muslims in Islam;

(ii) improvement in Islamic knowledge and inspiration of the grown-up Muslims;

(iii) dissemination of the knowledge of Islam among non-Muslims—all the non-Muslims of the world wherever they may be found—in order that they may know the Divine Message that has come for them, and those among them who are seriously dedicated to Truth may accept it for their own good; while, in the case of others, correct knowledge about Islam may dissipate their ignorance and the consequent misunderstandings, finally bringing about among them goodwill for Islam—which, in itself, forms a genuine contribution to the promotion of intercommunal and international goodwill.

Thus, *tabligh* stands out as a duty towards other individuals in respect of their spiritual and moral progress.

Also, it contributes simultaneously to the spiritual and moral development of the persons who undertake it, and thus it becomes a duty to Self.

Its role, however, as a collectivistic or societal duty, remains supreme. Indeed, from that point of view, it stands out as the foremost duty without which the very existence of Islam becomes jeopardised.

As the Holy Qur'ãn affirms, the Islamic Community is meant to continue to exist for all time—up to the Last Day. This is in the very nature of the case, because the Holy Prophet Muhammad (Peace be on him!) is the last and final Divine Messenger, and the Muslims are the last divinely raised religious Group. As such, disappearance of the Islamic Community at any time in human history is not conceivable. But, the dissipation of the energies of communities and nations—both ideological and non-ideological—being the Law of History, one of the most important instruments for keeping the Islamic community alive and functioning genuinely and truly is the repeated infusion of fresh blood into the body politic of Islam. This has already happened in Islamic history, as, for instance, when towards the end of the Abbaside period, the Muslim world began to show signs of lassitude and weakness, the conversion of the Turko-Tartars revitalised the Islamic community to an extent that it could maintain its glory for several centuries more. The same seems to be the crying need today. But this need cannot be fulfilled without resort to an *enlightened, dynamic and multidimensional* movement in the field of *tabligh,* and *not just a ritualistic or professional performance.*

V. Manners[16]

Manners may be defined as apparent modes of behaviour in relation to others, and may be evaluated as small coins of virtue.

The Qur'ãnic point of view, as emphasised already, is social. Consequently, in the Qur'ãnic moral code we find as much emphasis on manners as on morals; perhaps more, because indifference to manners may nullify a virtue itself. This is evident from the Qur'ãnic emphasis on the manners to be observed in the performance of one of the highest virtues in relation to others, *viz.*, charity:

"O ye who believe! make not your charity worthless by laying obligation and by hurt..." (II:264).

It is also evident from what has been said in connection with the manners to be observed in the presence of the Holy Prophet Muhammad (Peace be on him!):

"O ye who believe! raise not your voices above the voice of the Prophet, nor speak aloud to him in talk as ye may speak aloud to one another, lest your (good) deeds becomes vain and ye perceive not". (XLIX:2).

Coming to classification: In conformity with the comprehensive nature of the Qur'ãnic moral code, the Qur'ãnic duties in respect of manners belong to two categories: (i) those relating to religious manners, and (ii) those relating to social manners.

16. "Conduct may include inward activities like motives and desires as well as outward activities like speech and movements of the doer's limbs, and so these also will fall within the sphere of ethics. We so commonly think of these as causing outward bodily movements that we forget that they too are activities and liable to be judged good or bad even apart from the outward movements they produce." (W. Lillie: *Introduction to Ethics*, p. 4).

Book I

DUTIES TO SELF

Part I

DUTIES AS SPIRITUAL BEING

Part II

DUTIES AS PHYSICAL BEING

Part III

DUTIES AS RATIONAL BEING

Part IV

DUTIES AS AESTHETICAL BEING

Part V

DUTIES AS MORAL BEING

Part I

DUTIES AS SPIRITUAL BEING

Chapter I

DUTIES WITH REFERENCE TO GOD

(1) Duties of Respect; (2) Duties of Love

END:

(a) *Objective:*

Maintenance of a constant attitude of Respect and Love towards God for acquiring the Blessings of Divine Pleasure (*Ridwãn Allah*) and Divine Love (*Hubb Allah*).

as it has been said in the Holy Qur'ãn:

يَبْتَغُونَ فَضْلًا مِّنَ اللَّهِ وَرِضْوَانًا

".....seeking Grace from Allah and (His) Good Pleasure...."

(XLVIII:29).

Also:

يُحِبُّهُمْ وَيُحِبُّونَهُ

".....whom He will love and they will love Him....." (V:57).

(b) *Subjective:*

Creating in the moral agent:

(i) purity of will, leading to possible 'holiness' in the measure it may relate to human personality, as it has been said:

وَمَن يُؤْمِن بِاللَّهِ يَهْدِ قَلْبَهُ

" And whosoever believeth in Allah, He guideth his heart (aright)." (LXIV:11).

(ii) stability in, and enthusiasm for, the pursuit of moral

struggle, as we are told:

فَمَنْ يَّكْفُرْ بِالطَّاغُوْتِ وَ يُؤْمِنْ بِاللّٰهِ فَقَدِ اسْتَمْسَكَ بِالْعُرْوَةِ الْوُثْقٰى ۚ
لَا انْفِصَامَ لَهَا ۗ وَاللّٰهُ سَمِيْعٌ عَلِيْمٌ ○

".....And he who rejecteth false deities and believeth in Allah hath grasped a firm handhold which will never break. Allah is Hearer, Knower." (II:256).

(1) Duties of Respect

(a) <u>*Duties of Commission*</u>

(i) Cultivation of genuine and complete Faith in God and its inner realisation enjoined:

يٰۤاَيُّهَا الَّذِيْنَ اٰمَنُوْۤا اٰمِنُوْا بِاللّٰهِ وَرَسُوْلِهٖ وَالْكِتٰبِ الَّذِيْ نَزَّلَ عَلٰى
رَسُوْلِهٖ وَالْكِتٰبِ الَّذِيْۤ اَنْزَلَ مِنْ قَبْلُ ۗ وَمَنْ يَّكْفُرْ بِاللّٰهِ وَمَلٰۤئِكَتِهٖ وَكُتُبِهٖ
وَرُسُلِهٖ وَالْيَوْمِ الْاٰخِرِ فَقَدْ ضَلَّ ضَلٰلًاۢ بَعِيْدًا ○

"O ye who believe! believe (with all the richness of belief) in Allah[1] and His Messenger, and the Scripture which He hath sent to His Messenger and the Scripture which He sent to those before (him). And who denieth Allah, His Angels, His Books, His Messengers and the Day of Judgment, hath gone far far astray."[2] (IV:136).

(ii) Faith in the Unity of God—perfect monotheism—implying indivisible

---

1. The word "Allah", which is employed for the 'One True God' in Islamic terminology, is regarded as untranslatable in orthodox Muslim thought. Hence, while using the word God normally, I have avoided substituting it for "Allah" in quoting the Qur'ãnic verses.

2. Mark that belief in God is meaningless without:

(a) having faith in Him in accordance with what He has revealed about His Essence and His Attributes; and

(b) having faith in all the verities implied by the belief in Him.

It may also be noted that, according to the Holy Qur'ãn, belief in religious verities mentioned in the above verse is fruitless unless the possessor of that belief earns good by performing deeds of righteousness. (VI:158).

loyalty to Him, enjoined:

ذٰلِكُمُ اللّٰهُ رَبُّكُمْ ۚ لَآ اِلٰهَ اِلَّا هُوَ ۚ خَالِقُ كُلِّ شَيْءٍ فَاعْبُدُوْهُ ۚ

"That is Allah, your Lord! There is no God but He, the Creator of all things: then worship ye Him (alone)." (VI:102).

فَاِلٰهُكُمْ اِلٰهٌ وَّاحِدٌ فَلَهٗٓ اَسْلِمُوْا ؕ

".....and your God is One God, so unto Him submit (wholly and solely)." (XXII:34).

(iii) Maintenance of the attitude of respect for God enjoined:

اِنَّ الَّذِيْنَ اٰمَنُوْا وَعَمِلُوا الصّٰلِحٰتِ وَاَخْبَتُوْٓا اِلٰى رَبِّهِمْ ۙ اُولٰٓئِكَ اَصْحٰبُ الْجَنَّةِ ۚ هُمْ فِيْهَا خٰلِدُوْنَ ○

"Verily those who believe and work righteousness, and *humble themselves before their Lord,* they will be Companions of the Garden, to dwell therein for aye." (XI:23).

(iv) Cultivation of the fear of Displeasure of God and of the Final Accountability by Him, enjoined:

يٰٓاَيُّهَا الَّذِيْنَ اٰمَنُوا اتَّقُوا اللّٰهَ حَقَّ تُقٰتِهٖ وَلَا تَمُوْتُنَّ اِلَّا وَاَنْتُمْ مُّسْلِمُوْنَ ○

"O ye who believe! fear Allah[3] as He should be feared, and die not save as those who have surrendered (unto Him)." (III:102).

---

3. Fear of God is a necessary condition of our spiritual and moral development because fear is a vital element of respect. Again, fear of God does not relate to any inimical revenge from His side, but it is fear of being disowned by Him, as we read in the Holy Qur'ān:

وَقِيْلَ الْيَوْمَ نَنْسٰىكُمْ كَمَا نَسِيْتُمْ لِقَآءَ يَوْمِكُمْ هٰذَا

"It will be said (on the Day of Judgment): 'This Day We will forget you as ye forgot the meeting of this Day of yours!' (XLV:34).

Still again, it is the fear of Him who is 'Most Beneficent' and 'Most Merciful' (1:1, etc., etc.).

إِنَّمَا ذَٰلِكُمُ الشَّيْطَٰنُ يُخَوِّفُ أَوْلِيَآءَهُۥ فَلَا تَخَافُوهُمْ وَخَافُونِ إِن كُنتُم مُّؤْمِنِينَ ○

"It is only the devil that suggests to you the fear of his votaries: Be ye not afraid of them, but fear Me, if ye have faith." (III:175).

إِلَّا الَّذِينَ ظَلَمُوا مِنْهُمْ فَلَا تَخْشَوْهُمْ وَاخْشَوْنِي

".....except those that are bent on wickedness; so fear them not, but fear Me....." (II:150).

وَأَمَّا مَنْ خَافَ مَقَامَ رَبِّهِۦ وَنَهَى النَّفْسَ عَنِ الْهَوَىٰ ○ فَإِنَّ الْجَنَّةَ هِيَ الْمَأْوَىٰ ○

"And for such as had entertained the fear of standing before their Lord's (tribunal) (on the Day of Judgment)[4] and had restrained (their) souls from lower Desires, their Abode will be the Garden." (LXXIX:40, 41).

(v) Cultivation of Obedience to God enjoined:

يَٰٓأَيُّهَا الَّذِينَ ءَامَنُوٓا أَطِيعُوا اللَّهَ

"O ye who believe! Obey Allah...."[5] (IV:59).

يَٰٓأَيُّهَا الَّذِينَ ءَامَنُوا اسْتَجِيبُوا لِلَّهِ وَلِلرَّسُولِ إِذَا دَعَاكُمْ لِمَا يُحْيِيكُمْ

"O ye who believe! Give your response to (i.e., obey) Allah and His Messenger, when He calleth you to that which will give you life;...."[6] (VIII:24).

وَقُومُوا لِلَّهِ قَٰنِتِينَ ○

".....and stand before Allah in a devout (frame of mind)."[7] (II:238).

---

4. This is connected with the Islamic article of faith relating to belief in the Last Day—the Day of Final Accountability and of receiving final reward and punishment—emphasised over and again in the Holy Qur'ãn.

5,6,7. The words *tã'ah* and *istijãbah* and *qanût* used in the first, second and third verses respectively—all of them denote obedience. But *tã'ah* and *istijãbah* seem to emphasise *external* conformity to God's commands, while *qanût* seems to emphasise the *inwardness*, the purity of the heart—the Will—in submission to God.

وَأَنِيبُوا إِلَىٰ رَبِّكُمْ وَأَسْلِمُوا لَهُ مِن قَبْلِ أَن يَأْتِيَكُمُ الْعَذَابُ ثُمَّ لَا تُنصَرُونَ ۝

"Turn unto your Lord repentant, and *surrender* unto *Him*, before there cometh unto you the torment, and then ye shall not be helped."[8] (XXXIX:54).

يَا أَيُّهَا النَّاسُ اعْبُدُوا رَبَّكُمُ الَّذِي خَلَقَكُمْ وَالَّذِينَ مِن قَبْلِكُمْ لَعَلَّكُمْ
تَتَّقُونَ ۝

"O mankind! worship your Lord,[9] Who hath created you and those before you, so that ye may ward off (evil)."[10] (II:21).

(vi) Cultivation of trust in God's goodness, mercy and help enjoined:

أَمَّنْ هُوَ قَانِتٌ آنَاءَ اللَّيْلِ سَاجِدًا وَقَائِمًا يَحْذَرُ الْآخِرَةَ وَيَرْجُو رَحْمَةَ
رَبِّهِ ۗ قُلْ هَلْ يَسْتَوِي الَّذِينَ يَعْلَمُونَ وَالَّذِينَ لَا يَعْلَمُونَ ۗ إِنَّمَا يَتَذَكَّرُ
أُولُو الْأَلْبَابِ ۝

Mark also that the "devout frame of mind" should be eternally maintained by every Muslim. (III:17; XXXIII:35).

8. In another verse total submission to Allah has been emphasised:

بَلَىٰ مَنْ أَسْلَمَ وَجْهَهُ لِلَّهِ وَهُوَ مُحْسِنٌ فَلَهُ أَجْرُهُ عِندَ رَبِّهِ وَلَا خَوْفٌ عَلَيْهِمْ وَلَا هُمْ
يَحْزَنُونَ ۝

"Nay,—whoever submits his whole self to Allah and is a doer of good, he will get the reward with his Lord; on such shall be no fear nor shall they grieve." (II:112).

9. and Him alone:

وَقَضَىٰ رَبُّكَ أَلَّا تَعْبُدُوا إِلَّا إِيَّاهُ

"Thy Lord hath decreed that ye worship none but Him,...." (XVII:23).

10. The Holy Qur'ãn demands not merely formal obedience but obedience with all one's heart and it demands not obedience in certain matters only—as is demanded in the Christian maxim: "Give unto God what is God's and unto Caesar what is Caesar's"—but total surrender, surrender of the whole self and surrender with indivisible loyalty to God. Indeed, a Muslim's attitude towards God should be that of worship, in which his role is that of a humble slave only.

"Is one who worships devoutly during the hours of night prostrating himself or standing (in adoration), who takes heed of the Hereafter, and who places his hope in the Mercy of his Lord—(like one who does not)? Say: 'Are those equal, those who know and those who do not know? It is those who are endued with understanding that receive admonition."
(XXXIX:9).

إِنَّ الَّذِينَ آمَنُوا وَالَّذِينَ هَاجَرُوا وَجَاهَدُوا فِي سَبِيلِ اللَّهِ أُولَٰئِكَ يَرْجُونَ رَحْمَتَ اللَّهِ وَاللَّهُ غَفُورٌ رَحِيمٌ ○

"Lo! those who believe and those who suffer exile (in defence of Truth) and strive struggle in the path of Allah, they (i.e., such true Muslims) have hope of Allah's mercy; and Allah is Oft - Forgiving, Most Merciful." (II:218).

Then, there is the command:

وَعَلَى اللَّهِ فَتَوَكَّلُوا إِنْ كُنْتُمْ مُؤْمِنِينَ ○

".....and on Allah (i.e., in Allah's goodness, mercy and help) put your trust if ye are believers." (V:26).

(vii) Affirmation of one's dependence on God: Prayer to Him, enjoined:

وَقَالَ رَبُّكُمُ ادْعُونِي أَسْتَجِبْ لَكُمْ إِنَّ الَّذِينَ يَسْتَكْبِرُونَ عَنْ عِبَادَتِي سَيَدْخُلُونَ جَهَنَّمَ دَاخِرِينَ ○

"And your Lord hath said: Call on Me, I will answer your prayer. Verily those who are stiff-necked against My worship (i.e., against acknowledging Me as their Lord and Benefactor), will enter hell in humiliation." (XL:60).

ادْعُوا رَبَّكُمْ تَضَرُّعًا وَخُفْيَةً إِنَّهُ لَا يُحِبُّ الْمُعْتَدِينَ ○

"Call on your Lord with humility and in secret: Lo! Allah loveth not those who trespass beyond (rational and respectful) limits." (VII:55).

وَادْعُوهُ خَوْفًا وَطَمَعًا إِنَّ رَحْمَتَ اللَّهِ قَرِيبٌ مِنَ الْمُحْسِنِينَ ○

".....and call on Him with fear and longing (in your hearts): for the Mercy of Allah is (always) near to those who do good (to others)."
(VII:56).

(viii) Seeking Help and Grace from God, the Possessor and the Source of all Power, enjoined:

Says the Holy Qur'ãn:

اسْتَعِينُوا بِاللَّهِ

".....seek help from Allah....." (VII:128).

Now, help should be sought basically from God alone. Muslims have been commanded to pray to God in these words:

إِيَّاكَ نَعْبُدُ وَإِيَّاكَ نَسْتَعِينُ ۝

"Thee (alone) do we worship, and of Thee (alone) do we seek help." (I:5).

Again:

وَسْئَلُوا اللَّهَ مِنْ فَضْلِهِ ۚ

"And ask Allah of His Grace....." (IV:32).

And this seeking of Grace from God is a constant attribute of the life of a Muslim:

تَرَاهُمْ رُكَّعًا سُجَّدًا يَبْتَغُونَ فَضْلًا مِّنَ اللَّهِ وَرِضْوَانًا ۚ

"Thou will see them bow and prostrate themselves (in prayer) seeking Grace from Allah and (His) Good pleasure....." (XLVIII:29).

(ix) Seeking Guidance from God, the Possessor and Source of all Knowledge, enjoined:

It is a duty of every Muslim to pray to God for guidance in the following words:

اهْدِنَا الصِّرَاطَ الْمُسْتَقِيمَ ۝

"Guide us Thou (O Allah) unto the path straight....." (I:6).

(x) Following the Divine Guidance revealed in the Holy Qur'ãn, enjoined:

اتَّبِعُوا مَا أُنْزِلَ إِلَيْكُمْ مِّنْ رَّبِّكُمْ

"Follow the Revelation given unto you (in the Holy Qur'ãn) from your Lord....." (VII:3).

(xi) Showing respect to God by believing in all the Messengers and all the Scriptures sent by Him for the guidance of man, enjoined:

فَآمِنُوا بِاللَّهِ وَرُسُلِهِ

"So believe in Allah and (all) His Messengers." (III:179).

وَالَّذِينَ يُؤْمِنُونَ بِمَا أُنزِلَ إِلَيْكَ وَمَا أُنزِلَ مِن قَبْلِكَ

"(Muslims are those) who believe in the Revelation sent to thee (O Muhammad), and that which was sent before thee....." (II:4).

(b) <u>Duties of Omission</u>:

(i) Attributing any quality to God which is profane and blasphemous, prohibited:

وَلِلَّهِ الْأَسْمَاءُ الْحُسْنَىٰ فَادْعُوهُ بِهَا ۖ وَذَرُوا الَّذِينَ يُلْحِدُونَ
فِي أَسْمَائِهِ ۚ سَيُجْزَوْنَ مَا كَانُوا يَعْمَلُونَ ○

"The most excellent Names belong to Allah: so call on Him by them; and shun the company[11] (and the blasphemies) of those who use profanity in His names. They will be requited what they do." (VII:180).

(ii) Associating any partner with God and limiting His uniqueness and supremacy in any manner, prohibited:

وَاعْبُدُوا اللَّهَ وَلَا تُشْرِكُوا بِهِ شَيْئًا

"And worship Allah and associate not aught with Him (either in His Person or in His Attributes). (IV:36).

وَلَا تَدْعُ مَعَ اللَّهِ إِلَٰهًا آخَرَ ۘ لَا إِلَٰهَ إِلَّا هُوَ ۚ

"And call not, besides Allah, on another god. There is no god but He....." (XXVIII:88).

---

11. Mark here that not only their blasphemies but even their company is to be shunned.

(iii) Saying anything concerning God without the authority of Revelation, prohibited:

قُلْ إِنَّمَا حَرَّمَ رَبِّيَ الْفَوَاحِشَ مَا ظَهَرَ مِنْهَا وَمَا بَطَنَ وَالْإِثْمَ وَالْبَغْيَ بِغَيْرِ الْحَقِّ وَأَنْ تُشْرِكُوا بِاللَّهِ مَا لَمْ يُنَزِّلْ بِهِ سُلْطَانًا وَأَنْ تَقُولُوا عَلَى اللَّهِ مَا لَا تَعْلَمُونَ ○

"Say: The things that my Lord hath indeed forbidden are: shameful deeds, whether open or secret; sins and trespasses against truth or reason; assigning of partners to Allah, for which ye are given no authority: and *saying about Allah of which ye have no knowledge*." (VII:33).

(iv) Disobedience to and arrogance in respect of God, prohibited:

وَهُمْ لَا يَسْتَكْبِرُونَ ○

".....and they (i.e., the Believers) are not arrogant (in respect of worshipping Allah)." (XXXII:15).

وَأَمَّا مَنْ بَخِلَ وَاسْتَغْنَىٰ ○ وَكَذَّبَ بِالْحُسْنَىٰ ○ فَسَنُيَسِّرُهُ لِلْعُسْرَىٰ ○

"But he who is a greedy miser and *deemeth himself free from need* (*of Allah*), and gives the lie to the Best (i.e., dishonours Truth), We will indeed make for him smooth the Path to Misery." (XCII:8-10).

Again:

وَمَنْ يَعْصِ اللَّهَ وَرَسُولَهُ فَقَدْ ضَلَّ ضَلَالًا مُبِينًا ○

"If anyone disobeys (the Commands of) Allah and His Messenger, he is indeed on a clearly wrong Path." (XXXIII:36).

(v) Despairing of the Mercy of God prohibited:

وَلَا تَيْأَسُوا مِنْ رَوْحِ اللَّهِ ۖ إِنَّهُ لَا يَيْأَسُ مِنْ رَوْحِ اللَّهِ إِلَّا الْقَوْمُ الْكَافِرُونَ ○

".....and *never give up hope of Allah's Soothing Mercy*: truly no one despairs of Allah's Soothing Mercy except those who have no Faith." (XII:87).

قُلْ يٰعِبَادِيَ الَّذِيْنَ اَسْرَفُوْا عَلٰٓى اَنْفُسِهِمْ لَا تَقْنَطُوْا مِنْ رَّحْمَةِ اللّٰهِ ۭ اِنَّ اللّٰهَ
يَغْفِرُ الذُّنُوْبَ جَمِيْعًا ۭ اِنَّهٗ هُوَ الْغَفُوْرُ الرَّحِيْمُ ○

"Say: 'O My Servants who have transgressed against their souls! despair not of the Mercy of Allah, for Allah forgiveth all sins: verily He is Oft-Returning, Most Merciful." (XXXIX:53).

(vi) Believing in superstitions and seeking help from superstitious objects, thereby indirectly insulting God,[12] prohibited:

فَاجْتَنِبُوا الرِّجْسَ مِنَ الْاَوْثَانِ

".....so shun the abomination of idols (i.e., evils of idolatrous practices)....." (XXII:30).

يٰٓاَيُّهَا الَّذِيْنَ اٰمَنُوْٓا اِنَّمَا الْخَمْرُ وَالْمَيْسِرُ وَالْاَنْصَابُ وَالْاَزْلَامُ رِجْسٌ
مِّنْ عَمَلِ الشَّيْطٰنِ فَاجْتَنِبُوْهُ لَعَلَّكُمْ تُفْلِحُوْنَ ○

"O ye who believe! Intoxicants and games of chance (i.e., all forms of gambling), *and stone altars*[13] *and* (*divination by*) *arrows*[14], are an abomination,—of Satans' handiwork: shun it therefore, that ye may prosper." (V:93).

---

12. It may be noted that anyone who indulges in superstitions insults also his own dignity as a human being.

13. The stone altars were objects of superstitious worship in pre-Islamic Arabia. Oil was poured on them for consecration. They were also used for sacrifices to idols. Says Robertson Smith: "In Arabia, where sacrifice by fire is almost unknown, we find no proper altar, but in its place a rude pillar or heap of stones, besides which the victim is slain, the blood being poured out over the stone or its base.....The sacred stones.....are called *ansãb*, i.e., stones set up, pillars." (*Religion of the Semites*, p. 281).

14. Divination by arrows was a superstitious practice prevalent among the pre-Islamic Arabs. *Zalam* is "an arrow without a head and without feather: plural *Azlãm*, which was applied to those arrows by means of which the Arabs in the time of ignorance sought to know that which was allotted to them; .....and they put them in a receptacle, and when any of them desired to make a journey, or to accomplish a want, or when he desired to perform some affairs, he put his hand into that receptacle, and took forth an arrow; and if the arrow upon which was

مَا جَعَلَ اللّٰهُ مِنْۢ بَحِيْرَةٍ وَّلَا سَآئِبَةٍ وَّلَا وَصِيْلَةٍ وَّلَا حَامٍ ۙ وَّلٰكِنَّ الَّذِيْنَ كَفَرُوْا يَفْتَرُوْنَ عَلَى اللّٰهِ الْكَذِبَ ؕ وَاَكْثَرُهُمْ لَا يَعْقِلُوْنَ ۝

"It is not Allah Who hath instituted (superstitions like those of) a slit-ear she-camel, or a she-camel let loose for free pasture, or idol sacrifices for twin-births in animals, or stallion-camels freed from work. It was blasphemers who invented a lie against Allah, and most of them lack wisdom."[15] (V:106).

(vii) Magic, being evil practice and opposed to godliness, condemned; hence to abstain from it is duty:

Speaking of the practice of magic by the Jews, the Holy Qur'ãn says:

وَمَا هُمْ بِضَآرِّيْنَ بِهٖ مِنْ اَحَدٍ اِلَّا بِاِذْنِ اللّٰهِ ؕ وَيَتَعَلَّمُوْنَ مَا يَضُرُّهُمْ وَلَا يَنْفَعُهُمْ ؕ وَلَقَدْ عَلِمُوْا لَمَنِ اشْتَرٰىهُ مَا لَهٗ فِى الْاٰخِرَةِ مِنْ خَلَاقٍ ؕ

".....and they could harm none thereby (i.e., with their Magic) save by Allah's Will (i.e., in accordance with His laws). And they (i.e., the Jews) have learnt that which harmeth them (spiritually and morally), and profiteth them not; and assuredly they knew (from their Scripture) that the buyers of Magic would have no share in the happiness of the Hereafter." (II:102).

(2) Duties of Love

(a) Duties of Commission:

(i) Seeking in all actions the Pleasure of God, Who is the Moral Sovereign of the Universe, enjoined:

'Command' came forth, he went to accomplish his purpose, but if that upon which was 'Prohibition' came forth, he refrained; and if the blank came forth, they shuffled them a second time." (Lane's *Lexicon*).

15. This verse condemns four superstitions that were prevalent among the pagan Arabs. There are other superstitious notions and practices of the pagan Arabs also which have been condemned by the Holy Prophet Muhammad (Peace be on him) in his Sayings. Thus Islam has actually condemned all types of superstitions.

وَمِنَ النَّاسِ مَنْ يَّشْرِىْ نَفْسَهُ ابْتِغَاءَ مَرْضَاتِ اللّٰهِ ؕ وَاللّٰهُ رَءُوْفٌۢ بِالْعِبَادِ ○

"And of mankind is he (i.e., the true Muslim) who would sell (even) his life to earn the Pleasure of Allah. And Allah is full of kindness to His devotees." (II:207).

Nay: a true Muslim, in his highest spiritual effort, goes even beyond, and seeks God Himself:

وَمَا لِاَحَدٍ عِنْدَهٗ مِنْ نِّعْمَةٍ تُجْزٰٓى ○ اِلَّا ابْتِغَآءَ وَجْهِ رَبِّهِ الْاَعْلٰى ○

".....and (the righteous) have in their minds no favour from anyone for which a reward is expected in return but only the yearning to seek the Countenance of their Lord Most High." (XCII:19, 20).

(ii) Cultivation of Gratefulness to God enjoined:

وَ اشْكُرُوْا لِلّٰهِ اِنْ كُنْتُمْ اِيَّاهُ تَعْبُدُوْنَ ○

".....and express gratefulness to Allah, if it is (indeed) He Whom ye worship." (II:172).

وَاشْكُرُوْا نِعْمَتَ اللّٰهِ

".....and be grateful for the favour of Allah....." (XVI:114).

(iii) Cultivation of sincere devotion to God enjoined:

فَاعْبُدِ اللّٰهَ مُخْلِصًا لَّهُ الدِّيْنَ ○

".....so serve Allah offering Him sincere devotion." (XXXIX:2).

(iv) Steadfastness in devotion to God enjoined:

وَ اعْتَصِمُوْا بِاللّٰهِ ؕ هُوَ مَوْلٰىكُمْ ۚ فَنِعْمَ الْمَوْلٰى وَنِعْمَ النَّصِيْرُ ○

".....and hold fast by Allah (without swerving)! He is your Patron: an excellent Patron and an excellent Helper." (XXII:78).

اِلٰهُكُمْ اِلٰهٌ وَّاحِدٌ فَاسْتَقِيْمُوْٓا اِلَيْهِ

".....Your God is One God: so stand true to Him....." (XLI:6).

إِنَّ الَّذِينَ قَالُوا رَبُّنَا اللَّهُ ثُمَّ اسْتَقَامُوا فَلَا خَوْفٌ
عَلَيْهِمْ وَلَا هُمْ يَحْزَنُونَ ○

"Verily those who say: 'Our Lord is Allah', and remain steadfast thereto, on them shall be no fear, nor shall they grieve." (XLVI:13).

(v) Seeking nearness to God, the Source of all Goodness and Holiness, enjoined:

(a) *Through turning penitently unto Him:*

وَأَنِيبُوا إِلَىٰ رَبِّكُمْ وَأَسْلِمُوا لَهُ مِن قَبْلِ أَن يَأْتِيَكُمُ الْعَذَابُ ثُمَّ لَا تُنصَرُونَ ○

"*And turn penitently unto your Lord and submit unto Him* before there cometh unto you the torment, and then ye shall not be succoured."[16] (XXXIX:54).

(b) *Through seeking ardently the means of approach:*

يَا أَيُّهَا الَّذِينَ آمَنُوا اتَّقُوا اللَّهَ وَابْتَغُوا إِلَيْهِ الْوَسِيلَةَ وَجَاهِدُوا فِي
سَبِيلِهِ لَعَلَّكُمْ تُفْلِحُونَ ○

"O ye who believe! fear Allah and *seek the means of approach unto Him* and strive with might and main in His cause: that ye may prosper."[17] (V:38).

---

16. *Cf.* the Qur'ãnic verse:

مَّنْ خَشِيَ الرَّحْمَٰنَ بِالْغَيْبِ وَجَاءَ بِقَلْبٍ مُّنِيبٍ ○ ادْخُلُوهَا بِسَلَامٍ ذَٰلِكَ
يَوْمُ الْخُلُودِ ○

"....who feareth (Allah) Most Gracious in secret and cometh with a heart penitent (turned to Him): enter it (*i.e.*, Heaven) in Peace and Security. This is the Day of Eternal Life." (L:33, 34).

17. Mark that God is such an object of fear that, instead of being avoided, He is to be approached by us with all our Love. 'Fear of Allah' is thus the fear of our own deprivation of Divine Blessings which occurs when we remove ourselves away from Him.

Also mark that the way of approach lies in striving with might and main in His cause, something which even the pious Muslims of today seems to have forgotten, and hence the degeneration of the Muslim community everywhere.

(c) *Through detaching from wordly things and engaging in remembrance of and communion with Him:*

وَاذْكُرِ اسْمَ رَبِّكَ وَتَبَتَّلْ إِلَيْهِ تَبْتِيلًا ۝ رَّبُّ الْمَشْرِقِ وَالْمَغْرِبِ
لَآ إِلَٰهَ إِلَّا هُوَ فَاتَّخِذْهُ وَكِيلًا ۝

"And remember thou the name of thy Lord, and devote thyself to Him with an *exclusive* devotion.[18] Lord of the East and the West! No God is there but He. Take Him therefore for (thy) Disposer of Affairs." (LXXIII:8, 9).

فَاذْكُرُونِيٓ أَذْكُرْكُمْ

"Therefore remember Me, I will remember you....." (II:152).

يَٰٓأَيُّهَا الَّذِينَ آمَنُوا اذْكُرُوا اللَّهَ ذِكْرًا كَثِيرًا ۝ وَسَبِّحُوهُ بُكْرَةً وَأَصِيلًا ۝

"O ye who believe! Remember Allah with much remembrance and glorify Him early and late." (XXXIII:41, 42).

وَسَبِّحْ بِحَمْدِهِۦ

".....and celebrate His praise." (XXV:58).

وَاذْكُر رَّبَّكَ فِي نَفْسِكَ تَضَرُّعًا وَخِيفَةً وَدُونَ الْجَهْرِ مِنَ الْقَوْلِ بِالْغُدُوِّ
وَالْآصَالِ وَلَا تَكُن مِّنَ الْغَٰفِلِينَ ۝

"And remember thou thy Lord in thy (very) soul, with humility and in reverence, without loudness in word, in the mornings and evenings; and be not thou of those who are neglectful (of Allah's remembrance)."[19] (VII:205)

---

18. *tabattala il-allah* means: "He detached himself from wordly things and devoted himself to God;.....or he forsook every other thing, and applied himself to the service of God." (Lane's *Lexicon*).

19. Indeed, God's remembrance should be constant. *Cf.* the Qur'ãnic verse which says that the wise are "those who remember Allah standing, sitting and reclining" (III:191), because: "Lo! in the remembrance of Allah hearts do find serene tranquillity and steady peace." (XIII:28).

This remembrance should take the form of regular prayers also:

إِنَّنِي أَنَا اللَّهُ لَا إِلَٰهَ إِلَّا أَنَا فَاعْبُدْنِي وَأَقِمِ الصَّلَاةَ لِذِكْرِي ○

"Verily I! I am Allah! no God there is but I; so worship Me and *establish regular prayer for My remembrance*." (XX:14).

These regular, or, obligatory, prayers should be performed punctually at the appointed times:[20]

إِنَّ الصَّلَاةَ كَانَتْ عَلَى الْمُؤْمِنِينَ كِتَابًا مَوْقُوتًا ○

"Verily regular prayers are enjoined on the Believers at fixed times." (IV:103).

The regular prayers are to be followed (and preceded) by as much remembrance of God as possible and practicable:

فَإِذَا قَضَيْتُمُ الصَّلَاةَ فَاذْكُرُوا اللَّهَ قِيَامًا وَقُعُودًا وَعَلَىٰ جُنُوبِكُمْ ۚ

"Then when ye have finished the prayer, remember Allah, standing and sitting and lying on your sides....." (IV:103).

Also, besides the regular and repeated daily communion and constant remembrance of Allah during the normal waking hours of the day and the night, devoted Muslims should sacrifice their comfort during the sleeping hours of the night, according to their individual capacity, for communion with their Lord:

إِنَّمَا يُؤْمِنُ بِآيَاتِنَا الَّذِينَ إِذَا ذُكِّرُوا بِهَا خَرُّوا سُجَّدًا وَسَبَّحُوا بِحَمْدِ
رَبِّهِمْ وَهُمْ لَا يَسْتَكْبِرُونَ ○ تَتَجَافَىٰ جُنُوبُهُمْ عَنِ الْمَضَاجِعِ يَدْعُونَ
رَبَّهُمْ خَوْفًا وَطَمَعًا وَمِمَّا رَزَقْنَاهُمْ يُنْفِقُونَ ○

"Only those believe in Our revelations, who, when they are recited to them, fall down in adoration and celebrate the praises of their Lord, and they are not puffed up with pride. Their limbs do forsake their beds of sleep (while yet there is night), the while they call on their Lord, in Fear and Hope, and of that wherewith We have provided them they

20. Five times a day: at dawn, immediately afternoon, late afternoon, immediately after sunset, and before retirement to bed (in the first quarter of the night).

expend (for the welfare of others)." (XXXII:15, 16).

Indeed, the 'Servants of God' are:

وَالَّذِينَ يَبِيتُونَ لِرَبِّهِمْ سُجَّدًا وَقِيَامًا ۝

".....those who spend the night in adoration of their Lord, prostrate and standing....." (XXV:64).

(vi) Cultivation of love[21] *for God enjoined:*

Allah is the loving One (*al-Wadûd*)[22] and the cultivation of, and absorption in, His love forms the highest pursuit of a Muslim. The Holy Qur'ãn speaks of the true Believers as "a people whom Allah loves and they love Him." (V:57).

It is a relationship which is cultivated through right belief and right conduct:

إِنَّ الَّذِينَ آمَنُوا وَعَمِلُوا الصَّالِحَاتِ سَيَجْعَلُ لَهُمُ الرَّحْمَٰنُ وُدًّا ۝

"Verily those who believe and work deeds of righteousness, for them (Allah) Most Gracious will appoint (in this world as well as in the next) Love (i.e., His own love and the love of fellow-creatures)." (XIX:96).

This relationship is consciously and assiduously cultivated at a level where it surpasses a Muslim's love for everything else:

وَالَّذِينَ آمَنُوا أَشَدُّ حُبًّا لِلَّهِ ط

".....but the Believers are strongest in love for Allah." (II:165).

It forms the highest achievement for a Muslim, gives the direction to his will, and functions as the motivating force—equally with 'fear of God'—for all the actions of his life.

---

21. The Qur'ãnic concept of love for God has no affinity whatsoever with sensuous love. God is Most Sublime, according to the Holy Qur'ãn. As such, love for Him should be of sublime nature—namely, love modified by extreme respect. That is why the Qur'ãnic teaching combines 'Love for Allah' with 'fear of Allah'.

22. LXXXV:14.

(b) <u>*Duties of Omission*</u>:

(i) Following lusts of the heart, thereby incurring God's Displeasure, prohibited:

وَلَا تَتَّبِعِ الْهَوَىٰ فَيُضِلَّكَ عَن سَبِيلِ اللَّهِ ۚ إِنَّ الَّذِينَ يَضِلُّونَ عَن سَبِيلِ اللَّهِ
لَهُمْ عَذَابٌ شَدِيدٌ بِمَا نَسُوا يَوْمَ الْحِسَابِ ○

".....and follow not the lusts (of thy heart) that it beguile thee from the Way of Allah. Lo! those who wander from the Way of Allah have an awful doom, for as much as they forgot the Day of Reckoning." (XXXVIII:26).

(ii) Ungratefulness to God, prohibited:

وَاشْكُرُوا لِي وَلَا تَكْفُرُونِ ○

".....and unto Me give thanks, and *be not ungrateful* to Me." (II:152).

(iii) Behaving disloyally (as opposed to, sincere devotion) to God, prohibited:

يَا أَيُّهَا الَّذِينَ آمَنُوا لَا تَخُونُوا اللَّهَ

"O ye who believe! be not disloyal to (or, betray not the trust of) Allah....." (VIII:27).

(iv) Worshipping false gods, whether those of the polytheists and idol-worshippers or those that reside within the human self, prohibited:

وَلَقَدْ بَعَثْنَا فِي كُلِّ أُمَّةٍ رَّسُولًا أَنِ اعْبُدُوا اللَّهَ وَاجْتَنِبُوا الطَّاغُوتَ ۚ

"And assuredly We sent among every people a Messenger (with the Command:) 'Serve God, and eschew Evil and shun false gods'[23]." (XVI:36).

(v) Fickle-mindedness in respect of faith in God's Goodness, condemned: hence to abstain from it is duty:

---

23. *ijtanibû al-tãgût* implies both meanings. Abdullah Yusuf Ali's version is: 'eschew evil', while Marmaduke Pickthall's version is: 'shun false gods'.

al-tãgût is "whatever is worshipped instead, or to the exclusion, of God". (Lane's *Lexicon*).

وَمِنَ النَّاسِ مَنْ يَعْبُدُ اللَّهَ عَلَىٰ حَرْفٍ ۖ فَإِنْ أَصَابَهُ خَيْرٌ
اطْمَأَنَّ بِهِ ۖ وَإِنْ أَصَابَتْهُ فِتْنَةٌ انْقَلَبَ عَلَىٰ وَجْهِهِ خَسِرَ الدُّنْيَا
وَالْآخِرَةَ ۚ ذَٰلِكَ هُوَ الْخُسْرَانُ الْمُبِينُ ○

"And of mankind is he who worshippeth Allah, as it were, on the verge: if there befalleth him good, he is contented therewith; but if there befalleth him a trial, he turneth round on his face; he loseth the world and the Hereafter: that indeed is a loss manifest." (XXII:11).

(vi) Allowing preoccupation with and engrossment in worldly things to stand in the way of God's remembrance, prohibited:

يَا أَيُّهَا الَّذِينَ آمَنُوا لَا تُلْهِكُمْ أَمْوَالُكُمْ وَلَا أَوْلَادُكُمْ عَنْ ذِكْرِ اللَّهِ ۚ وَمَنْ
يَفْعَلْ ذَٰلِكَ فَأُولَٰئِكَ هُمُ الْخَاسِرُونَ ○

"O ye who believe! let not your riches or your children (—the two worldly things having a wide range of engrossment—) divert you from the remembrance of Allah. And whosoever doth that, the loss is their own". (LXIII:9).

(vii) Lack of earnestness in prayer and in the remembrance of God in general, condemned as the way of the Hypocrites: hence abstinence from it is duty:

وَإِذَا قَامُوا إِلَى الصَّلَاةِ قَامُوا كُسَالَىٰ يُرَاءُونَ النَّاسَ وَلَا يَذْكُرُونَ
اللَّهَ إِلَّا قَلِيلًا ○

".....(The Hypocrites) when they stand up in prayer, stand without earnestness, making a show to the people, and they remember not Allah but little." (IV:142).

(viii) Befriending the forces of evil, thereby violating our duty of love for God, condemned:

وَمَنْ يَتَّخِذِ الشَّيْطَانَ وَلِيًّا مِنْ دُونِ اللَّهِ فَقَدْ خَسِرَ خُسْرَانًا مُبِينًا ○

"Whosoever befriends Satan (who represents all the forces of evil), instead of Allah, hath of a surety suffered a loss that is manifest". (IV:119).

This is so because:

يُرِيدُ الشَّيْطٰنُ اَنْ يُّضِلَّهُمْ ضَلٰلًا ۢ بَعِيْدًا ○

".....Satan's wish is to lead them astray far away (from the Right)." (IV:60).

(ix) Loving any object of wordly life in preference to love for God, severely condemned: hence abstinence from it is duty:

قُلْ اِنْ كَانَ اٰبَآؤُكُمْ وَ اَبْنَآؤُكُمْ وَ اِخْوَانُكُمْ وَ اَزْوَاجُكُمْ وَ عَشِيْرَتُكُمْ
وَ اَمْوَالُ ۨاقْتَرَفْتُمُوْهَا وَ تِجَارَةٌ تَخْشَوْنَ كَسَادَهَا وَ مَسٰكِنُ
تَرْضَوْنَهَآ اَحَبَّ اِلَيْكُمْ مِّنَ اللّٰهِ وَ رَسُوْلِهٖ وَ جِهَادٍ فِيْ سَبِيْلِهٖ
فَتَرَبَّصُوْا حَتّٰى يَاْتِيَ اللّٰهُ بِاَمْرِهٖ ۭ وَاللّٰهُ لَا يَهْدِي الْقَوْمَ الْفٰسِقِيْنَ ○

"Say (O Muhammad! to the Muslims): If your fathers, and your sons, and your brothers, and your mates, and your kindred, and the wealth ye have acquired, and the commerce in which ye fear a decline, and the dwellings in which ye delight—(these) are dearer to you than Allah, or His Messenger, or the striving in His cause: then wait until Allah brings about His decision: and Allah guideth not the rebellious." (IX:24).

Chapter II

DUTIES TO THE HOLY PROPHET[1] MUHAMMAD (PEACE BE ON HIM)

(1) Duties of Respect; (2) Duties of Love

END:

(a) *Objective:*

Maintenance of the attitude of obedience and loyalty through the constant cultivation of respect and love for the Teacher and Exemplar of Qur'ãnic morals, in order to be able to act enthusiastically on the Qur'ãnic Moral Code.

(b) *Subjective:*

Maintenance of assurance, through the remembrance of the Example of the Holy Prophet (Peace be on him), in respect of his personal conduct and his achievements in the moral domain, that the moral idea set forth by the Holy Qur'ãn is realisable.

We have seen in the foregoing that Love for God is a Muslim's highest pursuit and the highest duty. In that connection, the Holy Qur'ãn states further that this love should manifest itself in loyalty following and imitating the communicator and exemplar of God's Guidance for mankind, namely, the Holy Prophet Muhammad (Peace be on him). It says:

قُلْ إِنْ كُنْتُمْ تُحِبُّوْنَ اللهَ فَاتَّبِعُوْنِيْ يُحْبِبْكُمُ اللهُ وَيَغْفِرْ لَكُمْ ذُنُوْبَكُمْ ۚ
وَاللهُ غَفُوْرٌ رَّحِيْمٌ ۝

---

1. According to the Holy Qur'ãn, the status of the Holy Prophet Muhammad (Peace be on him) is that of *nabî* and *rasûl*. Unfortunately, there is no English word capable of conveying the connotation of these terms properly. As regards the word "Prophet", it means, according to English lexicon, "a spokesman of the deity, one who proclaims a divine message, a preacher, a foreteller whether claiming to be inspired or not." Thus it can be adopted as an Islamic term only in a qualified manner—signifying there: "a spokesman of the One True God, who receives the Message from Him through Revelation, and proclaims and preaches it as a divinely appointed Teacher and as the possessor of flawless, sublime and extra-ordinary spiritual and moral personality".

In the Qur'ãnic verses quoted in this book, the words *nabî* and *rasûl* have been translated as "Prophet" and "Messenger" respectively.

"Say thou (O Muhammad)! If ye do love Allah, follow me (and build up your moral and spiritual life on my model): Allah will love you and forgive you your sins: For Allah is Oft-Forgiving, Most merciful." (III:31).

Following and imitating the Holy Prophet (Peace be on him) is not possible, however, without maintaining the attitudes of respect and love towards him,—these, in their turn, giving rise respectively to obedience and absolute loyalty. Thus we arrive at four duties relating to our relation with the Holy Prophet (Peace be on him), namely:

(1) to respect him above all created beings;

(2) to love him above all created beings;

(3) to obey him without demur;

(4) to be absolutely loyal to him.

Starting from the side of man, these four duties form the *essential condition* of the moral agent's Moral Perfection and of the Moral Perfection and Happiness of others—humanity at large, because true Guidance in that connection is available only through the Holy Prophet (Peace be on him) and that Guidance cannot be truly accepted and enthusiastically followed without maintaining the attitude implied in those duties.

We may now state the duties in the language of the Qur'ãn:

(1) Duties of Respect

(a) Subjective:

To regard the Holy Prophet with respect.

(i) Duty of Commission:

Maintaining the attitude of positive respect enjoined:

فَالَّذِينَ آمَنُوا بِهِ وَعَزَّرُوهُ وَنَصَرُوهُ وَاتَّبَعُوا النُّورَ الَّذِي أُنزِلَ
مَعَهُ ۙ أُولَٰئِكَ هُمُ الْمُفْلِحُونَ ○

".....So it is those who believe in him (i.e., Muhammad), and *honour him*, and help him, and follow the Light which is sent down with him,—it is they who will prosper." (VII:157).

(ii) Duty of Omission:

Directly or indirectly insulting the Holy Prophet prohibited:

وَمَا كَانَ لَكُمْ أَنْ تُؤْذُوا رَسُولَ اللَّهِ

"And it is not right for you to insult[2] Allah's Messenger (Muhammad)....." (XXXIII:53).

Worthy of note in this respect is the following stern commands of God given to the Muslims of the Holy Prophet's time:

يَاأَيُّهَا الَّذِينَ آمَنُوا لَا تُقَدِّمُوا بَيْنَ يَدَيِ اللَّهِ وَرَسُولِهِ وَاتَّقُوا اللَّهَ ۚ
إِنَّ اللَّهَ سَمِيعٌ عَلِيمٌ ۝ يَاأَيُّهَا الَّذِينَ آمَنُوا لَا تَرْفَعُوا أَصْوَاتَكُمْ فَوْقَ
صَوْتِ النَّبِيِّ وَلَا تَجْهَرُوا لَهُ بِالْقَوْلِ كَجَهْرِ بَعْضِكُمْ لِبَعْضٍ أَنْ تَحْبَطَ
أَعْمَالُكُمْ وَأَنْتُمْ لَا تَشْعُرُونَ ۝ إِنَّ الَّذِينَ يَغُضُّونَ أَصْوَاتَهُمْ عِنْدَ
رَسُولِ اللَّهِ أُولَٰئِكَ الَّذِينَ امْتَحَنَ اللَّهُ قُلُوبَهُمْ لِلتَّقْوَىٰ ۚ لَهُمْ مَغْفِرَةٌ
وَأَجْرٌ عَظِيمٌ ۝

"O ye who believe! put not yourselves forward[3] before Allah and His Messenger; and fear Allah: for Allah hears and knows all things.

"O ye who believe! raise not your voice above the voice of the Prophet (Muhammad), nor speak aloud to him in talk as ye may speak aloud to one another, lest your deeds (of righteousness) be rendered vain (thereby) and ye perceive not (the loss).

"Verily those who lower their voice in the presence of Allah's Messenger—these are they whose hearts Allah hath disposed unto Piety: For Them is Forgiveness and a great Reward." (XLIX:1-3).

Also: the following guidance to the socially uncouth people of those days:

إِنَّ الَّذِينَ يُنَادُونَكَ مِنْ وَرَاءِ الْحُجُرَاتِ أَكْثَرُهُمْ لَا يَعْقِلُونَ ۝ وَلَوْ أَنَّهُمْ
صَبَرُوا حَتَّىٰ تَخْرُجَ إِلَيْهِمْ لَكَانَ خَيْرًا لَهُمْ ۚ وَاللَّهُ غَفُورٌ رَحِيمٌ ۝

---

2. Insult: *'Azã*, the Arabic word used here, may equally mean: to annoy, to vex, to cause hurt or injury, to ill-treat by slander or unseemly conduct, or hurt the feelings.

3. i.e., do not attempt to give your advice in any matter before you are asked to do so by the Holy Prophet himself.

"Verily those who shout out to thee (O Muhammad) from without the inner apartments—most of them lack proper sense. If only they had patience until thou couldst come out to them, it would be best for them: but Allah is Oft-Forgiving, Most-Merciful." (XLIX:4, 5).

(b) Objective:

To obey the Holy Prophet without demur.

(i) <u>Duty of Commission</u>:

Practising positive obedience enjoined:

وَأَطِيعُوا الرَّسُولَ

".....and obey the Messenger (Muhammad)....." (IV:59).

إِنَّمَا كَانَ قَوْلَ الْمُؤْمِنِينَ إِذَا دُعُوا إِلَى اللَّهِ وَرَسُولِهِ لِيَحْكُمَ بَيْنَهُمْ أَنْ
يَقُولُوا سَمِعْنَا وَأَطَعْنَا ۚ وَأُولَٰئِكَ هُمُ الْمُفْلِحُونَ ۝

"The answer of the Believers, when summoned to Allah and His Messenger, in order that he may judge between them, is no other than this: they say, 'we hear and we obey': It is such as these that will attain felicity." (XXIV:51).

(ii) Duty of Omission:

Disobedience in any manner whatsoever, prohibited:

وَمَنْ يَعْصِ اللَّهَ وَرَسُولَهُ فَقَدْ ضَلَّ ضَلَالًا مُبِينًا ۝

".....and whosoever disobeys Allah and His Messenger, he verily goeth astray in error manifest." (XXXIII:36).

وَمَنْ يُشَاقِقِ الرَّسُولَ مِنْ بَعْدِ مَا تَبَيَّنَ لَهُ الْهُدَىٰ وَيَتَّبِعْ غَيْرَ
سَبِيلِ الْمُؤْمِنِينَ نُوَلِّهِ مَا تَوَلَّىٰ وَنُصْلِهِ جَهَنَّمَ ۖ وَسَاءَتْ مَصِيرًا ۝

"And whosoever opposeth the Messenger even after Guidance hath been plainly conveyed unto him, and follows a path other than that becoming to men of Faith, We shall leave him in the path he hath chosen, and land him in Hell,—what an evil refuge!" (IV:115).

(2) Duties of Love

(a) Subjective:

To regard the Holy Prophet with love.

(i) Duty of Commission:

Maintaining the attitude of positive love—a love which transcends the love for any other created being, emphasised; hence it is duty:

النَّبِيُّ أَوْلَىٰ بِالْمُؤْمِنِينَ مِنْ أَنفُسِهِمْ

"The Prophet is closer to the Believers than their own selves (—this spiritual relationship entitling him to more love and respect from the Believers than for any created being related in any way)."[1] (XXXIII:6).

This personal spiritual love for the Holy Prophet (on whom be Peace and the Blessings of Allah) is to be cultivated, besides obeying him in all things with overflowing love, through forming spiritual contact with him by reciting *salãt* and *salãm*, as commanded by God in the following verse:

إِنَّ اللَّهَ وَمَلَائِكَتَهُ يُصَلُّونَ عَلَى النَّبِيِّ ۚ يَا أَيُّهَا الَّذِينَ آمَنُوا صَلُّوا عَلَيْهِ وَسَلِّمُوا تَسْلِيمًا

"Lo! Allah and His angels shower blessings on the Prophet. O ye who believe! Send your benedictions on him (i.e., ask Allah for His blessings on him) and salute him with a worthy salutation (i.e., with respect and love.)"[5] (XXXIII:56).

4. Cf. the Saying of the Holy Prophet (Peace be on him):

لا يؤمن احدكم حتى اكون احب اليه من والده وولده والناس اجمعين

"None of you can have Faith unless I become to him dearer than his parents, his offspring and (in fact) all human beings." (Bukhãrî: *Sahîh*); Chapter on: *Hubb al Rasûl min al-Imãn.*

5. The shortest formula in this connection is:

صلى الله عليه وسلم

i.e., "Allah has bestowed on him His Blessings and Peace". This formula has

(b) Objective:

To foster absolute loyalty to the Holy Prophet (Peace be on him).

(i) <u>Duty of Commission</u>:

To be positively loyal to him emphasised as a condition of Faith; hence it is duty:

فَلَا وَرَبِّكَ لَا يُؤْمِنُونَ حَتّٰى يُحَكِّمُوكَ فِيمَا شَجَرَ بَيْنَهُمْ ثُمَّ لَا يَجِدُوا فِيٓ أَنْفُسِهِمْ حَرَجًا مِّمَّا قَضَيْتَ وَيُسَلِّمُوا تَسْلِيمًا ۝

"But nay, by thy Lord, they can have no (real) Faith, until they make thee judge in all dispute between them, and find in their souls no resistance against thy decisions, but accept them with the fullest submission." (IV:65).

وَمَا كَانَ لِمُؤْمِنٍ وَّلَا مُؤْمِنَةٍ إِذَا قَضَى اللّٰهُ وَرَسُولُهٗٓ أَمْرًا أَنْ يَّكُونَ لَهُمُ الْخِيَرَةُ مِنْ أَمْرِهِمْ ۭ

"And it becometh not a believing man or a believing woman, when Allah and His Messenger have decided an affair (for them), that they should (after that) claim any say in their affair;....." (XXXIII:36).

(ii) <u>Duty of Omission</u>:

Being disloyal to him in any manner, prohibited:

يٰٓأَيُّهَا الَّذِينَ اٰمَنُوا لَا تَخُونُوا اللّٰهَ وَالرَّسُولَ

"O ye who believe! *be not disloyal to* Allah and *His Messenger.....*" `(VIII:27).

---

been further condensed in the form: "Peace is with him", and is employed in the form of prayer: "Peace be on him."

These words should be repeated whenever a Muslim hears or mentions his sacred name.

Chapter III

DUTIES TO THE ANGELS

END:

(a) *Objective:*

Maintenance of the attitude of respect and love for purity of will and holiness wherever found in God's creatures.

(b) *Subjective:*

Constant consciousness of the fact that the world is a moral order, the angels being the functionaries of God's moral scheme.

(i) Nature and Functions of the Angels:

The angels, according to the Holy Qur'ãn, are neither impersonal forces in the sense of physical science, nor gods or demi-gods or sons or daughters of God, as some of the old mythologies conceived them to be. They are celestial beings endowed with personality[1] having been created[2] by God to act as His functionaries in the universe.[3]

The establishment of relation with the spiritual world, which is a vital condition of the spiritual development of a human being, is not conceivable without faith in the existence of the angels (—which, therefore, forms one of the cardinal articles of Islamic Belief—) and without a proper attitude towards them.

The angels are sinless beings—incapable of committing any sin—and as such possessors of purity, because their function is only to behave as God's absolutely obedient servants:

وَالْمَلٰٓئِكَةُ وَهُمْ لَا يَسْتَكْبِرُوْنَ ۝ يَخَافُوْنَ رَبَّهُمْ مِّنْ فَوْقِهِمْ وَيَفْعَلُوْنَ مَا يُؤْمَرُوْنَ ۝

".....and the angels; they are not arrogant (before their Lord). (Rather,) they fear their Lord, High above them, and they do whatever they are commanded." (XVI:49, 50).

They are honoured servants of God:

1,2,3. XXXV:1.

بَلْ عِبَادٌ مُّكْرَمُونَ ۝ لَا يَسْبِقُونَهُ بِالْقَوْلِ وَهُم بِأَمْرِهِ يَعْمَلُونَ ۝

"They (*i.e.*, the angels) are (but) servants raised to honour. They precede Him not in word and they act (in all things) by His command." (XXI:26, 27).

Besides their numerous functions mentioned in the Holy Qur'ãn, they, out of love for the Believers, ask for God's blessings on them:

هُوَ الَّذِي يُصَلِّي عَلَيْكُمْ وَمَلَائِكَتُهُ لِيُخْرِجَكُم مِّنَ الظُّلُمَاتِ إِلَى النُّورِ
وَكَانَ بِالْمُؤْمِنِينَ رَحِيمًا ۝

"He it is Who sends blessings on you, *as do His angels*, that He may bring you out from the depths of Darkness into Light: and He is Full of Mercy for the Believers." (XXXIII:43).

Also, they pray to God for forgiveness for all beings on the earth:

وَالْمَلَائِكَةُ يُسَبِّحُونَ بِحَمْدِ رَبِّهِمْ وَيَسْتَغْفِرُونَ لِمَن فِي الْأَرْضِ ۗ

".....and the angels celebrate the praises of their Lord, and ask forgiveness for those on the earth." (XLII:5).

(ii) Duties

Thus, because they are honoured beings, they deserve respect; and because they are noble and pure, they deserve love. They deserve love and respect specially from the Believers, whom they love and for whom their solicitude is great.

Part II

DUTIES AS PHYSICAL BEING

I. Duties of Omission:

(or, Duties of Respect for the Self).

END:

Natural Self-Preservation—as the Holy Qur'ãn commands:

وَلَا تُلْقُوا بِأَيْدِيكُمْ إِلَى التَّهْلُكَةِ

".....and be not cast by your own hands to ruin..."[1] (II:195).

(i) All things which harm physical health, prohibited:

يَا أَيُّهَا النَّاسُ كُلُوا مِمَّا فِي الْأَرْضِ حَلَالًا طَيِّبًا وَلَا تَتَّبِعُوا خُطُوَاتِ
الشَّيْطَانِ ۚ إِنَّهُ لَكُمْ عَدُوٌّ مُبِينٌ ۝

"O mankind! eat of whatsoever is on the earth, lawful and wholesome, and *follow not the footsteps of Satan* (*by using unlawfully acquired and unclean and unwholesome foods*[2]). Lo! he is to you an avowed enemy". (II:168).

---

1. This verse has the context of participation in collective welfare. But it also lays down a general principle which covers all situations and aspects of life.

2. Some of the unclean and unwholesome foods expressly mentioned in the Holy Qur'ãn are:

حُرِّمَتْ عَلَيْكُمُ الْمَيْتَةُ وَالدَّمُ وَلَحْمُ الْخِنْزِيرِ وَمَا أُهِلَّ لِغَيْرِ اللَّهِ بِهِ وَ
الْمُنْخَنِقَةُ وَالْمَوْقُوذَةُ وَالْمُتَرَدِّيَةُ وَالنَّطِيحَةُ وَمَا أَكَلَ السَّبُعُ إِلَّا مَا ذَكَّيْتُمْ
وَمَا ذُبِحَ عَلَى النُّصُبِ

"Forbidden unto you (for food) are carrion, and blood, and swineflesh, and that over which is invoked the name of other than Allah, and the strangled, the felled (*i.e.*, killed by a blow), and the dead through falling from a height, and that which hath been killed by (the goring of) horns, and that which hath been (partly) eaten by wild beasts—saving that which ye make lawful (by the death-stroke), and that which hath been slaughtered on the altars (according to the

(ii) Self-stupefaction, gluttony and intoxication, prohibited:

يَاأَيُّهَا الَّذِينَ آمَنُوا لَا تُحَرِّمُوا طَيِّبَاتِ مَا أَحَلَّ اللَّهُ لَكُمْ وَلَا تَعْتَدُوا ۚ
إِنَّ اللَّهَ لَا يُحِبُّ الْمُعْتَدِينَ ○

"O ye who believe! Make not unlawful the good things (whether they be foods or drinks or any other lawful pleasures) which Allah hath made lawful for you, nor transgress (in respect of your physical, mental, moral, spiritual and social health by making lawful for yourselves harmful foods, drinks, etc.); verily Allah loveth not the transgressors."[3] (V:90).

وَكُلُوا وَاشْرَبُوا وَلَا تُسْرِفُوا ۚ إِنَّهُ لَا يُحِبُّ الْمُسْرِفِينَ ○

".....and eat and drink, but *be not immoderate and intemperate*: verily He loveth not those who are immoderate and intemperate." (VII:31).

كُلُوا مِنْ طَيِّبَاتِ مَا رَزَقْنَاكُمْ وَلَا تَطْغَوْا فِيهِ فَيَحِلَّ عَلَيْكُمْ غَضَبِي ۖ وَمَنْ
يَحْلِلْ عَلَيْهِ غَضَبِي فَقَدْ هَوَىٰ ○

"Eat of the good things We have provided for your sustenance, but *commit no excess therein*, lest My wrath should justly descend on you; and those on whom descends My wrath do perish indeed." (XX:81).

يَاأَيُّهَا الَّذِينَ آمَنُوا إِنَّمَا الْخَمْرُ وَالْمَيْسِرُ وَالْأَنْصَابُ وَالْأَزْلَامُ رِجْسٌ
مِنْ عَمَلِ الشَّيْطَانِ فَاجْتَنِبُوهُ لَعَلَّكُمْ تُفْلِحُونَ ○

"O ye who believe! Intoxicants[4] and gambling, (dedication of) stones, and divination by arrows, (all these) are an abomination,—of

---

custom of pagan Arabs)...." (V:4).

وَلَا تَأْكُلُوا مِمَّا لَمْ يُذْكَرِ اسْمُ اللَّهِ عَلَيْهِ وَإِنَّهُ لَفِسْقٌ ۗ

"And eat not of that whereon Allah's name hath not been mentioned, for lo! it is abomination." (VI:121).

3. This verse forbids:—(i) self-mortification, upheld by asceticism; (ii) self-indulgence, and the consequent self-stupefaction, upheld by the hedonistic attitude.

4. The word *Khamr* used in the Arabic text stands, according to Lane, for "any intoxicating thing that clouds or obscures (lit. covers) the intellect." (*Arabic-English Lexicon*). Thus the Prohibition here relates to all intoxicants.

Of course, the most immediate reference here is to alcohol, or, wine, which was used as an intoxicant by the Arabs of those days and which is the scourge of the modern civilisation also.

The total prohibition of wine by the Qur'ãn is a fact of history, to which all historians of Islam, including its worst critics, have borne testimony. For instance, D.S. Margoliouth says: "When the revelation came, zealous followers went round the houses of the Muslims and emptied their vessels of all liquor which was supposed to be intoxicating, in many cases breaking the vessels themselves.....The prohibition was extended, to vinegar made of wine and a categorical denial was given to the suggestion that wine had medicinal value." (*Muhammad*, p. 283).

Still there are some "Muslims" today who, under the impact of the irreligious and the hedonistic influences of Western culture, not only drink wine but try to believe themselves and make others believe that, according to the Holy Qur'ãn, wine is not something totally evil,—wrongly taking shelter in the Qur'ãnic verse which says:

يَسْـَٔلُونَكَ عَنِ ٱلْخَمْرِ وَٱلْمَيْسِرِ قُلْ فِيهِمَآ إِثْمٌ كَبِيرٌ وَمَنَٰفِعُ لِلنَّاسِ
وَإِثْمُهُمَآ أَكْبَرُ مِن نَّفْعِهِمَا

"They ask thee (O Prophet) about wine and gambling. Tell (them): in both is a great sin, and *some benefit, for men,* but the sin of them is (far) greater than their benefit...." (II:219).

The vehement condemnation of wine even in this verse is very definite. However, coming to the words 'some benefits', what has been really affirmed is not any benefit in respect of human consumption but the other benefits to which a scientist refers thus: "Alcohol's most useful sphere of action is as a solvent in industrial concerns. (Dastur, *Alcohol: Its Use and Misuse*, p. 109).

The truth, based on all available evidence, is that all intoxicants, including alcohol, are among the greatest enemies of mankind. As the medical scientist whom we have just quoted says: "Alcohol belongs to a family of poisonous chemicals. Its theoretic food-value is of no value in practical dietics. It is never a stimulant. It has a sedative drug-action in moderate doses, and a narcotic poison-action in excess.....Its use as a beverage is physiologically unsound, economically disastrous, socially disruptive, and materially poisonous." (*op.cit.*, pp. 108, 109). As regards the social evils promoted by alcohol, the *Encyclopaedia of Religion and Ethics* pronounces the verdict that: "There is universal testimony as to the close relationship between excessive drinking the breaches of the moral law and the laws of the State. This is a direct consequence of the paralysis of the higher faculties, intellectual and moral, and the resulting free-play given to the

Satan's handiwork: shun such (abomination), therefore, that ye may prosper." (V:93).

(iii) Considering lawful pleasures relating to natural appetites as illegitimate, prohibited:[5]

يَا أَيُّهَا الَّذِينَ آمَنُوا لَا تُحَرِّمُوا طَيِّبَاتِ مَا أَحَلَّ اللَّهُ لَكُمْ

---

lower inclinations." (vol. I, p. 301). This verdict is confirmed by the *Jewish Encyclopaedia*, which says (I; p. 333): ".....the statistics of Baer, Kurelia, Gallavandis, and Sichart show that from 25 to 85 percent of all malefactors are drunkards."

We may observe here in passing the very unfortunate fact that certain religious groups, which have wielded a tremendous influence in human history, should have been responsible for patronising an evil that has engulfed a large part of mankind today. We may refer, for instance, to the Jews and the Christians. In the estimation of the Bible, wine 'cheereth God and man'. (*Judg*. 9:14). As for the Jewish religious practice, Friendler says in *The Jewish Religion* that: "it has been ordered (in the Jewish religion) that our meal on the eve of Sabbath and Festival should begin with a cup of wine in the honour of the day..... The *kidduah* consists of two blessings: one over the wine, one that refers to the holiness of the day." (p. 341). Coming to the Christian Church and clergy, the use of alcohol "was never absent from the Church nor from its clergy." (Smith and Cheetam's *Dictionary of Christian Antiquities*, I, p. 585). According to Cheyne and Black's *Encyclopaedia Biblica* (c. 1569), in the case of fire on the Sabbath day, only three necessaries of life are to be rescued by the good Christians, viz., "a basket of loaves, a cake of dried figs and a jar of wine."

5. The following verse is more explicit in disapproving Asceticism as a philosophy of life:

وَرَهْبَانِيَّةً ابْتَدَعُوهَا مَا كَتَبْنَاهَا عَلَيْهِمْ إِلَّا ابْتِغَاءَ رِضْوَانِ اللَّهِ فَمَا رَعَوْهَا
حَقَّ رِعَايَتِهَا ۚ فَآتَيْنَا الَّذِينَ آمَنُوا مِنْهُمْ أَجْرَهُمْ ۚ وَكَثِيرٌ مِنْهُمْ
فَاسِقُونَ ۝

"But (the institution of) Asceticism (Monasticism) which they (i.e., the early Christians) invented for themselves, We prescribed it not for them: (We commanded) only the seeking of Divine Pleasure; but that they did not foster as they should have done. Yet We bestowed, on those among them who believed, their (due) reward, but many of them are transgressors." (LVII:27).

That the unnatural suppression of sexual appetite by the institution of Asceticism promotes sexual vice, rather than cubring it, is borne out by the history of Christianity. As Scott says: "With the passing of the concubine, the nuns in the convents provided the 'holy men' with the means of satisfying their sexual cravings." (*History of Prostitution*, p. 112).

"O ye who believe! Make not unlawful (for yourselves) the good things (relating to lawful pleasures) which Allah hath made lawful for you....." (V:90)

(iv) Abusing or damaging any limb of one's body, including Castration, prohibited:

The Holy Qur'ãn says:

لَا ..... تَخُونُوٓا أَمَٰنَٰتِكُمْ

".....and defraud not your trusts....." (VIII:27).

The various limbs of the body, and the talents of a Muslim, are the "property" of God and he possesses them in "trust" for Him. A Muslim should not, therefore, abuse or damage any limb of his body[6].

(v) Committing suicide prohibited:

وَلَا تَقْتُلُوٓا أَنفُسَكُمْ ۚ إِنَّ ٱللَّهَ كَانَ بِكُمْ رَحِيمًا ۝

"And kill not (or, destroy not) yourselves; verily Allah is unto you ever Merciful."[7] (IV:29).

(2) <u>Duties of Commission</u>:

(or, Duties of Love for the Self).

***<u>END</u>*:**

Happiness of the moral agent through the maintenance and promotion of his physical well-being:

(i) Proper satisfaction of natural appetites enjoined:

(a) *Satisfaction of Hunger and Thirst:*

---

6. Those spiritualists who have regarded the body as an impediment in the way of their so-called spiritual progress have practised, as among a sect of the Hindus, the "drying up", or deliberate emaciation, of the limbs. Similarly, castration has been considered a means of curbing the sexual appetite and thereby acquiring the freedom to pursue "spirituality".

7. Speaking of this Qur'ãnic injunction, which prohibits suicide in all its forms, Professor Lecky says: "Suicide, which is never expressly condemned in the Bible, is more than once forbidden in the Koran." (*History of European Morals*, II, p. 23).

وَكُلُوا وَاشْرَبُوا وَلَا تُسْرِفُوا ۚ

".....and eat and drink, but be not immoderate and intemperate....."
(VII:31).

يَسْأَلُونَكَ مَاذَا أُحِلَّ لَهُمْ ۖ قُلْ أُحِلَّ لَكُمُ الطَّيِّبَاتُ ۙ

"They ask thee (O Muhammad!) what is lawful to them (as food). Say: Lawful unto you are all things good and pure." (V:5).

(b) *Satisfaction of sexual appetite:*

Satisfaction of sexual appetite has been permitted by the Holy Qur'ãn through lawful marriage *only*, and marriage has been enjoined:

وَأَنكِحُوا الْأَيَامَىٰ مِنكُمْ

"Marry those among you who are single."[8] (XXIV:32).

A very important point should be noted here. Although the union of man and woman in marriage involves the satisfaction of sexual appetite, it is *not*, in the view of the Qur'ãn, the end of marriage—the end being spiritual companionship and mutual love to which the sexual union itself should contribute, but which is marked off distinctly from mere sexual pleasure. The Holy Qur'ãn says:

وَمِنْ آيَاتِهِ أَنْ خَلَقَ لَكُم مِّنْ أَنفُسِكُمْ أَزْوَاجًا لِّتَسْكُنُوا إِلَيْهَا وَجَعَلَ
بَيْنَكُم مَّوَدَّةً وَرَحْمَةً ۚ إِنَّ فِي ذَٰلِكَ لَآيَاتٍ لِّقَوْمٍ يَتَفَكَّرُونَ ۝

"And among His Signs is this, that He created for you mates from among yourselves, that ye might obtain tranquillity and solace in them, and He hath ordained between you love and mercy. Verily in that are Signs for those who reflect." (XXX:21).

(c) *Rest and Sleep:*

وَمِن رَّحْمَتِهِ جَعَلَ لَكُمُ اللَّيْلَ وَالنَّهَارَ لِتَسْكُنُوا فِيهِ وَلِتَبْتَغُوا مِن
فَضْلِهِ وَلَعَلَّكُمْ تَشْكُرُونَ ۝

---

8. i.e., not in the bond of wedlock: they may be those who are unmarried, or those who have been lawfully divorced, or those who have been widowed.

"It is of His Mercy that he hath made for you Night and Day, *that therein* (*i.e., in the night*) *ye may enjoy rest*, and that ye may seek of His Grace (during the day);—and in order that ye may be grateful (to Him)." (XXVIII:73).

(ii) Physical cleanliness[9] *enjoined:*

فَاطَّهَّرُوْا ؕ

".....then purify (yourselves) (with physical cleanliness)....." (V:7).

مَا يُرِيْدُ اللّٰهُ لِيَجْعَلَ عَلَيْكُمْ مِّنْ حَرَجٍ وَّلٰكِنْ يُّرِيْدُ لِيُطَهِّرَكُمْ
وَلِيُتِمَّ نِعْمَتَهٗ عَلَيْكُمْ لَعَلَّكُمْ تَشْكُرُوْنَ ۝

"Allah intendeth not to lay upon you a hardship, but intendeth to purify you (with physical cleanliness) and to complete His favour to you, ye may be grateful (for His bounties)." (V:7).

---

9. The Holy Qur'ãn emphasis on physical cleanliness stands in sharp contrast with the "merit of uncleanliness" emphasised in the life of the followers of certain other religions, *e.g.*, Christianity. Writing of the medieval Christian aspirants of holiness, Professor Licky says: "The cleanliness of the body was regarded as a pollution of the soul, and the saints who were most admired had become one hideous mass of clotted filth. St. Athanasius relates with enthusiasm how St. Anthony, the patriarch of monarchism, had never, to extreme old age, been guilty of washing his feet....St. Euphraxia joined a convent of one hundred and thirty nuns, who never washed their feet, and who shuddered at the mention of a bath." (*op.cit.*, II, p. 47). Of a Christian pilgrim of the 4th century, the *Encyclopaedia Britannica* informs: "(she) boasted that she had not washed her face for 18 years for fear of removing the baptismal chrism." (I, p. 49).

"Dirt and disease became (in Christendom) the honourable insignia of saintship; loathsome fakirs exhibited their filth and their sores for the veneration of the faithful." (Hammerton: *Universal History of the World*, IV, p. 2333).

"Certainly," says another Western scholar, "the maxim which places cleanliness next to godliness, has no place in the biographies of the saints and heroes of monasticism even in climates where bathing would seem almost one of the necessities of life. Jerome warns ascetics against warm bath as morally enervating, and in a letter to one of his female disciples denounces every sort of bathing for women. Augustine allows a bath once a month only." (*Dictionary of Christian Antiquities,* II, p. 939).

وَيُنَزِّلُ عَلَيْكُم مِّنَ السَّمَاءِ مَاءً لِّيُطَهِّرَكُم بِهِ وَيُذْهِبَ عَنكُمْ رِجْزَ الشَّيْطَانِ

".....and He sent down water upon you from heaven that He might cleanse you thereby and remove from you the stain of Satan (—dirt being physically a symbol of evil)....." (VIII:11).

إِنَّ اللَّهَ يُحِبُّ التَّوَّابِينَ وَيُحِبُّ الْمُتَطَهِّرِينَ ۝

"Verily Allah loveth those who turn to him constantly, and He loveth those who practise cleanliness (in body, mind and spirit)." (II:222).

وَاللَّهُ يُحِبُّ الْمُطَّهِّرِينَ ۝

"And Allah loveth those who always keep themselves clean." (IX:108).

(iii) Physical development enjoined:

وَأَعِدُّوا لَهُم مَّا اسْتَطَعْتُم مِّن قُوَّةٍ

"Against them (i.e., the enemies of Islam, or, the forces of evil) prepare your Power (as individuals and as a community) to the utmost of your capacity....." (VIII:60).

Development of power by an individual includes the building up of a powerful physique. Hence, the command for the physical development of the individual is contained in the above comprehensive verse. This fact is corroborated by a *hadīth* of the Holy Prophet (Peace be on him), reported by Muslim in his *Sahīh* in the following words:

المؤمن القوىّ خير واحب الى الله من المؤمن الضعيف وفى كلٍّ خير
احرص على ما ينفعك واستعن بالله ولا تعجز

"A physically strong Believer is better and more loved by Allah than a physically weak Believer. And there is good in either of them. Be enthusiastic for everything which brings thee good, and seek therein Divine Help, and do not lose heart in thine endeavour....." (*Kitāb al-Qadr*).

Part III

DUTIES AS RATIONAL BEING

END:

(*i*) *Subjective:*

Balanced and healthy development of human knowledge in all dimensions.

(*ii*) *Objective:*

Service to humanity in terms of correct and comprehensive Guidance.

(*1*) *Duty of Commission:*

Pursuit of knowledge enjoined, with emphasis on:

(i) *its sublimity and unavoidable necessity—basically and for proper moral life.*

(ii) *its importance for spiritual development:*

(iii) *its role in conferring greatness on individuals and communities:*

(iv) *its compatibility with Faith;*

(v) *the principles of observation and research;*

(vi) *the principle of continuous and ceaseless endeavour for rising to higher and higher levels of knowledge;*

(vii) *the principle of Objectivity;*

(viii) *the principle of Comprehensiveness;*

(ix) *the attainment of the stage* of al-Hikmah, *or, the Wisdom;*

(x) *the technique of attaining all Higher Knowledge.*

Thus:

(*i*) ***Sublimity of the pursuit of Knowledge and its unavoidable necessity—basically as also for proper moral life, emphasised:***

The Holy Qur'ãn says:

وَعَلَّمَ آدَمَ الْأَسْمَاءَ كُلَّهَا

"And He imparted to Adam knowledge of the nature of all things....." (II:31).

The story of Adam given in the Holy Qur'ãn (II:30-39) reveals that knowledge was imparted to him by God:

(a) at the transcendental or spiritual stage of his existence, —when his life was sublime because of the innocence and the serene tranquillity that he enjoyed, together with his wife, in the "Presence of God";

(b) before he embarked on his earthly career, i.e., before he had the occasion to engage himself in wordly pursuits,—nay, before he had acquired any wordly interests;

(c) before he was confronted with the moral struggle.

All this means that, in the estimation of the Holy Qur'ãn:

(*a*) Acquisition of knowledge is a sublime and a spiritual pursuit;

(*b*) Cultivation of knowledge is one of the most basic needs and, hence, one of the most basic duties of a human being;

(*c*) Proper knowledge forms one of the most basic requirements of proper moral life.

(ii) Spiritual achievement through Knowledge, especially of empirical Reality, emphasised:

The Hoy Qur'ãn says:

إِنَّمَا يَخْشَى اللَّهَ مِنْ عِبَادِهِ الْعُلَمَاؤُا

".....Those only among His Servants who are learned (i.e., possessors and pursuers of knowledge) truly fear Allah." (XXXV:28).

Here possession and pursuit of knowledge—all true knowledge[1]—has been mentioned as the condition for true fear of God,

1. It is necessary to note here that the theme which is sealed by this verse, being contained in the verses immediately preceding and joining it, relates to the study of natural phenomena—the theme of physical science—, which means that the knowledge which has been commended here so highly comprehends within itself the cultivation of knowledge of God's creation and through that

which, in its turn, is, together with the love for God, the motivating force in the life of every true Muslim. Thus pursuit of knowledge becomes a duty from the point of view of leading a good spiritual and moral life.

(iii) Acquisition of greatness through Knowledge emphasised:

The Holy Qur'ãn says:

يَرْفَعِ اللّٰهُ الَّذِيْنَ اٰمَنُوْا مِنْكُمْ ۙ وَالَّذِيْنَ اُوْتُوا الْعِلْمَ دَرَجٰتٍ

"Allah will exalt those who have Faith among you, and those who have knowledge to high ranks"[2]. (LVIII:11).

According to this verse, basis for exaltation in the estimation of God is not only Faith in God and all spiritual verities, which is the highest theme of Religion, but also Knowledge, which forms as high a theme in the religion presented by the Holy Qur'ãn. This honoured place given to knowledge makes it obligatory for a Muslim to devote himself to it whole-heartedly.

(iv). Compatibility of Knowledge and Faith emphasised.

A very important point should be noted here. Faith and Knowledge, in the view of the Holy Qur'ãn, are compatible with each other. Indeed they are complementary—wedded to one another, as another verse clearly establishes:

---

the realisation of the greatness and the majesty of God. The immediately preceding verses are:

اَلَمْ تَرَ اَنَّ اللّٰهَ اَنْزَلَ مِنَ السَّمَآءِ مَآءً ۚ فَاَخْرَجْنَا بِهٖ ثَمَرٰتٍ مُّخْتَلِفًا اَلْوَانُهَا ۚ
وَمِنَ الْجِبَالِ جُدَدٌۢ بِيْضٌ وَّحُمْرٌ مُّخْتَلِفٌ اَلْوَانُهَا وَغَرَابِيْبُ سُوْدٌ ۝ وَمِنَ
النَّاسِ وَالدَّوَآبِّ وَالْاَنْعَامِ مُخْتَلِفٌ اَلْوَانُهٗ كَذٰلِكَ ۗ

"Seest thou not that Allah sends down rain from the sky? With it We then bring out produce of various colours. And in the mountains are tracts white and red, of various shades of colour, and black intense in hue. And so amongst men and crawling creatures and cattle, are they of various colours....."

(XXXV:27, 28).

2. This verse lays down clearly the Divine law for all human communities that one of the major factors which can make them great and powerful in the world is the cultivation of knowledge.

وَالرّٰسِخُوْنَ فِی الْعِلْمِ یَقُوْلُوْنَ اٰمَنَّا بِهٖ كُلٌّ مِّنْ عِنْدِ رَبِّنَا ۚ
وَمَا یَذَّكَّرُ اِلَّآ اُولُوا الْاَلْبَابِ ○

"And those who are firmly grounded in knowledge say: 'We believe in the Book; the whole of it is from our Lord': and none will grasp the Message except men of understanding." (III:7).

This is a unique feature of the Qur'ãnic philosophy.

Thus, the Holy Qur'ãn demands acceptance and adherence to its teachings on rational basis. It proclaims most emphatically:

لِّیَهْلِكَ مَنْ هَلَكَ عَنْۢ بَیِّنَةٍ وَّیَحْیٰى مَنْ حَیَّ عَنْۢ بَیِّنَةٍ

"So that he who perisheth (spiritually) should perish by indisputable (rational) evidence (or, proof) and he who surviveth (spiritually) should survive by indisputable (rational) evidence (or, proof)". (VIII:42).

It challenges its opponents on the basis of reason and knowledge in these words:

قُلْ هَلْ عِنْدَكُمْ مِّنْ عِلْمٍ فَتُخْرِجُوْهُ لَنَا ۚ اِنْ تَتَّبِعُوْنَ اِلَّا الظَّنَّ وَاِنْ
اَنْتُمْ اِلَّا تَخْرُصُوْنَ ○ قُلْ فَلِلّٰهِ الْحُجَّةُ الْبَالِغَةُ ۚ

"Say: 'Have ye any (certain) knowledge? If so, produce it before us. Lo! ye follow naught but opinion. Lo! ye do but guess".

"Say: With Allah is the argument that reaches home'." (VI:148, 149).

Again:

اَفَلَا یَتَدَبَّرُوْنَ الْقُرْاٰنَ ؕ

"Will they not then ponder on the Qur'ãn (i.e., examine its teachings rationally)." (IV:82; XLVII:24).

In fact, the Holy Qur'ãn appeals to humanity not less than forty-eight times--and at numerous places on the basis of the physical, the psychical and the social phenomena—to employ reason, emphasising regarding the truth of its teaching that:

وَتِلْكَ الْأَمْثَالُ نَضْرِبُهَا لِلنَّاسِ ۚ وَمَا يَعْقِلُهَا إِلَّا الْعَالِمُونَ ۝

"And these similitudes We set forth for mankind. But their import is grasped by the reason of only those who possess knowledge."

(XXIX:43).

(v) Observation and Research emphasised:

Similarly, the Holy Qur'ãn appeals not less than seventeen times to contemplate and meditate on the natural phenomena as well as on the truth of its own teachings. In that connection, it emphasises also the joint exploration of truth:

قُلْ إِنَّمَا أَعِظُكُم بِوَاحِدَةٍ ۖ أَن تَقُومُوا لِلَّهِ مَثْنَىٰ وَفُرَادَىٰ ثُمَّ تَتَفَكَّرُوا ۚ

"Say: I admonish you on one point: that ye awake, for Allah's sake, by twos and singly, and then contemplate." (XXXIV:46).

This contemplation is to be pursued in the form of search and *research* for arriving at the truth:

مَا تَرَىٰ فِي خَلْقِ الرَّحْمَٰنِ مِن تَفَاوُتٍ ۖ فَارْجِعِ الْبَصَرَ هَلْ تَرَىٰ مِن فُطُورٍ ۝
ثُمَّ ارْجِعِ الْبَصَرَ كَرَّتَيْنِ

"Thou shalt not behold want of proportion in the Creation of (Allah) Most Gracious. So turn thy vision again: seest thou any flaw? Then respect thy look twice over....." (LXVII:3, 4).

(vi) Endeavour to rise higher and higher in knowledge emphasised:

The Holy Qur'ãn has taught the prayer:

وَقُل رَّبِّ زِدْنِي عِلْمًا ۝

".....and say: O my Lord! advance me in knowledge." (XX:114).

It is evident that to pray for advance in knowledge and not to strive for it with might and main would be the height of irrationality. Therefore, this prayer implies the Divine Command for striving after knowledge. Hence, the duty to strive with a devoted and sincere heart for continuous progress in knowledge.

(vii) Objectivity in Knowledge emphasised:

But this duty has to be pursued, as the wordings of the above verse establish clearly, with reference to God, Who is the Source of all Truth. In other words, quest for knowledge should be based on unflinching faith in God and in His Guidance, and should be inspired purely by the motive of search for Reality and love for Truth. All preconceived notions, superficial opinions and conjectures should be avoided. In other words, the pursuit should be based on *objectivity*. Persons undertaking this pursuits should strive to be, as the Holy Qur'ãn states:

أُولُوا الْعِلْمِ قَائِمًا بِالْقِسْطِ ۚ

"Those possessing knowledge with devotion to justice (or, objectivity in knowledge)"—in other words, "the learned who are balanced (in their view of Reality)", being spiritually as well as rationally illumined. (III:18).

According to the Holy Qur'ãn this is rationally possible only for a devotee of God, Who is the Source of all Knowledge. It says:

إِنَّ فِي خَلْقِ السَّمٰوٰتِ وَالْأَرْضِ وَاخْتِلَافِ الَّيْلِ وَالنَّهَارِ لَآيٰتٍ لِأُولِي
الْأَلْبَابِ ۝ الَّذِينَ يَذْكُرُونَ اللّٰهَ قِيٰمًا وَّقُعُودًا وَّعَلٰى جُنُوبِهِمْ
وَيَتَفَكَّرُونَ فِي خَلْقِ السَّمٰوٰتِ وَالْأَرْضِ ۚ رَبَّنَا مَا خَلَقْتَ هٰذَا
بَاطِلًا ۚ سُبْحٰنَكَ فَقِنَا عَذَابَ النَّارِ ۝

"Behold! in the constitution of the heavens and the earth, and in the alternation of the Day and the Night,—there are indeed Signs for the possessors of understanding (i.e., the wise),—such as celebrate the praises of Allah, standing, sitting, and reclining, and reflect on (the problems relating to) the constitution of the heavens and the earth (finally) acquiring that stage of understanding the Reality where the conviction bursts out from them): 'Our Lord! Thou createst not (all) this in vain? Glory be to Thee! Give us salvation from the Penalty of the Fire'." (III:190, 191).

Thus the pursuit of knowledge should have, as its technique, non-capricious penetrating observation of the universe and man.

(viii) Comprehensive pursuit of Knowledge emphasised:

Observation relating to the Universe as a whole has been emphasised, among other verses, in III:191 quoted above. Observation of man's immediate environment—natural as well as social—and of his inner self has been emphasised in the following verses:

وَفِي الْأَرْضِ آيَاتٌ لِّلْمُوقِنِينَ ۝ وَفِي أَنفُسِكُمْ ۚ أَفَلَا تُبْصِرُونَ ۝

"On the earth are Signs for those who have sure faith (in the meaningfulness of all things), as also (there are Signs) in your own selves: will ye not, then, observe?" (LI:20, 21).

(ix) Quest for the stage of 'Wisdom' emphasised:

Such quest for knowledge will bear the fruit of *al-Hikmah*, or the Wisdom, about which the Holy Qur'ãn says:

وَمَن يُؤْتَ الْحِكْمَةَ فَقَدْ أُوتِيَ خَيْرًا كَثِيرًا ۗ وَمَا يَذَّكَّرُ إِلَّا أُولُو الْأَلْبَابِ ۝

".....and whoso is granted the Wisdom, receives indeed abundant Good, but none receives admonition save those possessing understanding." (II:269).

They will finally be blessed with guiding mankind aright on the basis of sure knowledge contained in the Divine Guidance, even as the Holy Prophet (Peace be on him) has been asked by God to declare:

قُلْ هَٰذِهِ سَبِيلِي أَدْعُو إِلَى اللَّهِ ۚ عَلَىٰ بَصِيرَةٍ أَنَا وَمَنِ اتَّبَعَنِي ۖ وَسُبْحَانَ
اللَّهِ وَمَا أَنَا مِنَ الْمُشْرِكِينَ ۝

"Say: 'This is my Way. I call to Allah with sure knowledge, I and whoever follows after me. To Allah be glory! And I am not among the idolaters'." (XII:108).

(x) The correct technique of attaining Higher Knowledge:

The process of education for acquiring higher knowledge, deducible from the Holy Qur'ãn, may also be mentioned here for further edification. Speaking of the functions of the Holy Prophet (Peace be on him) as Divine *Teacher*, the holy book informs us:

هُوَ الَّذِي بَعَثَ فِي الْأُمِّيِّينَ رَسُولًا مِّنْهُمْ يَتْلُو عَلَيْهِمْ آيَاتِهِ وَيُزَكِّيهِمْ وَيُعَلِّمُهُمُ
الْكِتَابَ وَالْحِكْمَةَ

"It is He Who has sent among the Unlettered a Messenger (Muhammad) from among them, to rehearse His revelations to them, to purify them, and to teach them the Book and the Wisdom...." (LXII:2).

Thus, we are given three stages of education for the acquisition of higher knowledge:

(1) The stage of basic and general education, represented in the Holy Prophet's mission by communicating Divine Revelations to the people;

(2) The stage of spiritual and moral purification for the sake of eradicating all subjective perversions and acquiring absolute devotion to truth, even as it was ordained in the Holy Prophet's mission;

(3) The stage of pursuing knowledge at the higher level where research is undertaken on the different facets of Reality and direct conviction is acquired on the basis of personal observation and insight, represented in the Holy Prophet's mission by 'teaching the Book and the Wisdom'.

The sum up: Cultivation of all knowledge, employing the method laid down for ensuring the service to truth, is a duty, according to the Holy Qur'ãn, commanded by the Holy Prophet Muhammad (Peace be on him) in the following words:

طلب العلم فريضة على كل مسلم ومسلمة

"Quest for knowledge is a duty for every Muslim man and woman." (Muslim's *Sahîh, Kitãb al-'Ilm*, p. 34).

(2) Duty of Omission:

Subjectivity and capriciousness in the pursuit of knowledge, as also lack of the spirit of observation and open-minded understanding to Truth, condemned:

According to the Holy Qur'ãn, those who employ subjectivity and caprice in the domain of knowledge remain misguided, in spite of the apparent scholarly tone of their endeavour:

أَفَرَءَيْتَ مَنِ اتَّخَذَ إِلَٰهَهُ هَوَىٰهُ وَأَضَلَّهُ اللَّهُ عَلَىٰ عِلْمٍ وَخَتَمَ عَلَىٰ سَمْعِهِ وَقَلْبِهِ وَجَعَلَ عَلَىٰ بَصَرِهِ غِشَٰوَةً فَمَن يَهْدِيهِ مِنۢ بَعْدِ اللَّهِ ۚ أَفَلَا تَذَكَّرُونَ ○

"Hast thou seen him who has taken his caprice to be his god, and Allah has left him astray despite his knowledge, and has sealed up his hearing and his heart (and understanding), and has set on his sight a covering? Who, then, will guide him after Allah (has withdrawn guidance)? Will ye not receive admonition?" (XLV:23).

This is so because:

وَمَا لَهُم بِهِ مِنْ عِلْمٍ ۖ إِن يَتَّبِعُونَ إِلَّا الظَّنَّ ۖ وَإِنَّ الظَّنَّ
لَا يُغْنِي مِنَ الْحَقِّ شَيْئًا ۝

".....they have no knowledge therein. They follow nothing but conjecture; and conjecture avails nothing against Truth." (LIII:28).

As to those who lack the spirit of observation and open-minded understanding of the Truth, they are led to, or remain in, nothing less than infidelity. We are told:

وَكَأَيِّن مِّنْ آيَةٍ فِي السَّمَاوَاتِ وَالْأَرْضِ يَمُرُّونَ عَلَيْهَا وَهُمْ عَنْهَا
مُعْرِضُونَ ۝ وَمَا يُؤْمِنُ أَكْثَرُهُم بِاللَّهِ إِلَّا وَهُم مُّشْرِكُونَ ۝

"How many a Sign there is in the heavens and in the earth that they pass by, turning away from it. And most of them believe not in God without associating other gods with Him!" (XII:105, 106).

This is so, because:

لَهُمْ قُلُوبٌ لَّا يَفْقَهُونَ بِهَا وَلَهُمْ أَعْيُنٌ لَّا يُبْصِرُونَ بِهَا وَلَهُمْ
آذَانٌ لَّا يَسْمَعُونَ بِهَا ۚ أُولَٰئِكَ كَالْأَنْعَامِ بَلْ هُمْ أَضَلُّ ۚ أُولَٰئِكَ هُمُ
الْغَافِلُونَ ۝

"...They have hearts, but understand not with them (*i.e.*, do not exert their will to understand); they have eyes, but perceive not with them; they have ears, but hear not with them. They are like cattle; nay, they are worse (in their listlessness). They are heedless." (VII:179).

Part IV

DUTIES AS AESTHETICAL BEING

Chapter I

PRELIMINARY OBSERVATIONS

The Holy Qur'ãn has given to humanity a theory of Aesthetics of its own. The present is not, however, the proper occasion to expound it. Only the following five points may be mentioned here:

(1) The Qur'ãnic concept of Beauty is wedded to spirituality or godliness.

(2) According to the Qur'ãnic teaching, the essential attributes of Beauty are:

Piety, Purity, Sublimity, Harmony, Balance, Proportion, Order and Perfection.

(3) The Holy Qur'ãn upholds only that Art which is noble and sublime, both in its conception and its goal, and it regards as vulgar and inadmissible all those forms of Art which do not enshrine the essential attributes of Beauty, as it understands and acknowledges.

(4) According to the Holy Qur'ãn, the spiritual value, or, religion, is the highest, and below it stand in serial order the moral, the intellectual and the physical values.

(5) As regards the aesthetic value, it should permeate and pervade all the aspects of human life: physical intellectual, moral, spiritual and social.

Our concern in the present discourse being the duties of man as the possessor of aesthetic consciousness, however, we may first of all observe with advantage the emphasis on aesthetic value found in the Holy Qur'ãn in respect of God, universe and man.

We find in the Holy Writ as follows:

(1) *GOD*:

God is the Possessor of Absolute Beauty:

The Holy Qur'ãn says:

اَللّٰهُ نُوْرُ السَّمٰوٰتِ وَ الْاَرْضِ ؕ

"Allah is the Light of the heavens and the earth." (XXIV:35).

This is one of the most profound verses, endowed with depths of meaning that are unfathomable. In understanding its implication from the point of view of the problem before us, however, the guidance for us lies in the fact that, according to the Holy Qur'ãn, darkness is ugliness, as the following verse denotes:

وَالَّذِيْنَ كَسَبُوا السَّيِّاٰتِ جَزَآءُ سَيِّئَةٍۢ بِمِثْلِهَا ۙ وَتَرْهَقُهُمْ ذِلَّةٌ ؕ مَا لَهُمْ مِّنَ اللّٰهِ مِنْ عَاصِمٍ ۚ كَاَنَّمَآ اُغْشِيَتْ وُجُوْهُهُمْ قِطَعًا مِّنَ الَّيْلِ مُظْلِمًا ؕ اُولٰٓئِكَ اَصْحٰبُ النَّارِ ۚ هُمْ فِيْهَا خٰلِدُوْنَ ○

"But those who have earned evil will have a reward (in the Hereafter) of like evil: ignominy will cover them: no protector they shall have from (the wrath of) Allah: (*ugliness will be their lot*) *as if their faces had been covered with a cloak of darkest night*. Such are the Companions of the Fire; they will abide therein." (X:27).

Now, if darkness relates to ugliness, light relates to beauty,— and thus the transcendental Light of God implies the possession of transcendental Beauty by Him.

Again, God is the Absolute, as we have seen elsewhere. Hence His beauty is Absolute Beauty.

The Holy Prophet (Peace be on him) has, as the expounder of the Holy Qur'ãn *par excellence*, made a very explict and direct statement in this regard. He says:

الله جميل ويحب الجمال

"Allah is Beautiful and He loves Beauty." (Muslim's *Sahîh, Bãb Tahrîm al-Kibr,* p. 65).

(2) *UNIVERSE*:

Being the Possessor of Absolute Beauty, God has very naturally created everything of the world in the frame of beauty, as the following verse says:

الَّذِيٓ أَحْسَنَ كُلَّ شَيْءٍ خَلَقَهُ

".....He Who has made everything which He has created most Good and Beautiful." (XXXII:7).

This is a statement about the universe as a whole and covers all things in the heavens and on the earth.

The Holy Qur'ãn goes, however, beyond this universal statement and embarks, in order to emphasise the existence of beauty further, on certain details with reference to: (i) the earth, its plant life and animal life, (ii) the heavenly bodies that surround the earth, and (iii) Heaven in the World Hereafter, or, what is called, the next world.

(i) *The earth, its plant life and animal life:*

The Holy Qur'ãn says:

(a) in respect of *all things*:

إِنَّا جَعَلْنَا مَا عَلَى الْأَرْضِ زِينَةً لَّهَا

"That which is on the earth We have made but as an adornment[1] for it...." (XVIII:7).

(b) in respect of *minerals and plants:*

وَأَنۢبَتْنَا فِيهَا مِن كُلِّ شَيْءٍ مَّوْزُونٍ

".....and We produced therein (i.e., in the earth) all kinds of things in due balance.[2]" (XV:19).

(c) in respect of *plants only:*

حَتَّىٰٓ إِذَآ أَخَذَتِ الْأَرْضُ زُخْرُفَهَا وَازَّيَّنَتْ

"(vegetation grows) till the earth is clad with its golden ornaments and is decked out in beauty......" (X:24).

(d) in respect of *animals:*

---

1. Mark that 'adorn' means 'add beauty to'.

2. Mark that 'balance' is an essential attribute of beauty.

وَالْأَنْعَامَ خَلَقَهَا ۚ لَكُمْ فِيهَا دِفْءٌ وَمَنَافِعُ وَمِنْهَا تَأْكُلُونَ ۝ وَلَكُمْ فِيهَا جَمَالٌ حِينَ تُرِيحُونَ وَحِينَ تَسْرَحُونَ ۝

"And cattle He hath created for you (O mankind): from them ye derive warmth, and numerous benefits, and of their (meat) ye eat. And *therein is beauty of you as* ye drive them home in evening, and as ye lead them forth to pasture in the morning." (XVI:5, 6).

وَالْخَيْلَ وَالْبِغَالَ وَالْحَمِيرَ لِتَرْكَبُوهَا وَزِينَةً ۚ وَيَخْلُقُ مَا لَا تَعْلَمُونَ ۝

"And (God hath created) horse, mules, and donkeys, that ye may ride them, and as *adornment;* and He will create (in future, through the mind and ingenuity of man, other vehicles) that ye know not (at the time of the revelation of the Qur'ān)". (XVI:8).

فَاقِعٌ لَوْنُهَا تَسُرُّ النَّاظِرِينَ ۝

"(The sacrificial cow, ordered by Moses, was to be) bright in her colour, providing pleasure to the beholders." (II:69).

(ii) The heavenly bodies that surround the earth:

In this respect, the Holy Qur'ān says:

وَلَقَدْ جَعَلْنَا فِي السَّمَاءِ بُرُوجًا وَزَيَّنَّاهَا لِلنَّاظِرِينَ ۝

"And assuredly We have set constellations in the heaven and We have beautified it for beholders." (XV:16).

إِنَّا زَيَّنَّا السَّمَاءَ الدُّنْيَا بِزِينَةٍ الْكَوَاكِبِ ۝

"We have indeed decked the lower heaven with beauty (in) the stars....." (XXXVII:6).

(iii) Heaven in the World Hereafter:

The Holy Qur'ān says about Heaven:

حَسُنَتْ مُسْتَقَرًّا وَمُقَامًا ۝

".....how beautiful an abode and place of rest!" (XXV:76).

وَحُسْنَ مَاٰبٍ ۝

"…..beautiful Place of (final) Return." (XXXVIII:25).

فَلَا تَعْلَمُ نَفْسٌ مَّآ اُخْفِيَ لَهُمْ مِّنْ قُرَّةِ اَعْيُنٍ جَزَآءًۢ بِمَا كَانُوْا يَعْمَلُوْنَ ۝

"Now no person knows what delight of the eyes (—what aesthetic satisfaction—) is kept hidden (in reserve) for them (in Heaven)—as a reward for their (good) deeds." (XXXII:17).

فَوَقٰىهُمُ اللّٰهُ شَرَّ ذٰلِكَ الْيَوْمِ وَلَقّٰىهُمْ نَضْرَةً وَّسُرُوْرًا ۝

"But Allah will deliever them from the evil of that Day, and will shed over them a Light of Beauty and a (blissful) Joy." (LXXVI:11).

وُجُوْهٌ يَّوْمَئِذٍ نَّاضِرَةٌ ۝ اِلٰى رَبِّهَا نَاظِرَةٌ ۝

"Some faces, that Day, will beam (in brightness and beauty), looking towards their Lord (Who is the Source of all Beauty and the Bestower of all Blessings)." (LXXV:22, 23).

(3) *MAN*:

According to the Holy Qur'ãn, human beings are possessors of Beauty, both outwardly and inwardly. It says:

لَقَدْ خَلَقْنَا الْاِنْسَانَ فِيْٓ اَحْسَنِ تَقْوِيْمٍ ۝

"We have indeed created man in the best and the most beautiful[3] constitution.[4]"[5] (XCV:4)

وَصَوَّرَكُمْ فَاَحْسَنَ صُوَرَكُمْ

---

3. *Ahsan* means: the best, the most beautiful.

4. *Taqwîm* means: constitution, mould, form, nature, symmetry.

5. Man is, therefore, "the comeliest specimen of God's handiwork", according to Maulana Abdul Majid Daryabadi (*English Translation and Commentary of the Holy Qur'ãn*, p. 956, n. 438); and, according to Allama Abdullah Yusuf Ali (*English Translation and Commentary of the Holy Qur'ãn*, p. 1759, n. 6199), "to man God gave the purest and the best nature." Mark here that symmetry and purity are the attributes of beauty.

"And (it is Allah Who hath) given you shape (O mankind!), and made your shapes beautiful...." (XL:64).

وَنَفْسٍ وَّمَا سَوّٰىهَا ۝

"By the Soul and Him Who endowed it with proportion and order[6]...." (XCI:7).

The above discussion proves that the Holy Qur'ãn is vehemently emphatic on the aesthetic value, affirming as it does, beauty in God, universe and man.

6. Mark that proportion and order are attributes of Beauty. Hence this verse refers definitely to the beauty of the inner personality of the human being.

Chapter II

DUTIES

The facts stated in the preceding chapter being what they are, the question is: Has the Holy Qur'ãn prescribed any duties relating to the aesthetic aspect of human life?

The answer is: yes.

Let us look into the details.

1. *The Holy Qur'ãn wants its followers to beautify their Faith and their actions,* and strive to obtain beautiful reward from God, as the following verses reveal:

وَمَنْ أَحْسَنُ دِينًا مِّمَّنْ أَسْلَمَ وَجْهَهُ لِلَّهِ وَهُوَ مُحْسِنٌ

"Who can be more beautiful in religion (—Faith and Action—) than one who surrendereth his whole self to Allah while doing good (to mankind)....." (IV:125).

وَأَنِ اسْتَغْفِرُوا رَبَّكُمْ ثُمَّ تُوبُوا إِلَيْهِ يُمَتِّعْكُم مَّتَاعًا حَسَنًا إِلَىٰ
أَجَلٍ مُّسَمًّى

".....and that, seek the forgiveness of your Lord, and turn to Him in repentance, He will grant you enjoyment, good and beautiful, for a term appointed." (XI:3).

لِّلَّذِينَ أَحْسَنُوا الْحُسْنَىٰ وَزِيَادَةٌ ۖ وَلَا يَرْهَقُ وُجُوهَهُمْ قَتَرٌ وَلَا ذِلَّةٌ ۚ أُولَٰئِكَ
أَصْحَابُ الْجَنَّةِ ۖ هُمْ فِيهَا خَالِدُونَ ○

"Those who do good (beautifying their deeds) obtain a (like) beautiful (reward)—and more (through Divine Grace). No darkness (of ugliness and sorrow) nor shame shall cover their faces (on the Day of Judgment)! They are Companions of the Garden: therein they will abide." (X:26).

وَمَن يَقْتَرِفْ حَسَنَةً نَّزِدْ لَهُ فِيهَا حُسْنًا ۚ

"And if anyone earns any good, We shall give him an increase in beauty (or, of good) in respect thereof." (XLII:23).

مَنْ ظَلَمَ ثُمَّ بَدَّلَ حُسْنًا بَعْدَ سُوْٓءٍ فَاِنِّيْ غَفُوْرٌ رَّحِيْمٌ ۝

"But if any have done wrong and have thereafter substituted beauty (in conduct) to take the place of evil, truly, I am Oft-Forgiving, Most Merciful." (XXVII:11).

2. *In respect of beauty in conduct*, the Qur'ãnic verses bear reference in the form of command to certain specific situations also. For instance:

(i) Beauty in Speech:

وَقُوْلُوْا لِلنَّاسِ حُسْنًا

"Speak to people employing beauty (in your speech)." (II:83).

(ii) Beauty in behaviour towards Parents:

وَوَصَّيْنَا الْاِنْسَانَ بِوَالِدَيْهِ حُسْنًا

"We have enjoined on man beauty (in conduct) in respect of his parents." (XXIX:8).

(iii) Beauty in Preaching and Argument:

اُدْعُ اِلٰى سَبِيْلِ رَبِّكَ بِالْحِكْمَةِ وَالْمَوْعِظَةِ الْحَسَنَةِ وَجَادِلْهُمْ بِالَّتِيْ
هِيَ اَحْسَنُ ۗ

"Invite (all to the Way of thy Lord with wisdom and beautiful preaching; and argue with them in ways that are best and most beautiful." (XVI:125).

3. *As regards physical life*, the following emphatic verse refers to the duty of beautifying it in all manner, of course, in harmony with the Qur'ãnic norms and principles:

قُلْ مَنْ حَرَّمَ زِيْنَةَ اللّٰهِ الَّتِيْٓ اَخْرَجَ لِعِبَادِهٖ وَالطَّيِّبٰتِ مِنَ
الرِّزْقِ ۗ قُلْ هِيَ لِلَّذِيْنَ اٰمَنُوْا فِي الْحَيٰوةِ الدُّنْيَا خَالِصَةً يَّوْمَ
الْقِيٰمَةِ ۗ كَذٰلِكَ نُفَصِّلُ الْاٰيٰتِ لِقَوْمٍ يَّعْلَمُوْنَ ۝

"Say: Who hath forbidden[1] things of beauty which Allah hath brought forth for His servants, and the things, clean and pure, which He hath provided for sustenance? Say: They are, in the life of this world, for those who believe (and) purely for them on the Day of Judgment. Thus do We explain the Signs in detail for those who have knowledge." (VII:32).

4. *In respect of dress*, we are told first that one of the functions of dress is beautification of the human personality:

يٰبَنِيْٓ اٰدَمَ قَدْ اَنْزَلْنَا عَلَيْكُمْ لِبَاسًا يُّوَارِيْ سَوْاٰتِكُمْ وَرِيْشًا ۭ وَلِبَاسُ التَّقْوٰى ۙ ذٰلِكَ خَيْرٌ ۭ ذٰلِكَ مِنْ اٰيٰتِ اللّٰهِ لَعَلَّهُمْ يَذَّكَّرُوْنَ ۝

"O children of Adam! We have bestowed upon you raiment to cover your shame[2] and as a means of beautification[3]; and the raiment of piety (which covers and beautifies the inner self) is the best.[4] That is of the Signs of Allah that haply they may be admonished." (VII:26).

Then, as if to emphaise the element of *sanctity* in beautification through dress, and to emphasise it for rectifying the wrong notion

---

1. The religious view of life has often been based on asceticism which stands for the negation of beauty. According to the Holy Qur'ãn, it is a wrong view of sanctity.

2. Here the Holy Qur'ãn condemns the cult of nudism, which is a product of the psychological perversions of modern times.

3. (*a*) Note here a relevant *hadîth* the Holy Prophet (Peace be on him) used to praise God when putting on a new dress in these words:

الحمد لله الذی کسانی ما اواری به عورتی واتجمل بها فی حیوتی

"Praise be to Allah who gave me to wear that which covers the part of the body that should remain hidden, and whereby I acquire beauty in my life." (Tirmizi: *Jãme'*). (*Al-Tãj al-Jãme' lî al-Usûl, fi Ahadîth al-Rusûl, Kitãb al-Libãs*, p. 174).

(*b*) Dress, according to Westermarck, "owes its origin, at least in great many cases, to the desire of men and women to make themselves mutually attractive". (Quoted in *Ency., Br.* VII, p. 649).

4. Here we obtain the principle that the garments we wear should never transgress the bounds of piety; otherwise, they will become source of ugliness.

Thus, the Holy Qur'ãn voices a masculine protest against those perversions in dress which have plagued modern womanhood in the West and in the countries coming under the influence of the West.

preached by certain other religions, it says, referring to worship, and, because a Muslim must compulsorily pray five times during the day and the night, referring, actually to all the twenty-four hours of one's daily life, as follows:

يَٰبَنِيٓ ءَادَمَ خُذُواْ زِينَتَكُمۡ عِندَ كُلِّ مَسۡجِدٖ وَكُلُواْ وَٱشۡرَبُواْ وَلَا تُسۡرِفُوٓاْۚ إِنَّهُۥ لَا يُحِبُّ ٱلۡمُسۡرِفِينَ ○

"O Children of Adam! look to your adornment[1] at every time and place of prayer: eat and drink: (Enjoy) but waste not by excess;[2] for Allah loveth not the wasters." (VII:31).

5. To conclude: *The Holy Qur'ãn demands and commands positive beautification of every aspect of human life*: spiritual, moral, intellectual and physical. Its teaching in this respect has been beautifully summed up by the Holy Prophet (Peace be on him) in these words:

إن الله كتب الإحسان على كل شيئ

"Verily Allah hath made obligatory the employment of beauty in respect of evrerything."[3] (*Sahîh al-Muslim*). (*Mishkãt al-Masãbîh, Kitãb al-Said, al-Fasl al-awwal*, p. 357).

---

1. It means not only dressing for grace and piety but also keeping the hair in proper form, and toilet and cleanliness.

   The following incident of the Holy Prophet's time may be quoted here with advantage, as it reveals the attitude of Islam in practice:

   "The Prophet (Peace be on him) was in the mosque, when a person came there with the hair of his head and beard in a dishevelled condition. The Prophet (Peace be on him) made a sign towards him which implied that he was ordering him to set his hair in order. That person (left the mosque), obeyed the command and returned. Then the Prophet (Peace be on him) remarked: 'Is it not better than that someone among you comes with dishevelled hair as if he is Satan'." (*Mishkãt al-Masãbih*, vol. I, p. 384).

2. Mark that the Holy Qur'ãn allows aesthetic fulfilment but not luxury, which is vice.

3. The Holy Prophet (Peace be on him) has commanded Muslims to fulfil aesthetic requirements even in respect of such matters as putting on the clothing over the dead body, preparing a grave, slaughtering an animal and killing an enemy soldier on the battlefield. (See: *Miskãt al-Masãbih, Bãb Ghusl al-Mayyit*, p. 143; and *Kitãb al-Said*, p. 357).

And let every Muslim artist and artisan remember the following Prophetic exhortation:

إنّ العبد اذا عمل عملا احبّ الله أن يتقنه

"Verily, when a servant (of Allah) executes any task, Allah loves that he executes it with thorough skill and for stability and perfection."[4] (*Kanz al-'Ummãl*).

4. Mark that 'perfection' is the attribute of beauty.

Part V

DUTIES AS MORAL BEING

(*or, Duties to Self Relating Strictly to Morality*)

I. Duties of Omission

(Duties of Respect for the Self)

2. Duties of Commission

(Duties of Love for the Self)

Chapter I

Duties of Omission

END :

Moral Self-Preservation.

(i) *Lying, or false speech, prohibited:*

وَاجْتَنِبُوا قَوْلَ الزُّورِ ۝

".....and shun the word that is false." (XXII:30).

إِنَّ اللَّهَ لَا يَهْدِي مَنْ هُوَ كَاذِبٌ كَفَّارٌ ۝

"Verily Allah guideth not those who are false and ungrateful." (XXXIX:3).

هَلْ أُنَبِّئُكُمْ عَلَىٰ مَنْ تَنَزَّلُ الشَّيَاطِينُ ۝ تَنَزَّلُ عَلَىٰ كُلِّ أَفَّاكٍ أَثِيمٍ ۝

"Shall I inform you (O people!) on whom it is that the evil ones descend? They descend on every sinful liar."[1] (XXVI:221, 222).

(ii) *Mixing up truth with falsehood prohibited:*

وَلَا تَلْبِسُوا الْحَقَّ بِالْبَاطِلِ

"And confound not truth with falsehood." (II:42).

---

1. Cf. XLV:7.

(iii) Concealing truth prohibited:

لَا .....تَكْتُمُوا الْحَقَّ وَأَنْتُمْ تَعْلَمُونَ ○

"And conceal not the truth while ye know (it)". (II:42).

(iv) Concealing evidence prohibited:

وَلَا تَكْتُمُوا الشَّهَادَةَ ، وَمَنْ يَكْتُمْهَا فَإِنَّهُ آثِمٌ قَلْبُهُ ، وَاللَّهُ بِمَا تَعْمَلُونَ عَلِيمٌ ○

"Conceal not evidence; for whoever conceals it,—his heart is tainted with sin. And Allah knoweth all that ye do." (II:283).

(v) Aversion to truth (—a state of mental perversion—a moral disease—) condemned:

لَقَدْ جِئْنٰكُمْ بِالْحَقِّ وَلٰكِنَّ أَكْثَرَكُمْ لِلْحَقِّ كٰرِهُونَ ○

"Verily We have brought the Truth to you: But most of you have hatred for truth (—truth being always bitter for those who become accustomed to living on and benefitting from falsehoods)." (XLIII:78).

(vi) Assisting falsehood or fraud, and giving false evidence, ruled out from Islamic conduct: hence abstinence from it is duty:

وَالَّذِينَ لَا يَشْهَدُونَ الزُّورَ ٧

"....and (the servants of the Most Gracious are those) who witness no falsehood." (XXV:72).

Note: 'Witnessing no falsehood' implies in the wordings of the Arabic text: (1) 'do not give false evidence'; and (2) 'do not assist falsehood or fraud'.

(vii) Spirit of hypocrisy condemned: hence abstinence from it is duty:

وَمِنَ النَّاسِ مَنْ يَقُولُ آمَنَّا بِاللَّهِ وَ بِالْيَوْمِ الْآخِرِ وَمَا هُمْ بِمُؤْمِنِينَ ○
يُخٰدِعُونَ اللَّهَ وَ الَّذِينَ آمَنُوا ، وَمَا يَخْدَعُونَ إِلَّا أَنْفُسَهُمْ وَمَا يَشْعُرُونَ ○ فِي قُلُوبِهِمْ
مَرَضٌ لا فَزَادَهُمُ اللَّهُ مَرَضًا ، وَلَهُمْ عَذَابٌ أَلِيمٌ لا بِمَا كَانُوا يَكْذِبُونَ ○

"And of the people there are some who say: 'We believe in Allah and the Last Day'; but they do not (really) believe. Fain would they deceive Allah and those who believe, but they only deceive themselves, and how little they perceive! In their hearts is a disease, so Allah hath increased unto them (that) disease; and grievous is the penalty they (incur), because they have been lying." (II:8-10).

These verses speak of the hypocrites of the Holy Prophet's time, who were practising deception in respect of the Muslims. They, however, lay down the moral principle that practising deception in human relations is strongly condemnable, and he who practises it becomes morally diseased. Thus, it is duty not only to others, but also to one's own self, to abstain from adopting hypocritical attitude in any matter whatsoever.

(viii) Deeds not conforming to words condemned: hence abstinence from the same is duty:

يَٰٓأَيُّهَا الَّذِينَ آمَنُوا لِمَ تَقُولُونَ مَا لَا تَفْعَلُونَ ○ كَبُرَ مَقْتًا عِندَ اللَّهِ
أَن تَقُولُوا مَا لَا تَفْعَلُونَ ○

"O ye who believe! why say ye that which ye do not? Grievously odious is it in the sight of Allah that ye say that which ye do not". (LXI:2, 3).

Disparity between word and the deed of a person may bring harm to others who may repose confidence in him in any matter, but it damages that person also, because: (1) he loses the capacity to stick to truth; and (2) he loses the confidence of his fellow-beings and, hence his prestige.

(ix) The spirit of duplicity condemned: hence abstinence from it is duty:

وَإِذَا لَقُوا الَّذِينَ آمَنُوا قَالُوا آمَنَّا وَإِذَا خَلَوْا إِلَىٰ شَيَاطِينِهِمْ قَالُوا إِنَّا
مَعَكُمْ إِنَّمَا نَحْنُ مُسْتَهْزِئُونَ ○ اللَّهُ يَسْتَهْزِئُ بِهِمْ وَيَمُدُّهُمْ فِي طُغْيَانِهِمْ
يَعْمَهُونَ ○ أُولَٰئِكَ الَّذِينَ اشْتَرَوُا الضَّلَالَةَ بِالْهُدَىٰ فَمَا رَبِحَت تِّجَارَتُهُمْ
وَمَا كَانُوا مُهْتَدِينَ ○.

"When they (*i.e.*, the Hypocrites) meet those who believe, they say: 'We believe'; but when they are alone with their evil ones, they say: 'We are really with you: we were only jesting'. Allah will throw back their mockery on them and give them rope in their trespasses; so they will wander like blind ones (to and fro). These are they who have bartered guidance for error: but their traffic is profitless, and they have lost true direction." (II:14-16).

Although these verses refer to the Hypocrites of Madinah, they lay down a universal principle, namely, that duplicity, which is a deeper phase of hypocrisy, corrupts a person's moral tone, on the one hand, and brings loss of face to him, on the other. Thus, side by side with being unjust to others, he who practise duplicity also damages himself. Hence it is a 'duty to self' to abstain from it completely.

(x) Making a show of hollow acts of goodness, devotion and charity, condemned; hence abstinence from that is duty:

Making a show of hollow acts of goodness, devotion and charity is a form of hypocrisy and, as such has been condemned by the Holy Qur'ãn:

فَوَيْلٌ لِّلْمُصَلِّينَ ۝ الَّذِينَ هُمْ عَن صَلَاتِهِمْ سَاهُونَ ۝ الَّذِينَ هُمْ
يُرَاءُونَ ۝ وَيَمْنَعُونَ الْمَاعُونَ ۝

"So woe to the worshippers who are neglectful of their Prayers, *those who do (good) to be seen*, but refuse (to supply) (even) small kindnesses (or, neighbourly needs)." (CVII:4-7).

(xi) Oath-mongering condemned; hence abstinence from it is duty:

All habitual liars lose the faith of their fellow-beings and hence resort to habitual and false swearing in order to create belief and confidence in their word: while "the true man's word is as good as his bond". Oath-mongering is thus related to evil character and a false personality, and is disapproved by the Holy Qur'ãn:

وَلَا تُطِعْ كُلَّ حَلَّافٍ مَّهِينٍ ۝

"Heed not the type of despicable man,—ready with oaths...."
(LXVIII:10).

(xii) Following one's lusts of the heart prohibited:

The Holy Qur'ãn enjoins:

فَلَا تَتَّبِعُوا الْهَوَىٰ أَن تَعْدِلُوا ۚ

"So follow not lusts of the heart[2] lest ye lapes (from truth)...." (IV:135).

(xiii) Desiring false appreciation and being pleased with flattery condemned; hence abstinence from it is duty:

The Holy Qur'ãn says:

لَا تَحْسَبَنَّ الَّذِينَ يَفْرَحُونَ بِمَا أَتَوا وَّيُحِبُّونَ أَن يُحْمَدُوا بِمَا لَمْ يَفْعَلُوا فَلَا تَحْسَبَنَّهُم بِمَفَازَةٍ مِّنَ الْعَذَابِ ۖ وَلَهُمْ عَذَابٌ أَلِيمٌ ۝

"Think not that those who exult in what they have brought about, and *love to be praised for what they have not done,*—think not that they can escape the penalty. For them is a penalty grievous indeed." (III:188).

(xiv) Flattery, as embodying self-debasement of the flatterer[3] ruled out in Islamic conduct; hence abstinence from it is duty:

The Holy Qur'ãn says:

يَا أَيُّهَا الَّذِينَ آمَنُوا اتَّقُوا اللَّهَ وَقُولُوا قَوْلًا سَدِيدًا ۝ يُصْلِحْ لَكُمْ أَعْمَالَكُمْ

"O ye who believe! Guard your duty to Allah and speak a straight speech: He will (on that account) make your conduct whole and sound....." (XXXIII:70, 71).

The Arabic word *Sadîd*, used in this verse, when applied to speech, means[4] 'true' and 'directed to the right point'. Now true speech is 'statement according to fact', as also 'sincere speech'. Moreover, a speech which is according to fact and sincere shall be a dignified speech. As for 'directed to the right point', it connotes a 'speech which has no

---

2. The word *Hawã* used in the Arabic text does not mean simple desire but "blameable or evil inclination". (Lane's *Arabic-English Lexicon*). It is "lusts of the heart" when related to morality; and "caprice" when related to knowledge.

3. It damages morally the other party also. We shall deal with it in "duties to others".

4. Lane's *Lexicon*. It also means: correct, right, relevant, pertinent.

exaggeration or its opposite'. It also contains the sense of straightforwardness[5].

The English word 'flattery' means: 'treating with insincere and exaggerated praise and servile attentions'.[6]

Flattery is, therefore, the very opposite of the 'straight speech' mentioned in the above verse.

Moreover, according to the above verse, 'straight speech' renders one's conduct whole and sound, which means that flattery renders conduct unsound.

Therefore, viewing it in the light of the Qur'ãnic teaching, flattery is immoral, and a Muslim should abstain from it totally. Condemning this vice, the Holy Prophet (Peace be on him) says:

اذا رأيتم المدّاحين فاحثوا فى افواههم التّراب

"When you meet the flatterers, throw dust into their mouths." (Muslim's *Sahîh*; Abû Dã'ûd's *Sunan*, Chap. on "Disapprobation of Flattery").

(xv) Love for pomp and show—ostentation[7]*, prohibited:*

وَلَا تَكُونُوا كَالَّذِينَ خَرَجُوا مِن دِيَارِهِم بَطَرًا وَرِئَاءَ النَّاسِ

"And be not like those who started from their homes insolently and to be seen of men (i.e., in vainglory and ostentation)." (VIII:47).

Referring to the unseemly conduct of the enemies of Islam at the battle of Badr, this verse lays down the moral injunction that a Muslim should always abstain from vainglory and ostentation.

(xvi) Conceit condemned; hence abstinence from it is duty:

The Holy Qur'ãn disapproves conceit in the following reference:

وَيَوْمَ حُنَيْنٍ إِذْ أَعْجَبَتْكُمْ كَثْرَتُكُمْ فَلَمْ تُغْنِ عَنكُمْ شَيْئًا وَضَاقَتْ
عَلَيْكُمُ الْأَرْضُ بِمَا رَحُبَتْ ثُمَّ وَلَّيْتُم مُّدْبِرِينَ

---

5. The other implications of 'straight speech' shall be dealt with in connection with the duty of truthfulness.

6. See Chambers, *Twentieth Century Dictionary*.

7. i.e., display to draw attention or admiration.

"....and on the day of (the battle of) Hunain: Behold! your superiority in numbers elated you; then it availed you naught, and the earth, for all that it is wide, straitened unto you; then ye turned back in retreat." (IX:25).

This verse relates to the battle of Hunain, in which for the first time the Muslim army outnumbered the enemy forces; yet it was in this battle that the Muslim forces suffered a severe set-back first, which has been ascribed to the spirit of elation, as opposed to the spirit of faith in God, which overtook the minds of a part of them, i.e., the new converts and the less disciplined.

The moral principle contained in that event is that God disapproves and punishes conceit and self-elation. Hence the duty to abstain from the same.

(xvii) *Exultation in one's achievements condemned; hence abstinence from it is duty:*

لَا تَحْسَبَنَّ الَّذِيْنَ يَفْرَحُوْنَ بِمَآ اَتَوْا وَّ يُحِبُّوْنَ اَنْ يُّحْمَدُوْا بِمَا لَمْ يَفْعَلُوْا
فَلَا تَحْسَبَنَّهُمْ بِمَفَازَةٍ مِّنَ الْعَذَابِ ۚ وَلَهُمْ عَذَابٌ اَلِيْمٌ ○

"Think not that *those who exult in what they have brought about*, and love to be praised for what they have not done,—think not that they can escape the penalty. For them is a penalty grievous indeed." (III:188).

Exultation in one's achievements has been condemned here because it breeds pride which leads to a person's ruin at least in damaging his character. In fact, it also blocks further progress.

A Muslim should always attribute his achievements to the favour of God and maintain the state of mind known as humility.

(xviii) *Self-goodness—self-piousness* (*piety-complex*) *condemned; hence abstinence from it is duty:*

The Holy Qur'ãn lays down the rule:

فَلَا تُزَكُّوْٓا اَنْفُسَكُمْ ۖ هُوَ اَعْلَمُ بِمَنِ اتَّقٰى ○

"Therefore ascribe not purity (i.e., goodness and righteousness) unto yourselves. He is Best Aware of him who wardeth off evil.[8]" (LIII:32).

---

8. *zakã'un*, i.e., purity, goodness, righteousness....and *zakã nafsahu*: "He praised himself." (Lane's *Lexicon*).

Many of those who are strict in conformity to external religious behaviour, without imbibing thoroughly the inner spirit of religious life, develop consciously or unconsciously, what may be termed as 'piety-complex', which is actually a form of self-esteem culminating in contempt for others.

Many others who strive to be morally good develop a feeling of self-esteem in that respect.

Both of those wrong attitudes have been disapproved by the Holy Qur'ãn and should be shunned by every Muslim.

(xix) Haughtiness prohibited:

Haughtiness in all forms has been regarded as a basic evil by the Holy Qur'ãn. *Iblîs*, who enjoyed the prerogative of the holy company of angels, became Devil because he compared himself with Adam and said:

أَنَا خَيْرٌ مِّنْهُ ؕ

".....I am better that he." (XXXVIII:76).

and thus:

اِسْتَكْبَرَ وَكَانَ مِنَ الْكٰفِرِيْنَ ۝

"he was haughty, and became one of those who reject Faith (—indeed, became the Devil)." (XXXVIII:74).

As regards mankind:

اِنَّهٗ لَا يُحِبُّ الْمُسْتَكْبِرِيْنَ ۝

"Verily He (i.e., God) loveth not those who are haughty." (XVI:23).

and:

فَلَبِئْسَ مَثْوَى الْمُتَكَبِّرِيْنَ ۝

"....evil indeed is the abode of those who are haughty." (XVI:29).

Hence, it is a Qur'ãnic moral duty to abstain from haughtiness in all forms. It should be shunned in thought, word and deed. The Holy

Qur'ãn lays down the rules:

لَا تُصَعِّرْ خَدَّكَ لِلنَّاسِ وَلَا تَمْشِ فِي الْأَرْضِ مَرَحًا ۖ إِنَّ اللَّهَ لَا يُحِبُّ كُلَّ
مُخْتَالٍ فَخُورٍ ۝ وَاقْصِدْ فِي مَشْيِكَ وَاغْضُضْ مِنْ صَوْتِكَ ۚ إِنَّ أَنْكَرَ
الْأَصْوَاتِ لَصَوْتُ الْحَمِيرِ ۝

"Swell not thy cheek (for pride) at the people, and walk not in insolence through the earth[9]; for Allah loveth not any vainglorious[10] boastful[11] (person). And be modest in thy gait, and lower thy voice (in humility)[12]; for the harshest of sounds without doubt is the braying of an ass." (XXXI:18, 19).

Another verse which condemns the demonstration of haughtiness in very strong terms may also be quoted:

وَلَا تَمْشِ فِي الْأَرْضِ مَرَحًا ۖ إِنَّكَ لَنْ تَخْرِقَ الْأَرْضَ وَلَنْ تَبْلُغَ الْجِبَالَ طُولًا ۝

"And walk not in insolence through the earth. Verily, thou wilt by no means rend the earth, nor canst thou attain to the mountains in stature." (XVII:37).

(xx) Obstinacy, perverseness, self-righteousness ruled out; hence abstinence from the same is duty:

In emphasising the qualities of the righteous, the Holy Qur'ãn says:—

وَلَمْ يُصِرُّوا عَلَىٰ مَا فَعَلُوا وَهُمْ يَعْلَمُونَ ۝

".....and they are never obstinate in persisting knowingly in (the wrong) they have done." (III:135).

It is thus a duty to abstain from obstinancy, perverseness and self-righteousness in all the situations of life.

---

9. These injunctions relate to behaviour in general.

10. Vainglorious; i.e., proud in the heart. This emphasises condemnation of haughtiness as it is to be found in the haughty person's thought.

11, 12. The reference here is to abstain from employing haughty tone in talk.

(xxi) Quarrelsomeness prohibited:

The Holy Qur'ãn has mentioned quarrelsomeness as the opposite of righteousness:—

فَإِنَّمَا يَسَّرْنَٰهُ بِلِسَانِكَ لِتُبَشِّرَ بِهِ الْمُتَّقِينَ وَتُنذِرَ بِهِ قَوْمًا لُّدًّا ۝

"So have We made the (Qur'ãn) easy in thine own tongue, that with it thou mayest give glad tidings to the righteous, and warn therewith the vehemently quarrelsome folk." (XIX:97).

The holy book also says about true Muslims:—

وَإِذَا خَاطَبَهُمُ الْجَٰهِلُونَ قَالُوا سَلَٰمًا ۝

"....and when the ignorant address them (in arrogance and lack of culture), they say, 'Peace! (avoiding thus all quarrel with them)...." (XXV:63).

Finally, there is the command, given to the Holy Prophet (Peace be on him), but meant to be obeyed by all Muslims, according to their situation:—

وَأَعْرِضْ عَنِ الْجَٰهِلِينَ ۝

".....and keep away from the (disputations raked up by the) ignorant."[13] (VII:199).

It is, therefore, a duty for everyone who aims at righteousness, i.e., every true follower of the Qur'ãn, to abstain completely from quarrelsomeness.

(xxii) Being overpowered by wrath ruled out; hence abstinence from it is duty:

In emphasising the qualities of the righteous, the Holy Qur'ãn says:—

---

13. It should be noted that in its relation to the Holy Prophet (Peace be on him), which forms its real context, this command has a more comprehensive implication. He was commanded not to engage in fruitless controversies with his ignorant strong-headed opponents, nor to conciliate them, but to ignore them; "holding to forgiveness and commanding what was right." (VII: 199, first part of the verse).

وَالْكٰظِمِيْنَ الْغَيْظَ

".....and (those) who control their wrath...." (III:134).

Hence, it is a Qur'ãnic duty of omission not to permit oneself under any circumstance to be overpowered by wrath.

(xxiii) Light-heartedness prohibited:

The Holy Qur'ãn says:

... وَلَا تَفْرَحُوْا بِمَآ اٰتٰكُمْ ط

".....and (in order that) ye may not (lose the balance of your mind in) joy because of that (wordly good) which hath been given (to you)...." (LVII:23).

Exultation over the good things of the world is wedded to light-heartedness. The man of God should regard all wordly good fortune as illusory (LVII:20)[14]. Hence he should not suffer from emotional disturbance on such occasions, and should maintain his serenity, knowing, as he does, its true value. In other words, he should avoid light-heartedness.

(xxiv) Pessimism, i.e., being overpowered by despair, prohibited:

The Holy Qur'ãn says:

لِّكَيْلَا تَاْسَوْا عَلٰى مَا فَاتَكُمْ

"That ye may not despair over matters which have escaped you...." (LVII:23).

Elsewhere, the exhortation is in the form of the emphatic command:

وَلَا تَايْئَسُوْا مِنْ رَّوْحِ اللّٰهِ اِنَّهٗ لَا يَايْئَسُ مِنْ رَّوْحِ اللّٰهِ اِلَّا الْقَوْمُ الْكٰفِرُوْنَ ○

---

14. The verse reads:

وَمَا الْحَيٰوةُ الدُّنْيَآ اِلَّا مَتَاعُ الْغُرُوْرِ ○

"What is the life of this world but a matter of illusion."

"and never give up hope of Allah's Soothing Mercy: Truly no one despairs of Allah's Soothing Mercy except those who have no faith." (XII:87).

This should be so, because every true Muslim is a man of God and devotion to him is the end-all and be-all of his life:

قُلْ إِنَّ صَلَاتِي وَنُسُكِي وَمَحْيَايَ وَمَمَاتِي لِلَّهِ رَبِّ الْعَالَمِينَ ۝
لَا شَرِيكَ لَهُ ۚ

"Say: 'Truly, my prayer and my service of sacrifice, my life and my death are (all) for Allah, the Cherisher of the Worlds: No partner hath He." (VI:162, 163).

It is through this intense devotion that the light of Faith and Hope continues to burn constantly in his heart, and despair can never overtake him. Indeed, he is, in his religious make-up, out and out an optimist, and pessimism is the very negation of his Faith.

Hence the Qur'ãnic duty of shunning Pessimism completely and thoroughly.

(xxv) Being overpowered by fear ruled out; hence the effort to eradicate it is duty:

Fear is one of the greatest scourges of human life, and he who can overcome it is really a fortunate man. The Holy Qur'ãn has given a teaching which ensures this merit thoroughly.

According to the holy book, a true Muslim is he who has absolute faith in God and cultivates true devotion to Him. (VI:162)[15]. This faith and this devotion lend a strength to his will, a balance to his emotions and a grace to the personality which never fail him in life, because God's help and protection is unfailingly and always available to him:

فَمَن يَكْفُرْ بِالطَّاغُوتِ وَيُؤْمِن بِاللَّهِ فَقَدِ اسْتَمْسَكَ بِالْعُرْوَةِ الْوُثْقَىٰ لَا انفِصَامَ لَهَا ۗ

"So whoever rejects Evil and believes in Allah hath grasped the most trustworthy hand-hold that never breaks". (II:256).

Thus a true Muslim is never afraid of anything of this world. He

---

15. Quoted above.

leads a life free of fear in proportion to the strength of his faith and trust in God:

أَلَآ إِنَّ أَوْلِيَآءَ اللّٰهِ لَا خَوْفٌ عَلَيْهِمْ وَلَا هُمْ يَحْزَنُونَ ۝ الَّذِينَ آمَنُوا
وَكَانُوا يَتَّقُونَ ۝ لَهُمُ الْبُشْرَىٰ فِي الْحَيٰوةِ الدُّنْيَا وَفِي الْآخِرَةِ ۚ لَا تَبْدِيلَ
لِكَلِمٰتِ اللّٰهِ ۚ ذٰلِكَ هُوَ الْفَوْزُ الْعَظِيمُ ۝

"Behold! verily on the friends of Allah there is no fear, nor shall they grieve; those who believe and (constantly) guard against evil; for them are Glad Tidings in the life of the Present and in the Hereafter: No change can there be in the Words of Allah. This is indeed the supreme Felicity." (X:62-64).

For them, the Comforting Message and the Command is:

وَلَا تَحْزَنُوا

"Entertain no fear!" (XLI:30).

Because: all things and the consequences of all events are under the control and command of the All-Powerful, the All-Just and Most Merciful God:

تَبٰرَكَ الَّذِي بِيَدِهِ الْمُلْكُ ز وَهُوَ عَلَىٰ كُلِّ شَيْءٍ قَدِيرٌ ۝

"Blessed be He in Whose hands is Dominion; and He over all things hath Power...." (LXVII:1).

وَلِلّٰهِ عَاقِبَةُ الْأُمُورِ ۝

".....and with Allah rests the end of (all) affairs". (XXII:41).

It is thus the duty of a Muslim not to allow himself to be overpowered by fear.

(xxvi) Cowardice on the battlefield prohibited:

A true Muslim develops the strength of his heart through a dynamic and vibrant faith in God to such an extent that cowardice on the battlefield is inconceivable in his case:

وَالصّٰبِرِينَ فِي الْبَأْسَآءِ وَالضَّرَّآءِ وَحِينَ الْبَأْسِ ۗ أُولٰٓئِكَ الَّذِينَ صَدَقُوا ۖ
وَأُولٰٓئِكَ هُمُ الْمُتَّقُونَ ۝

".....and those who are firm and patient, in pain (or suffering) and adversity, and throughout all periods of panic and violence.[16] These are they who are proven true (in their faith in God); and these are they who are (truly) righteous". (II:177).

Therefore, the Holy Qur'ãn lays down the command:

يَٰٓأَيُّهَا ٱلَّذِينَ ءَامَنُوٓا۟ إِذَا لَقِيتُمُ ٱلَّذِينَ كَفَرُوا۟ زَحْفًا فَلَا تُوَلُّوهُمُ ٱلْأَدْبَارَ ۝ وَ
مَن يُوَلِّهِمْ يَوْمَئِذٍ دُبُرَهُۥٓ إِلَّا مُتَحَرِّفًا لِّقِتَالٍ أَوْ مُتَحَيِّزًا إِلَىٰ فِئَةٍ
فَقَدْ بَآءَ بِغَضَبٍ مِّنَ ٱللَّهِ وَمَأْوَىٰهُ جَهَنَّمُ ۖ وَبِئْسَ ٱلْمَصِيرُ ۝

"O ye who believe! When ye meet the Unbelievers[17] in hostile array, *never turn your backs to them.*

"If any do turn his back to them on such a day, unless it be in a stratagem of war or to retreat to a troop (of his own), he draws on himself the wrath of Allah, and his abode is Hell,—an evil refuge (indeed)!" (VIII:15, 16).

Thus, to abstain from cowardice is a duty.

(xxvii) Fear of opponents of truth and justice ruled out; hence abstinence from it is duty:

The Holy Qur'ãn mentions it as one of the essential qualities of a true Muslim that, in upholding truth and justice, he is never afraid of those who may be opposed to him:

وَلَا يَخَافُونَ لَوْمَةَ لَآئِمٍ ۚ

"and (they are) never afraid of the reproaches of such as find fault....." (V:57).

Thus, to abstain from fear of opposition in respect of upholding truth and justice is a duty.

(xxviii) Cultivation of sadness, anxiety and worry in respect of worldly events and things prohibited:

---

16. i.e., in war.

17. War between Muslim states is inconceivable in Islam.

A true Muslim is, as we have already noted, a man of God, and his motto in life is to commit all his affairs to His care:

وَأُفَوِّضُ أَمْرِيٓ إِلَى ٱللَّهِۚ إِنَّ ٱللَّهَ بَصِيرُۢ بِٱلۡعِبَادِ ۝

"(He said:) and I commit my affair to Allah: for Allah (ever) watches over His Servants." (XL:44).

This motto, taught by the Holy Qur'ãn, cuts at the very root of that attitude of mind which subjects a person to indulge irrationally in sadness, anxiety and worry, thereby damaging him in many ways.

Speaking directly of the problem, the holy book says:

لِّكَيۡلَا تَحۡزَنُواْ عَلَىٰ مَا فَاتَكُمۡ وَلَا مَآ أَصَٰبَكُمۡۗ

"....that (He might teach) you not to grieve for that which ye missed or for that which befell you...." (III:153).

Thus it is the duty of every true Muslim not to cultivate sadness, anxiety and worry in respect of what happens to him in his life.

(xxix) (a) *Capriciousness,*

(b) *indulgence in fancies and phantasms divorced from the realities of life,*

and (c) *harbouring evil thoughts,*

—all ruled out in Islamic conduct; hence abstinence from them is duty:

The Holy Qur'ãn regards *waswãs* as a great evil, so much so that it teaches a definite prayer for seeking God's protection against it. The prayer is:

قُلۡ أَعُوذُ بِرَبِّ ٱلنَّاسِ ۝ مَلِكِ ٱلنَّاسِ ۝ إِلَٰهِ ٱلنَّاسِ ۝ مِن شَرِّ
ٱلۡوَسۡوَاسِ ٱلۡخَنَّاسِ ۝ ٱلَّذِي يُوَسۡوِسُ فِي صُدُورِ ٱلنَّاسِ ۝ مِنَ ٱلۡجِنَّةِ
وَٱلنَّاسِ ۝

"Say: I seek refuge with the Lord and Cherisher of Mankind, the King (or Ruler) of Mankind, the God (or Judge) of Mankind from the evil of the *waswãs* of (or caused by) the slinking (devil), who whispereth in the hearts of Mankind,—among jinns and among men." (CXIV).

The word *'waswãs'* which has been left untranslated by the present writer comprehends within it several meanings that relate to different aspects of evil in the thoughts and feelings of human beings. The "*Dictionary of Modern Written Arabic*" gives the following meanings:

"devilish insinuation, temptation, wicked thoughts, doubt, misgiving, suspicion; delusion, fixed idea; uneasiness, anxiety, concern, melancholy."

The word '*waswãs*' covers, therefore: (*i*) depression of spirits through thoughts of sadness (—melancholy): (*ii*) anxiety; worry (—uneasiness and concern); (*iii*) capriciousness (—doubt, misgiving, suspicion); (*iv*) indulgence in delusions; (*v*) harbouring of evil thoughts.

Thus, the above prayer, while it emphasises the duty of abstaining from cultivation of sadness, anxiety and worry—stated in the immediately preceding section, also emphasises the duty of (*i*) shunning of capriciousness, and (*ii*)[18] abstaining from indulgence in delusions, namely, in fancies and phantasms divorced from the realities of life and consequently living in an imaginary world of one's own making, and (*iii*) guarding oneself against harbouring evil thoughts.

(xxx) Perversion—straying, and leading others, into evil courses condemned; hence abstinence from it is duty:

The Holy Qur'ãn condemns perversion in all its forms in the following verses:

وَاتْلُ عَلَيْهِمْ نَبَأَ الَّذِيٓ اٰتَيْنٰهُ اٰيٰتِنَا فَانْسَلَخَ مِنْهَا فَاَتْبَعَهُ الشَّيْطٰنُ فَكَانَ مِنَ الْغٰوِيْنَ ○

"And relate to them the story[19] of the man to whom We sent Our Signs, but he passed them by: So Satan followed him up, and he became of the perverted". (VII:175).

---

18. With regard to this duty, refer also to XXVI:225 where the word *wahm* has been employed.

19. "The story is preferably to be taken in a general sense, and not with reference to any particular individual." (Abdul Majid Daryabadi, *op.cit*, p. 298, n. 295).

وَبُرِّزَتِ الْجَحِيمُ لِلْغٰوِينَ ۝

"And the Fierce Fire shall be placed in full view before the perverted ones." (XXVI:91).

Hence, it is a duty to abstain from perversion in all its forms.

(xxxi) Indulgence in everything vain ruled out; hence abstinence from it is duty:

Emphasising certain essential attributes of Islamic conduct, the Holy Qur'ãn says:

وَالَّذِينَ هُمْ عَنِ اللَّغْوِ مُعْرِضُونَ ۝

".....and those (Believers) who from (everything) vain keep away....." (XXIII:3).

At another place, the same trait of Muslim character has been mentioned in these words:

وَإِذَا مَرُّوا بِاللَّغْوِ مَرُّوا كِرَامًا ۝

".....and when they pass by some vanity (like vain random talk, unedifying jokes, vain 'recreations', etc.), they pass by it with dignified (avoidance[20])". (XXV:72).

(xxxii) Idle discourse disapproved; hence abstinence from it is duty:

The following verse of the Holy Qur'ãn, though it relates to a particular event, also lays down a general rule of conduct:

وَمِنَ النَّاسِ مَنْ يَشْتَرِي لَهْوَ الْحَدِيثِ لِيُضِلَّ عَنْ سَبِيلِ اللَّهِ بِغَيْرِ عِلْمٍ ۖ وَيَتَّخِذَهَا هُزُوًا ۚ أُولَٰئِكَ لَهُمْ عَذَابٌ مُهِينٌ ۝

"And of mankind are those who purchase (i.e., are occupied with) idle discourse[21], to mislead (men) from Allah's Way (—which is

---

20. i.e., neither indulging in it nor being fussy about it.

21. "Life is taken seriously by men who realize the issues that hang upon it. But there are men of a frivolous turn of mind who prefer idle tales to true Realities and they are justly rebuked here". (A. Yusuf Ali, *op.cit.*, p. 1080).

the way of beneficial spending of time and energy) without knowledge (i.e., on the basis of vain fanciful stories), and throw ridicule on it: for such there will be a humiliating Penalty." (XXXI:6).

It is, therefore, duty to abstain from wasting time and energy in vain talks, frivolous discourses and idle tales.

(xxxiii) Recklessness prohibited:

One of the attributes of the unrighteous mentioned by the Holy Qur'ãn is that of being '*musrif*' (XL:28), which word comprehends 'recklessness' in its meanings.

Also, the injunction has been laid down:

وَلَا تُسْرِفُوْا ط

".....Do not practice recklessness....." (VII:31).

(xxxiv) Abstinence enjoined in respect of:

(*i*) Idle curiosity;

(*ii*) Believing in unfounded reports;

(*iii*) Spreading unfounded reports;

(*iv*) Entering into discussions without correct knowledge of the problem;

(*v*) Entertaining opinions for which no strong reason to believe exists;

(*vi*) Proffering uncertain opinion;

(*vii*) Tendering uncertain advice.

In the following pithy verse, whose Arabic text can be but poorly translated into English, the Holy Qur'ãn lays down a comprehensive duty of omission which covers all the above vices:

وَلَا تَقْفُ مَا لَيْسَ لَكَ بِهٖ عِلْمٌ ط

"Pursue not and follow not that whereof thou hast no knowledge." (XVII:36).

(xxxv) Idleness ruled out; hence abstinence from it is duty:

The Holy Qur'ãn commands the Muslims in these words:

يَٰٓأَيُّهَا الَّذِينَ آمَنُوا اصْبِرُوا وَصَابِرُوا وَرَابِطُوا وَاتَّقُوا اللَّهَ لَعَلَّكُمْ تُفْلِحُونَ ○

"O ye who believe! persevere, and excel in perseverance, and be (always) in a state of readiness, and observe your duty to Allah that haply ye may prosper." (III:200).

Idleness, or aversion to labour, is possible in a physically normal person only when: (*a*) he has no serious end in view, and (*b*) he possesses a tone of mind whereby he suffers from lack of perseverance.

The Holy Qur'ãn cuts at the root of both of these shortcomings when it commands the Muslims, in the above verse, to develop the very opposite character, namely, maximum of perseverance and the most serious end, *i.e.,* making observance of the duty to God the goal of life.

Thus, idleness is definitely a vice in the Qur'ãnic moral system and should, as such, be shunned by every Muslim.

Expounding this Qur'ãnic teaching, the Holy Prophet (Peace be on him) has taught the Muslims to seek God's refuge from idleness. The wordings of the prayer are:

اللهم إني أعوذ بك من الهمّ والحزن والعجز والكسل والبخل وضلع الدّين وغلبة الرّجال

"O Allah! I seek refuge with Thee from worry and grief and incompetence (in the performance of duties) and *idleness* and cowardice and miserliness and the burden of debt and the tyranny of the people." (Bukhãrî's *Sahîh*).

(xxxvi) Abstinence enjoined in respect of false endeavour in earning livelihood:

(a) through beggary;

(b) through acquiring money falsely by religious pretences and superstitious practices;

(c) through gambling.

(a) Beggary:

The qualities of the needy person who deserves financial help have been laid down thus:

لِلْفُقَرَآءِ الَّذِيْنَ اُحْصِرُوْا فِيْ سَبِيْلِ اللّٰهِ لَا يَسْتَطِيْعُوْنَ ضَرْبًا فِي
الْاَرْضِ يَحْسَبُهُمُ الْجَاهِلُ اَغْنِيَآءَ مِنَ التَّعَفُّفِ تَعْرِفُهُمْ بِسِيْمٰهُمْ
لَا يَسْئَلُوْنَ النَّاسَ اِلْحَافًا

"(Voluntary financial help is[22]) for those in need, who, in Allah's cause[23], are restricted, and cannot move about in the land (seeking for trade or work). The ignorant man thinks because of their modesty (in respect of asking for help), that they are free from want. Thou shalt know them from their (unfailing) mark. They beg not importunately from all and sundry....." (II:273).

Thus: the person who deserves help should fulfil the following conditions:

(*i*) his need for money should be genuine;

(*ii*) it should arise from some honourable or acceptable cause, including inability to work due to physical ailments or non-availability of employment;

(*iii*) he should be respectable in his demeanour;

(*iv*) he should not beg from all and sundry, namely, should not adopt beggary as a profession.

Professional beggary, which is a debasing form of acquiring easy money, is, therefore, completely ruled out by the Holy Qur'ãn. Indeed, it has no place in Muslim society[24].

(b) Acquiring money falsely through religious pretences and superstitious practices:

---

22. (Primarily).

23. All genuine service to mankind, specially religious service, is included here.

24. The fact is affirmed further by the uncompromising verdict of the Holy Prophet (Peace be on him) against beggary. (See: e.g., Abû Dã'ûd: *Sunan*, Vol. I, pp. 232, 247).

The Holy Qur'ãn points out condemningly another false means of earning money which damages both the recipient and the giver of money,—the means, namely, of employing religious pretences and superstitions, or, so-called "spiritual" practices. It says:

يا أيها الذين آمنوا إن كثيرا من الأحبار والرهبان ليأكلون
أموال الناس بالباطل

"O ye who believe! verily many of the priests and the monks devour the substances of the people in falsehood (i.e., on false pretences)....." (IX:34).

This verse refers to the Jewish priest and divines and the Christian monks and clergy. The false pretences consisted in that the Jewish priests used to misinterpret the law for the benefit of obtaining money from the interested parties[25], and the Christian monks and clergy used to issue indulgences and dispensations and had made the shrines of their saints a source of revenue for themselves.[26]

The condemnation by the Holy Qur'ãn means that it is the duty of a Muslim to abstain from acquiring money from all types of false pretences and practices in the name of spirituality and religion.

(c) Gambling, as embodying the spirit of earning wealth without labour, prohibited:

Another way of acquiring easy money is through the different forms of gambling. The Holy Qur'ãn commands the Muslims to shun all those forms of false earning, when it says:

يا أيها الذين آمنوا إنما الخمر والميسر والأنصاب والأزلام رجس
من عمل الشيطان فاجتنبوه لعلكم تفلحون ○

"O ye who believe! intoxicants and *gambling*[27], (dedication of)

---

25. Cf. *Is.* 1:23, *Je.* 6:13; *Mi.* 3:11.

26. See: Prof. Lecky's *History of European Morals.*

27. Gambling: the word *maisir*, used in the Arabic text, denotes literally: a means of getting something too easily—getting profit without labour and on the basis of chance. Finally, it is 'any game of hazard, or play of stakes, or wagers, so that even the game of children with walnut is included under this name by Mujahid'. (Lane's *Arabic-English Lexicon*). The most familiar form of gambling

stones, and (divination by) arrows, are *an abomination*—of *Satan's handiwork: Shun it, therefore,* that ye may prosper.[28]" (V:93).

Thus, it is a duty to abstain totally from all forms of gambling.

(xxxvii) Love of wealth for its won sake[29] vehemently condemned; hence abstinence from it is duty:

The Holy Qur'ãn, while condemning unrighteousness, recounts love of wealth as one of the vices:

وَتُحِبُّونَ الْمَالَ حُبًّا جَمًّا

".....and ye love wealth with inordinate love." (LXXXIX:20).

وَإِنَّهُ لِحُبِّ الْخَيْرِ لَشَدِيدٌ

---

among the Arabs was based on the principle of lottery through the employment of arrows. The Greeks used knuckle-bones. The Roman children employed 'head-or-tail' system with the coins. The Israelites used to draw lots. Certain other communities, like the Aryans, used dice. (*Encyclopaedia of Religion and Ethics*, VI, pp. 163, 164).

28. The total abolition of this evil practise in Muslim society by the Holy Prophet (Peace be on him) has been admitted even by his worst critics as one of the "most celebrated" reforms accomplished by him. (See: D.S. Margoliouth in: *Encyclopaedia Brit.*, XVII, p. 407, 11th Ed.). As for the non-Muslim communities, even of the present 'age of enlightenment': "The extent to which gambling prevails at the present time is difficult to assess.....Most of it is centered in the horse-racing....On the whole, it may safely be asserted that little short of £100,000,000 changes hands every year in England in connection with gambling transactions.....Side by side with the betting odds and betting tips, the newspapers record the tragic results on those who yield to the temptation. In 13 years (1895-96 to 1906-7) there were 156 suicides in England assigned to this cause, as well as 719 cases of theft on embezzlement, and 442 bankruptcies". (*Encyclopaedia of Religion and Ethics*, VI, pp. 164, 168). Indeed, the close relationship between gambling and crime, including sexual crime and crime against life and property, is an established fact of human history and can be perused in the cultural histories of the different communities who have indulged in this devastating vice.

29. It should be noted that the verses which voice condemnation of love for wealth are all to be found in the closing part of the Holy Qur'ãn. This fact seems to emphasize that love for wealth may damage even an otherwise virtuous life. Hence, the greatest caution is necessary in that respect.

"and lo! in the love of wealth the (i.e., the unregenerate man who is ungrateful to God) is violent." (C:8).

أَلْهَاكُمُ التَّكَاثُرُ ۝ حَتَّىٰ زُرْتُمُ الْمَقَابِرَ ۝

"The emulous desire for abundance and increase (in wealth, status and other wordly possessions) distracts you (from the more serious and higher things), until ye visit the graves (*i.e.,* ye die)." (CII:1, 2).

وَيْلٌ لِّكُلِّ هُمَزَةٍ لُّمَزَةٍ ۝ الَّذِي جَمَعَ مَالًا وَعَدَّدَهُ ۝ يَحْسَبُ أَنَّ مَالَهُ أَخْلَدَهُ ۝
كَلَّا لَيُنبَذَنَّ فِي الْحُطَمَةِ ۝

"Woe to every kind of scandal-monger and backbiter, who amasseth wealth and counteth it (often out of love for it), thinking his wealth would make him last for ever. By no means! He will surely be thrown into that (Hell) which breaks to pieces." (CIV:1-4).

It is, therefore, the duty of a Muslim to shun love for wealth totally, regarding wealth only as a means to virtue.

(xxxviii) Abstinence enjoined in respect of Covetousness[30] *or, the spirit of Greed, which expresses itself in:*

(a) *Covetous Selfishness, or, withholding from others the goods possessed by one's own self (=miserliness);*

and (b) *Coveting other's goods.*

(a) *Covetous Selfishness*:

The Holy Qur'ãn has laid down the rule:

وَمَن يُوقَ شُحَّ نَفْسِهِ فَأُولَٰئِكَ هُمُ الْمُفْلِحُونَ ۝

"And those saved from the covetousness[31] of their own souls,—they are the ones that achieve prosperity." (LIX:9; LXIV:16).

Thus it is duty to abstain from harbouring the spirit of covetousness—covetous selfishness—in all things that we possess.

---

30. Synonymous words are: Avarice, avidity, cupidity, greed, greediness.

31. The word used here in the Arabic text is *shuhh*, which means 'covetousness combined with stinginess'. We may call it 'covetous selfishness'.

(b) Coveting other's goods prohibited:

By coveting others' goods:

(i) one damages his spirit of contentment and, as a consequence, his peace of mind; and

(*ii*) he cultivates the spirit of jealousy.

Both of these are vices.

The Holy Qur'ãn, therefore, says:

وَلَا تَتَمَنَّوْا مَا فَضَّلَ اللّٰهُ بِهٖ بَعْضَكُمْ عَلٰى بَعْضٍ

"And in no wise covet those things in which Allah hath made some of you excel others." (IV:32).

It is, thus, a duty to abstain from coveting the goods that others possess.

(xxxix) Permitting oneself the very Spirit of Miserliness, prohibited:

The Holy Qur'ãn commands:

وَلَا تَجْعَلْ يَدَكَ مَغْلُوْلَةً اِلٰى عُنُقِكَ

"Make not thy hand tied (in miserliness) to thy neck....."
(XVII:29).

Because, the true Muslims are those who:

وَلَمْ يَقْتُرُوْا

"are not niggardly". (XXV:67).

And every Muslim should always remember that :

وَالَّذِيْنَ يَكْنِزُوْنَ الذَّهَبَ وَالْفِضَّةَ وَلَا يُنْفِقُوْنَهَا فِيْ سَبِيْلِ اللّٰهِ فَبَشِّرْ
هُمْ بِعَذَابٍ اَلِيْمٍ ۝ يَوْمَ يُحْمٰى عَلَيْهَا فِيْ نَارِ جَهَنَّمَ فَتُكْوٰى بِهَا
جِبَاهُهُمْ وَجُنُوْبُهُمْ وَظُهُوْرُهُمْ ۭ هٰذَا مَا كَنَزْتُمْ لِاَنْفُسِكُمْ فَذُوْقُوْا
مَا كُنْتُمْ تَكْنِزُوْنَ ۝

"....there are those who bury gold and silver and spend it not in the Way of Allah: announce unto them a most grievous penalty—on the Day when heat will be produced out of that (wealth) in the fire of Hell, and with it will be branded their foreheads, their flanks, and their backs: (And it will be said to them:) 'This is the (treasure) which ye buried for yourselves: taste ye, then, the (treasure) ye buried'." (IX: 34, 35).

and:

وَلَا يَحْسَبَنَّ الَّذِينَ يَبْخَلُونَ بِمَآ اٰتٰهُمُ اللّٰهُ مِنْ فَضْلِهٖ هُوَ خَيْرًا لَّهُمْ ۚ بَلْ هُوَ
شَرٌّ لَّهُمْ ۚ سَيُطَوَّقُوْنَ مَا بَخِلُوْا بِهٖ يَوْمَ الْقِيٰمَةِ ۚ وَلِلّٰهِ مِيْرَاثُ السَّمٰوٰتِ
وَالْاَرْضِ ۚ وَاللّٰهُ بِمَا تَعْمَلُوْنَ خَبِيْرٌ ۝

"Let not those who are niggardly in respect of the gifts which Allah hath given of His Grace, think it is good for them: nay! it is bad for them. Soon shall the things withheld in niggardliness be tied to their necks like a collar (—the callar of agonising misery—) on the Day of Judgment. To Allah belongs the heritage of the heavens and earth; and Allah is well acquainted with what ye do." (III:180).

It is, therefore, a duty to self to keep one's heart absolutely clear of the spirit of miserliness.

(xl) Practising miserliness in respect of one's self specifically condemned; hence abstinence from it is duty:

People are generally miserly in respect of others. But there are those also who are miserly, not only towards others, but even towards themselves. Namely, they deprive themselves of rationally and justly benefiting from those means of healthy living which God bestows on them. Such persons have been condemned by the Holy Qur'ān:

اِنَّ اللّٰهَ لَا يُحِبُّ مَنْ كَانَ مُخْتَالًا فَخُوْرًا ۝ الَّذِيْنَ يَبْخَلُوْنَ
وَيَاْمُرُوْنَ النَّاسَ بِالْبُخْلِ وَيَكْتُمُوْنَ مَآ اٰتٰهُمُ اللّٰهُ مِنْ
فَضْلِهٖ ۚ وَاَعْتَدْنَا لِلْكٰفِرِيْنَ عَذَابًا مُّهِيْنًا ۝

"Verily, Allah loveth not the arrogant, the vainglorious;—nor those who are niggardly and command mankind to niggardliness and *hide the bounties which Allah hath bestowed on them*; and We have prepared for the ungrateful a punishment that steeps them in contempt...." (IV:36, 37).

"Hiding the bounties which Allah hath bestowed on them" implies:

(*i*) Withholding bounties from others;

(*ii*) Disallowing those bounties from manifesting themselves on one's person and in the different aspects of one's personal life.

There is a *hadith* which clarifies the duty in respect of the second implication directly:

إِنَّ اللّٰهَ يُحِبُّ أَنْ يَرٰى أَثَرَ نِعْمَتِهٖ عَلٰى عَبْدِهٖ

"Allah loves to see the effects of His bounties on the person of His Servant." (Tirmizi).

It is, therefore, the duty of a Muslim to abstain from practising miserliness towards his own self.

(xli) (a) Squandering—Vain Spending, prohibited:

The Holy Qur'ãn says:

وَلَا تُبَذِّرْ تَبْذِيرًا ۝ إِنَّ الْمُبَذِّرِينَ كَانُوٓا إِخْوَانَ الشَّيٰطِينِ ۖ وَكَانَ الشَّيْطٰنُ لِرَبِّهٖ كَفُورًا ۝

"....but squander not (your wealth) in the manner of a spendthrift. Verily spendthrifts are associates of (*i.e.*, of the same family as) the Evil Ones; and the Evil One is to his Lord (Himself) ungrateful'[32]."[33] (XVII:26, 27).

It is, therefore, a duty to abstain totally from squandering one's wealth, whether of one's own self and defendants or for others.

---

32. Hence those who squander their wealth commit no less a sin than that of being ungrateful to God by misusing His bounty.

33. Cf. another verse:

وَلَا تَبْسُطْهَا كُلَّ الْبَسْطِ فَتَقْعُدَ مَلُومًا مَّحْسُورًا ۝

".....nor open it (*i.e.,* the hand) with a complete opening lest thou become blameworthy and destitute." (XVII:29).

(b) Insincerity in acts seemingly of charity and spending one's wealth for show in general, condemned:

إِنَّ اللّٰهَ لَا يُحِبُّ مَنْ كَانَ مُخْتَالًا فَخُوْرًا ۙ . . . . وَالَّذِيْنَ يُنْفِقُوْنَ أَمْوَالَهُمْ رِئَاءَ النَّاسِ

"Verily Allah loveth not the arrogant, the vainglorious.....those who expend their substance to show off to men...." (IV: 36, 38).

(xlii) Impatience, or want of calm endurance and perseverance, disapproved; hence abstinence from it is duty;

وَلَوْ أَنَّهُمْ صَبَرُوْا حَتّٰى تَخْرُجَ إِلَيْهِمْ لَكَانَ خَيْرًا لَّهُمْ ط

"If only they had patience until thou (O Prophet) could come out to them, it would have been good for them. (That they behaved impatiently was bad for them)". (XLIX:5).

This verse indicates that impatience, namely, want of calm endurance and perseverance, is bad for one's self. Hence to abstain from it is duty to self.

(xliii) Spirit of Ungratefulness condemned; hence abstinence from it is duty:

The Holy Qur'ãn says:

إِنَّ اللّٰهَ لَا يُحِبُّ كُلَّ خَوَّانٍ كَفُوْرٍ

"Verily, Allah loveth not any treacherous, ungrateful (person)." (XXII:38).

This verse emphasises basically the *spirit* of ungratefulness. Of Course, active ungratefulness, whether towards God or towards fellow-beings, is also definitely included.

It is, therefore, duty to eschew the spirit of ungratefulness and to abstain from being ungrateful to anyone, whereby the moral purity of one's own inner personality is damaged.

(xliv) Indecency, lewdness and everything abominable in thought and word and deed, prohibited:

The Holy Qur'ãn has commanded:

وَلَا تَقْرَبُوا الْفَوَاحِشَ مَا ظَهَرَ مِنْهَا وَمَا بَطَنَ ۚ

"....and draw not nigh to indecencies, whether open or secret...."[34] (VI:151).

Again:

وَيَنْهَىٰ عَنِ الْفَحْشَاءِ وَالْمُنكَرِ وَالْبَغْيِ ۚ

"....and He forbidden lewdness and abomination and wickedness...."[35] (XVI:90).

It is, thus, duty to abstain totally from indecency, lewdness and everything abominable in thought, in speech and in action.

(xlv) *The very Spirit of Sexual Immodesty prohibited:*

The Holy Qur'ãn says:

وَلَا تَقْرَبُوا الزِّنَىٰ ۖ إِنَّهُ كَانَ فَاحِشَةً وَسَاءَ سَبِيلًا ۝

"And come not nigh to adultery: for it is a shameful (deed) and an evil, opening the road (to other evils)." (XVII:32).

The words "come not nigh to" imply abstinence from the very *spirit* of sexual immodesty, as also the attitude and the behaviour in which it manifests itself. Thus it is a duty to shun[36] they very spirit of sexual

---

34, 35. The words *fawãhish* and *fahshã'* used in the above verses for shameful things are very rich in their meanings and cannot be translated into English.

36. This stern moral attitude of Islam may be compared with the spirit, the attitude, and the consequent behaviour, nurtured in the Western communities, where, because of freedom of promiscuity, adultery "has become fashionable in both England and America" and elsewhere. (Scott: *History of Prostitution*, p. 226). Indeed, because of the absence of the spirit of sexual modesty and of the cultivation of general licence in respect of sexual manners, sexual morality has been damaged to such an extent that: "The old type of prostitute who pranced about gaudily and drunkenly in the Strand, Leicester Square, Piccadily and Regent Street, is a thing of the past..... There has been a huge increase in promiscuity among men and even greater increase among women....The results are that more and more every year is man turning to so-called girls of respectability in order to satisfy his sexual appetite.... Virginity among women is becoming something to sneer at.... Where all the practising what is virtually prostitution there can be no such thing as prostitution." (*Ibid.*, pp. 224, 225, 228). There is a lesson in this for all those Muslims who advocate the adoption

immodesty, as also the immodest attitudes and behaviour that cause temptation in relations between the sexes.

(xlvi) *Defiling one's spiritual and moral purity through illicit sexual gratification, including homosexuality and self-abuse, prohibited:*

Abstinence from lewdness has already been included in the duty mentioned in the previous section. Here we may quote the verse where the command has been given with particular reference to sexual appetite. The Holy Qur'ãn says:

قُلْ لِّلْمُؤْمِنِيْنَ يَغُضُّوْا مِنْ اَبْصَارِهِمْ وَيَحْفَظُوْا فُرُوْجَهُمْ ۭ ذٰلِكَ اَزْكٰى
لَهُمْ ۭ اِنَّ اللّٰهَ خَبِيْرٌۢ بِمَا يَصْنَعُوْنَ ۝ وَقُلْ لِّلْمُؤْمِنٰتِ يَغْضُضْنَ مِنْ
اَبْصَارِهِنَّ وَيَحْفَظْنَ فُرُوْجَهُنَّ

"Say thou (O Prophet!) to the believing men that they should lower their gaze (in the spirit of sexual modesty) and guard their private parts (against misuse): that will make for greater purity for them. And Allah is well acquainted with all that ye do.

"And say to the believing women that they should lower their gaze and guard their private parts (against misuse)." (XXIV:30, 31).

These verse lay down the duty of abstaining from defiling one's purity by illicit sexual relations and sexual self-abuse.[37]

(xlvii) *Indifference to self-reform condemned; hence abstinence from it is duty:*

The greatest of moral diseases consists in the attitude of indifference to self-reform. The Holy Qur'ãn takes full cognizance of it and, in order to warn the Muslims of its evil implications and consequences, condemns the presence of this disease among the clergy and the people of a previous religious community.

Addressing their clergy, it says:

---

of western culture. Alas! the social evils of the West are only too fast penetrating the Muslim communities also under the spell of modernisation!

37. The only way of satisfying the sexual appetite recognised by the Holy Qur'ãn as legitimate and chaste is that of marriage between man and woman duly solemnised. (XXIII: 5-7; LXX:29-31). All other ways are totally prohibited.

أَتَأْمُرُونَ النَّاسَ بِالْبِرِّ وَتَنْسَوْنَ أَنْفُسَكُمْ وَأَنْتُمْ تَتْلُونَ الْكِتٰبَ ۚ أَفَلَا تَعْقِلُونَ ۝

"Do ye enjoin right conduct on the people, and forget (to practise it) yourselves, and yet ye study the Scripture? Will ye not understand?" (II:44).

ثُمَّ قَسَتْ قُلُوبُكُمْ مِنْ بَعْدِ ذٰلِكَ فَهِيَ كَالْحِجَارَةِ أَوْ أَشَدُّ قَسْوَةً ۚ وَإِنَّ مِنَ الْحِجَارَةِ لَمَا يَتَفَجَّرُ مِنْهُ الْأَنْهٰرُ ۚ وَإِنَّ مِنْهَا لَمَا يَشَّقَّقُ فَيَخْرُجُ مِنْهُ الْمَاءُ ۚ وَإِنَّ مِنْهَا لَمَا يَهْبِطُ مِنْ خَشْيَةِ اللّٰهِ ۗ وَمَا اللّٰهُ بِغَافِلٍ عَمَّا تَعْمَلُونَ ۝

"Thenceforth your hearts hardened: they became like a rock and even worse in hardness. For among rocks there are some from which rivers gush forth; others there are which when split asunder send forth water; and others which sink for fear of Allah: and Allah is not unmindful of your actions." (II:74).

It is, therefore, the duty of a Muslim to abstain from cultivating or retaining an attitude which may disable him from reforming himself in respect of his weaknesses and deficiencies.

Chapter II

DUTIES OF COMMISSION

END :

Moral Development ensuring Moral Perfection.

(i) Cultivation and practice of Truthfulness enjoined:

The Holy Qur'ãn lays down the command in the following two verses:

يَا أَيُّهَا الَّذِينَ آمَنُوا اتَّقُوا اللَّهَ وَكُونُوا مَعَ الصَّادِقِينَ ۝

"O ye who believe! Guard your duty to Allah (in respect of truthfulness) and be with those who are true (in thought, word and deed.)" (IX:119).

يَا أَيُّهَا الَّذِينَ آمَنُوا اتَّقُوا اللَّهَ وَقُولُوا قَوْلًا سَدِيدًا ۝ يُصْلِحْ لَكُمْ
أَعْمَالَكُمْ وَيَغْفِرْ لَكُمْ ذُنُوبَكُمْ ۗ وَمَن يُطِعِ اللَّهَ وَرَسُولَهُ فَقَدْ فَازَ فَوْزًا
عَظِيمًا ۝

"O ye who believe! Guard your duty to Allah and speak words (that are) true and directed to the right point: that He may make your conduct whole and sound and forgive you your sins. He that obeys Allah and His Messenger, hath indeed attained the highest achievement." (XXXIII:70, 71).

The first commands the Muslims:

(a) to be most conscientiously truthful, namely, through guarding their duty of obedience to God Who is all time a witness even to their innermost thoughts and feelings, not to speak of speech and action;

(b) to be comprehensively truthful, because conscientious truthfulness means truthfulness in every respect, namely, in thought, word and deed;

(c) to develop the spirit and activity of truthfulness by upholding the cause of truthfulness and by loving the company of those who are genuinely truthful.

The second verse commands, not only conscientious truthfulness in speech, but also guarding against even unconscious slip from truth by making the speech "directed to the right point."[1]

Truthfulness in thought, word and deed is, therefore, a duty. Indeed, it is such an important duty that it forms one of essential attributes of righteousness (III:14-16), and Heaven has been promised to those who uphold truth in their hearts and practise it in their actions (XXXIII:35). In Heaven itself, the righteous will enjoy their blissful life in "*an Assembly of Truth* in the Presence of the Sovereign Omnipotent." (LIV:55).

(ii) Guarding of Oaths enjoined:

Taking lightly one's oaths is the quality of the person who is deficient in moral earnestness and lacks in true devotion to truthfulness. Hence, in order to maintain sound moral outlook and character, it is a duty to guard one's oaths, i.e., to be true to one's oaths; and this is what the Holy Qur'ãn has commanded:

وَاحْفَظُوْٓا اَيْمَانَكُمْ ؕ

".....and guard your oaths." (V:92).

(iii) Cultivation of the spirit of Sincerity and Uprightness enjoined:

Sincerity means freedom from pretence. Uprightness (or, *honesty*) means freedom from fraud. Both these qualities are actually forms of truthfulness, implying that there should be sameness in reality as in appearance. In other words, what we express in words should be the same as we feel in our hearts, and in no way should we do injustice to our speech by making it immoral through making it discordant with what we believe to be true. The Holy Qur'ãn has thus commanded sincerity and uprightness (side by side with truthfulness in giving evidence and with justice in pronouncing judgment), in the following verse:

وَاِذَا قُلْتُمْ فَاعْدِلُوْا

".....and when ye utter a word, do justice thereunto...."
(VI:152).

---

1. "Directed to the right point" also means employing accuracy in expression, which is a part of wisdom—another great excellence upheld by the Holy Qur'ãn. (II:269).

(iv) Steadfastness in everything good and true enjoined:

The Holy Qur'ãn has commanded the Muslims to be steadfast in the cause of Truth:

وَرَابِطُوا

".....and be ever ready (*i.e.,* fixed in your resolve)...." (III:200).

Again:

يَآيُّهَا الَّذِينَ آمَنُوا إِذَا لَقِيتُمْ فِئَةً فَاثْبُتُوا

"O ye who believe! when ye meet a (hostile) force, stay firm...." (VIII:45).

This should be so, because firmness is one of the basic qualities of true Believers:

يُثَبِّتُ اللّٰهُ الَّذِينَ آمَنُوا بِالْقَوْلِ الثَّابِتِ فِي الْحَيٰوةِ الدُّنْيَا وَفِي الْآخِرَةِ

"Allah keepeth firm those who believe, with the Word that stands firm, in this world and in the Hereafter..." (XIV:27).

Hence, steadfastness in all that is good and true is duty.

(v) Modesty enjoined:

Modesty, which means "restraint by a sense of seemliness" and which implies spiritual purity and moral decency in one's inner attitudes and outward behaviour *in respect of moral decorum*, has been emphasised in a beautiful manner in the following Qur'ãnic verses:

يٰبَنِي آدَمَ قَدْ أَنْزَلْنَا عَلَيْكُمْ لِبَاسًا يُّوَارِي سَوْاٰتِكُمْ وَرِيْشًا ۖ وَلِبَاسُ التَّقْوٰى ۙ ذٰلِكَ خَيْرٌ ۚ ذٰلِكَ مِنْ اٰيٰتِ اللّٰهِ لَعَلَّهُمْ يَذَّكَّرُوْنَ ۝ يٰبَنِيْٓ اٰدَمَ لَا يَفْتِنَنَّكُمُ الشَّيْطٰنُ كَمَآ اَخْرَجَ اَبَوَيْكُمْ مِّنَ الْجَنَّةِ يَنْزِعُ عَنْهُمَا لِبَاسَهُمَا لِيُرِيَهُمَا سَوْاٰتِهِمَا ۚ

"O ye children of Adam! We have bestowed raiment upon you to conceal your shame, and as an adornment. But *the raiment of piety, that is the best.* Such are among the Signs of Allah, that ye may be admonished.

"O ye children of Adam! *Let not Satan seduce you,* in the same manner as he got your parents out of the Garden (of felicity), stripping them of the raiment (of innocence and purity), that he might manifest their shame to them....." (VII:26, 27).

'Raiment of piety', in verse 26, emphasises the observance of modesty in the inner attitude as well as outward behaviour; while the words: 'let not Satan seduce you' in verse 27, proclaim the duty of the observance of modesty.[2]

(vi) Marriage enjoined for providing the protection of the moral fortress of married life to the individual:

The law has been laid down:

وَأَنكِحُوا الْأَيَامَىٰ مِنكُمْ وَالصَّالِحِينَ مِنْ عِبَادِكُمْ وَإِمَائِكُمْ ۚ إِن يَكُونُوا
فُقَرَاءَ يُغْنِهِمُ اللَّهُ مِن فَضْلِهِ ۗ وَاللَّهُ وَاسِعٌ عَلِيمٌ ۝

"Marry those among you who are single, or the virtuous ones among your slaves, male or female: If they are in poverty Allah will give them Means out of His Grace: for Allah encompasseth all, and He knoweth all things." (XXIV:32).

That marriage provides a moral fortress, a fortress of chastity, has been emphasised by the Holy Qur'ãn in the word *muhsin—hisn* meaning fortess—employed in the verse which points out the true motive with which a Muslim should marry:

مُّحْصِنِينَ غَيْرَ مُسَافِحِينَ ۚ

".....desiring chastity, not lust....." (IV:24).

(vii) Chastity under all conditions: Preservation of sexual sanctity enjoined:

Chastity implies maintenance of purity in thought, word and deed, and in respect of the sexual passion. The Holy Qur'ãn makes it a duty when it commands:

2. The Holy Qur'ãn has not only laid down this duty in fundamental terms, but has also given certain rules in that respect. We shall state those rules in the section on "Manners."

وَلْيَسْتَعْفِفِ الَّذِيْنَ لَا يَجِدُوْنَ نِكَاحًا

"Those who find not the wherewithal of marriage shall keep themselves chaste (in thought, word and deed)...." (XXIV:33).

Elsewhere, the womenfolk have been specifically commanded:

وَاَنْ يَّسْتَعْفِفْنَ خَيْرٌ لَّهُنَّ ط

".....and that they shall observe the principle of chastity (even in respect of the most distantly related aspects of attitude and behaviour), that is best for them...." (XXIV:60).

(viii) Labouring for earning one's livelihood enjoined:

The Holy Qur'ãn has commanded:

وَابْتَغُوْا مِنْ فَضْلِ اللّٰهِ وَاذْكُرُوا اللّٰهَ كَثِيْرًا لَّعَلَّكُمْ تُفْلِحُوْنَ○

".....*and seek of* (*i.e., strive and labour for*) *Allah's bounty* (*i.e., means of livelihood*): and remember Allah much, that ye may prosper." (LXII:10).

The above command to strive and labour for earning one's livelihood has actually been given in the context of the observance of special weekly congregational worship on Fridays. This does not mean, however, that the command is confined only to Fridays. On the contrary, the Holy Qur'ãn has emphasised the virtue of labouring for earning one's livelihood by repudiating the Jewish-Christian notion of the Sabbath—of the false belief as to the sanctity of idleness and abstinence from work—and asserting that labour for honest earning is most definitely a part of worship.

Expounding the Qur'ãnic view, the Holy Prophet (Peace be on him) says:

طلب كسب الحلال فريضة ....

"To engage in labour for honest livelihood is duty...." (*Mishkãt al-Masabîh*, vol. II., p. 7).

(ix) Earning livelihood through honest means enjoined:

The verse quoted in the preceding injunction[3] implies one more

3. LXII:10.

command also: namely, to earn one's livelihood by honest means and in honest manner, because it has to be earned as "God's Bounty" and not as Satan's favour. Moreover, the command to earn has been combined with the command to "remember Allah much, that ye may prosper", thereby commanding spiritualisation of the effort for earning, which alone can truly guarantee the maintenance of one's conscience as sound and unblemished.

(x) Benefiting oneself from only that which has been lawfully acquired, enjoined:

The most basic need of man is food, and hence it is hunger in respect of which it is most difficult to observe lawfulness. Even an honest person finds it most difficult to abstain from employing debasing or illegitimate means, like theft, when he is confronted with death by starvation. Hence, the Holy Qur'ãn has mentioned food when laying down the duty of benefiting oneself from only that which has been lawfully acquired. It says:

يَٰٓأَيُّهَا ٱلنَّاسُ كُلُوا۟ مِمَّا فِى ٱلْأَرْضِ حَلَٰلًا طَيِّبًا

"O mankind! eat of whatsoever is on the earth (provided it is) lawfully acquired, and good (*i.e.*, lawful for your health)...." (II:168).

Then the Holy Qur'ãn goes beyond food and lays down the general law:

يَٰٓأَيُّهَا ٱلَّذِينَ ءَامَنُوٓا۟ أَنفِقُوا۟ مِن طَيِّبَٰتِ مَا كَسَبْتُمْ وَمِمَّآ أَخْرَجْنَا لَكُم مِّنَ ٱلْأَرْضِ

"O ye who believe! Spend out of the good things which ye have lawfully earned and out of that which We have brought forth for you from the earth...." (II:267).

According to Qur'ãnic commentators, this verse relates to spending in charity for others[4], from which a person benefits spiritually. But, spending on one's personal needs should all the more strictly be based on what one has lawfully earned, because in that way alone can the spiritual health—the integrity of personality—be properly maintained.

---

4. Actually speaking, there is nothing in the wordings of the verse whereby personal expenditure should be excluded.

(xi) Virtue of industry enjoined:

To lead a hard life, to engage in perpetual endeavour for the flowering up of one's talents and faculties, to struggle incessantly through honest labour for higher and higher achievement: that is the law of life in Islam, emphasised time and again in the Holy Qur'ãn and enshrined in the life of the Holy Prophet (Peace be on him). Emphasising this law, the Holy Qur'ãn says:

وَاَنْ لَّيْسَ لِلْاِنْسَانِ اِلَّا مَا سَعٰى ۝ وَاَنَّ سَعْيَهٗ سَوْفَ يُرٰى ۝

".....and that for man shall be naught (*i.e.,* no man deserves) save that wherefor he maketh effort, and that (the fruit of) his effort will soon come in sight." (LIII:39, 40).

Again:

وَلِكُلٍّ دَرَجٰتٌ مِّمَّا عَمِلُوْا ۭ وَمَا رَبُّكَ بِغَافِلٍ عَمَّا يَعْمَلُوْنَ ۝

"For each (human being) is a rank according to the *deeds* which he doth: for thy Lord is not unaware of what they do". (VI:132).

The first verse says that no human being deserves any success in life except what he labours for. The second verse emphasises progress on the basis of genuine, practical endeavour.

Industry is, therefore, an important duty to self, according to the Holy Qur'ãn.

(xii) Virtue of pursuing stable and sound Progress in life, through:

(i) Planning one's life and activity soundly;

(ii) Aiming at consequential (as opposed to wasteful) activity;

(iii) Aiming at the highest and the soundest productivity in one's activity,

enjoined:

The Holy Qur'ãn commands:

يٰٓاَيُّهَا الَّذِيْنَ اٰمَنُوا اتَّقُوا اللّٰهَ وَلْتَنْظُرْ نَفْسٌ مَّا قَدَّمَتْ لِغَدٍ ۚ وَ
اتَّقُوا اللّٰهَ ۭ اِنَّ اللّٰهَ خَبِيْرٌۢ بِمَا تَعْمَلُوْنَ ۝

"O ye who believe! Fear Allah (in wasting your life and talents in vain or wrong pursuits and through unsound planning and execution), and (in all types of actions) let every soul look to what (resulting good and worthiness for success and progress) he has sent forth for the morrow. Yea, fear Allah (for making your activity positive, planned, consequential and progressive, thereby manifesting your true and active thankfulness to Him for His bounties): for Allah is well acquainted with (all) that ye do." (LIX:18).

That the human outlook should be progressive, which necessitates aiming at the highest and the soundest productivity, is borne out by the fact that man, according to the Holy Qur'ãn, is an evolutionary being and the character of human life is evolutionary:[5]

فَلَآ أُقْسِمُ بِالشَّفَقِ ۝ وَالَّيْلِ وَمَا وَسَقَ ۝ وَالْقَمَرِ إِذَا اتَّسَقَ ۝ لَتَرْكَبُنَّ طَبَقًا عَنْ طَبَقٍ ۝١٩

"So I do call to witness the ruddy glow of Sunset; the Night and its Homing; and the Moon in her Fulness: Ye shall surely travel from stage to stage." (LXXXIV:16-19).

(xiii) Cultivation and maintenance of Optimism enjoined:

Optimism, or maintaining an unflinching attitude of hope, is based, in a Muslim's life, on his unswerving faith in, and sincere reliance on, God, and has been mentioned in the Holy Qur'ãn as an essential attribute of Islamic life:[6]

أَمَّنْ هُوَ قَانِتٌ آنَاءَ الَّيْلِ سَاجِدًا وَّ قَائِمًا يَّحْذَرُ الْآخِرَةَ وَيَرْجُوا رَحْمَةَ رَبِّهِ ؕ

"Is one who worships devoutly during the hours of the night prostrating himself and standing (in adoration), who takes heed of the

---

5. A critical study of the Holy Qur'ãn reveals that it is not only the human personality which is evolutionary but also the universe wherein humanity originated and has to fulfil its destiny.

6. That Pessimism, as mentioned before (on page 71), amounts to infidelity (*Kufr*) also shows that, according to the Holy Qur'ãn, the Faithful is he for whom Optimism is an inseparable quality of character.

Hereafter, and *who places his hope in the Mercy of his Lord* (like one who does not)?...." (XXXIX:9).

To maintain optimistic attitude in life, is, therefore, duty.

(xiv) Cultivation and maintenance of the spirit of and the attitude of Generosity (or, Spirit of Benevolence) enjoined:

Actual generosity is a duty to others. But the cultivation and maintenance of the spirit and the attitude of generosity is a duty towards self because of the purity and enrichment that it acquires thereby. It is this spirit and this attitude that have been emphasised together with actual generosity, as essential attributes of righteousness, in the following verses:

وَسَارِعُوٓا إِلَىٰ مَغْفِرَةٍ مِّن رَّبِّكُمْ وَجَنَّةٍ عَرْضُهَا السَّمٰوٰتُ وَالْأَرْضُ
أُعِدَّتْ لِلْمُتَّقِينَ ۝ الَّذِينَ يُنفِقُونَ فِي السَّرَّآءِ وَالضَّرَّآءِ

"And view with one another, hastening to forgiveness from your Lord, and to a Garden whose breadth is that (of the whole) of the heavens and of the earth, prepared for the righteous,—those who spend (freely), whether in prosperity or in adversity....." (III:133, 134).

الَّذِينَ يُنفِقُونَ أَمْوٰلَهُم بِالَّيْلِ وَالنَّهَارِ سِرًّا وَعَلَانِيَةً فَلَهُمْ أَجْرُهُمْ
عِندَ رَبِّهِمْ وَلَا خَوْفٌ عَلَيْهِمْ وَلَا هُمْ يَحْزَنُونَ ۝

"Those who spend (in Charity) of their goods by night and by day, in secret and in public, have their reward with their Lord; on them shall be no fear, nor shall they grieve." (II:274).

(xv) Constancy in Life commanded; hence its observance is duty:

Success and productivity in life demands constancy in our effort, and hence devotion to the principle of constancy is a duty to self. The Holy Qur'ãn enjoins it in respect of Prayer, saying that life is truly and ultimately successful of those "who," besides possessing other virtues, "are constant at their worship."[7] (LXX:23).

Now, Prayer being the most basic character-building exercise according to the Holy Qur'ãn, the above verse refers indirectly to the

---

7. الَّذِينَ هُمْ عَلَىٰ صَلَاتِهِمْ دَآئِمُونَ ۝

merit of cultivation and maintenance of the principle of constancy in respect of all virtues. This fact has been directly emphasised by the Holy Prophet (Peace be on him) when he says:

إِنَّ أَحَبَّ الْعَمَلِ إِلَى اللهِ أَدْوَمُهُ

"The action (of goodness) most loved by God is that in which the principle of Constancy is observed most." (Bukhãri: *Sahîh*, Vol. II., p. 957).

(xvi) Punctuality and Regularity in life enjoined:

The Holy Qur'ãn has enjoined punctuality in respect of Prayer:

إِنَّ الصَّلٰوةَ كَانَتْ عَلَى الْمُؤْمِنِيْنَ كِتٰبًا مَّوْقُوْتًا ۝

"Verily the Prayer is prescribed unto the Believers at definite times (or, at appointed hours)". (IV:103).

In this manner the Holy Qur'ãn trains and accustoms the Muslims to punctuality in all the affairs of life.

Moreover, the holy book appeals repeatedly to the Believers to observe the principle of regularity found in Nature and within their own selves, and take lesson from it all. For instance:

وَفِي الْأَرْضِ اٰيٰتٌ لِّلْمُوْقِنِيْنَ ۝ وَفِيْ أَنْفُسِكُمْ ۚ أَفَلَا تُبْصِرُوْنَ ۝

"On the earth are Signs for those of assured Faith, as also in your own selves: will ye not then observe?" (LI:20, 21).

إِنَّ فِيْ خَلْقِ السَّمٰوٰتِ وَالْأَرْضِ وَاخْتِلَافِ الَّيْلِ وَالنَّهَارِ لَاٰيٰتٍ لِّأُولِي الْأَلْبَابِ ۝

"Behold! In the constitution of the heavenly bodies and the earth, and the alternation of the Day and the Night, there are indeed Signs for the possessors of understanding...." (III:190).

Such being the importance of punctuality and regularity according to the Holy Qur'ãn, it is a duty to observe them in life to the best of one's ability.

(xvii) Observance of the principle of Moderation enjoined:

According to the Holy Qur'ãn, conformity to the just mean in all things of life is one of the basic distinguishing marks of Islamic conduct. God says:

وَكَذَٰلِكَ جَعَلْنَٰكُمْ أُمَّةً وَسَطًا

"Thus We have exalted you as a community (*ummah*) conforming to the just mean...." (II:143).

Having laid down the principle basically and for universal application in life, the holy book also refers to certain concrete instances of its application. For instance:

(a) Concerning prayer:

وَلَا تَجْهَرْ بِصَلَاتِكَ وَلَا تُخَافِتْ بِهَا وَابْتَغِ بَيْنَ ذَٰلِكَ سَبِيلًا ۝

"Neither speak the Prayer aloud, nor speak it in a low tone, but seek a middle course between." (XVII:110).

(b) Concerning spending:

The true servants of God are:

وَالَّذِينَ إِذَا أَنفَقُوا لَمْ يُسْرِفُوا وَلَمْ يَقْتُرُوا وَكَانَ بَيْنَ ذَٰلِكَ قَوَامًا ۝

"those who, when they spend[8] (their wealth, talents, time, energy, etc.), are neither extravagant nor sparing, but hold a just (balance) between those (extremes)." (XXV:67).

(c) Concerning walking:

وَاقْصِدْ فِي مَشْيِكَ

"And be moderate in thy pace....." (XXXI:19).

Thus, observance of the principle of moderation in all things is a duty.

(xviii) Observance and maintenance of Discipline enjoined:

A true Muslim's life is a disciplined life. It is hedged in by

8. Here there is no specific mention of wealth. Hence the reference is general.

principles, rules and laws from all sides, named by the Holy Qur'ãn as 'limits ordained by God', and it is a duty to maintain life strictly within those limits. Discipline is thus the hallmark of Islamic life. Speaking of the true Believers the Holy Qur'ãn says:

وَالْحٰفِظُوْنَ لِحُدُوْدِ اللّٰهِ ؕ وَبَشِّرِ الْمُؤْمِنِيْنَ ۝

"....and those who keep the limits ordained by Allah. So proclaim the glad tidings to the Believers." (IX:112).

As regards those who are undisciplined and violate those limits, we are told:

تِلْكَ حُدُوْدُ اللّٰهِ فَلَا تَعْتَدُوْهَا ۚ وَمَنْ يَّتَعَدَّ حُدُوْدَ اللّٰهِ فَاُولٰٓئِكَ هُمُ الظّٰلِمُوْنَ ۝

"These are the limits (ordained by) Allah. Transgress them not. For whoso transgresses Allah's limits: such are wrongdoers." (II:229).

Again:

وَمَنْ يَّتَعَدَّ حُدُوْدَ اللّٰهِ فَقَدْ ظَلَمَ نَفْسَهٗ ؕ

".....and any who transgresses the limits ordained by Allah, does verily wrong his own soul....." (LXV:1).

Observance of strict discipline in life is, therefore, duty to self.

(xix) *Cultivation and Practice of Moral Courage enjoined:*

Moral courage consists in upholding and advocating truth without fear.

According to the Holy Qur'ãn, it forms one of the essential attributes of Islamic conduct. For, the true Believers are those who are:

لَا يَخَافُوْنَ لَوْمَةَ لَآئِمٍ ؕ

".....never afraid (in upholding Truth) of the reproaches of such as find fault." (V:57).

Hence, cultivation and maintenance of moral courage is duty.

(xx) *Remaining pitched in battle against the forces of evil enjoined:*

A true Muslim is a man of God and, as such, his function is to enjoin what is right and to forbid what is wrong[9]. He cannot perform this function, however, unless he remains pitched in battle against the forces of evil. And this he has been commanded by the Holy Qur'ãn:

إِنَّ الشَّيْطَٰنَ لَكُمْ عَدُوٌّ فَاتَّخِذُوهُ عَدُوًّا

"Verily Satan is an enemy to you: so treat him (constantly) as an enemy (remaining engaged in perpetual fight with him)." (XXXV:6).

Shaitãn or, Satan, is according to Lane's *Arabic-English Lexicon*, not only 'the devil', but 'any that is exceedingly, or inordinately, proud or corrupt or unbelieving or rebellious.' As such, Satan represents all evils, whatever their form, wherever they are found, and whenever they manifest themselves. Used as a proper noun, i.e., as 'the Satan', the word signifies the personification of Evil. In any case, the promptings to evil are there all the time: the forces of evil, in their multifarious forms, are perpetually at work. Those who do not treat evil as their enemy fall a victim to it. But every Muslim is, so to say, born to destroy evil and to establish the good. He cannot treat evil even with indifference, not to speak of befriending it. He must fight, fight continuously and with all his might, against evil, wherever it is within his reach and whatever its form. It is his unavoidable duty.

Expounding this duty, the Holy Prophet (Peace be on him) says:

من رأى منكم منكرًا فليغيّره بيده ومن لم يستطع فبلسانه ومن لم يستطع فبقلبه وذالك اضعف الإيمان

"Whoever observe evil it is his duty to eradicate it with his hand (or, power of authority). But he who is unable to do that, let him employ (the power of) his tongue. In case there is one who is unable even to do that, let him (at least detest it) with his heart. This last, however, is the weakest degree of Faith". (Muslim: *Sahîh*, vol. I, p. 51).

(xxi) Cultivation and Practice of Bravery enjoined:

True Muslims, according to the Holy Qur'ãn, are those who face all hardships and trials, and the forces of the enemy at the battlefield, bravely:

---

9. III:110; IX:71; IX:112; etc.

وَالْمُوفُونَ بِعَهْدِهِمْ إِذَا عَاهَدُوا ۚ وَالصَّابِرِينَ فِي الْبَأْسَاءِ وَالضَّرَّاءِ
وَحِينَ الْبَأْسِ ۗ أُولَٰئِكَ الَّذِينَ صَدَقُوا ۖ وَأُولَٰئِكَ هُمُ الْمُتَّقُونَ ۝

".....and those who observe firmness and calmness in pain (or suffering) and adversity, and throughout all periods of panic and violence (i.e., in war): Such are they who are true (in their Faith[10]). Such are the God-fearing." (II:177).

Muslims have been, therefore, commanded:

يَا أَيُّهَا الَّذِينَ آمَنُوا إِذَا لَقِيتُمْ فِئَةً فَاثْبُتُوا وَاذْكُرُوا اللَّهَ كَثِيرًا
لَعَلَّكُمْ تُفْلِحُونَ ۝

"O ye who believe! When ye meet a force (of the enemy on the battlefield), hold firm (i.e., face the enemy bravely), and call Allah in remembrance much[11] (and often), that ye may be successful). (VIII:45).

Again:

يَا أَيُّهَا الَّذِينَ آمَنُوا إِذَا لَقِيتُمُ الَّذِينَ كَفَرُوا زَحْفًا فَلَا تُوَلُّوهُمُ الْأَدْبَارَ ۝

"O ye who believe! When ye meet the Unbelievers in battle, never turn your backs to them." (VIII:15).

(xxii) Observance of Self-Respect, Magnanimity and Sobriety enjoined:

It is the duty of every Muslim to cultivate and observe self-respect, side by side with humility; because the very fact that he is a Muslim makes every true follower of Islam honourable. The Holy Qur'ãn says:

كُنْتُمْ خَيْرَ أُمَّةٍ

---

10. Mark that bravery belongs to the heart and not to the body. It is the true faith and the true spirit (i.e., true devotion to an ideal) that makes a man brave. In the case of a Muslim, it is Faith in God in all its aspects which is the only motivating force in his life; and Faith in God is the highest and the most unfailing source of strength.

11. Mark that bravery is cultivated at higher and higher levels through devotion to God.

"Ye are the best community (in respect of your ideology and your mission)....." (III:110).

وَ لِلّٰهِ الْعِزَّةُ وَ لِرَسُوْلِهٖ وَ لِلْمُؤْمِنِيْنَ

"Honour belongs to Allah and His Messenger (Muhammad) and the (true) Believers;...." (LXIII:8).

That is why God has commended the self-respecting attitude of the *Ashãb-us-Suffah* (People of the Platform) in II:273, already quoted[12], and has referred to the virtues of self-respect, magnanimity and sobriety as the virtues which should be practised by all of His true Servants:

وَ اِذَا مَرُّوْا بِاللَّغْوِ مَرُّوْا كِرَامًا ۝

".....and when they pass by what is nonsense, they pass by it observing self-respect, magnanimity and sobriety." (XXV:72).

(xxiii) Self-defence against wrong enjoined:

Self-respect makes self-defence necessary, wherever required. Of course, all mischief is to be avoided (VII:56; XXVIII:77, etc.) and nothing should be done which violates any of the virtues that have been enjoined (II:208). With these precautions, self-defence is a duty, because it has been mentioned by the Holy Qur'ãn as a quality of the Believer's conduct:

وَ الَّذِيْنَ اِذَآ اَصَابَهُمُ الْبَغْيُ هُمْ يَنْتَصِرُوْنَ ۝

"and those who, when an oppressive wrong is inflicted on them, help and defend themselves."[13] (XLII:39).

(xxiv) Observance of the spirit of Contentment enjoined:

Discontentment can be in respect of:

(a) one's resources, or, (b) one's possessions.

(a) As to the first one may feel that if he is able to acquire the patronage of the high-ups, he can increase his resourcefulness for

---

12. See page 80.

13. This verse relates to individual as well as collective action, according to the form of the wrong inflicted.

increasing his possessions: wealth, prestige, power, etc. Such an ambition leads almost always to debasement of the self, and consequently to the violation of the virtue of self-respect. Hence, a Muslim has been commanded to direct all his needs and all his ambitions to God and God alone, as, for instance, in the basic Muslim prayer:

إِيَّاكَ نَعْبُدُ وَإِيَّاكَ نَسْتَعِينُ ۝

"Thee alone (O Allah) do we worship and Thine help alone we seek." (I:5).

The Holy Qur'ãn wants a Muslim to be absolutely contented with the Patronage of God, Who is the Source of all Good, when it asks emphatically:

أَلَيْسَ اللَّهُ بِكَافٍ عَبْدَهُ ۖ

"Is not Allah enough for His servant?" (XXXIX:36).

(b) The usual form of discontentment is in respect of what one possesses, and it becomes more damaging morally when one starts cultivating jealousy in relation to what others possess. The Holy Qur'ãn has forbidden it outright:

وَلَا تَتَمَنَّوْا مَا فَضَّلَ اللَّهُ بِهِ بَعْضَكُمْ عَلَىٰ بَعْضٍ ۚ لِلرِّجَالِ نَصِيبٌ مِمَّا
اكْتَسَبُوا ۖ وَلِلنِّسَاءِ نَصِيبٌ مِمَّا اكْتَسَبْنَ ۚ وَاسْأَلُوا اللَّهَ مِنْ فَضْلِهِ ۗ
إِنَّ اللَّهَ كَانَ بِكُلِّ شَيْءٍ عَلِيمًا ۝

"And covet not the thing in which Allah hath made some of you excel others (but cultivate the spirit of contentment). Unto men a fortune from that which they have earned, and unto women a fortune from that which they have earned. (Be not jealous of one another) but ask Allah of his bounty (through positive, rational effort and the fulfilment of your genuine needs). Lo! Allah is ever Knower of all things (including your innermost feelings; so be careful)." (IV:32).

Cultivation and maintenance of the spirit of contentment[14] is, therefore, a duty to self for keeping it morally healthy.

---

14. Contentment should be clearly distinguished from want of effort for improving one's life in all those things which have been approved or commended by God, including rational possession of the goods of this world.

(xxv) Practice of Selflessness in doing good enjoined:

The Prophets of God, who have embodied service to humanity at its highest, were asked by God to proclaim in unequivocal terms that they did not want any reward for it. The Holy Qur'ãn has mentioned this time and again[15], thus laying down the principle that it is a duty to observe selflessness in doing a duty to others.

In fact, all good to others should be done purely out of love for God[16], and therefore, never, never for any selfish end. Or else, the merit of the otherwise virtuous deed will become null and void, as the Holy Qur'ãn warns:

يٰٓاَيُّهَا الَّذِيْنَ اٰمَنُوْا لَا تُبْطِلُوْا صَدَقٰتِكُمْ بِالْمَنِّ وَ الْاَذٰى

"O ye who believe! Render not vain your charity by reminders of your generosity or by injury..." (II:264).

On the positive side, the following motto of selflessness has been laid down as the guiding light for all true Muslims. Their attitude, whenever they do any good to others, should invariably be:

لَا نُرِيْدُ مِنْكُمْ جَزَآءً وَّ لَا شُكُوْرًا ۝

".....No reward do we desire from you, nor thanks." (LXXVI:9).

(xxvi) Soft-heartedness, gentleness and kindness enjoined:

A Muslim, while he has been commanded to be stiff and mighty against evil[17], has to be, in his basic character, soft-hearted. This is what the Holy Qur'ãn has taught. A Muslim should practise humility (XXXIII:35) which means showing respect to others. That makes it

---

15. VI:90; XI:29; XI:51; XXV:57; XXVI:109; XXVI:127; XXVI:145; XXVI:164; XXVI:180; XXXVIII:86; XLII:23; etc. The words mentioned in connection with the Holy Prophet Muhammad (Peace be on him) are:

قُلْ لَّآ اَسْـَٔلُكُمْ عَلَيْهِ اَجْرًا ۭ

".....Say: No reward for this (i.e., my service to humanity as Prophet of God) do I ask of you...." (VI:90).

16. II:177; etc.

17. See page 103. Also: XLVIII:29.

impossible for him to be of harsh temperament. Then, he is to be the pursuer of "compassion and kindness" (XC:17). Taking both of these qualities into consideration, the basic tone of his character should not but be that of soft-heartedness, gentleness and kindness, unless any exceptional situation justly demands otherwise.

Moreover, he has to follow the examples of the Prophets whose conduct has been set for him as a pattern. Now, the Holy Qur'ãn says, on the one hand, that: "there is for you an excellent pattern (of conduct) in Abraham and those with him...." (LX:4); and on the other hand, it informs us: "Lo! Abraham was soft-hearted, long-suffering." (IX:114). Therefore, to cultivate and maintain soft-heartedness is duty.

Concerning the Holy Prophet Muhammad (Peace be on him) the Holy Qur'ãn emphasises his soft-heartedness in these words:

فَبِمَا رَحْمَةٍ مِّنَ اللَّهِ لِنتَ لَهُمْ

"It is part of the Mercy of Allah that thou dost deal soft-heartedly with them...." (III:159).

Indeed, he is:

رَحْمَةً لِّلْعٰلَمِيْنَ ○

"Mercy (and Blessing) unto all the worlds." (XXI:107).

And:

بِالْمُؤْمِنِيْنَ رَءُوْفٌ رَّحِيْمٌ ○

".....To the Believers he is most kind, merciful." (IX:128).

".....To follow the Holy Prophet Muhammad (Peace be on him) is duty[18]. To cultivate and maintain soft-heartedness, gentleness and kindness is, therefore, also duty.

(xxvii) Patience, Forbearance, Perseverance, Composure, Equanimity, Steadfastness, Self-control and Hardiness enjoined:

The virtues mentioned above are very closely related to one another and are included in the Arabic word *sabr*[19], which has been

18. III:31; XXXIII:21.

19. See: *A Dictionary of Modern Written Arabic*, published by Cornell University Press, U.S.A.

repeatedly emphasised by the Holy Qur'ãn in different contexts and has been enjoined forcefully.

The Holy Book says:

يٰٓأَيُّهَا الَّذِينَ اٰمَنُوا اسْتَعِينُوا بِالصَّبْرِ وَالصَّلٰوةِ ۚ إِنَّ اللّٰهَ مَعَ الصّٰبِرِينَ ○.....
وَلَنَبْلُوَنَّكُمْ بِشَيْءٍ مِّنَ الْخَوْفِ وَالْجُوعِ وَنَقْصٍ مِّنَ الْأَمْوَالِ وَالْأَنْفُسِ وَ
الثَّمَرٰتِ ۗ وَبَشِّرِ الصّٰبِرِينَ ○ الَّذِينَ إِذَآ أَصَابَتْهُمْ مُّصِيبَةٌ ۙ قَالُوٓا إِنَّا لِلّٰهِ وَ
إِنَّآ إِلَيْهِ رٰجِعُونَ ○ أُولٰٓئِكَ عَلَيْهِمْ صَلَوٰتٌ مِّنْ رَّبِّهِمْ وَرَحْمَةٌ ۟ وَأُولٰٓئِكَ
هُمُ الْمُهْتَدُونَ ○

"O ye who believe! seek help in *sabr* and prayer; verily Allah is with those who practise *sabr*.....

"Be sure We shall test you with something of fear and hunger, some loss in goods or lives or the fruits (of your toil), but give glad tidings to those who practise *sabr*,—who say, when afflicted with calamity: 'To Allah we belong and to Him is our return': They are those on whom (descend) the Blessings and the Mercy of Allah; and they are the rightly guided." (II:153, 155-157).

وَالصّٰبِرِينَ فِي الْبَأْسَآءِ وَالضَّرَّآءِ وَحِينَ الْبَأْسِ ۗ أُولٰٓئِكَ الَّذِينَ
صَدَقُوا ۖ وَأُولٰٓئِكَ هُمُ الْمُتَّقُونَ ○

".....and those who practise *sabr* in pain (or suffering) and adversity, and throughout all periods of panic and violence. Such are the people of truth, the God-fearing." (II:177).

وَاللّٰهُ يُحِبُّ الصّٰبِرِينَ ○

".....and Allah loveth those who practise *sabr*." (III:146).

الصّٰبِرِينَ وَالصّٰبِرٰتِ . . . أَعَدَّ اللّٰهُ لَهُمْ مَّغْفِرَةً وَّأَجْرًا عَظِيمًا ○

".....the men and the women who practise *sabr*,.....for them Allah hath prepared forgiveness and great reward." (XXXIII:35).

وَالَّذِينَ صَبَرُوا ابْتِغَآءَ وَجْهِ رَبِّهِمْ . . . أُولٰٓئِكَ لَهُمْ عُقْبَى الدَّارِ ○

"Those who observe *sabr*, seeking their Lord's Countenance (i.e., Divine Pleasure).....for such there is the final attainment of the (Eternal) Home." (XIII:22).

It is, therefore, the duty of every Muslim to practise *sabr* with a view to attain perfection in it:

يا أيها الذين آمنوا اصبروا وصابروا ورابطوا واتقوا الله لعلكم تفلحون ○

"O ye who believe! practise *sabr*, vie in the practise of *sabr* and be (ever) ready (in the cause of Truth); and be careful of your duty to Allah; that ye may succeed and prosper." (III:200).

(xxviii) Cultivating the spirit of Humility and Modesty enjoined:

The Holy Qur'ãn refers to, and enjoins the duty of, cultivating and observing humility and modesty in the following verses:

والخاشعين والخاشعات ... أعد الله لهم مغفرة وأجرا عظيما

"......the men and the women who posses the spirit of humility..... for them Allah hath prepared forgiveness and mighty reward." (XXXIII:35).

وعباد الرحمن الذين يمشون على الأرض هونا وإذا خاطبهم الجاهلون
قالوا سلاما ○

"And the servants of (God) Most Gracious are those who walk on the earth with humility, and when the ignorant address them (in arrogance), they (do not insult them or engage with them, but) say (or, wish them) 'Peace!' (separating themselves from them calmly)[20]. (XXV:63).

ولا تصعر خدك للناس ولا تمش في الأرض مرحا إن الله لا يحب
كل مختال فخور ○ واقصد في مشيك واغضض من صوتك
إن أنكر الأصوات لصوت الحمير ○

20. *i.e.*, "Peace, and Good-bye; let me leave you." (Abdullah Yusuf Ali, *op.cit.*, p. 941, n. 3123).

"And swell not thy cheek (for pride) at the fellow-beings,[21] nor walk in insolence through the earth[22]; for Allah loveth not any arrogant boaster. And be moderate in thy pace, and lower thy voice[23]; for the harshest of sounds without doubt is the braying of the ass."

(XXXI:18, 19).

(xxix) Observance of the spirit of Thankfulness[24] enjoined:

The Holy Qur'ãn contains the command, originally given by God to the Holy Prophet Moses (Peace be on him) but meant to be obeyed by every Muslim:

وَكُن مِّنَ الشّٰكِرِينَ ○

".... and be of those who are thankful." (VII:144).

Speaking directly to its addresses, the holy book has commanded:

وَاشْكُرُوا نِعْمَتَ اللّٰهِ إِن كُنتُمْ إِيَّاهُ تَعْبُدُونَ ○

"....and be thankful for the favours of Allah, if it is He Whom ye serve." (XVI:114).

It should be noted here that all the goods that a man receives in his life, through whatever medium they might be delivered to him, are God's favours according to the Qur'ãnic teaching. When a person bestows his favours on anyone, not only the thing that he bestows, but he himself becomes God's favour in that respect. It is thus a duty to thank God for every good that one receives, as also to thank him who acts as the agency for obtaining that good.[25]

---

21. This is the command to observe humility in one's behaviour in general.

22. This is the command to observe humility in walking.

23. This is the command to observe humility in the tone of one's talk.

24. Thankfulness comes into operation with regard to others, and as such it is a duty to others. But the spirit of thankfulness enriches the inner personality of the moral agent himself. Hence it forms a duty to self also.

25. This has been emphasised in direct terms by the Holy Prophet (Peace be on him) when he says:—

لا يشكر الله من لا يشكر الناس

"He who does not express thankfulness to human beings is not (really) thankful to Allah (also)." (Bukhãrî: *Adab al-Mufrad*, p. 34).

(xxx) Struggle to achieve Self-Purification, along with its Qur'ãnic technique, enjoined:

(1) According to the Holy Qur'ãn, the servants of God, namely, true Muslims, are those who not only practise righteousness but constantly yearn for perfection in it:

وَالَّذِينَ يَقُولُونَ رَبَّنَا هَبْ لَنَا مِنْ أَزْوَاجِنَا وَذُرِّيَّاتِنَا قُرَّةَ أَعْيُنٍ وَّ
اجْعَلْنَا لِلْمُتَّقِينَ إِمَامًا ۝

"And those who pray, 'Our Lord! bestow on us coolness of eyes from our wives and our offspring, and make us (so perfect in virtue that we may be) unto the righteous a pattern (to be followed)." (XXV:74).

And this yearning becomes a reality in the case of those who strive for it truly:

وَمِنْهُمْ سَابِقٌ بِالْخَيْرَاتِ بِإِذْنِ اللَّهِ ۗ ذَٰلِكَ هُوَ الْفَضْلُ الْكَبِيرُ ۝

".....and among them (i.e., the followers of the Qur'ãn) there are those who, by Allah's leave, are foremost in virtues. That is the great Grace (i.e., the most honourable achievement)." (XXXV:32).

For that achievement, however, it is necessary to purify the self. Hence, true Muslims are those who:

الَّذِينَ هُمْ لِلزَّكَاةِ فَاعِلُونَ ۝

"act aiming at (self-) purification." (XXIII:4).

And, thereby they develop:

قَلْبٍ سَلِيمٍ ۝

"a sound heart." (XXVI:89).

Hence, Self-purification and development of Conscientiousness is duty.

(2) But the human heart cannot be developed into a morally sound heart without:

(a) Constant self-examination; and

(b) The consequent struggle directed at abstaining from evil of every type and practising good in every way.

The Holy Qur'ãn commands its followers in respect of both:

(a) As to constant self-examination:

يٰٓاَيُّهَا الَّذِيْنَ اٰمَنُوا اتَّقُوا اللّٰهَ وَلْتَنْظُرْ نَفْسٌ مَّا قَدَّمَتْ لِغَدٍ ۚ وَاتَّقُوا اللّٰهَ ۭ اِنَّ اللّٰهَ خَبِيْرٌۢ بِمَا تَعْمَلُوْنَ ○

"O ye who believe! Fear Allah, and let every soul look to (i.e., examine) what it has sent forth for the morrow. Yea! fear Allah: for Allah is well acquainted with what ye do." (LIX:18).

(b) As regards the struggle:

(i) against all evil within and without the self:

اِنَّ الشَّيْطٰنَ لَكُمْ عَدُوٌّ فَاتَّخِذُوْهُ عَدُوًّا

"Verily Satan (who represents and prompts all evils within and without the self) is an enemy to you: so treat him (constantly) as an enemy (remaining engaged in perpetual fight with him)." (XXXV:6).

(ii) in favour of all that is good;

وَجَاهِدُوْا فِي اللّٰهِ حَقَّ جِهَادِهٖ ۭ هُوَ اجْتَبٰىكُمْ

"And strive for Allah (i.e., for the establishment of the highest good within and without the self) as is due unto Him, hard striving. He has chosen you (for it).... (XXII:78).

Thus, constant Self-examination and the Struggle to destroy evil and to establish the good are Qur'ãnic duties to self.

(3) But the Struggle (*Jihãd*) mentioned above is not possible without a living and dynamic faith in God and devotion[26] to Him, i.e., without maintaining the heart as:

قَلْبٍ مُّنِيْبٍ ○

"a heart turned in devotion to God." (L:33).

---

26. Duty in this respect has been mentioned on pp. 3-8.

For that, however, it is necessary:

(a) to conscientiously and devotedly practise:

(i) Communion with God;

(ii) Fasting; and

(iii) Charity; —and

(b) to fulfil all duties rigorously, whether they are to self or to others.

The Holy Qur'ãn has enjoined all the above as duty:

(a) (i) As to communion with God, it has prescribed three forms and has enjoined their observance:

(*i*) Constant remembrance of God:

يٰٓاَيُّهَا الَّذِيْنَ اٰمَنُوا اذْكُرُوا اللّٰهَ ذِكْرًا كَثِيْرًا ۙ وَّسَبِّحُوْهُ بُكْرَةً وَّاَصِيْلًا ۝

"O ye who believe! Celebrate the remembrance of Allah, remembring (Him) much (in word and in thought), and glorify Him morning and evening." (XXXIII:41, 42).

(*ii*) Observance of Regular Prayer, in congregation and otherwise.

وَاَقِيْمُوا الصَّلٰوةَ

"And establish regular prayer....."[27] (II:110).

(*iii*) Congregational worship at the highest level:

وَلِلّٰهِ عَلَى النَّاسِ حِجُّ الْبَيْتِ مَنِ اسْتَطَاعَ اِلَيْهِ سَبِيْلًا ؕ

"And pilgrimage to the House (i.e., the *Ka'bah* at Makkah) (for congregational worship at world-level) is a duty unto Allah for mankind,— for him who can afford the journey...." (III:97).

(ii) As to fasting, which is the most potent exercise for the practise of self-control, the Holy Qur'ãn orders it in these words:

يٰٓاَيُّهَا الَّذِيْنَ اٰمَنُوْا كُتِبَ عَلَيْكُمُ الصِّيَامُ كَمَا كُتِبَ عَلَى الَّذِيْنَ مِنْ
قَبْلِكُمْ لَعَلَّكُمْ تَتَّقُوْنَ ۝

27. This command has been repeated at numerous places in the Holy Qur'ãn.

"O ye who believe! Fasting is prescribed to you, even as it was prescribed to those before you, that ye may (learn) self-restraint." (II:183).

(iii) As to charity, the Holy Qur'ãn enjoins:

(a) compulsory charity (*Zakat*, etc.),

as well as

(b) optional charity.

It says:

وَآتُوا الزَّكٰوةَ

".....and pay the poor-due....."[28] (II:110).

يٰٓأَيُّهَا الَّذِينَ آمَنُوٓا أَنفِقُوا مِن طَيِّبٰتِ مَا كَسَبْتُمْ وَمِمَّآ أَخْرَجْنَا لَكُم مِّنَ الْأَرْضِ

"O ye who believe! Spend (for helping those in need) but of the good things which ye have (honourably) earned, and of that which We bring forth from the earth for you....[29] (II:267).

(b) As regards fulfilment of all duties rigorously, whether they are to self or to others, the Holy Qur'ãn lays down the command:

يٰٓأَيُّهَا الَّذِينَ آمَنُوا ادْخُلُوا فِي السِّلْمِ كَآفَّةً

"O ye who believe! Enter into Islam wholly (i.e., fulfil all the duties prescribed by Islam, including those related to apparently trivial issues of life)." (II:208).

---

28. This command has been repeated at numerous places in the Holy Qur'ãn. It shall be properly referred to in the "Duties to Others."

29. This command has been repeated at numerous places in the holy book.

Appendix

DUTIES TO ANIMALS AND THINGS

Note: Duties to animals and things are really duties to Self, because in the final analysis, they form part of "duty of Conscientiousness". Hence they have been included as appendix to "Duties to Self."

God says in the Holy Qur'ãn:

(1)

وَبِالْوَالِدَيْنِ إِحْسَانًا . . . وَمَا مَلَكَتْ أَيْمَانُكُمْ

".....and do good to parents....and to what your right hands own...." (IV:36).

According to the celebrated commentator Imam Fakhr al-Din al-Razi[1], the expression "what your right hands own," stands for all those that have no civil rights, including the dumb animals. Thus this verse lays down the duty[2] of being good towards, and doing good to, the animals.

(2)

هُوَ الَّذِي خَلَقَ لَكُم مَّا فِي الْأَرْضِ جَمِيعًا

"It is He Who hath created for you all things that are on the earth....." (II:29).

All things having been created for our benefit, it becomes our natural duty:

(i) to protect everything from damage;

(ii) to employ it for our benefit in keeping with its dignity as God's creation;

---

1. See *al-Tafsir al-Kabir*, vol. III, p. 323.

2. This duty has been taught in an elaborate form in the *Hadîth*.

(iii) to promote its well-being, as far as possible, thereby establishing our thankfulness to God for His Blessing in a practical manner.

Book II

DUTIES TO OTHER INDIVIDUALS

Part I

FUNDAMENTAL DUTIES TOWARDS ALL HUMAN BEINGS

Part II

DUTIES OF CONDITION TOWARDS OTHER INDIVIDUALS

Part III

DUTIES IN RESPECT OF MANNERS

Part I

FUNDAMENTAL DUTIES TOWARDS ALL HUMAN BEINGS

I. Duties Relating to the Happiness of Others.

II. Duties Relating to the Moral Perfection of Others.

Chapter I

DUTIES RELATING TO THE HAPPINESS OF OTHERS

(1) Duties of Omission (2) Duties of Commission

(I) DUTIES OF OMISSION

END: Abstinence from ill-wishing and ill-doing to fellow-beings:

(A) Comprehensive Commands;

(B) Specific Commands:

I. Duties of Love. II. Duties of Respect.

(A) *Comprehensive Commands relating to the duty of abstaining from all evil against fellow-beings:*

(i) *With regard to the duties of omission pertaining to the happiness of other individuals, in their capacity basically and purely as human beings, the Holy Qur'ãn has laid down certain comprehensive commands through which Muslims have been ordered to abstain from committing every conceivable form of evil against them. For instance:*

وَيَنْهٰى عَنِ الْفَحْشَآءِ وَالْمُنْكَرِ وَالْبَغْيِ يَعِظُكُمْ لَعَلَّكُمْ تَذَكَّرُوْنَ ۝

".....and He (i.e., God) forbiddeth lewdness and wickedness (i.e., all evil conduct) and infringement (of the rights of others). He exhorteth you that haply ye may be admonished." (XVI:90).

وَلَا تَبْخَسُوا النَّاسَ اَشْيَآءَهُمْ

"....and wrong not mankind in their things[1]....." (VII:85).

وَالَّذِينَ يَنقُضُونَ عَهْدَ اللَّهِ مِن بَعْدِ مِيثَاقِهِ وَيَقْطَعُونَ مَا أَمَرَ اللَّهُ بِهِ
أَن يُوصَلَ وَيُفْسِدُونَ فِي الْأَرْضِ أُولَٰئِكَ لَهُمُ اللَّعْنَةُ وَ
لَهُمْ سُوءُ الدَّارِ ۝

"And those who break the Covenant of Allah after having plighted their world thereto, and sever that which Allah hath commanded should be joined[2], and work mischief (i.e., cause moral corruption and material disorder) in the land: on them is the Curse and for them is the terrible Abode (i.e., Hell)." (XIII:25).

قُلْ إِنَّمَا حَرَّمَ رَبِّيَ الْفَوَاحِشَ مَا ظَهَرَ مِنْهَا وَمَا بَطَنَ وَالْإِثْمَ
وَالْبَغْيَ بِغَيْرِ الْحَقِّ

"Say (O Muhammad): my Lord forbiddeth only indecencies, such of them as are open and such as are secret, and sin, and infringement (of the rights of others) without justice....." (VII:33).

وَلَا تُفْسِدُوا فِي الْأَرْضِ بَعْدَ إِصْلَاحِهَا وَادْعُوهُ خَوْفًا وَطَمَعًا
إِنَّ رَحْمَتَ اللَّهِ قَرِيبٌ مِّنَ الْمُحْسِنِينَ ۝

"Work not confusion in the earth after the fair ordering (thereof), and call on Him in fear and hope. Lo! the Mercy of Allah is (always) near to those who do right." (VII:56).

وَوَضَعَ الْمِيزَانَ ۝ أَلَّا تَطْغَوْا فِي الْمِيزَانِ ۝

".....and He hath set up the Balance, that ye transgress not the balance (of justice in your actions)" (LV: 7,8).

---

1. According to Baidawi, things imply 'rights' of human beings. (See his *Tafsir*, p. 300).

2. According to the commentators of the Holy Qur'ān, it refers to the non-fulfilment of duties which men owe to God and to parents, family, neighbours, community, country and fellow-creatures in general. (See Abdul Majid Daryabadi, *op.cit.*, Vol. I, n. 118).

لَا تَظْلِمُونَ وَلَا تُظْلَمُونَ ○

"....ye shall neither wrong nor be wronged." (II:279).

(ii) Wrongdoing has not been allowed even against worst enemies :

وَلَا يَجْرِمَنَّكُمْ شَنَاٰنُ قَوْمٍ عَلٰٓى اَلَّا تَعْدِلُوْا ؕ

"....and let not the hatred of others to you make you swerve to wrong and depart from justice.... (V:9).

(iii) Wrongdoing to anyone is so severely abhorred that even befriending the wrongdoer is most severely condemned:

وَلَا تَرْكَنُوْٓا اِلَى الَّذِيْنَ ظَلَمُوْا فَتَمَسَّكُمُ النَّارُ ۙ وَمَا لَكُمْ مِّنْ دُوْنِ اللّٰهِ
مِنْ اَوْلِيَآءَ ثُمَّ لَا تُنْصَرُوْنَ ○

"And incline not to those who do wrong, or else the Fire will seize you—ye have no protectors other than Allah,—and ye shall not be succoured." (XI:113).

(B) <u>*Specific Commands relating to specific duties of commission*</u>:

I. Duties of Love:

(i) Violating others' right to life prohibited:

(*a*) *The Holy Qur'ãn commands the Muslims never to commit murder*:

وَلَا تَقْتُلُوا النَّفْسَ الَّتِىْ حَرَّمَ اللّٰهُ اِلَّا بِالْحَقِّ ؕ ذٰلِكُمْ وَصّٰىكُمْ
بِهٖ لَعَلَّكُمْ تَعْقِلُوْنَ ○

"....Take not life, which Allah hath made sacred, except by way of justice and law: Thus doth He command you, that ye may learn wisdom." (VI:151).

وَلَا تَقْتُلُوا النَّفْسَ الَّتِىْ حَرَّمَ اللّٰهُ اِلَّا بِالْحَقِّ ؕ وَمَنْ قُتِلَ مَظْلُوْمًا فَقَدْ جَعَلْنَا
لِوَلِيِّهٖ سُلْطٰنًا فَلَا يُسْرِفْ فِّى الْقَتْلِ ؕ اِنَّهٗ كَانَ مَنْصُوْرًا ○

"And take not life, which Allah hath made sacred, except by way of justice and law. And if anyone is slain wrongfully, We have given his heir authority (to demand redress through law or to forgive): but let him not exceed bounds in the matter of taking life; for he is helped (by the law)[3]." (XVII:33).

(b) *The following verse stresses the gravity of the crime of murder in the strongest possible terms*:

مَنْ قَتَلَ نَفْسًا بِغَيْرِ نَفْسٍ أَوْ فَسَادٍ فِي الْأَرْضِ فَكَأَنَّمَا قَتَلَ النَّاسَ جَمِيعًا ۚ

".....if anyone killeth a human being—unless it be for murder or for spreading mischief in the land—it shall be as if he killed all mankind....." (V:35).

(c) *The Holy Qur'ãn condemns not only murder in general but also human sacrifice to idols and false deities, and the custom of female infanticide, practised by the pagan communities, including the pre-Islamic Arabs*[4]:

وَكَذَٰلِكَ زَيَّنَ لِكَثِيرٍ مِّنَ الْمُشْرِكِينَ قَتْلَ أَوْلَادِهِمْ شُرَكَاؤُهُمْ لِيُرْدُوهُمْ وَلِيَلْبِسُوا عَلَيْهِمْ دِينَهُمْ ۖ

"Even so, in the eyes of many of the Pagans, their (so-called) 'partners' (of God) made alluring the slaughter of their offspring, in order to lead them to their own destruction, and cause confusion in their religion." (VI:137).

وَلَا تَقْتُلُوا أَوْلَادَكُمْ خَشْيَةَ إِمْلَاقٍ ۖ نَّحْنُ نَرْزُقُهُمْ وَإِيَّاكُمْ ۚ إِنَّ قَتْلَهُمْ كَانَ خِطْئًا كَبِيرًا ۝

3. In this respect, there is no discrimination in Islam. "According to *Hanafis*, the life of a slave stands on equal footing with that of a free-man, of a woman with that of a man, of a non-Muslim with that of a Muslim." (Abdur Rahim: *Muhammadan Jurisprudence*, p. 359).

4. For the wide-spread practice of infanticide among different ancient nations, including the Greeks and the Romans, see *Encyclopaedia Britannica*, XII, p. 332. The Qur'ãnic law in respect of this almost universal evil is actually a world-reform.

"Kill not your children for fear of want: We shall provide sustenance for them as well as for you. Verily killing of them is a great sin." (XVII:31).

(ii) Violating the Rights of Others in respect of wealth prohibited:

(*a*) *The Holy Qur'ãn forbids all illegal methods, including dishonesty, theft, dacoity, etc., in acquiring what belongs to others:*

وَلَا تَبْخَسُوا النَّاسَ أَشْيَاءَهُمْ

".....and wrong not mankind in their goods....." (VII:85).

يَا أَيُّهَا الَّذِينَ آمَنُوا لَا تَأْكُلُوا أَمْوَالَكُمْ بَيْنَكُمْ بِالْبَاطِلِ

"O ye who believe! devour not your property among yourselves (i.e., consume not one another's belongings) unlawfully....." (IV:29).

It is generally the demands of one's family for higher standard of living which induce a person to acquire wealth by unlawful means. The Holy Qur'ãn makes a pointed reference to it and asks the Muslims not to succumb to their wives' and children's wrong requests or desires—though treating them with affection—and to stick to absolute honesty in respect of one's earnings:

يَا أَيُّهَا الَّذِينَ آمَنُوا إِنَّ مِنْ أَزْوَاجِكُمْ وَأَوْلَادِكُمْ عَدُوًّا لَكُمْ
فَاحْذَرُوهُمْ ۚ وَإِنْ تَعْفُوا وَتَصْفَحُوا وَتَغْفِرُوا فَإِنَّ اللَّهَ غَفُورٌ
رَحِيمٌ ۝ إِنَّمَا أَمْوَالُكُمْ وَأَوْلَادُكُمْ فِتْنَةٌ ۚ وَاللَّهُ عِنْدَهُ
أَجْرٌ عَظِيمٌ ۝ فَاتَّقُوا اللَّهَ مَا اسْتَطَعْتُمْ

"O ye who believe! Truly, among your wives and children are (some that are) enemies to yourselves: so beware of them! But if ye forgive and overlook and cover up (their faults), verily Allah is Forgiving, Merciful. Your wealth and your children may be but a trial, whereas Allah! with Him is an immense Reward. So keep your duty to Allah as best as ye can....." (LXIV:14-16).

(*b*) *Loot and arson have been specifically condemned and prohibited:*

وَإِذَا تَوَلَّىٰ سَعَىٰ فِي الْأَرْضِ لِيُفْسِدَ فِيهَا وَيُهْلِكَ الْحَرْثَ وَالنَّسْلَ ۗ
وَاللَّهُ لَا يُحِبُّ الْفَسَادَ ۝

"And when he (i.e., the enemy of Truth) turneth away, he speedeth through the land that he may act corruptly therein and destroy the crops and the cattle. And Allah approveth not mischief." (II:205).

وَلَا تَقْعُدُوا بِكُلِّ صِرَاطٍ

"Beset not the highways menacing (wayfarers)...." (VII:86).

(*c*) *With regard to theft, its prohibition is covered fully in* IV: 29. *It has, however, been specifically prohibited also in the following verse:*

وَلَا يَسْرِقْنَ

"(that).....they will not steal....."[5] (LX:12).

The stern view that the Holy Qur'ãn takes in respect of theft is evident from the punishment it has prescribed in V:38. We shall mention it at its suitable place.

(*d*) *Depriving other persons of their inheritance condemned:*

In counting the vices which shall lead human beings to Hell, the Holy Qur'ãn says:

وَتَأْكُلُونَ التُّرَاثَ أَكْلًا لَّمًّا ۝

"And ye devour Inheritance (of the weak), devouring greedily." (LXXXIX:19).

(*e*) *To take by deceit more than one's share out of a thing jointly deserved or owned by several persons, condemned:*

وَمَنْ يَغْلُلْ يَأْتِ بِمَا غَلَّ يَوْمَ الْقِيٰمَةِ ۚ ثُمَّ تُوَفّٰى كُلُّ نَفْسٍ مَّا كَسَبَتْ وَهُمْ لَا يُظْلَمُونَ ۝

".....whosoever is false to his trust (as a co-sharer), he shall restore on the Day of Resurrection (and Judgment) what he misappropriated.

---

5. This verse forms part of the pledge which the women converts from paganism took at the hands of the Holy Prophet (Peace be on him). It applies, however, equally to men. (Ref: *Tafsir al-Jalãlain*, p. 458).

Then every soul will receive its due, whatever (good or evil) it earned, and none shall be dealt with unjustly." (III:161).

(*f*) *Defrauding in general in mutual relations of business prohibited:*

وَلَا تُخْسِرُوا الْمِيزَانَ ۝

"....and make not deficient the balance (by diminishing what is due to the buyer)". (LV:9).

وَلَا تَكُونُوا مِنَ الْمُخْسِرِينَ ۝

"....and cause no loss (to others in trade through fraud)". (XXVI:181).

وَلَا تَنْقُصُوا الْمِكْيَالَ وَالْمِيزَانَ

"....And give not short measure or weight....." (XI:84).

وَيْلٌ لِلْمُطَفِّفِينَ ۝ الَّذِينَ إِذَا اكْتَالُوا عَلَى النَّاسِ يَسْتَوْفُونَ ۝ وَإِذَا كَالُوهُمْ
أَوْ وَزَنُوهُمْ يُخْسِرُونَ ۝

"Woe to those that deal in fraud,—those who, when they have to receive by measure from men, exact full measure, but when they have to give by measure or weight to men, give less than due."(LXXXIII:1-3).

(g) *Misappropriating things entrusted, prohibited:*

يَا أَيُّهَا الَّذِينَ آمَنُوا لَا تَخُونُوا اللَّهَ وَالرَّسُولَ وَتَخُونُوا أَمَانَاتِكُمْ
وَأَنْتُمْ تَعْلَمُونَ ۝

"O ye who believe! Betray not the trust of Allah and the Messenger, *nor misappropriate knowingly things entrusted to you.*" (VIII:27).

Also, *favouring and supporting the misappropriator is prohibited:*

وَلَا تَكُنْ لِلْخَائِنِينَ خَصِيمًا ۝

"....and be not thou an advocate for those who betray their trust...." (IV:105).

(*h*) *Hoarding commodities and withholding them from free circulation for exploiting fellow-beings through the creation of artificial scarcity and the consequent shooting up of prices, condemned.*

In counting the vices that will lead human beings to Hell, the Holy Qur'ãn says:

وَجَمَعَ فَأَوْعٰى ○

"He hoarded and withheld it (from circulation)." (LXX:18).

(*i*) *Exploiting the needs of others by lending money on interest*[6] *vehemently condemned and prohibited:*

اَلَّذِيْنَ يَأْكُلُوْنَ الرِّبٰوا لَا يَقُوْمُوْنَ اِلَّا كَمَا يَقُوْمُ الَّذِيْ يَتَخَبَّطُهُ
الشَّيْطٰنُ مِنَ الْمَسِّ ۚ ذٰلِكَ بِاَنَّهُمْ قَالُوْٓا اِنَّمَا الْبَيْعُ مِثْلُ الرِّبٰوا ۘ وَ
اَحَلَّ اللّٰهُ الْبَيْعَ وَحَرَّمَ الرِّبٰوا ۚ فَمَنْ جَآءَهٗ مَوْعِظَةٌ مِّنْ رَّبِّهٖ فَانْتَهٰى
فَلَهٗ مَا سَلَفَ ۚ وَ اَمْرُهٗٓ اِلَى اللّٰهِ ۚ وَمَنْ عَادَ فَاُولٰٓئِكَ اَصْحٰبُ النَّارِ ۚ
هُمْ فِيْهَا خٰلِدُوْنَ ○ يَمْحَقُ اللّٰهُ الرِّبٰوا وَيُرْبِي الصَّدَقٰتِ ۚ وَاللّٰهُ لَا يُحِبُّ
كُلَّ كَفَّارٍ اَثِيْمٍ ○

"Those who devour *ribã*[7] (usury and interest) will not stand (on the Day of Resurrection) except as stands one whom the Evil One by his touch hath driven to madness. That is because they say: 'Trade is like *ribã*'. But Allah hath permitted trade and forbidden *ribã.* Those who after receiving direction from their Lord desist, shall be pardoned for the past; their case is for Allah (to Judge); but those who repeat the offence are Companions of the Fire: they will abide therein.

"Allah will deprive *ribã* of all blessings, but will give increase for deeds of charity: For He loveth not creatures ungrateful and wicked." (II:275, 276).

---

6. The economy which Islam offers is interest-free economy, and therefore, Islam condemns not only usury but all forms of interest-bearing transactions.

7. *Ribã* means "any addition, however slight, over and above the principal," and thus includes both usury and interest. (See: Lane's *Arabic-English Lexicon.*)

يَا أَيُّهَا الَّذِينَ آمَنُوا لَا تَأْكُلُوا الرِّبَا أَضْعَافًا مُضَاعَفَةً ۖ وَاتَّقُوا اللَّهَ
لَعَلَّكُمْ تُفْلِحُونَ ۝

"O ye who believe! Devour not *ribã*, doubled and multiplied; but fear Allah that ye may (really) prosper." (III:130).

(iii) Corrupting others in respect of wealth, prohibited:

(a) Through Bribery:

وَلَا تَأْكُلُوا أَمْوَالَكُمْ بَيْنَكُمْ بِالْبَاطِلِ وَتُدْلُوا بِهَا إِلَى الْحُكَّامِ لِتَأْكُلُوا فَرِيقًا
مِنْ أَمْوَالِ النَّاسِ بِالْإِثْمِ وَأَنْتُمْ تَعْلَمُونَ ۝

"Do not consume your property among yourselves iniquitously; neither proffer it to the judges, that you may sinfully consume a portion of other men's goods, and that wittingly." (II:188).

In the *Hadith* we find that the Holy Prophet (Peace be on him) has very strongly condemned the acceptor of bribe, the giver of bribe and the middleman. (See: *Mishkãt al-Masãbîh, Bãb a'-Rizq al-Wulãt*, p. 326).

(b) Through Gambling:

يَا أَيُّهَا الَّذِينَ آمَنُوا إِنَّمَا الْخَمْرُ وَالْمَيْسِرُ وَالْأَنْصَابُ وَالْأَزْلَامُ رِجْسٌ
مِنْ عَمَلِ الشَّيْطَانِ فَاجْتَنِبُوهُ لَعَلَّكُمْ تُفْلِحُونَ ۝

"O ye who believe! Intoxicants and gambling, and (dedication of) stones, and divination by arrows, are an abomination,—of Satan's handiwork: Eschew such (abomination), that ye may prosper." (V:93).

(iv) Want of Helpfulness and Charitableness towards others condemned; hence abstinence from it is duty:

(a) *Hoarding gold and silver, thereby keeping it out of circulation and thus damaging collective economy, on the one hand, and abstaining from rendering economic assistance in deserving individual cases, on the other, vehemently condemned:*

وَالَّذِينَ يَكْنِزُونَ الذَّهَبَ وَالْفِضَّةَ وَلَا يُنْفِقُونَهَا فِي سَبِيلِ اللَّهِ
فَبَشِّرْهُمْ بِعَذَابٍ أَلِيمٍ ۝ يَوْمَ يُحْمَىٰ عَلَيْهَا فِي نَارِ جَهَنَّمَ فَتُكْوَىٰ
بِهَا جِبَاهُهُمْ وَجُنُوبُهُمْ وَظُهُورُهُمْ ۖ هَٰذَا مَا كَنَزْتُمْ لِأَنْفُسِكُمْ
فَذُوقُوا مَا كُنْتُمْ تَكْنِزُونَ ۝

".....those who hoard up gold and silver and spend it not in the Way of Allah (i.e., for the welfare of fellow-beings), announce to them (O Muhammad) a most grievous penalty—on the day when heat will be produced out of that (wealth) in the fire of Hell, and with it will be branded their foreheads (representing human thinking) and their flanks (which support the seat of greed, i.e., the stomach) and their backs (as symbolising stability and strength)—(and it will be said unto them:) Here is that which ye hoarded for yourselves. Now taste of what ye used to hoard."

(IX:34, 35).

(b) *Practising niggardliness and promoting it as a creed condemned:*

وَلَا تَجْعَلْ يَدَكَ مَغْلُولَةً إِلَىٰ عُنُقِكَ

"Make not thy hand tied (in niggardliness) to thy neck....."

(XVII:29).

إِنَّ اللَّهَ لَا يُحِبُّ مَن كَانَ مُخْتَالًا فَخُورًا ۝ الَّذِينَ يَبْخَلُونَ وَ
يَأْمُرُونَ النَّاسَ بِالْبُخْلِ وَيَكْتُمُونَ مَا آتَاهُمُ اللَّهُ مِن فَضْلِهِ ۗ
وَأَعْتَدْنَا لِلْكَافِرِينَ عَذَابًا مُّهِينًا ۝

"Verily Allah loveth not such as are vainglorious, boasters—those who are niggardly and command mankind to niggardliness and hide that which Allah hath vouchsafed to them of His Bounty; and We have prepared for the infidels torment ignominious." (IV:36, 37).[8]

(c) *Refusing small kindness to Others condemned:*

فَوَيْلٌ لِّلْمُصَلِّينَ ۝ الَّذِينَ هُمْ عَن صَلَاتِهِمْ سَاهُونَ ۝ الَّذِينَ هُمْ
يُرَاءُونَ ۝ وَيَمْنَعُونَ الْمَاعُونَ ۝

"Ah, woe unto the worshippers, who are heedless of their Prayers; who would be seen (at worship) *yet refuse small kindnesses* to (others)."

(CVII:4-7).

(d) *Well-doing to Others with a view to getting more in return disapproved as worthless act of goodness:*

---

8. Cf. LVII: 23, 24.

وَمَآ اٰتَيْتُمْ مِّنْ رِّبًا لِّيَرْبُوَاْ فِيْٓ اَمْوَالِ النَّاسِ فَلَا يَرْبُوْا عِنْدَ اللّٰهِ ۚ وَمَآ اٰتَيْتُمْ مِّنْ زَكٰوةٍ تُرِيْدُوْنَ وَجْهَ اللّٰهِ فَاُولٰٓئِكَ هُمُ الْمُضْعِفُوْنَ ○

"And whatsoever ye give in gift[9] in order that it may increase among the substance of men (and return to you augmented) increaseth not with Allah (i.e., is not accepted as virtue and blessed by Allah); but that which ye give out for charity, seeking the Countenance (i.e., Pleasure) of Allah, (will increase): it is these who will get a recompense multiplied." (XXX:39).

(e) *Charity with laying obligation on the recipient and/or, hurting him in any way, prohibited:*

يٰٓاَيُّهَا الَّذِيْنَ اٰمَنُوْا لَا تُبْطِلُوْا صَدَقٰتِكُمْ بِالْمَنِّ وَ الْاَذٰى

"O ye who believe! Render not vain your charity by reminders of your generorsity or by injury....." (II:264).

(v) Want of Goodwill towards Others prohibited:

(a) *Breaking promises, pledges and covenants and violating oaths taken in mutual dealings prohibited:*

وَلَا تَنْقُضُوا الْاَيْمَانَ

".....And break not your oaths (when ye pledge your word in any matter)....." (XVI:91).

اِنَّمَا يَتَذَكَّرُ اُولُوا الْاَلْبَابِ ○ الَّذِيْنَ يُوْفُوْنَ بِعَهْدِ اللّٰهِ وَلَا يَنْقُضُوْنَ الْمِيْثَاقَ ○

".....It is those who are endued with understanding that receive admonition;—those who fulfil the Covenant of Allah and fail not in their plighted word." (XIII:19, 20).

(b) *Abstaining from giving false evidence made a condition of Faith, and thereby a duty:*

Recounting the fundamental virtues of true Muslims, the Holy Qur'ãn says:

---

9. This is the rendering of the word *ribã* here by Maulana Abdul Majid Daryabadi. (See in *English Translation of the Holy Qur'ãn*, p. 651).

وَالَّذِيْنَ لَا يَشْهَدُوْنَ الزُّوْرَ

".....and those who witness no falsehood (i.e., do not give false evidence)[10]...." (XXV:72).

(c) Concealing evidence prohibited:

وَلَا تَكْتُمُوا الشَّهَادَةَ ، وَمَنْ يَّكْتُمْهَا فَاِنَّهٗٓ اٰثِمٌ قَلْبُهٗ ، وَاللّٰهُ بِمَا تَعْمَلُوْنَ عَلِيْمٌ ۝

"Conceal not evidence; for whoever conceals it, his heart is tainted with sin. And Allah knoweth all that ye do." (II:283).

(d) Treachery condemned; hence abstinence from it is duty:

The Holy Qur'ān says:

اِنَّ اللّٰهَ لَا يُحِبُّ كُلَّ خَوَّانٍ كَفُوْرٍ ۝

"Verily, *Allah loveth not any that is treacherous,* or shows ingratitude." (XXII:38).

Also:

وَالَّذِيْنَ لَا يَشْهَدُوْنَ الزُّوْرَ

"(The servants of God are)....those who witness no falsehood (i.e., deal not falsely or treacherously with anyone)...." (XXV:72).

(e) Ingratitude for the good received from others condemned; hence abstinence from it is duty:

The Holy Qur'ān says:

اِنَّ اللّٰهَ لَا يُحِبُّ كُلَّ خَوَّانٍ كَفُوْرٍ ۝

"Verily, Allah loveth not any that is treacherous, or *shows ingratitude.*" (XXII:38).

II. Duties of Respect:

(i) (*a*) *Showing contempt for others; and*

---

10. The other meaning of this verse has been quoted below 142.

(b) *Oppressing others,*

prohibited:

وَلَا تُصَعِّرْ خَدَّكَ لِلنَّاسِ وَلَا تَمْشِ فِي الْأَرْضِ مَرَحًا إِنَّ اللَّهَ لَا يُحِبُّ كُلَّ مُخْتَالٍ فَخُورٍ

"And swell not thy cheek at human beings (i.e., do not treat others contemptuously and do not oppress them), nor walk in insolence through the earth; for Allah loveth not any vainglorious, boaster." (XXXI:18).

Arrogance and oppression are such grave vices that the hearts of those who indulge in them are sealed up to influences for good:

كَذَٰلِكَ يَطْبَعُ اللَّهُ عَلَىٰ كُلِّ قَلْبِ مُتَكَبِّرٍ جَبَّارٍ

"Thus doth Allah seal up every heart—of (him who is) stiff-necked, oppressor." (XL:35).

Indeed, they alone who abstain from belittling and oppressing others will go to Heaven:

تِلْكَ الدَّارُ الْآخِرَةُ نَجْعَلُهَا لِلَّذِينَ لَا يُرِيدُونَ عُلُوًّا فِي الْأَرْضِ وَلَا فَسَادًا ۚ وَالْعَاقِبَةُ لِلْمُتَّقِينَ

"That Home of the Hereafter We shall give to those who intend not high-handedness or mischief (i.e., evil in general) on earth: And the End is (best) for the righteous." (XXVIII:83).

(ii) Damaging the honour of Others through defaming them in any way, even though the defamatory remarks are based on truth, prohibited:

(a) Defamation in general forbidden:

وَلَا تَلْمِزُوا أَنْفُسَكُمْ

"....and defame not (nor be sarcastic to) each other...." (XLIX:11).

The only exception in speaking ill of others is where a person has been wronged mischievously and he has to defend his honour by exposing his wicked enemy. Even in that case, however, such a wronged person has been advised to practise forgiveness and to abstain from exposing the evils of his enemy—leaving the affair to God and hoping for His Reward—because God is 'Forgiving, Powerful'.

The Holy Qur'ãn says:

لَا يُحِبُّ اللَّهُ الْجَهْرَ بِالسُّوءِ مِنَ الْقَوْلِ إِلَّا مَن ظُلِمَ ۚ وَكَانَ اللَّهُ سَمِيعًا عَلِيمًا ○
إِن تُبْدُوا خَيْرًا أَوْ تُخْفُوهُ أَوْ تَعْفُوا عَن سُوءٍ فَإِنَّ اللَّهَ كَانَ عَفُوًّا قَدِيرًا ○

"Allah approveth not the utterance of evil speech (directed at defaming others), unless by one who hath been wronged; and Allah is ever Hearing, Knowing.

"If ye do good openly or keep it secret, or cover evil with pardon, lo! Allah is ever Forgiving, Powerful." (IV:148, 149).

(b) Scandalmongering specifically condemned; hence abstinence from it is duty:

وَيْلٌ لِّكُلِّ هُمَزَةٍ لُّمَزَةٍ ○

"Woe to every (kind of) scandalmonger[11], backbiter...." (CIV:1).

وَلَا تُطِعْ كُلَّ حَلَّافٍ مَّهِينٍ ○ هَمَّازٍ مَّشَّاءٍ بِنَمِيمٍ ○

"Heed not thou any (who is) ready with oaths, (is) a slanderer, (and) goes about with calumnies...." (LXVIII:10, 11).

(c) Fabrication of lies against Others condemned; hence abstinence from it is duty:

وَيْلٌ لِّكُلِّ أَفَّاكٍ أَثِيمٍ ○

"Woe to every sinful fabricator of falsehoods." (XLV:7).

(d) Transferring one's guilt to Others condemned; hence abstinence from it is duty:

وَمَن يَكْسِبْ خَطِيئَةً أَوْ إِثْمًا ثُمَّ يَرْمِ بِهِ بَرِيئًا فَقَدِ احْتَمَلَ بُهْتَانًا
وَإِثْمًا مُّبِينًا ○

"But if anyone earns a fault or a sin and throws it on to one that

---

11. The vice of scandalmongering covers "talking or suggesting evil of men or women by word, or innuendo, or behaviour, or mimicry, or sarcasm, or insult."

is innocent, he carries (on himself) (both) a falsehood and a flagrant sin." (IV:112).

(e) Attacking the honour of chaste women through slandering them condemned vehemently; hence abstinence from it is duty:

إِنَّ الَّذِينَ يَرْمُونَ الْمُحْصَنٰتِ الْغٰفِلٰتِ الْمُؤْمِنٰتِ لُعِنُوا فِي الدُّنْيَا وَالْاٰخِرَةِ ۖ وَلَهُمْ عَذَابٌ عَظِيمٌ ۝ يَوْمَ تَشْهَدُ عَلَيْهِمْ أَلْسِنَتُهُمْ وَأَيْدِيهِمْ وَأَرْجُلُهُمْ بِمَا كَانُوا يَعْمَلُونَ ۝ يَوْمَئِذٍ يُوَفِّيهِمُ اللّٰهُ دِينَهُمُ الْحَقَّ وَيَعْلَمُونَ أَنَّ اللّٰهَ هُوَ الْحَقُّ الْمُبِينُ ۝

"Those who slander chaste women, indiscreet but believing, are cursed in this life and in the Hereafter; for them is a grievous Penalty,—on the day when their tongues, their hands, and their feet will bear witness against them as to their actions. On that Day Allah will pay them back (all) their just dues, and they will realize that Allah is the (very) Truth that makes all things manifest." (XXIV:23-25).

(iii) Backbiting others prohibited:

وَلَا يَغْتَبْ بَعْضُكُمْ بَعْضًا ۚ أَيُحِبُّ أَحَدُكُمْ أَنْ يَأْكُلَ لَحْمَ أَخِيهِ مَيْتًا فَكَرِهْتُمُوهُ ۚ وَاتَّقُوا اللّٰهَ ۚ إِنَّ اللّٰهَ تَوَّابٌ رَحِيمٌ ۝

"....and speak not ill of each other behind their backs. Would any of you like to eat the flesh of his dead brother? Nay, ye would abhor it. So fear Allah. Verily, Allah is Relenting, Merciful."

(XLIX:12).

(iv) Using obscene language against anyone prohibited:

وَيَنْهٰى عَنِ الْفَحْشَاءِ وَالْمُنْكَرِ وَالْبَغْيِ ۚ

"....and (God) forbiddeth all shameful, abominable deeds...." (XVI:90).

Using obscene language is in itself shameful. To use it for insulting another person is all the more shameful, and it is, therefore, absolutely forbidden to a Muslim.

(v) Cultivation of rancour against anyone ruled out; hence abstinence from it is duty:

The Holy Qur'ãn commands in relation to the worst ideological enemies of the Muslims who were in a state of perpetual war with them, thus:

وَإِنْ جَنَحُوا لِلسَّلْمِ فَاجْنَحْ لَهَا وَتَوَكَّلْ عَلَى اللّٰهِ ۚ إِنَّهُ
هُوَ السَّمِيعُ الْعَلِيمُ ۝

"And if they (i.e., the enemies at war) incline to peace, incline thou also to it, and trust in Allah. Lo! He is the Hearer, the Knower. (VIII:61).

This command implies that a Muslim should not cultivate rancour against anyone, but should always be ready to establish peace even with his worst ideological enemies, not to speak to enemies at lower level, namely, the level of simple social relations.

(vi) Jealousy prohibited in its very basis:

Jealousy is a widely prevalent moral shortcoming of human beings. Its goal is the deprivation of others of the good things that they may have in excess of what one may possess, and it emerges and entrenches itself in the character of those who are not blessed with true faith in God and genuine moral refinement. Its roots lie in covetousness. Consequently, those who do not efface covetousness from their lives fall victim to it.

The Holy Qur'ãn mentions its evil and teaches the prayer for being saved from it. (CXIII:5). Then going to its root, it lays down the command that it is the duty of a Muslim to abstain from covetousness and the consequent jealousy under all circumstances:

وَلَا تَتَمَنَّوْا مَا فَضَّلَ اللّٰهُ بِهِ بَعْضَكُمْ عَلَىٰ بَعْضٍ ۚ لِلرِّجَالِ نَصِيبٌ مِمَّا
اكْتَسَبُوا ۖ وَلِلنِّسَاءِ نَصِيبٌ مِمَّا اكْتَسَبْنَ ۚ وَسْئَلُوا اللّٰهَ مِنْ فَضْلِهِ ۗ
إِنَّ اللّٰهَ كَانَ بِكُلِّ شَيْءٍ عَلِيمًا ۝

"And in no wise covet those things in which Allah hath bestowed His gifts more freely on some of you than on others. Unto men a fortune from that which they have earned, and unto women a fortune from that which they have earned. (All this is with Allah's permission. Therefore, never wish or try that the good things which others have may be diminished for them), but ask (for yourselves) Allah of His Bounty (with a positive healthy outlook). Lo! Allah is ever Knower of all things." (IV:32).

(vii) Observance of Duplicity[12] *condemned; hence abstinence from it is duty:*

Duplicity is a deeper phase of insincerity, which has its roots in hypocrisy. The Holy Qur'ãn condemns it in very strong terms:

وَإِذَا لَقُوا الَّذِينَ آمَنُوا قَالُوا آمَنَّا وَإِذَا خَلَوْا إِلَىٰ شَيَاطِينِهِمْ قَالُوا إِنَّا مَعَكُمْ
إِنَّمَا نَحْنُ مُسْتَهْزِئُونَ ○ اللَّهُ يَسْتَهْزِئُ بِهِمْ وَيَمُدُّهُمْ فِي طُغْيَانِهِمْ
يَعْمَهُونَ ○ أُولَٰئِكَ الَّذِينَ اشْتَرَوُا الضَّلَالَةَ بِالْهُدَىٰ فَمَا رَبِحَتْ تِجَارَتُهُمْ
وَمَا كَانُوا مُهْتَدِينَ ○

"When they meet those who believe, they say: 'We believe'. But when they are alone with their evil ones, they say: 'We are really with you; we were only jesting'.

"Allah will throw back their mockery on them, and give them rope in their trespasses; so they will wander like blind ones (to and fro).

"These are they who bartered Guidance for error; but their traffic is profitless, and they have lost true direction." (II:14-16).

It should be noted that, though the particular reference in these verses is to the Hypocrites of Madinah, they contain the general law that duplicity, wherever practised, is a grave vice, and it is the duty of a Muslim to abstain from it totally if he has to be true to his Faith.

(viii) Cultivating the habit of suspecting the motives of Others prohibited:

يَا أَيُّهَا الَّذِينَ آمَنُوا اجْتَنِبُوا كَثِيرًا مِنَ الظَّنِّ إِنَّ بَعْضَ
الظَّنِّ إِثْمٌ

"O ye who believe! Shun as much suspicion (as possible); for lo! some suspicion is a crime (because it involves cruel injustice to innocent

11. We have mentioned this vice in connection with 'Duties to Self' also. This is so because duplicity is a two-edged vice. It injures, on the one hand, the moral tone of him who indulges in it; and, on the other hand, the interests of him against whom it is practised.

and well-meaning people).....” (XLIX:12).

(ix) Spying, i.e., probing into the affairs of Others, prohibited:

وَلَا تَجَسَّسُوا

“.....and spy not (into the affairs of others for fault-finding)....” (XLIX:12).

(x) Deriding and ridiculing Others prohibited:

يَا أَيُّهَا الَّذِينَ آمَنُوا لَا يَسْخَرْ قَوْمٌ مِّن قَوْمٍ

“O ye who believe! let not a folk deride a folk....” (XLIX:11).

(xi) Giving offensive nicknames to Others prohibited:

وَلَا تَنَابَزُوا بِالْأَلْقَابِ

“And offend not others by nicknames.....” (XLIX:11).

(xii) Corrupting others through flattery to be avoided:

The Holy Qur'ãn condemns those who love to be flattered and warns them of grievous consequences. (III:188). Now, to be the cause of the commission of sin by someone else is also a sin. Thus to flatter anyone and thereby corrupt his mentality is a sin, and hence to abstain from it is duty.

(ii) Duties of Commission

END:

Positive well-wishing and well-doing to fellow-beings.

(A) Comprehensive command relating to the duty of practising well-wishing and well-doing towards fellow-beings, enjoined:

The Holy Qur'ãn says:

يَا أَيُّهَا الَّذِينَ آمَنُوا ارْكَعُوا وَاسْجُدُوا وَاعْبُدُوا رَبَّكُمْ وَافْعَلُوا الْخَيْرَ لَعَلَّكُمْ تُفْلِحُونَ

“O ye who believe! Bow down, prostrate yourselves and adore

your Lord, and (always) do good (to others), that ye may prosper."
(XXII:77).

(B) *Specify Commands relating to specific Duties of Commission:*

(a) Duties of Love;

(b) Duties of Respect.

(*a*) *Duties of Love*:

(i) *Duties relating to life:*

(a) *Protecting and preserving human life: an act of sublime goodness; hence, an important duty:*

The Holy Qur'ãn says:

وَمَنْ أَحْيَاهَا فَكَأَنَّمَا أَحْيَا النَّاسَ جَمِيعًا ؕ

"....and whoso saveth (i.e., protects and preserves) the life of one, it shall be as if he had saved the life of all mankind...." (V:35).

(b) *The Qur'ãnic law of Equality, combining permission for blood-wit, in cases of murder, also directed to saving of human lives as far as equitable:*

يَا أَيُّهَا الَّذِينَ آمَنُوا كُتِبَ عَلَيْكُمُ الْقِصَاصُ فِي الْقَتْلَى ؕ الْحُرُّ بِالْحُرِّ وَ
الْعَبْدُ بِالْعَبْدِ وَالْأُنْثَى بِالْأُنْثَى ؕ فَمَنْ عُفِيَ لَهُ مِنْ أَخِيهِ شَيْءٌ فَاتِّبَاعٌ
بِالْمَعْرُوفِ وَأَدَاءٌ إِلَيْهِ بِإِحْسَانٍ ؕ

"O ye who believe! the law of Equality is prescribed to you in cases of murder: the free for the free, the slave for the slave, the woman for the woman. But if any remission is made by the brother (i.e., the heirs of the murdered person), then grant any reasonable demand, and compensate him (in the form of blood-money) with handsome gratitude....." (II:178).[13]

(c) *Active sympathy with Others for the amelioration and removal of their sufferings in respect of their health—as also in other respects—, enjoined:*

---

13. The legal implications of this verse have been discussed in Penal Ethics.

Recounting the moral qualities of true Muslims, the Holy Qur'ãn says:

ثُمَّ كَانَ مِنَ الَّذِينَ آمَنُوا وَتَوَاصَوْا بِالصَّبْرِ وَتَوَاصَوْا بِالْمَرْحَمَةِ ○

"Then will he be of those who believe, and enjoin patience (i.e., constancy and self-restraint), and enjoin compassion and active sympathy (with others for the amelioration and removal of their sufferings and misfortunes)". (XC:17).

Thus visiting the sick, not as a mere formality but for active sympathy in their suffering, and participation, according to one's capacity, in all collective efforts directed at the preservation and promotion of human health is a duty, without the fulfilment of which no one can aspire to be a true Muslim.

(ii) *Duties in respect of wealth of Others*:

To regard the weaith of others as absolutely inviolable, enjoined:

(a) *Only that which has been acquired by a Muslim lawfully can be owned and utilized by him:*

يَا أَيُّهَا النَّاسُ كُلُوا مِمَّا فِي الْأَرْضِ حَلَالًا طَيِّبًا وَلَا تَتَّبِعُوا خُطُوَاتِ
الشَّيْطَانِ إِنَّهُ لَكُمْ عَدُوٌّ مُبِينٌ ○ إِنَّمَا يَأْمُرُكُمْ بِالسُّوءِ وَالْفَحْشَاءِ

"O humankind! consume, out of that which is (found) on the earth, (only) that which is lawful and good; and do not follow the footsteps of the devil, for he is to you an avowed enemy. He enjoineth upon you only the evil and the foul....."[14] (II:168, 169).

(b) *Protecting the wealth of Others entrusted to one's custody, enjoined:*

إِنَّ اللَّهَ يَأْمُرُكُمْ أَنْ تُؤَدُّوا الْأَمَانَاتِ إِلَىٰ أَهْلِهَا

"Lo! Allah commandeth you to render back your Trusts to those to whom they are due....." (IV:58).[15]

---

14. Cf. XVI:90; XXIV:21.

15. Cf. II;283.

(c) Complete honesty in commercial transactions enjoined:

وَأَوْفُوا الْكَيْلَ إِذَا كِلْتُمْ وَزِنُوا بِالْقِسْطَاسِ الْمُسْتَقِيمِ ۚ ذَٰلِكَ خَيْرٌ وَ
أَحْسَنُ تَأْوِيلًا ۝

"Give full measure when ye measure, and weigh with an even balance, (in short, be fully honest in all your commercial dealings): That is most fitting and most advantageous in the final determination".

(XVII:35).

وَأَوْفُوا الْكَيْلَ وَالْمِيزَانَ بِالْقِسْطِ ۖ

".....Give measure and weight with full justice....." (VI:152).[16]

(iii) Duty in respect of spending one's wealth for Others:

(A) Charitableness and generosity towards Others enjoined:

(a) All that belongs to a Muslim belongs actually to God and is, therefore, meant to be generously spent for the benefit of God's creatures:

إِنَّ اللَّهَ اشْتَرَىٰ مِنَ الْمُؤْمِنِينَ أَنفُسَهُمْ وَأَمْوَالَهُم بِأَنَّ لَهُمُ الْجَنَّةَ ۚ

"Allah hath purchased of the Believers their persons and their wealth because the Garden (of Paradise) will be theirs." (IX:111).

(b) The basis of a Muslim's charity and generosity is purely "love for God" and "fear of the Hereafter" and hence the economic assistance which he renders to anyone is to be from the highest motive and without the least tinge of worldliness:

وَآتَى الْمَالَ عَلَىٰ حُبِّهِ

".....(but it is righteousness).....to spend wealth (in charity) *out of love for Him* (i.e., God) (alone)....." (II:177).

. . . . . الَّذِي يُؤْتِي مَالَهُ يَتَزَكَّىٰ ۝ وَمَا لِأَحَدٍ عِندَهُ
مِن نِّعْمَةٍ تُجْزَىٰ ۝ إِلَّا ابْتِغَاءَ وَجْهِ رَبِّهِ الْأَعْلَىٰ ۝
وَلَسَوْفَ يَرْضَىٰ ۝

---

16. Cf. XXVI:181, 182.

".....(the righteous) who spend their wealth (on others) for increase in self-purification, and have in their minds no favour from anyone for which a reward is expected in return, but only the desire to seek for the countenance of their Lord Most High; and soon will they attain (complete) satisfaction." (XCII:18-21).

وَالَّذِينَ يُؤْتُونَ مَا آتَوا وَّ قُلُوبُهُمْ وَجِلَةٌ أَنَّهُمْ إِلَىٰ رَبِّهِمْ رَاجِعُونَ ۝
أُولَٰئِكَ يُسَارِعُونَ فِي الْخَيْرَاتِ وَهُمْ لَهَا سَابِقُونَ ۝

"And those who dispense their charity with their hearts full of fear, because they will return to their Lord;—it is these who hasten in every good work, and these who are foremost in them." (XXIII:60-61).

(c) Charity—a Basic Virtue:

لَن تَنَالُوا الْبِرَّ حَتَّىٰ تُنفِقُوا مِمَّا تُحِبُّونَ ۚ وَمَا تُنفِقُوا مِن شَيْءٍ
فَإِنَّ اللَّهَ بِهِ عَلِيمٌ ۝

"By no means shall ye attain righteousness unless ye give (freely) of that which ye love; and whatever ye give, of a truth Allah knoweth it well." (III:92).

(d) Measure of charity defined: To spend what is superfluous from one's rational needs:

وَيَسْأَلُونَكَ مَاذَا يُنفِقُونَ ۚ قُلِ الْعَفْوَ ۗ كَذَٰلِكَ يُبَيِّنُ اللَّهُ لَكُمُ الْآيَاتِ
لَعَلَّكُمْ تَتَفَكَّرُونَ ۝ فِي الدُّنْيَا وَالْآخِرَةِ ۗ

"They ask thee (O Muhammad!) how much they are to spend; say: 'What is beyond your needs.' Thus Allah maketh clear to you His signs: in order that ye may consider (their bearings) on this life and the Hereafter." (II:219, 220).

(e) Mode of giving charity defined:

إِن تُبْدُوا الصَّدَقَاتِ فَنِعِمَّا هِيَ ۖ وَإِن تُخْفُوهَا وَتُؤْتُوهَا
الْفُقَرَاءَ فَهُوَ خَيْرٌ لَّكُمْ ۚ وَيُكَفِّرُ عَنكُم مِّن سَيِّئَاتِكُمْ ۗ وَاللَّهُ بِمَا تَعْمَلُونَ
خَبِيرٌ ۝

"If ye disclose (acts of) charity, even so it is well, but if ye conceal them, and make them reach those (really) in need, that is best for you. It will atone for some of your evil deeds. And Allah is well acquainted with what ye do." (II:271).

(f) Blessings of charity emphasised through parables:

مَثَلُ الَّذِيْنَ يُنْفِقُوْنَ اَمْوَالَهُمْ فِيْ سَبِيْلِ اللّٰهِ كَمَثَلِ حَبَّةٍ اَنْۢبَتَتْ
سَبْعَ سَنَابِلَ فِيْ كُلِّ سُنْۢبُلَةٍ مِّائَةُ حَبَّةٍ ؕ وَاللّٰهُ يُضٰعِفُ لِمَنْ
يَّشَآءُ ؕ وَاللّٰهُ وَاسِعٌ عَلِيْمٌ ○ اَلَّذِيْنَ يُنْفِقُوْنَ اَمْوَالَهُمْ فِيْ سَبِيْلِ اللّٰهِ ثُمَّ
لَا يُتْبِعُوْنَ مَآ اَنْفَقُوْا مَنًّا وَّلَآ اَذًى ۙ لَّهُمْ اَجْرُهُمْ عِنْدَ رَبِّهِمْ ۚ وَلَا
خَوْفٌ عَلَيْهِمْ وَلَا هُمْ يَحْزَنُوْنَ ○

"The parable of those who spend their substance in the Way of Allah is that of a grain of corn: it groweth seven ears, and each ear hath a hundred grains. Allah giveth manifold increase to whom He pleaseth: for Allah careth for all, and He knoweth all things. Those who spend their substance in the cause of Allah, and follow not up their gifts with reminders of their generosity or with injury,—their reward is with their Lord: on them shall be no fear, nor shall they grieve." (II:261, 262).

وَمَثَلُ الَّذِيْنَ يُنْفِقُوْنَ اَمْوَالَهُمُ ابْتِغَآءَ مَرْضَاتِ اللّٰهِ وَتَثْبِيْتًا مِّنْ اَنْفُسِهِمْ
كَمَثَلِ جَنَّةٍۢ بِرَبْوَةٍ اَصَابَهَا وَابِلٌ فَاٰتَتْ اُكُلَهَا ضِعْفَيْنِ ۚ فَاِنْ لَّمْ
يُصِبْهَا وَابِلٌ فَطَلٌّ ؕ وَاللّٰهُ بِمَا تَعْمَلُوْنَ بَصِيْرٌ ○

"And the likeness of those who spend their substance, seeking to please Allah and to strengthen their souls, is as a garden, high and fertile: heavy rain makes it yield a double increase of harvest, and if it receives not heavy rain, light moisture sufficeth it. Allah seeth well whatever ye do." (II:265).

(g) Charity should be practised at all times and under all circumstances:

اَلَّذِيْنَ يُنْفِقُوْنَ اَمْوَالَهُمْ بِالَّيْلِ وَالنَّهَارِ سِرًّا وَّعَلَانِيَةً فَلَهُمْ اَجْرُهُمْ
عِنْدَ رَبِّهِمْ ۚ وَلَا خَوْفٌ عَلَيْهِمْ وَلَا هُمْ يَحْزَنُوْنَ ○

"Those who (in charity) spend of their goods by night and by day, in secret and in public, have their reward with their Lord: on them shall be no fear, nor shall they grieve." (II:274).

وَ سَارِعُوْٓا اِلٰى مَغْفِرَةٍ مِّنْ رَّبِّكُمْ وَ جَنَّةٍ عَرْضُهَا السَّمٰوٰتُ وَ الْاَرْضُ
اُعِدَّتْ لِلْمُتَّقِيْنَ ۙ الَّذِيْنَ يُنْفِقُوْنَ فِى السَّرَّآءِ وَ الضَّرَّآءِ وَ الْكٰظِمِيْنَ
الْغَيْظَ وَ الْعَافِيْنَ عَنِ النَّاسِ ؕ وَ اللّٰهُ يُحِبُّ الْمُحْسِنِيْنَ ۚ

"Be quick in race for forgiveness from your Lord, and for a Garden whose width is that (of the whole) of the heavens and of the earth, prepared for the righteous,—those who spend (freely), whether in prosperity, or in adversity; who restrain anger, and pardon (all) men;—for Allah loves those who do good". (III:133, 134).

(h) A very forceful appeal made for practising charity:

اَيَوَدُّ اَحَدُكُمْ اَنْ تَكُوْنَ لَهٗ جَنَّةٌ مِّنْ نَّخِيْلٍ وَّ اَعْنَابٍ تَجْرِىْ مِنْ تَحْتِهَا
الْاَنْهٰرُ ۙ لَهٗ فِيْهَا مِنْ كُلِّ الثَّمَرٰتِ ۙ وَ اَصَابَهُ الْكِبَرُ وَ لَهٗ ذُرِّيَّةٌ ضُعَفَآءُ ۖ
فَاَصَابَهَآ اِعْصَارٌ فِيْهِ نَارٌ فَاحْتَرَقَتْ ؕ كَذٰلِكَ يُبَيِّنُ اللّٰهُ لَكُمُ الْاٰيٰتِ
لَعَلَّكُمْ تَتَفَكَّرُوْنَ ۚ

"Does any of you wish that he should have a garden with date-palms and vines and streams flowing underneath, and all kinds of fruit, while he is stricken with old age, and his children are not strong (enough to look after themselves)—that it should be caught in a whirlwind with fire therein, and be burnt up? Thus doth Allah make clear to you His Sings (in respect of possible economic misery and the way to remedy it through the universal practise of economic well-doing to others), that they may consider." (II:266).

(i) Specific categories of those who deserve charitable economic assistance, mentioned:

The following categories have been specified:

The kinsfolk, the orphans, the needy; 'those who ask'; the poverty-stricken persons in general; those in bondage (as slaves or as prisoners of war), (including the task of their emancipation through payment of ransom); those suffering from the burden of debt (and have to be relieved through the payment of that debt); the wayfarers; and recent converts to Islam." (II:177; IX:60).

(j) Command given to use one's talents and possessions for, and practise assistance of all kinds to, all:

يَٰٓأَيُّهَا ٱلَّذِينَ ءَامَنُوٓا أَنفِقُوا مِمَّا رَزَقْنَٰكُم مِّن قَبْلِ أَن يَأْتِىَ يَوْمٌ لَّا
بَيْعٌ فِيهِ وَلَا خُلَّةٌ وَلَا شَفَٰعَةٌ ۗ وَٱلْكَٰفِرُونَ هُمُ ٱلظَّٰلِمُونَ ۝

"O ye who believe! spend out of (the bounties) We have provided for you, before the Day comes when no bargaining (will avail), nor friendship nor intercession. Those who reject Faith injure (only themselves)."[17] (II:254).

(B) Charitableness towards one's debtor enjoined:

وَإِن كَانَ ذُو عُسْرَةٍ فَنَظِرَةٌ إِلَىٰ مَيْسَرَةٍ ۚ وَأَن تَصَدَّقُوا
خَيْرٌ لَّكُمْ إِن كُنتُمْ تَعْلَمُونَ ۝

"If the debtor is in a difficulty, grant him time till it is easy for him to repay. But if ye remit it by way of charity, that is best for you if ye only knew." (II:280).

(C) Giving of free gifts to cultivate and to enhance love enjoined:

The Holy Qur'ãn says:

وَلَا تَنسَوُا ٱلْفَضْلَ بَيْنَكُمْ ۚ

"....and do not forget grace amongst yourselves...." (II:237).

The Arabic word used here for 'grace' means, according to Lane's *Lexicon*, "a free gift, or favour, a benefit, and bounty". Thus this verse includes the command of giving free gifts for cultivating generosity and for enhancing love.

(iv) Maintenance of goodwill towards Others:

(a) Absolute injustice enjoined, even though it means any amount of personal suffering for the moral agent, or the interests of those

---

17. Besides this verse, there are numerous other verses where the merit of helping others has been mentioned e.g., LVI:7, LXIII:10.

nearest and dearest to him are sacrificed, and even though the other party is his or Islam's worst enemy:

إِنَّ اللَّهَ يَأْمُرُ بِالْعَدْلِ

"Verily, Allah enjoineth justice (to all and under all circumstances)....." (XVI:90).

يَٰٓأَيُّهَا الَّذِينَ ءَامَنُوا كُونُوا قَوَّٰمِينَ بِالْقِسْطِ شُهَدَآءَ لِلَّهِ وَلَوْ عَلَىٰٓ أَنفُسِكُمْ أَوِ الْوَٰلِدَيْنِ وَالْأَقْرَبِينَ ۚ إِن يَكُنْ غَنِيًّا أَوْ فَقِيرًا فَاللَّهُ أَوْلَىٰ بِهِمَا ۖ فَلَا تَتَّبِعُوا الْهَوَىٰٓ أَن تَعْدِلُوا ۚ وَإِن تَلْوُۥٓا أَوْ تُعْرِضُوا فَإِنَّ اللَّهَ كَانَ بِمَا تَعْمَلُونَ خَبِيرًا ۝

"O ye who believe! Be ye staunch in justice, witnesses for Allah, even though it be against yourselves or (your) parents or (your) kindred, whether (the case be of) a rich man or a poor man, for Allah is nearer unto both (than ye are). So follow not passion lest ye lapse (from truth); and if ye lapse or fall away, then lo! Allah is ever informed as to what ye do." (IV:135).

يَٰٓأَيُّهَا الَّذِينَ ءَامَنُوا كُونُوا قَوَّٰمِينَ لِلَّهِ شُهَدَآءَ بِالْقِسْطِ ۖ وَلَا يَجْرِمَنَّكُمْ شَنَـَٔانُ قَوْمٍ عَلَىٰٓ أَلَّا تَعْدِلُوا ۚ اعْدِلُوا هُوَ أَقْرَبُ لِلتَّقْوَىٰ ۖ وَاتَّقُوا اللَّهَ ۚ إِنَّ اللَّهَ خَبِيرٌۢ بِمَا تَعْمَلُونَ ۝

"O ye who believe! Be steadfast witnesses for Allah in equity, and let not the hatred of any people seduce you that ye deal not justly. Deal justly, that is nearer to your duty. Observe your duty to Allah. Lo! Allah is informed of what ye do." (V:9).

(b) *Bearing witness firmly and without fear or favour and thereby assisting those who are in the right made a basic virtue and, hence, duty:*

وَالَّذِينَ هُم بِشَهَٰدَٰتِهِمْ قَآئِمُونَ ۝

"And those who stand firm in their testimonies." (LXX:33).

(c) *Fulfilling all promises, agreements, pledges, covenants, contracts, engagements and treaties, enjoined:*

وَأَوْفُوا بِالْعَهْدِ إِنَّ الْعَهْدَ كَانَ مَسْئُولًا

".....and fulfil (every) promise (and engagement); for (every) promise (and engagement) will be enquired into (on the Day of Reckoning)." (XVII:34).

يَا أَيُّهَا الَّذِينَ آمَنُوا أَوْفُوا بِالْعُقُودِ

"O ye who believe! Fulfil (all) obligations (or compacts)[18]." (V:1).

(d) Sincerity and straightforwardness in general towards Others enjoined:

As we have already seen, a Muslim is required to do good to others purely for the sake of God, which alone is virtue according to the Holy Qur'ãn. But that is impossible without cultivating and maintaining absolute sincerity for God, as demanded in the Holy Qur'ãn:

وَادْعُوهُ مُخْلِصِينَ لَهُ الدِّينَ

".....and call upon Him, making your devotion sincere as in His sight...." (VII:29).

But genuine sincerity for God is impossible to maintain unless one possesses sincerity essentially. Hence cultivation and maintenance of essential sincerity, one channel of which is sincerity towards fellow-beings, is duty.

Thus the Holy Qur'ãn commands the Muslims to be sincere and straightforward in all their dealings with everyone:

وَأَنَّ هَٰذَا صِرَاطِي مُسْتَقِيمًا فَاتَّبِعُوهُ

"And (He commandeth you, saying): This is My straight Way (—the Way of Truth, Justice, Sincerity and Straightforwardness—): follow it....." (VI:153).

---

18. The Arabic word *'aqd*, used there, means literally: a contract, a compact, a covenant, and an engagement. Finally, it comprehends all duties towards God and man. (See: Lane's *Arabic-English Lexicon*).

(e) *Cultivating and maintaining the attitude of compassionate kindness towards others emphasized as one of the basic qualities of a true Muslim's character:*

وَتَوَاصَوْا بِالْمَرْحَمَةِ ۝

"....and enjoin on each other practice of compassionate kindness (towards all)....." (XC:17).

(f) *Gracefulness and liberality in dealing with Others enjoined:*

وَلَا تَنسَوُا الْفَضْلَ بَيْنَكُمْ ۚ

".....and forget not gracefulness and liberality in your mutual dealings....." (II:237).

(g) *Positive effort for the creation and maintenance of harmony and peace among human beings, emphasized as a great virtue which should never be avoided:*

لَا خَيْرَ فِي كَثِيرٍ مِّن نَّجْوَاهُمْ إِلَّا مَنْ أَمَرَ بِصَدَقَةٍ أَوْ مَعْرُوفٍ أَوْ
إِصْلَاحٍ بَيْنَ النَّاسِ ۚ وَمَن يَفْعَلْ ذَٰلِكَ ابْتِغَاءَ مَرْضَاتِ اللَّهِ فَسَوْفَ
نُؤْتِيهِ أَجْرًا عَظِيمًا ۝

"In most of their secret talks there is no good; but if one exhorts to a deed of charity or justice or conciliation between human beings, (secrecy is permissible). To him who does this, seeking the good pleasure of Allah, We shall soon give a reward of the highest (value)." (IV:114).

وَلَا تَجْعَلُوا اللَّهَ عُرْضَةً لِّأَيْمَانِكُمْ أَن تَبَرُّوا وَتَتَّقُوا وَتُصْلِحُوا بَيْنَ النَّاسِ ۗ
وَاللَّهُ سَمِيعٌ عَلِيمٌ ۝

"And make not Allah's (name) an excuse in your oaths against doing good, or acting rightly, or making peace between human beings; for Allah is He Who heareth and knoweth all things." (II:224).

إِنَّا لَا نُضِيعُ أَجْرَ الْمُصْلِحِينَ ۝

"....never shall We suffer the reward of the reformers to perish." (VII:170).

(h) Judging Others' motives in the best light, except when a definite reasonable cause exists, enjoined:

As we have already seen, the Holy Qur'ãn forbids guessing about others' motives:

يَٰٓأَيُّهَا ٱلَّذِينَ ءَامَنُوا ٱجْتَنِبُوا كَثِيرًا مِّنَ ٱلظَّنِّ إِنَّ بَعْضَ
ٱلظَّنِّ إِثْمٌ

"O ye who believe! Shun as much suspicion as possible; for lo! some suspicion is a crime....." (XLIX:12).

It means that a Muslim should cultivate basically the attitude of initially judging other's motives in the best light, except when a definite reasonable cause exists to the contrary.

(i) Speaking good of Others, while paying due regard to truth and justice, enjoined:

The Holy Qur'ãn says:

وَقُل لِّعِبَادِى يَقُولُوا ٱلَّتِى هِىَ أَحْسَنُ إِنَّ ٱلشَّيْطَٰنَ يَنزَغُ بَيْنَهُمْ إِنَّ ٱلشَّيْطَٰنَ
كَانَ لِلْإِنسَٰنِ عَدُوًّا مُّبِينًا ۝

"Say to My servants that they should (only) say (in general and about others) those things that are best; for Satan doth sow dissensions among them: lo! Satan is to man an avowed enemy." (XVII:53).

(j) Speaking to Others with courtesy and politeness enjoined:

وَقُولُوا لِلنَّاسِ حُسْنًا

".....and speak unto mankind with courtesy and politeness (according to best standards of human speech)...." (II:83).

(k) Gratefulness to Others for any good that one may receive from them, enjoined:

In asking the questions:

هَلْ جَزَآءُ ٱلْإِحْسَٰنِ إِلَّا ٱلْإِحْسَٰنُ ۝

"Is the reward of goodness aught save goodness?" (LV:60), the Holy Qur'ãn emphasises the principle that a Muslim should always reward goodness with goodness, and the least that he can do is to sincerely thank him who does him any good. And gratefulness brings reward from God:

وَسَنَجْزِي الشّٰكِرِينَ ○

"We (i.e., God) shall reward the thankful." (III:145).

(l) The most rational behaviour upheld and the highest moral standard enjoined in respect of evil emanating from Others:

(i) The Holy Qur'ãn permits equal redress of wrongs done to a Muslim by Others, at the same time commending forgiveness:

وَإِنْ عَاقَبْتُمْ فَعَاقِبُوا بِمِثْلِ مَا عُوقِبْتُمْ بِهِ ۖ وَلَئِنْ صَبَرْتُمْ لَهُوَ
خَيْرٌ لِلصّٰبِرِينَ ○

"If you punish (him who has wronged you) then punish with the like of that wherewith ye were afflicted. But if ye show patience, that is indeed the best (course) for those who are patient." (XVI:126).

وَجَزٰٓؤُا سَيِّئَةٍ سَيِّئَةٌ مِّثْلُهَا ۚ فَمَنْ عَفَا وَأَصْلَحَ فَأَجْرُهُ عَلَى اللّٰهِ ۚ إِنَّهُ
لَا يُحِبُّ الظّٰلِمِينَ ○ وَلَمَنِ انْتَصَرَ بَعْدَ ظُلْمِهِ فَأُولٰٓئِكَ مَا عَلَيْهِمْ مِّنْ سَبِيلٍ ○
إِنَّمَا السَّبِيلُ عَلَى الَّذِينَ يَظْلِمُونَ النَّاسَ وَيَبْغُونَ فِي الْأَرْضِ بِغَيْرِ
الْحَقِّ ۚ أُولٰٓئِكَ لَهُمْ عَذَابٌ أَلِيمٌ ○ وَلَمَنْ صَبَرَ وَغَفَرَ إِنَّ ذٰلِكَ لَمِنْ عَزْمِ
الْأُمُورِ ○

"The recompense for an injury is an injury equal (in degree) thereto; (i.e., when anyone is wronged and he stands up for his rights, the most he can claim is equal redress): but if a person (prefers the saintly character to that of the wordly-wise man, and) forgives (the offender) and makes reconciliation (in the interests of morality), his reward is due from Allah: Lo! He loveth not those who do wrong. And whosoever vindicateth himself (without transgressing limits of justice) after he hath suffered wrong—for such there is no way (of blame) against them. The way (of blame) is only against those who oppress mankind and insolently transgress beyond bounds through the land, defying right and justice. For such there will be a painful doom. And verily whoso showeth patience and forgiveth—lo! that (voluntary forbearance and clemency) would truly be an exercise of courageous will and solution in the conduct of affairs." (XLII:40-43).

(ii) Nay, the Holy Qur'ãn goes further. It enjoins repelling evil with goodness as the highest moral ideal—às a necessary condition of moral perfection:

وَلَا تَسْتَوِي الْحَسَنَةُ وَلَا السَّيِّئَةُ ۚ ادْفَعْ بِالَّتِي هِيَ أَحْسَنُ فَإِذَا الَّذِي بَيْنَكَ وَ
بَيْنَهُ عَدَاوَةٌ كَأَنَّهُ وَلِيٌّ حَمِيمٌ ۝ وَمَا يُلَقَّاهَا إِلَّا الَّذِينَ صَبَرُوا ۚ وَمَا يُلَقَّاهَا
إِلَّا ذُو حَظٍّ عَظِيمٍ ۝ وَإِمَّا يَنْزَغَنَّكَ مِنَ الشَّيْطَانِ نَزْغٌ فَاسْتَعِذْ بِاللَّهِ ۖ إِنَّهُ هُوَ
السَّمِيعُ الْعَلِيمُ ۝

"Nor can Goodness and Evil be equal. Repel (Evil) with what is better (i.e., Goodness): Then will he between whom and thee was hatred become as it were thy friend and intimate! And no one will be granted such goodness except those who exercise patience and self-restraint,—none but persons of the greatest good fortune. And if (at any time) an incitement to discord is made to thee by the Evil One, seek refuge in Allah. He is the One Who hears and knows all things." (XLI:34-36).

وَإِنَّ السَّاعَةَ لَآتِيَةٌ ۖ فَاصْفَحِ الصَّفْحَ الْجَمِيلَ ۝

"And the Hour (of Final Accountability and Divine Judgment) is surely coming. So overlook (any human faults) with gracious forgiveness."
(XV:85).

وَلْيَعْفُوا وَلْيَصْفَحُوا ۗ أَلَا تُحِبُّونَ أَنْ يَغْفِرَ اللَّهُ لَكُمْ ۗ وَاللَّهُ غَفُورٌ رَحِيمٌ ۝

"....Let them forgive (those who do any injury to them) and let them overlook (the offenders' faults). Do you not wish that Allah forgive you? For Allah is Oft-Forgiving, Most Merciful." (XXIV:22).

فَاعْفُوا وَاصْفَحُوا حَتَّىٰ يَأْتِيَ اللَّهُ بِأَمْرِهِ ۗ إِنَّ اللَّهَ عَلَىٰ كُلِّ شَيْءٍ قَدِيرٌ ۝

"....But forgive (the enemies of Islam) and overlook (their hostility) till Allah accomplisheth His purpose; for Allah hath power over all things." (II:109).

(*b*) *Duties of Respect*:

(i) Treating with respect all human beings in their fundamental rights as fellow-beings—irrespective of differences of sex, race, colour, etc., enjoined:

According to the Holy Qur'ãn every human being deserves respect in his capacity as a human being:

وَلَقَدْ كَرَّمْنَا بَنِيٓ اٰدَمَ

"Verily We have honoured the Children of Adam...." (XVII:70).

This aspect of the Qur'ãnic moral teaching includes:

(a) respecting the rights of all human beings with regard to life, honour and property.

Also: (b) respecting every human being's equality of status as a human being;

and, as a consequence:

(c) respecting his right to freedom,

(d) and the right to fraternise with all other human beings,

—except when a just moral cause intervenes.

The following verse of the Holy Qur'ãn prescribes it, in conjunction with other numerous relevant and connected verses that have been quoted in different contexts in the present dissertation, as a duty of all human beings to protect and promote the above human rights:

يٰٓاَيُّهَا النَّاسُ اتَّقُوْا رَبَّكُمُ الَّذِىْ خَلَقَكُمْ مِّنْ نَّفْسٍ وَّاحِدَةٍ وَّخَلَقَ
مِنْهَا زَوْجَهَا وَبَثَّ مِنْهُمَا رِجَالًا كَثِيْرًا وَّنِسَآءً ۚ وَاتَّقُوا اللّٰهَ الَّذِىْ تَسَآءَلُوْنَ
بِهٖ وَالْاَرْحَامَ ۚ اِنَّ اللّٰهَ كَانَ عَلَيْكُمْ رَقِيْبًا ۝

"O humankind! fear (in respect of the rights of fellow-beings) your Guardian-Lord (*i.e.*, Allah) Who created you from a single soul, and created, of like nature, his mate, and from them twain hath spread abroad countless men and women (everyone of whom is thus bound up in one fraternity—the human family—and possesses the birthright of basic human equality with his fellow-beings to have the freedom of equal opportunity for enjoying the blessings of life on earth). Reverence Allah, through Whom you claim your mutual (rights) (and, therefore, respect your fellow-beings' rights to life, honour, and property, as also those relating to liberty, equality and fraternity), and (reverence) the wombs (that bore you): for Allah ever watches over you." (IV:1).

Here we may also quote with advantage another important related verse which specifically repudiates the erroneous notion of inequality of human beings on physical bases—tribal, racial, etc.—and lays down the basic and the most just principle on the basis of which one human being *earns* more honour than another. God proclaims in the Holy Qur'ãn:

يَٰٓأَيُّهَا ٱلنَّاسُ إِنَّا خَلَقْنَٰكُم مِّن ذَكَرٍ وَأُنثَىٰ وَجَعَلْنَٰكُمْ شُعُوبًا وَ
قَبَآئِلَ لِتَعَارَفُوٓا۟ ۚ إِنَّ أَكْرَمَكُمْ عِندَ ٱللَّهِ أَتْقَىٰكُمْ ۚ إِنَّ ٱللَّهَ عَلِيمٌ
خَبِيرٌ ○

"O humankind! We created you from a single (pair) of a male and female, and made you into nations and tribes, that you may know each other (not that ye may despise each other). Verily the most honoured of you in the sight of Allah is (he who is) the most righteous of you and Allah has full knowledge and is well acquainted (with all things.)"

(XLIX:13).

(ii) Humility, forbearance and peacefulness have been mentioned in the Holy Qur'ãn as basic virtues; hence to practise them is duty:

وَعِبَادُ ٱلرَّحْمَٰنِ ٱلَّذِينَ يَمْشُونَ عَلَى ٱلْأَرْضِ هَوْنًا وَإِذَا خَاطَبَهُمُ ٱلْجَٰهِلُونَ
قَالُوا۟ سَلَٰمًا ○

"And the servants of (Allah) Most Gracious are those who walk on the earth in humility, and when the ignorant address them, they say, 'Peace!' " (XXV:63).

وَٱلْخَٰشِعِينَ وَٱلْخَٰشِعَٰتِ وَٱلْمُتَصَدِّقِينَ وَٱلْمُتَصَدِّقَٰتِ وَٱلصَّٰٓئِمِينَ وَٱلصَّٰٓئِمَٰتِ
وَٱلْحَٰفِظِينَ فُرُوجَهُمْ وَٱلْحَٰفِظَٰتِ وَٱلذَّٰكِرِينَ ٱللَّهَ كَثِيرًا وَٱلذَّٰكِرَٰتِ أَعَدَّ
ٱللَّهُ لَهُم مَّغْفِرَةً وَأَجْرًا عَظِيمًا ○

"*....for men and women who humble themselves*, for men and women who give in charity, for men and women who fast (and deny themselves), for men and women who guard their chastity, and for men and women who engage much in Allah's remembrance—, for them has Allah prepared forgiveness and great reward." (XXXIII:35).

The most important occasion when a person's spirit of humility is put to test is when he speaks to another person. Hence, humility in talk with others has been enjoined specifically also:

وَاغْضُضْ مِن صَوْتِكَ ۚ إِنَّ أَنكَرَ الْأَصْوَاتِ لَصَوْتُ الْحَمِيرِ

".....and lower thy voice (in humility); for the harshest of sounds without doubt is the braying of an ass." (XXXI:19).

Chapter II

DUTIES OF THE MORAL PERFECTION OF OTHERS

END:

Moral Perfection of Others.

(1) Duties of Omission;

(2) Duties of Commission.

I. Duties of Omission

END:

Abstinence from all forms of activity that might be conducive to the creation of, or might directly create, conditions of immorality.

(a) Duties of Love; (b) Duties of Respect.

(*a*) *Duties of Love*:

(*i*) *Creating conditions of moral corruption prohibited:*

وَلَا تُفْسِدُوا فِي الْأَرْضِ بَعْدَ إِصْلَاحِهَا وَادْعُوهُ خَوْفًا وَطَمَعًا ۚ
إِنَّ رَحْمَتَ اللَّهِ قَرِيبٌ مِّنَ الْمُحْسِنِينَ ○

"Do not mischief (moral or material) on the earth, after it hath been set in order, but call on Him with fear and hope: For the Mercy of Allah is always near to those who practise virtue." (VII:56).

(*ii*) *Obstructing the path of morality, as also other paths of goodness, prohibited:*

وَلَا تَكُونُوا كَالَّذِينَ خَرَجُوا مِن دِيَارِهِم بَطَرًا وَرِئَاءَ النَّاسِ
وَيَصُدُّونَ عَن سَبِيلِ اللَّهِ ۚ

"And be not like those who started from their homes insolently and to be seen of men, and to hinder (men) from the Way of Allah (i.e., the perfect System of Goodness which alone leads to God)." (VIII:47).

أَلْقِيَا فِي جَهَنَّمَ كُلَّ كَفَّارٍ عَنِيدٍ ۝ مَّنَّاعٍ لِّلْخَيْرِ

"(The sentence will be:) throw, throw into Hell every contumacious Rejector (of God)!—hinderer of good....." (L:24, 25).

وَلَا تُطِعْ كُلَّ حَلَّافٍ مَّهِينٍ ۝ هَمَّازٍ مَّشَّاءٍ بِنَمِيمٍ ۝ مَّنَّاعٍ لِّلْخَيْرِ

"Heed not the type of despicable man,—ready with oaths, a slanderer, going about with calumnies, hinderer of good....."
(LXVIII:10-12).

(iii) Co-operating with others in sin and transgression prohibited:

وَلَا تَعَاوَنُوا عَلَى الْإِثْمِ وَالْعُدْوَانِ ۚ وَاتَّقُوا اللَّهَ ۖ إِنَّ اللَّهَ شَدِيدُ الْعِقَابِ ۝

".....and help ye not one another in sin and transgression: Fear Allah: Lo! Allah is strict in punishment." (V:3).

(iv) Spreading lewdness in any form; and thereby enticing others in vice prohibited:

قُلْ إِنَّمَا حَرَّمَ رَبِّيَ الْفَوَاحِشَ مَا ظَهَرَ مِنْهَا وَمَا بَطَنَ

"Say: the things that my Lord hath indeed forbidden are: (indulging in and spreading[1], at any level and any type of,) shameful deeds (or lewdness), whether open or secret....." (VII:33).

وَيَنْهَىٰ عَنِ الْفَحْشَاءِ

"....and He forbids (indulging in and spreading, at any level and any type of,) shameful deeds (or lewdness)....." (XVI:90).

(*b*) *Duties of Respect*:

Duties in respect of illegitimate and immoral sexual relations whereby, side by side with one's own chastity, the chastity and honour of others as well as the sanctity of the institution of family[2], is violated:

---

1. Cf. XXIV:19.

2. It should be noted that one of the ends of "sexual duties" is the preservation and promotion of the "family" as the basic unit of society –a point which is

(i) *Adultery and Fornication prohibited*[3]:

وَلَا تَقْرَبُوا الزِّنٰىٓ اِنَّهٗ كَانَ فَاحِشَةً ۭ وَسَاۗءَ سَبِيْلًا ۝

"And come not nigh to fornication and adultery: For it is a shameful (deed) and an evil, opening the road (to other evils)." (XVII:32).

وَلَا يَزْنُوْنَ

"(The true servants of God are those who).....do not commit adultery (nor fornication)...." (XXV:68).

وَلَا يَزْنِيْنَ

"....that they will not commit adultery (nor fornication)...." (LX:12).

(ii) *Homosexuality vehemently condemned; hence abstinence from it is duty:*

Speaking of the Sodomites, the Holy Qur'ãn says:

وَلُوْطًا اِذْ قَالَ لِقَوْمِهٖٓ اَتَاْتُوْنَ الْفَاحِشَةَ مَا سَبَقَكُمْ بِهَا مِنْ اَحَدٍ مِّنَ الْعٰلَمِيْنَ ۝ اِنَّكُمْ لَتَاْتُوْنَ الرِّجَالَ شَهْوَةً مِّنْ دُوْنِ النِّسَاۗءِ ۭ بَلْ اَنْتُمْ قَوْمٌ مُّسْرِفُوْنَ ۝ . . . . وَاَمْطَرْنَا عَلَيْهِمْ مَّطَرًا ۭ فَانْظُرْ كَيْفَ كَانَ عَاقِبَةُ الْمُجْرِمِيْنَ ۝

"We also (sent) Lut: He said to his people: 'Do you commit lewdness such as no people in creation (ever) committed before you? For ye practise your lusts on men in preference to women: ye are indeed a people transgressing beyond bounds'.....And We rained down on them a shower (of brimstone): then see what was the end of those who indulged in sin and crime?" (VII:80, 81, 84).

(iii) *The institution of Prostitution condemned:*

Speaking of the women prisoners of war, the Holy Qur'ãn lays

basic to the Qur'ãnic social philosophy and which is of immense value in respect of its bearing on the moral health of human society.

3. "Polyandry" and "Noega" also come under this category. They are, therefore, prohibited. See p. 185.

down the following rule, thus promulgating the law condemning the business of prostitution in all its aspects:

وَلَا تُكْرِهُوا فَتَيٰتِكُمْ عَلَى الْبِغَاءِ إِنْ أَرَدْنَ تَحَصُّنًا لِّتَبْتَغُوا عَرَضَ الْحَيٰوةِ الدُّنْيَا

"....and force not your maids to prostitution (—a custom prevalent among the pagan Arabs in respect of their slave-girls—) their desire being for chastity, in order that ye may make a gain in the goods of this life....."
(XXIV:33).

(II) Duties of Commission

END:

Active struggle for creating an atmosphere conducive to morality and awakening the moral consciousness of one's fellow-beings by word and deed.

Preliminary:

The Holy Qur'ãn says:

وَالْعَصْرِ ۝ إِنَّ الْإِنسَانَ لَفِي خُسْرٍ ۝ إِلَّا الَّذِينَ آمَنُوا وَعَمِلُوا الصّٰلِحٰتِ وَتَوَاصَوْا بِالْحَقِّ ۙ وَتَوَاصَوْا بِالصَّبْرِ ۝

"By Time (as it has unfolded through the ages, recording man's successes and failures), verily man is in a state of loss, but not those who have Faith and do (constantly) righteous deeds, and exhort one another to Truth and exhort one another to endurance (in the service of Truth)."
(CIII:1-3).

The Holy Qur'ãn further warns that evasion of this active struggle leads to calamities of the highest magnitude, which afflict the innocent and the guilty alike:

وَاتَّقُوا فِتْنَةً لَّا تُصِيبَنَّ الَّذِينَ ظَلَمُوا مِنكُمْ خَاصَّةً ۚ وَاعْلَمُوا أَنَّ اللَّهَ شَدِيدُ الْعِقَابِ ۝

"And fear the chastisement that shall not afflict those alone who among you do wrong; and know that verily Allah is Severe in Chastising."
(VIII:25).

DUTIES:

(a) Duty of Love; (b) Duty of Respect.

(*a*) *Duty of Love*:

Active struggle for the fullest establishment of morality enjoined:

(i) The mission which has been entrusted by God to the Muslim community is the establishment of moral order in the world as a whole—a mission the fulfilment of which is the duty of every Muslim, man and woman:

كُنْتُمْ خَيْرَ أُمَّةٍ أُخْرِجَتْ لِلنَّاسِ تَأْمُرُونَ بِالْمَعْرُوفِ وَتَنْهَوْنَ عَنِ
الْمُنْكَرِ وَتُؤْمِنُونَ بِاللَّهِ

"Ye (O Muslim!) are the best (ideological) community that hath been raised up for mankind. Ye enjoin right conduct and forbid all that is wrong (=evil); and ye believe in Allah....." (III:110).

(ii) This mission entails, however, certain difficult conditions, which cannot be possible for every Muslim to fulfil. Consequently, while it is the duty of every Muslim to co-operate[4] in it to the best of his capacity and in the manner best suited to him, it is necessary that there should be a trained, disciplined and devoted band of Muslims who should lead the struggle. And this is what the Holy Qur'ãn has enjoined:

وَلْتَكُنْ مِنْكُمْ أُمَّةٌ يَدْعُونَ إِلَى الْخَيْرِ وَيَأْمُرُونَ بِالْمَعْرُوفِ وَيَنْهَوْنَ
عَنِ الْمُنْكَرِ وَأُولَٰئِكَ هُمُ الْمُفْلِحُونَ ○

"Let there arise out of you a band of people inviting to all that is good, enjoining what is right, and forbidding what is wrong: They are the ones who attain felicity." (III:104).

---

4. Co-operation is also participation according to the Holy Qur'ãn:

مَنْ يَشْفَعْ شَفَاعَةً حَسَنَةً يَكُنْ لَهُ نَصِيبٌ مِنْهَا وَمَنْ يَشْفَعْ شَفَاعَةً
سَيِّئَةً يَكُنْ لَهُ كِفْلٌ مِنْهَا وَكَانَ اللَّهُ عَلَىٰ كُلِّ شَيْءٍ مُقِيتًا ○

"Whoever recommends and helps a good cause becomes a partner therein: and whoever recommends and helps an evil cause shares in its burden: and Allah hath power over all things." (IV:85).

(iii) The basic struggle consists, thus, in propagating among mankind the Divine Teachings which form the very foundation and the life-blood of the moral order. This struggle has, however, to be pursued in the sublimest manner. The Holy Qur'ãn says:

ادْعُ إِلَىٰ سَبِيلِ رَبِّكَ بِالْحِكْمَةِ وَالْمَوْعِظَةِ الْحَسَنَةِ وَجَادِلْهُم بِالَّتِي هِيَ أَحْسَنُ إِنَّ رَبَّكَ هُوَ أَعْلَمُ بِمَن ضَلَّ عَن سَبِيلِهِ وَهُوَ أَعْلَمُ بِالْمُهْتَدِينَ ○

"Invite (all) to the Way of thy Lord with wisdom and beautiful preaching; and argue with them in ways that are best and most gracious: For thy Lord knoweth best who have strayed from His Path and who receive guidance." (XVI:125).

(iv) The establishment of the moral order necessitates finally the employment of state authority for this purpose. The Holy Qur'ãn enjoins this function on the Islamic State:

وَلَيَنصُرَنَّ اللَّهُ مَن يَنصُرُهُ إِنَّ اللَّهَ لَقَوِيٌّ عَزِيزٌ ○ الَّذِينَ إِن مَّكَّنَّاهُمْ فِي الْأَرْضِ أَقَامُوا الصَّلَاةَ وَآتَوُا الزَّكَاةَ وَأَمَرُوا بِالْمَعْرُوفِ وَنَهَوْا عَنِ الْمُنكَرِ وَلِلَّهِ عَاقِبَةُ الْأُمُورِ ○

"....Allah will certainly aid those who aid His (cause)—for verily Allah is Full of Strength, exalted in Might, (able to enforce His Will) (Muslims are) those who, if We give them authority in the land, establish regular prayer and give regular charity, enjoin the right and forbid wrong; and with Allah rests the end (and decision) of (all) affairs. (XXII:40, 41).

(v) The Holy Qur'ãn condemns the establishment of secret societies for evil ends. But it permits secret activity, if absolutely necessary, for the promotion of virtue:

لَّا خَيْرَ فِي كَثِيرٍ مِّن نَّجْوَاهُمْ إِلَّا مَنْ أَمَرَ بِصَدَقَةٍ أَوْ مَعْرُوفٍ أَوْ إِصْلَاحٍ بَيْنَ النَّاسِ وَمَن يَفْعَلْ ذَٰلِكَ ابْتِغَاءَ مَرْضَاتِ اللَّهِ فَسَوْفَ نُؤْتِيهِ أَجْرًا عَظِيمًا ○

"In most of their secret talks there is no good, but if one exhorts to a deed of charity or justice or conciliation between human beings, (secrecy is permissible): to him who does this, seeking the good pleasure of Allah, We shall soon give a reward of the highest (value)." (IV:114).

(*b*) *Duty of Respect*:

Marriage permitted as the only means of fulfilling sexual need and made obligatory for preserving the moral health of society:

وَأَنكِحُوا الْأَيَامَىٰ مِنكُمْ وَالصَّالِحِينَ مِنْ عِبَادِكُمْ وَإِمَائِكُمْ ۚ إِن يَكُونُوا
فُقَرَاءَ يُغْنِهِمُ اللَّهُ مِن فَضْلِهِ ۗ وَاللَّهُ وَاسِعٌ عَلِيمٌ ﴿٣٢﴾ وَلْيَسْتَعْفِفِ الَّذِينَ لَا
يَجِدُونَ نِكَاحًا حَتَّىٰ يُغْنِيَهُمُ اللَّهُ مِن فَضْلِهِ ۗ

"Marry those among you who are single, or the virtuous ones among your slaves, male or female :if they are in poverty, Allah will give them means out of His Grace: for Allah encompasseth all, and He knoweth all things. Let those who find not the wherewithal for marriage keep themselves chaste, until Allah gives them means out of His Grace."

(XXIV:32, 33).

(Secrecy is permissible) to him who does this, seeking the good pleasure of Allah, We shall soon give a reward of the highest (value)." (IV:114)

(b) Duty of Respect.

Marriage permitted as the only means of fulfilling sexual need and made obligatory for preserving the moral health of society.

وأنكحوا الأيامى منكم والصالحين من عبادكم وإمائكم إن
يكونوا فقراء يغنهم الله من فضله والله واسع عليم ۝ وليستعفف الذين
لا يجدون نكاحا حتى يغنيهم الله من فضله

Marry those among you who are single, or the virtuous ones among your slaves, male or female: if they are in poverty, Allah will give them means out of His Grace: for Allah encompasseth all, and He knoweth all things. Let those who find not the wherewithal for marriage keep themselves chaste, until Allah gives them means out of His Grace.
(XXIV:32, 33)

Part II

DUTIES OF CONDITION TOWARDS OTHER INDIVIDUALS

(A) Duties to Relatives and to the non-Relatives belonging to one's home;

(B) Duties with respect to Age and Rank;

(C) Duties to Particular Categories of non-Relatives;

(D) Duties to Muslims as Muslims;

(E) Duties to non-Muslims as non-Muslims.

In part I of the "Duties of Others", we have covered those duties of omission and commission which the Holy Qur'ãn has prescribed in respect of our dealings with our fellow-beings without consideration of the nature of our relationship with them. They are duties which, according to the Holy Qur'ãn, we owe to every human being in his capacity as human being. In other words, they are duties which relate to fundamental human rights.

The Holy Qur'ãn has prescribed, however, another set of duties also, which we owe to others in consideration of their specific relations with us. They may be called: "Duties of Condition". We shall deal with them now, classifying them first into five broad sections: A, B, C, D, and E, as given above. Of course, these sections are further subdivisible, as we shall see.

Chapter I

DUTIES TO RELATIVES AND TO THE NON-RELATIVES BELONGING TO ONE'S HOME

(1) Duties towards one's Parents.

(2) Duties towards one's Offspring.

(3) Respective duties of Husband and Wife.

(4) Duties towards Relatives in General.

(5) Duties towards Domestic Servants.

(1) Duties Towards One's Parents

(*a*) Duties of Commission

(*i*) *As the following verses show,* the Holy Qur'ãn enjoins:

(*a*) *doing good to parents in every way;*

(*b*) *obeying them without demur in everything good;*

(*c*) *behaving respectfully towards them;*

(*d*) *maintaining attitude of thankfulness towards them;*

(*e*) *caring for them with mercy—*
with special regard for the mother[1].

The Holy Qur'ãn says:

وَقَضٰى رَبُّكَ اَلَّا تَعْبُدُوْٓا اِلَّآ اِيَّاهُ وَبِالْوَالِدَيْنِ اِحْسَانًا ؕ اِمَّا يَبْلُغَنَّ
عِنْدَكَ الْكِبَرَ اَحَدُهُمَآ اَوْ كِلٰهُمَا فَلَا تَقُلْ لَّهُمَآ اُفٍّ وَّلَا تَنْهَرْهُمَا وَقُلْ لَّهُمَا
قَوْلًا كَرِيْمًا ۝ وَاخْفِضْ لَهُمَا جَنَاحَ الذُّلِّ مِنَ الرَّحْمَةِ وَقُلْ رَّبِّ ارْحَمْهُمَا كَمَا
رَبَّيٰنِيْ صَغِيْرًا ۝ رَبُّكُمْ اَعْلَمُ بِمَا فِيْ نُفُوْسِكُمْ ؕ اِنْ تَكُوْنُوْا صٰلِحِيْنَ فَاِنَّهٗ كَانَ
لِلْاَوَّابِيْنَ غَفُوْرًا ۝

"Thy Lord hath decreed that ye worship none but Him, and that ye be kind to parents. Whether one or both of them attain old age in thy life, say not to them a word of contempt, nor repel them, but address them in terms of honour. And, out of kindness, lower to them the wing of humility; and say, 'My Lord! bestow on them Thy Mercy even as they

1. Ref.: Footnote on p. 176.

cherished me in childhood'. Your Lord knoweth best what is in your hearts: if ye do deeds of righteousness, verily He is Most Forgiving to those who turn to Him again and again (in true penitence)."

(XVII:23-25).

وَوَصَّيْنَا الْإِنسَانَ بِوَالِدَيْهِ إِحْسَانًا ۖ حَمَلَتْهُ أُمُّهُ كُرْهًا وَوَضَعَتْهُ
كُرْهًا ۖ وَحَمْلُهُ وَفِصَالُهُ ثَلَاثُونَ شَهْرًا ۚ حَتَّىٰ إِذَا بَلَغَ أَشُدَّهُ وَبَلَغَ أَرْبَعِينَ
سَنَةً قَالَ رَبِّ أَوْزِعْنِي أَنْ أَشْكُرَ نِعْمَتَكَ الَّتِي أَنْعَمْتَ عَلَيَّ وَعَلَىٰ
وَالِدَيَّ وَأَنْ أَعْمَلَ صَالِحًا تَرْضَاهُ وَأَصْلِحْ لِي فِي ذُرِّيَّتِي ۖ إِنِّي تُبْتُ
إِلَيْكَ وَإِنِّي مِنَ الْمُسْلِمِينَ ○ أُولَٰئِكَ الَّذِينَ نَتَقَبَّلُ عَنْهُمْ أَحْسَنَ مَا
عَمِلُوا وَنَتَجَاوَزُ عَن سَيِّئَاتِهِمْ فِي أَصْحَابِ الْجَنَّةِ ۖ وَعْدَ الصِّدْقِ
الَّذِي كَانُوا يُوعَدُونَ ○

"We have enjoined on man kindness to his parents: In pain did his mother bear him, and in pain did she give him birth. The carrying of the (child) to his weaning is (a period of) thirty months. At length, when he reaches the age of full strength and attains forty years, he says, O my Lord! grant me that I may be grateful for Thy favour which Thou hast bestowed upon me, and upon both my parents, and that I may work righteousness such as Thou mayest approve; and be gracious to me in my issue. Truly have I turned to Thee and truly do I bow (to Thee) in Islam'. Such are they from whom we shall accept the best of their deeds and pass by their ill deeds: (they shall be) among the companions of the Gardenias promise of truth, which was made to them (in this life). (XLVI:15, 16).

(ii) Doing good to parents even if they are non-Muslims, regardless of their attitude to Islam, enjoined:

وَوَصَّيْنَا الْإِنسَانَ بِوَالِدَيْهِ حَمَلَتْهُ أُمُّهُ وَهْنًا عَلَىٰ وَهْنٍ وَفِصَالُهُ فِي عَامَيْنِ
أَنِ اشْكُرْ لِي وَلِوَالِدَيْكَ إِلَيَّ الْمَصِيرُ ○ وَإِن جَاهَدَاكَ عَلَىٰ أَن تُشْرِكَ بِي
مَا لَيْسَ لَكَ بِهِ عِلْمٌ فَلَا تُطِعْهُمَا ۖ وَصَاحِبْهُمَا فِي الدُّنْيَا مَعْرُوفًا ۖ وَاتَّبِعْ
سَبِيلَ مَنْ أَنَابَ إِلَيَّ ۚ ثُمَّ إِلَيَّ مَرْجِعُكُمْ فَأُنَبِّئُكُم بِمَا كُنتُمْ تَعْمَلُونَ ○

"And We have enjoined on man (to be good) to his parents: In travail upon travail did his mother bear him, and in years twain was his weaning: (hear the command), 'Show gratitude to Me and to thy parents':

to Me is (thy final) Goal. But if they strive to make thee join in worship with Me things of which thou hast no knowledge, obey them not; yet bear them company in this life with justice (and consideration), and follow the way of those who turn to Me (in love): In the end the return of you all is to Me, and I will tell you (the truth and meaning of) all that ye did." (XXXI:14, 15).

(*b*) Duty of Omission:

Abstinence from obeying non-Muslim parents in their anti-Islamic religious beliefs and practices, enjoined:

وَوَصَّيْنَا الْإِنسَانَ بِوَالِدَيْهِ حُسْنًا ۖ وَإِن جَاهَدَاكَ لِتُشْرِكَ بِي مَا لَيْسَ
لَكَ بِهِ عِلْمٌ فَلَا تُطِعْهُمَا ۚ إِلَيَّ مَرْجِعُكُمْ فَأُنَبِّئُكُم بِمَا
كُنتُمْ تَعْمَلُونَ ○

"We enjoined on man kindness to parents: but if they (either of them) strive (to force) thee to join with Me (in worship) anything of which thou hast no knowledge, obey them not. Ye have (all) to return to Me, and I will tell you (the truth) of all that ye did." (XXIX:8).

2. Duties Towards one's Offspring

A. Social and Spiritual Status of the Child:

(i) The Holy Qur'ãn teaches that the child is a respectable being:

(a) because of his humanity, concerning which it has been said:

وَلَقَدْ كَرَّمْنَا بَنِي آدَمَ

"Verily We have honoured the Children of Adam...." (XVII:70).

(b) because of his sinlessness, as it has been said:

لَقَدْ خَلَقْنَا الْإِنسَانَ فِي أَحْسَنِ تَقْوِيمٍ ○

"Assuredly We have created man in the goodliest constitution (i.e., pure and individually perfect)." (XCV:4).

وَلَا تَكْسِبُ كُلُّ نَفْسٍ إِلَّا عَلَيْهَا ۚ وَلَا تَزِرُ وَازِرَةٌ وِزْرَ أُخْرَىٰ

".....Every soul draws the need of its acts on none but itself: no bearer of burden can bear the burden of another....." (VI:164).

Thus the child is born singles, without inheriting the sins of his ancestors. And it is classed as innocent up to the age of discretion, as it has been said:

لَا يُكَلِّفُ اللّٰهُ نَفْسًا اِلَّا وُسْعَهَا ۚ

"On no soul doth Allah place a responsibility but to the extent of its ability....." (II:286).

And its categorisation as innocent makes it logically immune from receiving those punishments which are meant for adults in respect of commission of wrongs.

(ii) In its condemnation of infanticide, the Holy Qur'ãn teaches that the child is a 'gift from God'—a 'trust'[1] of God placed in the care of the child's elders, and should, therefore, be treated with love, understanding and extreme care:

قَدْ خَسِرَ الَّذِيْنَ قَتَلُوْٓا اَوْلَادَهُمْ سَفَهًاۢ بِغَيْرِ عِلْمٍ وَّ حَرَّمُوْا مَا رَزَقَهُمُ

اللّٰهُ افْتِرَآءً عَلَى اللّٰهِ ۚ قَدْ ضَلُّوْا وَ مَا كَانُوْا مُهْتَدِيْنَ ۝

"Lost are those who besottedly have murdered their children without knowledge, and forbidden (to themselves) that which Allah bestowed upon them (as gift), inventing a lie against Allah. They have indeed gone astray and heeded no guidance." (VI:140).

B. Duties

(*i*) <u>Duties of Omission</u>:

Infanticide had been practised by different communities of the world, including the pagan Arabs, the Hindus, the Greeks and the Romans, in the pre- Qur'ãnic era of human history.[2] When the Holy Qur'ãn came, it voiced its condemnation of that evil and inhuman practice in strong

---

1. A Muslim holds everything—his life, property, position, children, etc.—as trust from God. (IX:111).

2. See: *Encyclopaedia of Religion and Ethics* and *Encyclopaedia Britannica* (relevant portions).

terms and forbade it totally, as we have seen in verse VI:140 quoted above, and as we find in the following:

(a) *Killing of offspring for fear of poverty—before their birth: in the form of abortion, or after their birth: in the form of murder—forbidden:*

وَلَا تَقْتُلُوٓا أَوْلَادَكُمْ خَشْيَةَ إِمْلَاقٍ نَحْنُ نَرْزُقُهُمْ وَإِيَّاكُمْ إِنَّ
قَتْلَهُمْ كَانَ خِطْأً كَبِيرًا ○

"Kill not your children for fear of want: We shall provide sustenance for them as well as for you. Verily the killing of them is a great sin." (XVII:31).[3]

(b) *Killing of daughters for extra fear of dishonour specially condemned*:

وَإِذَا بُشِّرَ أَحَدُهُمْ بِالْأُنْثَىٰ ظَلَّ وَجْهُهُ مُسْوَدًّا وَهُوَ كَظِيمٌ ○
يَتَوَارَىٰ مِنَ الْقَوْمِ مِنْ سُوٓءِ مَا بُشِّرَ بِهِ أَيُمْسِكُهُ عَلَىٰ هُونٍ أَمْ يَدُسُّهُ
فِي التُّرَابِ أَلَا سَاءَ مَا يَحْكُمُونَ ○

"When news is brought to one of them, of (the birth of) a female (child), his face darkens, and he is filled with inward grief! With shame does he hide himself from his people, because of the bad news he has had! Shall he retain it on (sufferance and) contempt, or bury it in the dust! Ah! what an evil (choice) they decide on!" (XVI:58, 59).

وَإِذَا الْمَوْءُدَةُ سُئِلَتْ ○ بِأَيِّ ذَنْبٍ قُتِلَتْ ○

"When the female (infant), buried alive, is questioned (by God on the Day of Judgment)—for what crime she was killed!" (LXXXI:8, 9).

(c) *Infanticide with 'religious' motives condemned*:

وَكَذَٰلِكَ زَيَّنَ لِكَثِيرٍ مِنَ الْمُشْرِكِينَ قَتْلَ أَوْلَادِهِمْ شُرَكَاؤُهُمْ لِيُرْدُوهُمْ
وَلِيَلْبِسُوا عَلَيْهِمْ دِينَهُمْ وَلَوْ شَاءَ اللَّهُ مَا فَعَلُوهُ فَذَرْهُمْ وَمَا يَفْتَرُونَ ○

---

3. There is another verse also of the same import, *i.e.*, VI:151.

"Even so, in the eyes of most of the Pagans, their 'partners' made alluring the slaughter of their children, to lead them to their own destruction, and cause confusion in their religion. If Allah had willed, they would not have done so: But leave alone them and their inventions." (VI:137).

(*ii*) Duties of Commission:

Condemning contempt for one's children, forbidding their treatment as a burden, and teaching respect and love for them, the Holy Qur'ãn refers to their upbringing by their parents,—a function which all parents, including the animal parents, perform basically and naturally under the urge of the parental instinct, but wherein the outlook requires to be refined and enlightened in the interest of human well-being. In this connection:

(a) The Holy Qur'ãn commands the safeguarding of the interest of the child, in the most delicate period of his life, in respect of suckling him, which is specially jeopardised in case the parents are unfortunately separated from each other through divorce:

وَالْوَالِدَٰتُ يُرْضِعْنَ أَوْلَٰدَهُنَّ حَوْلَيْنِ كَامِلَيْنِ لِمَنْ أَرَادَ أَن يُتِمَّ الرَّضَاعَةَ ۚ
وَعَلَى الْمَوْلُودِ لَهُ رِزْقُهُنَّ وَكِسْوَتُهُنَّ بِالْمَعْرُوفِ ۚ

"The mothers shall give suck to their offspring for two whole years, if the father desires to complete the term. But he shall bear the cost of their food and clothing on equitable terms....." (II:233).

(b) Then it refers to the unselfish upbringing of the child by the parents up to the time of his maturity[4] as a virtue, in the following prayer which Muslim children are taught to make for their parents:

وَقُل رَّبِّ ارْحَمْهُمَا كَمَا رَبَّيَانِي صَغِيرًا

".....and say: 'My Lord! bestow on them Thy Mercy even as they (tenderly) cherished me (when I was) young." (XVII:24).

This verse refers to the fact that the parents have to look after the needs of the child until he is mature. It has been mentioned as a

---

4. The obligation of maintenance of the offspring upto the age of maturity is borne out by the law laid down for transferring to the orphans living in one's charge the administration of their properties. (See IV:6).

universal fact which occurs in a natural course,—namely, everyone whose outlook in respect of his children is rational and not perverted and whose circumstances do not force him to act against the true dictates of human nature[5], is bound to do it. However, although natural, it should be treated as a specific duty in the light of the general command of "doing good to all" and "taking special care of those who are related to one in blood" (XVI:90), in the interest of the moral health of human society.

(c) The Holy Qur'ãn teaches prayers which are highly instructive in guiding us to the parents' duties towards their children. The prayers are:

وَأَصْلِحْ لِي فِي ذُرِّيَّتِي

".....and be Thou good unto me in my progeny (O Lord!) (i.e., cause my progeny to be good and accomplished in every way)....."

(XLVI:15).

رَبَّنَا هَبْ لَنَا مِنْ أَزْوَاجِنَا وَذُرِّيَّاتِنَا قُرَّةَ أَعْيُنٍ وَاجْعَلْنَا لِلْمُتَّقِينَ إِمَامًا

"....Our Lord! Grant unto us the comfort of our eyes from our wives and our offspring, and give us (the grace) to lead the righteous."

(XXV:74).

Now, for the offspring to be "comfort of one's eyes" it is necessary that they should be good in every way; and they would not be normally so unless the parents exert to their full for building up their children in all aspects of their lives and to the highest stature possible.

We know that mere yearning expressed in prayer and left at that means nothing more than sheer idiocy and insult to God. Hence this verse refers to the duty of doing everything in the power of the parents to bring up their children healthy and strong physically, intellectually, morally, spiritually and economically. Of course, that would mean sacrifice for the parents. But, according to the Holy Qur'ãn, self-sacrifice is an essential quality of Muslim character (LIX:9), and it becomes a duty in the case of one's children.

5. In case of adverse circumstances the Qur'ãnic social philosophy makes it the duty of the state to look after the proper upbringing and development of the child, as we shall see later.

(d) Finally, the Holy Qur'ãn lays down the command:

يَٰٓأَيُّهَا ٱلَّذِينَ ءَامَنُوا۟ قُوٓا۟ أَنفُسَكُمْ وَأَهْلِيكُمْ نَارًا وَقُودُهَا ٱلنَّاسُ
وَٱلْحِجَارَةُ عَلَيْهَا مَلَٰٓئِكَةٌ غِلَاظٌ شِدَادٌ لَّا يَعْصُونَ ٱللَّهَ مَآ
أَمَرَهُمْ وَيَفْعَلُونَ مَا يُؤْمَرُونَ ۝

"O ye who believe! *protect yourselves and your wives and children from a (spiritual) Fire* whose fuel (unlike the fuel of physical fire) is human beings (who lead wrong lives) and stones (which have been worshipped as false deities by ancient communities) over which are (appointed) angels stern (and) severe, who fliench not (from executing) the Commands they receive from Allah, but do (precisely) what they are commanded." (LXVI:6).

In order to understand the implications of the above command truly and comprehensively, it is necessary to grasp deeply the constitution of the human personality and the dynamics of human activity. The fact is that the different aspects of the human personality are inter-related and, according to the Qur'ãnic concept of *tauhid*, they form an organic unity,—their inter-relationship and inter-dependence being expressible as follows:

Sound mind resides in a sound body.

Sound morality is possible only for a person of sound mind.

Sound spirituality is attainable only by a person of sound morals.

Sound economic pursuit requires at least the soundness of body and mind both.

Thus, saving one's children from the fire of Hell necessitates not only giving them formal teaching of certain religious beliefs and practices—which, if not integrated with other aspects of life, amounts for all practical purposes to a defective attempt—but taking all those steps which will make them good in every way, as taught by the Holy Qur'ãn and expounded in the present dissertation, in respect of human life, namely: *physically, intellectually, morally, spiritually and economically*: the comprehensive programme and the manner in which the Holy Prophet (Peace be on him) built up the despicable pagan Arabs into a community of righteous and progressive superhumans.[6]

---

6. Indeed, the Holy Prophet (Peace be on him) built up his followers in a most comprehensive way, as would be evident even from a perusal of the present dissertation. The same comprehensiveness should grace the programme of the parents for their children.

This means that the verse quoted above envisages the following rights of the child and their fulfilment:

(1) establishment of an atmosphere of love and understanding for the child's proper growth;

(2) protection against all evils; neglect, cruelty and exploitation;

(3) provision of adequate nutrition, proper housing, recreation, and medical service;

(4) provision of opportunities and facilities for the child's balanced development in freedom and dignity, according to the Qur'ãnic code of life;

(5) provision of the best available formal education, in keeping with the child's aptitude and capabilities;

(6) provision of comprehensive moral education and training;

(7) Above all and running through every phase of the child's life, there should be the provision of spiritual education and training—of as high an order as possible—for making him truly God-fearing: which is the most basic and the highest virtue that a Muslim should possess.

3. Respective Duties of the Husband and the Wife

For a proper understanding of the mutual rights and duties of the husband and the wife as taught by the Holy Qur'ãn, it is necessary to begin with a basic evaluation of woman's position in that teaching.[7]

---

7. It may be observed at the very outset that the Qur'ãnic teaching on this problem is in sharp contrast with the point of view of other religions. We may mention here the teaching of the Bible. "According to the Old Testament, woman is responsible for the fall of man, and this became the cornerstone of Christian teaching....It is a remarkable fact that the gospels (barring divorce, Matt. 19:9) contain not a word in favour of woman....The epistles of St. Paul definitely insist that no change can be permitted in the position of woman...St Jerome has aught but good to say of woman....'Woman is the gate of the devil, the road of evil, the sting of the scorpion'. Canon law declares: 'Man only is created to the image of God, not woman: therefore woman shall serve him and be his hand-maid'. The Provincial Council of Macon (sixth century) seriously discussed the question 'whether woman had a soul at all'." (Krafft-Ebing: *Psychopathia Sexualis*, p. 4. n.).

(A) Basic Guidance Constituting the Background of Duties

1. Position of Woman:

We have already seen that the Holy Qur'ãn makes no distinction between man and woman as regards the fundamental human rights. Here we may specifically state that:

Woman, like man, is the possessor of free personality, and enjoys equality with man, in respect of:

(a) Her spiritual and moral status:

لِلرِّجَالِ نَصِيبٌ مِّمَّا اكْتَسَبُوا ۚ وَلِلنِّسَاءِ نَصِيبٌ مِّمَّا اكْتَسَبْنَ ۚ

".....Unto men the benefit of what they earn (of virtue), and unto women the benefit of what they earn (of virtue) (i.e., in matters of spiritual grace both, man and woman, enjoy equal status and are independent of one another)." (IV:32).

إِنَّ الْمُسْلِمِينَ وَالْمُسْلِمَاتِ وَالْمُؤْمِنِينَ وَالْمُؤْمِنَاتِ وَالْقَانِتِينَ وَالْقَانِتَاتِ
وَالصَّادِقِينَ وَالصَّادِقَاتِ وَالصَّابِرِينَ وَالصَّابِرَاتِ وَالْخَاشِعِينَ وَ
الْخَاشِعَاتِ وَالْمُتَصَدِّقِينَ وَالْمُتَصَدِّقَاتِ وَالصَّائِمِينَ وَالصَّائِمَاتِ وَالْحَافِظِينَ
فُرُوجَهُمْ وَالْحَافِظَاتِ وَالذَّاكِرِينَ اللَّهَ كَثِيرًا وَالذَّاكِرَاتِ أَعَدَّ اللَّهُ لَهُم
مَّغْفِرَةً وَأَجْرًا عَظِيمًا

"Lo! men who surrender (unto Allah) and women who surrender, and men who believe and women who believe, and men who obey and women who obey, and men who speak the truth and women who speak the truth, and men who persevere (in righteousness) and women who persevere, and men who are humble and women who are humble, and men who give alms and women who give alms, and men who fast and women who fast, and men who guard their modesty and women who guard (their modesty), and men who remember Allah much and women who remember—Allah hath prepared for them forgiveness and vast reward." (XXXIII:35).

As regards the point of view of other religions, primitive as well as civilised, reference may be made to: *Encyclopaedia of Religion and Ethics*.

(b) Her economic rights:

لِلرِّجَالِ نَصِيبٌ مِّمَّا اكْتَسَبُوا ۖ وَلِلنِّسَاءِ نَصِيبٌ مِّمَّا اكْتَسَبْنَ ۚ

".....Unto men a fortune from what they have earned (of wealth), and unto women a fortune from what they have earned (of wealth) (both being free and equal with regard to the possession of their economic rights)....." (IV:32).[8]

لِلرِّجَالِ نَصِيبٌ مِّمَّا تَرَكَ الْوَالِدَانِ وَالْأَقْرَبُونَ وَلِلنِّسَاءِ نَصِيبٌ
مِّمَّا تَرَكَ الْوَالِدَانِ وَالْأَقْرَبُونَ مِمَّا قَلَّ مِنْهُ أَوْ كَثُرَ ۚ نَصِيبًا
مَّفْرُوضًا ○

"Unto the men (of a family) belongeth a share of that which parents and near kindred leave, and unto the women a share of that which the parents and near kindred leave, whether it be little or much—a legal share." (IV:7).

(c) Her legal rights:

وَلَهُنَّ مِثْلُ الَّذِي عَلَيْهِنَّ بِالْمَعْرُوفِ ۚ

".....And they (women) have rights similar to those (of men) over them, according to what is equitable...." (II:228).

لَا تُضَارَّ وَالِدَةٌ بِوَلَدِهَا وَلَا مَوْلُودٌ لَّهُ بِوَلَدِهِ ۚ

"A mother should not be made to suffer because of her child, nor he to whom the child is born (be made to suffer) because of his child (because both are equal before the law)...." (II:233).

2. Inequalities of Condition:

Indeed, as a *human being*, woman enjoys equality of status with man. With this, however, there are also "inequalities of condition" which have been necessitated by the differences in her physical constitution, mental make-up and her distinct roles in society as mother and as wife. Thus:

(a) as mother:

In the verses we have quoted concerning the duties to parents we find that the Holy Qur'ãn lays special emphasis on the role of the mother, thereby pointing to the superiority of her role in respect of the

8. It should be noted that this verse applies to worldly wealth as well as to virtue.

child—as a consequence of which she deserves devotion grater, and honour higher, than the father.[9]

(b) as wife:

As a wife, side by side with enjoying equal fundamental human rights, she has been placed one degree below the husband in the matter of administering the affairs of the family:

وَلِلرِّجَالِ عَلَيْهِنَّ دَرَجَةٌ ۚ

"....but men have a degree (of advantage) over them[10]...." (II:228).

---

9. This implication has been stated by the Holy Prophet (Peace be on him) in concrete terms when he singles out the mother and says:

ان الجنة عند رجليها

"Verily Paradise is by the side of her feet." (Mishkãt al-Masãbih, p. 421)

Also in the *hadith* where he (Peace be on him) emphasised service to the mother thrice and thereafter mentioned service to the father. (*Riyãd al-Sãlihîn*, p. 163).

10. Compare this with the following verdicts of the exponents of modern scientific thought on this problem:

Says Nemilov: "Man, perhaps even down to the protein molecules of his tissue cells, is biologically different from woman. From the very moment of sex formation in the embryo, the biological ducting of the sexes develops along entirely divergent paths..... We must recognize the unquestionable existence of the biological inequality of the sexex. It goes deeper and is of far greater import than it would appear to those not familiar with natural science."

(*Biological Tragedy of Woman*, pp. 75-78).

"The desires and conduct of the two sexes", says Mercier, "are not similar but are complementary and reciprocal. In courtship the male is active: his role is to court, to pursue, to possess, to control, to protect, to love. The role of the female is passive.....Consequent on this fundamental difference are certain others. For pursuit, greater ardour is necessary than for mere reception; and the courting activity of the male is, throughout the whole animal kingdom, more ardent than that of the female; and this greater ordour is connected with certain other differences." (*Conduct and its Disorders Biologically Considered*, pp. 289-290).

Julian Huxley observes: "I venture to prophesy not only that the inherent differences between the sexes will not tend to diminish in the course of evolution but that man will continue, as now and in the past, to emphasise them by custom and convention." (*Essays in Popular Science*, p. 63).

It should, however, be clearly kept in mind that, in the Qur'ãnic teaching, the husband and the wife stand in complementary relation to each other, and never in the relation of the ruler and the ruled (II:187).

In the presence of the husband, the Holy Qur'ãn has not chosen her to function as the head of the family, because owing to his masculine constitution and appropriate mental make-up, the husband is better equipped to earn livelihood for the family, to bear the physical strains, and to avert dangers to the family in general. The Holy Qur'ãn refers to these functions of the husband when, speaking of his role for the wife, it says:

الرِّجَالُ قَوّٰمُوْنَ عَلَى النِّسَآءِ بِمَا فَضَّلَ اللّٰهُ بَعْضَهُمْ عَلٰى بَعْضٍ وَّبِمَآ اَنْفَقُوْا مِنْ اَمْوَالِهِمْ

"Men are the protectors and maintainers of women, because Allah hath given the one more (strength) than the other, and because they spend of their wealth (for supporting them and other members of the family)....." (IV:34).

Of course, the husband has to administer the family jointly with the wife, according to the Qur'ãnic law:

وَاَمْرُهُمْ شُوْرٰى بَيْنَهُمْ

"....(Believers are those) who conduct their affairs by mutual consultation (and not arbitrarily)...." (XLII:38).

As a follower of the Qur'ãn, it is only in extreme cases that the husband may differ irreconcilably with the wife. But then too he cannot transgress the bounds of justice and mercy; for the Holy Qur'ãn commands him to be always just, merciful and considerate[12].

The second position of the wife as administrator is, thus, not a source of suffering for her but a source of strength and a blessing.

(c) as sharer in inheritance:

In respect of inheritance, the Holy Qur'ãn has laid down the law:

12. See references on absolute justice to all and mercifulness towards all (p. 156, 158).

يُوصِيكُمُ اللَّهُ فِي أَوْلَادِكُمْ ۖ لِلذَّكَرِ مِثْلُ حَظِّ الْأُنْثَيَيْنِ ۚ

"Allah (thus) directeth you as regards your children's inheritance: to the male a portion equal to that of two females...." (IV:11).

This, however, has nothing to do with the inferiority of woman, the real reason behind this inequality in share being that the male has been given the role of the bread-winner for the family and, as such, entrusted with the financial burden of himself and his wife and children, while the female has not been given the role of bread-winner and, as such, has not been entrusted with any financial obligations towards anyone, including her husband and children; indeed, not even her own, because that has been made the obligation of the husband. Thus, although getting half of the male's share, she, in most cases, remains at an advantage as compared with the male, rather than suffering loss.

(d) as giver of evidence in lawsuits:

In its law of evidence, the Holy Qur'ãn had laid down:

وَاسْتَشْهِدُوا شَهِيدَيْنِ مِنْ رِجَالِكُمْ ۖ فَإِنْ لَمْ يَكُونَا رَجُلَيْنِ فَرَجُلٌ
وَامْرَأَتَانِ مِمَّنْ تَرْضَوْنَ مِنَ الشُّهَدَاءِ أَنْ تَضِلَّ إِحْدَاهُمَا
فَتُذَكِّرَ إِحْدَاهُمَا الْأُخْرَىٰ ۚ

".....and get two witnesses out of your own men, and if there are not two men, then a man and two women, such as ye chose for witnesses, so that if one of them errs (in her judgment or in her memory), the other can remind her...." (II:282).

This law is based on the fact that unlike man, whose sphere of activity is mostly outside the home and who thereby gains a rich experience of and a sharp judgment about men and things, the natural sphere of activity for the woman is the home, which does not allow her to acquire the same richness of experience and sharpness of judgment regarding the affairs of the outside world. Hence, she is not likely to hold her own under the severe strain of cross-examination, because of which any possible short coming on her part as a witness to a case is required to be made up through a second woman's evidence.

This is the Muslim point of view, deducible from the above verse itself. And it bears no insult for womanhood.

The non-Muslim point of view with respect to woman's evidence is, however, harsh and insulting to her.

In the Judaic law, woman is completely debarred from giving evidence. We are told in the *Jewish Encyclopaedia*, (V, p. 177) that: "The witness must be a man and not woman." Indeed, "let not the testimony of women be admitted, on account of the levity and boldness of their sex." (Josephus: *Antiquities of the Jews*, v, 8:15).

The verdict of the sages of the modern age of enlightenment—of a civilisation that is referred to as "Christian", is:

The fact that women are difficult to deal with under cross-examination is well-known among lawyers, and their skill in drawing red herrings across the path of any enquiry directed against themselves, makes them stubborn and evasive witnesses at all times when they have anything to conceal". (Ludovici: *Woman*, p. 320).

"We are again and again forced to admit", says Bauer, "that a woman is not in a position to judge objectively, without being influenced by her emotions". (*Woman and Love*, I, p. 289).

In the view of Havelock Ellis: "In women deception is almost physiological....in some countries it has led to the legal testimony of women being placed on a lower footing than that of men". (*Man and Woman*, p. 196).

3. The Institution of Marriage:

The Qur'ãnic point of view with regard to the institution of Marriage is based on the following principles and laws:

(i) Interdependence of man and woman in ensuring fullness of life for each other through mutual affection, mutual confidence and mutual protection as husband and wife has been stressed by using a metaphor of profound beauty:

هُنَّ لِبَاسٌ لَّكُمْ وَأَنتُمْ لِبَاسٌ لَّهُنَّ

"....They are a garment unto you, and ye are a garment unto them...." (II:187).

(ii) For those who can afford it, marriage is an obligation:

وَأَنكِحُوا الْأَيَامَىٰ مِنكُمْ وَالصَّالِحِينَ مِنْ عِبَادِكُمْ وَإِمَائِكُمْ ۚ إِن يَكُونُوا فُقَرَاءَ
يُغْنِهِمُ اللَّهُ مِن فَضْلِهِ ۗ وَاللَّهُ وَاسِعٌ عَلِيمٌ

"Marry[13] those among you who are single, and the pious among your slaves, male or female: if they are in poverty, Allah will give them means out of His grace: Allah is of ample means, and He knoweth all things." (XXIV:32)[14]

(iii) Marriage is a social contract:

The word *nikāh*, used for marriage in the Holy Qur'ān, originally means *'aqd*, according to Imam Raghib (vide *Mufradāt al-Qur'ān*); and *'aqd* means contract. Thus the very word *nikāh* implies that marriage is a social contract, and not a sacrament, although it is a sacred contract. Moreover, the Qur'ānic permission to terminate the relation of marriage, if it becomes absolutely impossible for the husband and the wife to continue that relation, proves that the Qur'ān regards marriage as a social contract only.

(iv) Women are not to be treated as chattels:

يَٰٓأَيُّهَا ٱلَّذِينَ ءَامَنُوا۟ لَا يَحِلُّ لَكُمْ أَن تَرِثُوا۟ ٱلنِّسَآءَ كَرْهًا ۖ

---

13. As to those who cannot afford married life, they have been commanded to observe absolute chastity:

وَلْيَسْتَعْفِفِ ٱلَّذِينَ لَا يَجِدُونَ نِكَاحًا حَتَّىٰ يُغْنِيَهُمُ ٱللَّهُ مِن فَضْلِهِۦ ۗ

"Let those who find not the wherewithal for marriage keep themselves chaste, until Allah gives them means out of His grace...." (XXIV:33).

14. Contrast it with the attitude of those religions which advocate celibacy and idolise it as the ideal of perfection, considering sexual satisfaction even in the bond of marriage as positive evil from the spiritual point of view. Thus, in Christianity: "As an institution, Jesus regards marriage as essentially physical and intended only for the present age. Those who were to share in the blessings of the eschatological kingdom would neither marry nor be given in marriage but would be possessed of the non-physical body in the resurrection." (Hastings' *Dictionary of the Bible*, II, p. 138). "It was this outlook on sex which led to the rule that no man or woman, married or unmarried, who had performed the sex act the previous night, should take part in a Church festival or in the Eucharist." (Scott: *History of Prostitution*, pp. 72, 73). "Christianity", writes the sociologist Ludovici "......preaches that sex is to be deplored, to be avoided, and, if possible, negatived. And the Puritan, who may be regarded as the extreme Christian, is notorious for his implacable loathing of sex". (*Woman*, p. 5). It may be observed here in passing that it is this attitude of Christianity that has been responsible for the very dirty crusade of Western writers against Islam's affirmative attitude towards sex.

"O ye who believe! You are forbidden to inherit (as chattels) the women against their will...." (IV:19).

(v) Marriage with persons of certain categories has been prohibited:

The Holy Qur'ãn has prohibited marriage with all those who may stand in the relations of consanguinity, or affinity, or fosterage, in IV:23. Abdur Rahim explains that Qur'ãnic law thus: "By reason of consanguinity a man cannot marry any female ascendant or descendant of his or the daughter of any ascendant, how high soever, or of any descendant, how low soever, or the daughter of his brother or sister or the daughter of a brother's or sister's daughter, and so on. On the ground of affinity he is debarred from marrying a woman who has been the wife of any ascendant of his, and any ascendant or descendant of the wife if marriage has been consummated, or of any woman with whom he has had unlawful connection and any woman who has been the wife of his son or grandson. Generally speaking, fosterage induces the same limits of relationship prohibitive of marriage as consanguinity". (*Muhammadan Jurisprudence*, p. 329).

(vi) Relations between husband and wife have been conceived as based on mutual co-operation, love and compassion:

وَمِنْ اٰيٰتِهٖٓ اَنْ خَلَقَ لَكُمْ مِّنْ اَنْفُسِكُمْ اَزْوَاجًا لِّتَسْكُنُوْٓا اِلَيْهَا وَجَعَلَ بَيْنَكُمْ مَّوَدَّةً وَّرَحْمَةً ۭ اِنَّ فِيْ ذٰلِكَ لَاٰيٰتٍ لِّقَوْمٍ يَّتَفَكَّرُوْنَ ○

"And among His Signs is this, that He created your mates from among yourselves, that ye may dwell in transquillity with them, and He has put love and mercy between your (hearts); verily in that are Signs for those who reflect." (XXX:21).

It means that:—

(*a*) marriage is essentially a spiritual bond of union, rather than a mere physical relationship;

(*b*) marriage should be contracted with the firm resolve of maintaining that relation for life;

(*c*) monogamy should be the ideal[15], because that is the ideal

15. Polygamy has been permitted by the Holy Qur'ãn on humanitarian grounds, under exceptional circumstances, and with restrictive conditions, as we shall see later.

condition in which mutual co-operation, harmony and love can be practised normally and smoothly by the common man.

(vii) Polygamy permitted with severe restrictions:

The only Qur'ãnic verse which contains the permission for polygamous marriage, says:

وَإِنْ خِفْتُمْ أَلَّا تُقْسِطُوا فِي الْيَتٰمٰى فَانْكِحُوا مَا طَابَ لَكُمْ مِّنَ النِّسَآءِ مَثْنٰى
وَثُلٰثَ وَرُبٰعَ فَإِنْ خِفْتُمْ أَلَّا تَعْدِلُوا فَوَاحِدَةً أَوْ مَا مَلَكَتْ أَيْمَانُكُمْ
ذٰلِكَ أَدْنٰى أَلَّا تَعُولُوا ۝

"And if ye fear that ye shall not be able to deal justly with the orphans, marry of the women who seem good to you, two and three and four; and if ye fear that (in case of having more wives than one) ye shall not be able to deal justly (with them) then (marry) only one (free woman) or (a captive) that your right hands possess. That will be more suitable to prevent you from doing injustice." (IV:3).

Important points, worthy of being carefully noted, are:—

(*a*) This verse does not enjoin polygamy, but only permits it.

(*b*) Unrestricted polygamy, which had been rampant among the pre-Qur'ãnic Arabs and many other nations of the world.[16] has been restricted to the maximum of four.[17]

(*c*) The permission relates to situations of emergency[18], and not to normal conditions of life and society.

---

15. "Polygamy", says Roberts, "was the rule among the Eastern peoples before Muhammad's time." (*Social Laws of the Qur'ãn*. p. 8). As for a comprehensive discussion of the history of this institution among different nations of the world, see: *Encyclopaedia of Religion and Ethics*.

16. Fixing the maximum at four seems to be based on the natural law relating to monthly courses, whereby the husband can do justice in respect of conjugal relations even if he has the maximum of four wives.

17. This verse was revealed after the battle of Uhud, which gave rise to a situation of emergency. Appreciable number of Muslim men were killed in the battle, leaving behind orphans and widows, and giving to the preponderance of adult females. Also there were some women captives of war. Polygamy was prescribed for those who were God-fearing and whose sole mission in life was spiritual refinement and pursuit of Divine Pleasure.

(*d*) The permission is based, not on considerations of lust, nor on any benefit accruing to the marrying male, but on the principle of sacrifice—of providing protection and support to orphans, while undergoing a severe tension of dealing with all the wives.

(*e*) The permission is conditioned by one's ability to deal equitably with his wives, which even at the formal level is an extremely difficult condition to fulfil except for those who are thoroughly disciplined, stick to spiritual and moral values above everything else, and enter into marriage for spiritual considerations—for the sake of obtaining Divine Pleasure.

(*f*) Thus this verse, instead of inducing the men to practise polygamy, recommends to them monogamy.

(*g*) Finally, looking at the Qur'ãnic permission for polygamy with an unbiased mind, every rational person is bound to be convinced that in situations of emergency, namely, whenever there is a preponderance of females—as it happens after the wars—and wherever there is the problem of the uncured for and unsolicited widows and orphans, it becomes a moral duty of God-fearing people to practise polygamy, whereby alone the individuals can be saved from disaster and the community can escape the horrors of prostitution.

The verdict of human history in this behalf, coming down to the year 1970, is indisputable.

The *Natal Mercury* (Durban, Sept. 10, 1970) reports thus:—

"The people of a strongly Christian town near Calabar, capital of Nigeria's South-Eastern State, have agreed to relax the one-man-one-wife rule. At a mass meeting recently they decided that every man was free to marry from two to six women at the drastically reduced

---

A. Yusuf Ali says: "Notice the conditional clause about orphans, introducing the rules about marriage. This reminds us of the immediate occasion of the promulgation of this verse. It was after Uhud, when the Muslim community was left with many orphans and widows, and some captives of war. Their treatment was to be governed by principles of the greatest humanity and equity. The occasion is past, but the principles remain. Marry the orphans if you are quite sure that you will in that way protect their interests and their property, with perfect justice to them and to your own dependants, if you have any. If not, make other arrangements for the orphans." (*op.cit.*, p. 179).

price of R 10 a wife. Bride price in the area used to be between R 100 and R 300.

"The reason for the move is that the town has been swarming with unmarried girls and widows since the end of the Nigerian civil war. The town's elders believe that a general return to polygamy will help to keep women from turning to prostitution for a living.

"The decision, almost certain to be approved by the State's military Government, highlights one of the serious social problems now confronting Nigeria in the aftermath of the 30-month civil war.

"Japan and most of Europe faced similar situations after World War II....

"West Germany, which suffered most and made the most rapid post-war economic recovery, is still faced with the problem of surplus women. And the same is true today of Japan and Italy.

"For Nigeria the problem will be especially difficult to solve. The country is still underdeveloped. The surplus women are mostly illiterate.

"The matter is further complicated by the fact that most ex-soldiers now joining the ranks of the unemployed have no other professional training or skills.

"Federal and State leaders agree that a 'liberalisation of marriage law' will go a long way to minimising the problem.

"The main difficulty is the attitude of the Church, still a very powerful influence in the three states in former Eastern Nigeria where the problem is most acute. More than 75 per cent of the population is Christian.

"An Ibo leader told me: 'We would like our people to follow the example of the Calabar people because the problem is really serious in our area. One difficulty, of course, will be economic....But our main difficulty may be with the Christian missions, especially the Roman Catholic Church which still exercises a strong influence on our people. But we hope the Church will close its eyes, so that Christians can marry as many wives as they can afford just as the Muslims and pagans do. I can see no other way out'."

"There is", wrote Dr. Mrs. Annie Besant, the renowned English leader of the Theosophical Movement, "pretended monogamy in the West, but there is really polygamy without responsibility; the 'mistress' is cast out to be the 'woman of the street', for the first lover has no responsibility for her future and she is a hundred times worse off than the sheltered wife and mother in the polygamous home. When we see thousands of miserable women who crowd the streets of Western towns during the night, we must surely feel that it does not lie in the Western mouth to reproach Islam for polygamy. It is better for woman, happier for woman, more respectable for woman, to live in polygamy, united to one man only, with the legitimate child in her arms, and surrounded with respect, than to be seduced, cast out into the street—perhaps with an illegitimate child outside the pale of law—unsheltered and uncared for, to become the victim of any passerby, night after night, rendered incapable of motherhood, despised by all".

(Annie Besant, *The Life and Teachings of Muhammad*, p. 3).

(viii) Polyandry and Neoga ruled out:

Recounting the categories of women with whom marriage is forbidden, the Holy Qur'ãn says:

وَالْمُحْصَنٰتُ مِنَ النِّسَآءِ

"....and (forbidden also) are wedded women (i.e., women having husbands)....." (IV:24).

Thus the holy book repudiates polyandry (or, plurality of husbands) and the Hindu custom of *Neoga* (or, loaning the wife to another person for getting an issue), and the custom of exchanging wives practised by certain savage tribes[18].

(ix) Temporary and 'companionate' marriage prohibited:

Temporary conjugal relations are prompted purely by lust, and in no case for establishing that sublime spiritual relation between man and woman which alone can form the basis for building up the family. Therefore, the Holy Qur'ãn disallows temporary and 'companionate' marriages. It says:

وَأُحِلَّ لَكُمْ مَّا وَرَآءَ ذٰلِكُمْ أَنْ تَبْتَغُوْا بِأَمْوَالِكُمْ مُّحْصِنِيْنَ غَيْرَ مُسٰفِحِيْنَ

".....Except for these (prohibited relations), all others (i.e., other women) are lawful, provided ye seek (them in marriage) with gifts from

18. Refer to *Encyclopaedia of Religion and Ethics*, Vol. I., p. 125.

your property (as dower-money), desiring chastity (in permanent companionship), not lust (in any form of temporary marriage)...."[19] (IV:24).

(x) Dowry enjoined out of regard for woman's dignity[20] *and her economic interest:*

وَآتُوا النِّسَاءَ صَدُقَاتِهِنَّ نِحْلَةً ۚ

"And give the woman[21] (on marriage) their dower as a free gift...." (IV:4).

(B) Duties of Husband and Wife Towards One Another

1. *Duties of the Husband*:

Preliminary:

The Holy Qur'ãn stresses the extraordinary importance of, and hence the duty of extreme carefulness about, the relationship of marriage:

وَاتَّقُوا اللَّهَ الَّذِي تَسَاءَلُونَ بِهِ وَالْأَرْحَامَ ۚ إِنَّ اللَّهَ كَانَ عَلَيْكُمْ رَقِيبًا ○

"....and be careful of your duty to Allah, through Whom ye demand (your mutual rights), and to the wombs. Verily Allah ever watches over you." (IV:1).

It should be noted here that in the Arabic text the word 'womb' has been coupled grammatically with the word 'Allah' in respect of the observance of carefulness in duty, thus highlighting the position of the mother and the wife in the Qur'ãnic teaching.

---

19. "Real satisfaction", says Pollens, "Come not from mere sexual experience but from a relationship which is lasting and continuous and which is built on feelings of affection, devotion and tenderness." (*The Sex Criminal*, p. 196).

20. Says Abdur Rahim: "It is not a consideration proceeding from the husband for the contract of marriage, but it is an obligation imposed by the law on the husband as a mark of respect for the wife, as is evident from the fact that the non-specification of the dower at the time of marriage does not affect the validity of the marriage." (*Muhammadan Jurisprudence*, p. 334).

21. This should be clearly distinguished from the evil custom of paying the price of the bride to her parents, a custom prevalent in ancient times in many communities of the world, for which refer to Westermarck's *Short History of Marriage*, pp. 166-169.

(i) Duties of Commission:

(a) *Protecting and maintaining the wife stressed as an unavoidable function of the husband; hence fulfilments of this function is duty:*

اَلرِّجَالُ قَوّٰمُوْنَ عَلَى النِّسَآءِ بِمَا فَضَّلَ اللّٰهُ بَعْضَهُمْ عَلٰى بَعْضٍ وَّبِمَآ اَنْفَقُوْا مِنْ اَمْوَالِهِمْ

"Men are the protectors and maintainers of women, because Allah has given the one more (strength) than the other, and because they support them from their means....." (IV:34).

(b) *Treating the wife with kindness and equity enjoined:*

وَعَاشِرُوْهُنَّ بِالْمَعْرُوْفِ

"....and (O Believers!) live with them (*i.e.,* the wives) on a footing of kindness and equity....." (IV:19).

(c) *Toleration of the faults and the shortcomings*[22] *of the wife, enjoined:*

فَاِنْ كَرِهْتُمُوْهُنَّ فَعَسٰۤى اَنْ تَكْرَهُوْا شَيْـًٔا وَّيَجْعَلَ اللّٰهُ فِيْهِ خَيْرًا كَثِيْرًا

".....If ye take a dislike to them (i.e., the wives), it may be that ye dislike a thing, and Allah brings about through it a great good."(IV:19).

(d) *Spiritualisation of physical relation, abstaining from damaging wife's dignity through unnatural offence, and keeping the duty of parenthood in view with due regard to wife's health enjoined:*

نِسَآؤُكُمْ حَرْثٌ لَّكُمْ فَاْتُوْا حَرْثَكُمْ اَنّٰى شِئْتُمْ وَقَدِّمُوْا لِاَنْفُسِكُمْ وَاتَّقُوا اللّٰهَ وَاعْلَمُوْۤا اَنَّكُمْ مُّلٰقُوْهُ وَبَشِّرِ الْمُؤْمِنِيْنَ

"Your wives are a tilth unto you (like the soil which accepts the seed and brings forth the plants). So go in unto your tilth (and not anywhere

22. According to Nemilov: "Anyone familiar with the physiology and biology of woman will be less annoyed and irritated at her sudden change of mood, allegedly unreasonable flares of temper, her unmotivated acts. Understanding this, man will deeply sympathise with the bearers of the egg cells who, having the same aspirations and claims upon life, are burdened with more difficult biological tasks." (*Biological Tragedy of Woman*: pp. 187, 188).

else) when and in what manner ye like; but send (good deeds) before you for your souls; and fear Allah (in respect of your moral and spiritual obligations towards your wife, towards yourselves and towards the offspring that you may beget as a consequence); and know that ye will (one day) meet Him. And give (O Muhammad) glad tidings to the Believers (i.e., those who, as believers in the Qur'ãnic Guidance, remain devoted to spiritual and moral values even in carnal pleasures)." (II:223).

A commentator of the Holy Qur'ãn comments on this verse thus:—

"Sex is not a thing to be ashamed of, or to be treated lightly, or to be indulged to excess. It is as solemn a fact as any in life. It is compared to a husbandman's tilth; it is a serious affair to him: he sows the seed in order to reap the harvest. But he chooses his own time and mode of cultivation. He does not sow out of season nor cultivate in a manner which will injure or exhaust the soil. He is wise and considerate and does not run riot. Coming from the simile to human beings, every kind of mutual consideration is required, but above all, we must remember that even in these matters there is a spiritual aspect. We must never forget our souls, and that we are responsible to God.

"It was carnal-minded men who invented the doctrine of original sin: 'Behold', says the Psalmist, 'I was shapen in iniquity, and in sin did my mother conceive me' (*Psalms*, li:5). This is entirely repudiated by Islam, in which the office of father and mother is held in the highest veneration. Every child of pure love is born pure. Celibacy is not necessarily a virtue, and may be a vice". (A. Yusuf Ali, *op.cit.*, p. 88).

(e) *Concern for the welfare of the wife in all respects, specially the spiritual, stressed, and hence looking after the physical, mental, moral, spiritual and economic welfare of the wife is duty:*

The Holy Qur'ãn has taught the prayer:

رَبَّنَا هَبْ لَنَا مِنْ أَزْوَاجِنَا وَذُرِّيَّٰتِنَا قُرَّةَ أَعْيُنٍ وَاجْعَلْنَا لِلْمُتَّقِينَ إِمَامًا

"....Our Lord! *Grant to us the comfort of our eyes from our wives* and our offspring, and give us (the grace to lead the righteous." (XXV:74).

Moreover, the Muslim husband and fathers have been entrusted with the following duty:

يَا أَيُّهَا الَّذِينَ آمَنُوا قُوا أَنفُسَكُمْ وَأَهْلِيكُمْ نَارًا

"O ye who believe! protect yourselves and *your wives* and children from a (spiritual) Fire...." (LXVI:6).

While expounding the teaching contained in these verses with respect to "duties", in the section on "Duties to the Offspring", we have already seen that these verses relate to the duty of ensuring the physical, mental, moral, spiritual and economic welfare. (See. p. 172).

(ii) <u>*Duty of Omission*</u>:

There are several duties of omission which are directly and indirectly contained in the foregoing and the forthcoming discussions relating to the "Position of Woman" and the "Husband-Wife relation". One specific duty, which is not contained there, may, however, be mentioned here.

Accusing the wife falsely, or without proper evidence, has been regarded as a heinous crime; hence to abstain from it is duty[23]:

The Holy Qur'ãn says:

وَالَّذِينَ يَرْمُونَ الْمُحْصَنَاتِ ثُمَّ لَمْ يَأْتُوا بِأَرْبَعَةِ شُهَدَاءَ فَاجْلِدُوهُمْ
ثَمَانِينَ جَلْدَةً وَلَا تَقْبَلُوا لَهُمْ شَهَادَةً أَبَدًا ۚ وَأُولَٰئِكَ هُمُ الْفَاسِقُونَ

"And those who accuse clean women (of unchastity) and then produce not four (eye) witnesses, scourge them with eighty stripes and accept not their testimony for ever. And these! they are the transgressors." (XXIV:4).[24]

2. *Duties of the Wife:*

<u>Of Commission and Omission</u>:

(a) *Submissiveness to the husband as the head of the family—not in servile manner but with the spirit of dignified maintenance of harmony;*

(b) *guarding the conjugal rights of the husband through*

---

23. It is also a duty of all men towards all women.

24. The procedure of law in case of accusation of the wife by the husband of adultery, has been mentioned in the verses that follow. We shall deal with it when discussing punishments.

abstaining from doing anything that may, in the least measure, violate her chastity;

(c) *protecting the prestige and the property of her husband:*

The above three virtues form the unavoidable functions of the righteous wife, according to the Holy Qur'ãn; and hence constitute the basic duties of the wife.

The Holy Qur'ãn says:

فَالصّٰلِحٰتُ قٰنِتٰتٌ حٰفِظٰتٌ لِّلْغَيْبِ بِمَا حَفِظَ اللّٰهُ ؕ

"....So the righteous women are obedient (to God and submissive to their husbands), and guard in (the husband's) absence what Allah would have them guard (i.e., their chastity and the prestige and property of the husband)...." (IV:34).

(C) Laws Relating to Abnormal Situations and the Respective Duties:

1. *Efforts of the husband, in case of wife's refractoriness and fear of desertion, to bring her to the path of rectitude:*

وَالّٰتِيْ تَخَافُوْنَ نُشُوْزَهُنَّ فَعِظُوْهُنَّ وَاهْجُرُوْهُنَّ فِي الْمَضَاجِعِ وَ
اضْرِبُوْهُنَّ ۚ فَاِنْ اَطَعْنَكُمْ فَلَا تَبْغُوْا عَلَيْهِنَّ سَبِيْلًا ؕ اِنَّ اللّٰهَ كَانَ
عَلِيًّا كَبِيْرًا ○

".....As to those (wives) on whose part ye fear rebellion and desertion admonish them (first); (in case that does not reform their conduct) banish them to beds apart; (lastly, if they still prove to be incorrigible, ye are permitted to) beat them (with a tooth-brush or something like it, in order to awaken in them the sentiment of self-respect and the consciousness of the seriousness of their guilt in itself and in respect of its consequences for the family-life, and in a manner which causes no injury or pain to them). Then if they obey you (by returning to the path of rectitude), seek not a way (of harassment or ill-treatment) against them. Verily, Allah is Most High, Great (wherefore it does not behove you to tyrannise over your wives)." (IV:34).

This verse speaks of serious breach in loyalty to the marital bond on the part of the wife. Now, there can be three ways: (1) to divorce the wife offhand; (2) to take the matter to a court of law; (3) to deal with it at personal level. The Holy Qur'ãn prefers the last, and that for obvious reasons. The first is an extreme measure, and its consequences may be very damaging for the wife or for the family as a whole. The second alternative is scandalous and means 'washing dirty linen' in public. It invites accusations and counter-accusations, and it is specially damaging for the wife. It is the third alternative only, the one prescribed by the Holy Qur'ãn, which is the best in the interest of the wife and of public morality.

In connection with beating the rebellious wife, there are certain important facts which should be borne in mind:

Firstly, to resort to it as a last remedy has been merely *permitted, and not made obligatory.*

Secondly, although permitted in theory, it has been positively discouraged in practice, as, for instance, the Holy Prophet (Peace be on him), who alone has the original right to interpret the teachings of the Qur'ãn and whose interpretation alone can be absolutely correct, says: "You will not find these men (who beat their wives) as the good ones among you."[25] Again: "No one should ever beat his wife with a whip like a slave (who was beaten with the whip by non-Muslim masters)."[26] Still again: "The best of you is he who is best to his wife."[27]

Thirdly, it has been made absolutely clear by the Holy Prophet (Peace be on him) that the beating should be of a symbolic or norminal type. It should be "striking without injury of pain",[28] and it should be "with a tooth-brush or something like it."[29]

Fourthly, the function of the Holy Qur'ãn is to provide guidance to human beings belonging to all stages of social evolution. Consequently, this remedy, while it may be unthinkable in respect of people belonging to the higher stages of social evolution, may yet form the only proper and 'natural' corrective instrument in the case of those who stand at the lower ladders of social and psychological refinement. In fact, it has not only formed a vital part of marital life but has been regarded as a positive

---

25. Abû Dã'ûd: *Sunan*, vol. I, p. 292; etc.

26. Bukhãrî: *Sahîh*, vol. II, p. 784.

27. Ibn Mãjah: *Sunan; Bãb Husn ma'ãshrat al-Nisã*, p. 142.

28. Ibn Mãjah: Sunan, p. 133. Muslim: *Sahîh*, vol. I, p. 291.

29. See Tabarî's *Tafsir*, vol. V, p. 41, Egyptian edition.

contribution to marital success among many a community of the world, who have believed in the eminent philosopher Nietzsche's verdict: "When you go to a woman forget not your whip." And the testimony in this behalf is irrefutable.

Krafft-Ebing says: "Among peoples of a lower class of culture the subjection of woman is extended even to brutality. This flagrant proof of dependence is felt by woman even with sexual pleasure and accepted as a token of love". (*Psychopathia Sexualis*, p. 211).

" Among the Slaves of the lower class the wives feel hurt if they are not beaten by their husbands; the peasant women in some parts of Hungary do not think they are loved by their husbands until they have received the first box on the ear; among the Italian community a wife, if not beaten by her husband, regards him as a fool." (*Encyclopaedia of Religion and Ethics*, VIII: p. 156).

"The Englishman's privilege of beating his wife with a stick not thicker than his thumb, has become rather favourite." (Ludovici: *Woman*, p. 13).

According to the school of thought founded by Freud, the scientist, the father of Psychoanalysis, and the idol of the rebels against religion: "Helence Dentach has elaborated Freud's assumption and generalised it in calling masochism the elemental power in feminine mental life. She contends that what woman ultimately wants in intercourse is to be raped and violated, what she wants in mental life is to be humiliated: menstruation is significant to woman because it feeds masochistic fantasies: childbirth represents the climax of masochistic satisfaction." (Horney: *New Ways in Psychoanalysis*, p. 110).

2. *Procedure in case of serious disagreement and conflict between the husband and the wife:*

(i) Effort at reconciliation through arbitration by a Family Council composed of one representative from each side[30], enjoined:

وَإِنْ خِفْتُمْ شِقَاقَ بَيْنِهِمَا فَابْعَثُوا حَكَمًا مِّنْ أَهْلِهِ وَحَكَمًا مِّنْ
أَهْلِهَا ۚ إِن يُرِيدَا إِصْلَاحًا يُوَفِّقِ اللَّهُ بَيْنَهُمَا ۗ إِنَّ اللَّهَ كَانَ عَلِيمًا
خَبِيرًا ۝

"And if ye (O Muslims) fear a breach between them twain (i.e.,

30. Mark the healthy nature of this prescription, wherein scandal as well as chicaneries of the law have been avoided and the sanctity of the husband-wife relation has been fully maintained.

the husband and the wife), appoint two arbiters, one from his family, and the other from hers (—the two knowing the mentalities, the faults and the merits of both—); then if the two (arbiters) wish for rectification (i.e., strive for reconciliation earnestly and justly), Allah shall bring about harmony between the twain: For Allah hath full knowledge, and is acquainted with all things." (IV:35).

(ii)

(*a*) While lending its weight to the sanctity of the marriage-relation, the Holy Qur'ãn gives due consideration to the weaknesses and aberrations of human nature. Therefore, it allows divorce as a necessary evil[31], when that becomes the only remedy for rectifying a situation of irreconcilable incompatibility.

(*b*) In allowing the divorce, however, the Holy Qur'ãn prescribes a procedure which aims at eliminating the evils of idiosyncrasy and availing every possible opportunity and means for reconciliation before the final repture,—the procedure consisting in abstention from pronouncing divorce during the menstrual period, which is the period of least mutual husband-wife attraction, and pronouncing it in three stages at intervals of one month each, thereby preventing hasty step and providing the parties repeated opportunity for cool deliberation.

(*c*) Though pronouncement of divorce has been placed in the hands of the husband, the wife has also been given the right to sue for, and obtain, divorce.[32]

(*d*) In case of divorce, again the Holy Qur'ãn emphasises with full force the safeguarding of the welfare of the wife and treatment of the wife with generosity.

(*e*) The Qur'ãnic teachings is also emphatic in safeguarding the welfare of the unborn child, if that may be the case.

(*f*) When the marriage tie has been *finally* dissolved, the husband is not permitted to take back his wife, until she has married someone else sincerely and has thereafter become a widow or a divorce. This injunction is meant to check husbands from making fun of marriage, which is a

31. Cf. The Holy Prophet's exposition of the Qur'ãnic standpoint: "Of all things permitted by law, divorce is the most hateful in the sight of God." (Abu Dã'ûd: *Sunan*, XIII:3).

32. Marriage being a social contract, the Islamic law gives to the wife also the right to deprive the husband of the prerogative of pronouncing the divorce at his will. Says Abdur Rahim: "It is open to a woman at the time of marriage or subsequently thereto to stipulate for their (*i.e.*, husband's rights) curtailment or to get some of them transferred to herself, such as the right to dissolve the marriage." (*Muhammadan Jurisprudence*, p. 328).

serious affair according to the Holy Qur'ān.

(*g*) A period of waiting or probation, has been prescribed for the divorced women as a healthy gap in their sexual life, and for saving them from taking any hasty step in connection with their next marriage (which is necessary after the emotional disturbance caused by the shock of divorce), and for safeguarding the interests of the unborn child, if any.

(*h*) Cessation of relations with the wife without freeing her from the marriage-tie has been prohibited.

The following verses of the Holy Qur'ān contain injunctions in respect of the above:

يٰٓاَيُّهَا النَّبِيُّ اِذَا طَلَّقْتُمُ النِّسَآءَ فَطَلِّقُوْهُنَّ لِعِدَّتِهِنَّ وَ اَحْصُوا
الْعِدَّةَ ۚ وَاتَّقُوا اللّٰهَ رَبَّكُمْ ۚ لَا تُخْرِجُوْهُنَّ مِنْۢ بُيُوْتِهِنَّ وَ لَا يَخْرُجْنَ
اِلَّآ اَنْ يَّاْتِيْنَ بِفَاحِشَةٍ مُّبَيِّنَةٍ ۚ وَ تِلْكَ حُدُوْدُ اللّٰهِ ۚ وَ مَنْ
يَّتَعَدَّ حُدُوْدَ اللّٰهِ فَقَدْ ظَلَمَ نَفْسَهٗ ۚ لَا تَدْرِيْ لَعَلَّ اللّٰهَ يُحْدِثُ
بَعْدَ ذٰلِكَ اَمْرًا ۝ فَاِذَا بَلَغْنَ اَجَلَهُنَّ فَاَمْسِكُوْهُنَّ بِمَعْرُوْفٍ
اَوْ فَارِقُوْهُنَّ بِمَعْرُوْفٍ وَّ اَشْهِدُوْا ذَوَيْ عَدْلٍ مِّنْكُمْ وَ اَقِيْمُوا
الشَّهَادَةَ لِلّٰهِ ۚ ذٰلِكُمْ يُوْعَظُ بِهٖ مَنْ كَانَ يُؤْمِنُ بِاللّٰهِ وَ الْيَوْمِ
الْاٰخِرِ ۚ وَ مَنْ يَّتَّقِ اللّٰهَ يَجْعَلْ لَّهٗ مَخْرَجًا ۝ وَّ يَرْزُقْهُ مِنْ حَيْثُ
لَا يَحْتَسِبُ ۚ وَمَنْ يَّتَوَكَّلْ عَلَى اللّٰهِ فَهُوَ حَسْبُهٗ ۚ اِنَّ اللّٰهَ بَالِغُ اَمْرِهٖ ۚ قَدْ
جَعَلَ اللّٰهُ لِكُلِّ شَيْءٍ قَدْرًا ۝ وَ الّٰٓـِٔيْ يَئِسْنَ مِنَ الْمَحِيْضِ مِنْ نِّسَآئِكُمْ
اِنِ ارْتَبْتُمْ فَعِدَّتُهُنَّ ثَلٰثَةُ اَشْهُرٍ ۙ وَّ الّٰٓـِٔيْ لَمْ يَحِضْنَ ۚ وَ اُولَاتُ
الْاَحْمَالِ اَجَلُهُنَّ اَنْ يَّضَعْنَ حَمْلَهُنَّ ۚ وَ مَنْ يَّتَّقِ اللّٰهَ يَجْعَلْ لَّهٗ
مِنْ اَمْرِهٖ يُسْرًا ۝ ذٰلِكَ اَمْرُ اللّٰهِ اَنْزَلَهٗٓ اِلَيْكُمْ ۚ وَمَنْ يَّتَّقِ اللّٰهَ
يُكَفِّرْ عَنْهُ سَيِّاٰتِهٖ وَيُعْظِمْ لَهٗٓ اَجْرًا ۝ اَسْكِنُوْهُنَّ مِنْ حَيْثُ
سَكَنْتُمْ مِّنْ وُّجْدِكُمْ وَ لَا تُضَآرُّوْهُنَّ لِتُضَيِّقُوْا عَلَيْهِنَّ ۚ وَاِنْ كُنَّ
اُولَاتِ حَمْلٍ فَاَنْفِقُوْا عَلَيْهِنَّ حَتّٰى يَضَعْنَ حَمْلَهُنَّ ۚ فَاِنْ اَرْضَعْنَ
لَكُمْ فَاٰتُوْهُنَّ اُجُوْرَهُنَّ ۚ وَ اْتَمِرُوْا بَيْنَكُمْ بِمَعْرُوْفٍ ۚ وَ اِنْ تَعَاسَرْتُمْ
فَسَتُرْضِعُ لَهٗٓ اُخْرٰى ۝ لِيُنْفِقْ ذُوْ سَعَةٍ مِّنْ سَعَتِهٖ ۚ وَمَنْ قُدِرَ عَلَيْهِ
رِزْقُهٗ فَلْيُنْفِقْ مِمَّآ اٰتٰىهُ اللّٰهُ ۚ لَا يُكَلِّفُ اللّٰهُ نَفْسًا اِلَّا مَآ اٰتٰىهَا ۚ
سَيَجْعَلُ اللّٰهُ بَعْدَ عُسْرٍ يُّسْرًا ۝

" O Prophet! When ye (the Muslims) do divorce women, divorce them at their prescribed periods, and count (accurately) their prescribed periods; and fear Allah your Lord: and turn them not out of their houses, nor shall they (themselves) leave, except in case they are guilty of some open lewdness; those are the limits set by Allah: and any who transgresses the limits of Allah, does verily wrong his (own) soul: thou knowest not if perchance Allah will bring about thereafter some new situation.

"Thus when they fulfil their term appointed, either take them back on equitable terms or part with them on equitable terms; and take for witness two persons from among you, endued with justice, and establish the evidence (as) before Allah. Such is the admonition given to him who believes in Allah and the Last Day. And for those who fear Allah, He (ever) prepares a way out.

"And He provides for him from (sources) he never could imagine. And if anyone puts his trust in Allah, sufficient is (Allah) for him. For Allah will surely accomplish His purpose. Verily, for all things has Allah appointed a due proportion.

"Such of your women as have passed the age of monthly courses, for them the prescribed period, if ye have any doubt, is three months, and for those who have no courses (it is the same): For those who carry (life within their wombs), their period is until they deliver their burdens: and for those who fear Allah, He will make their path easy.

"That is the Command of Allah, which He has sent down to you: and if anyone fears Allah, He will remove his ills from him and will enlarge his reward.

"Let the women live (in *'Iddat*), in the same style as ye live, according to your means: Annoy them not, so as to restrict them. And if they carry (life in their wombs), then spend (your substance) on them until they deliver their burden: and if they suckle your (offspring), give them their recompense: And take mutual counsel together, according to what is just and reasonable, And if ye find yourselves in difficulties, let another woman suckle (the child) on the (father's) behalf.

"Let the man of means spend according to his means: and the man whose resources are restricted, let him spend according to what Allah has given him. Allah puts no burden on any person beyond what He has given him After a difficulty, Allah will soon grant relief." (LXV:1-7).

وَالْمُطَلَّقٰتُ يَتَرَبَّصْنَ بِاَنْفُسِهِنَّ ثَلٰثَةَ قُرُوْٓءٍ ؕ وَلَا يَحِلُّ لَهُنَّ اَنْ يَّكْتُمْنَ
مَا خَلَقَ اللّٰهُ فِىْٓ اَرْحَامِهِنَّ اِنْ كُنَّ يُؤْمِنَّ بِاللّٰهِ وَالْيَوْمِ الْاٰخِرِ ؕ وَ بُعُوْلَتُهُنَّ
اَحَقُّ بِرَدِّهِنَّ فِىْ ذٰلِكَ اِنْ اَرَادُوْٓا اِصْلَاحًا ؕ وَلَهُنَّ مِثْلُ الَّذِىْ عَلَيْهِنَّ
بِالْمَعْرُوْفِ ۪ وَلِلرِّجَالِ عَلَيْهِنَّ دَرَجَةٌ ؕ وَاللّٰهُ عَزِيْزٌ حَكِيْمٌ ۝ اَلطَّلَاقُ مَرَّتٰنِ
فَاِمْسَاكٌ ۢ بِمَعْرُوْفٍ اَوْ تَسْرِيْحٌ ۢ بِاِحْسَانٍ ؕ وَلَا يَحِلُّ لَكُمْ اَنْ تَاْخُذُوْا مِمَّآ
اٰتَيْتُمُوْهُنَّ شَيْـًٔا اِلَّآ اَنْ يَّخَافَآ اَلَّا يُقِيْمَا حُدُوْدَ اللّٰهِ ؕ فَاِنْ خِفْتُمْ اَلَّا
يُقِيْمَا حُدُوْدَ اللّٰهِ ۙ فَلَا جُنَاحَ عَلَيْهِمَا فِيْمَا افْتَدَتْ بِهٖ ؕ تِلْكَ حُدُوْدُ
اللّٰهِ فَلَا تَعْتَدُوْهَا ۚ وَمَنْ يَّتَعَدَّ حُدُوْدَ اللّٰهِ فَاُولٰٓئِكَ هُمُ الظّٰلِمُوْنَ ۝
فَاِنْ طَلَّقَهَا فَلَا تَحِلُّ لَهٗ مِنْ ۢ بَعْدُ حَتّٰى تَنْكِحَ زَوْجًا غَيْرَهٗ ؕ فَاِنْ طَلَّقَهَا
فَلَا جُنَاحَ عَلَيْهِمَآ اَنْ يَّتَرَاجَعَآ اِنْ ظَنَّآ اَنْ يُّقِيْمَا حُدُوْدَ اللّٰهِ ؕ وَتِلْكَ
حُدُوْدُ اللّٰهِ يُبَيِّنُهَا لِقَوْمٍ يَّعْلَمُوْنَ ۝ وَاِذَا طَلَّقْتُمُ النِّسَآءَ فَبَلَغْنَ اَجَلَهُنَّ
فَاَمْسِكُوْهُنَّ بِمَعْرُوْفٍ اَوْ سَرِّحُوْهُنَّ بِمَعْرُوْفٍ ۪ وَّلَا تُمْسِكُوْهُنَّ ضِرَارًا
لِّتَعْتَدُوْا ۚ وَمَنْ يَّفْعَلْ ذٰلِكَ فَقَدْ ظَلَمَ نَفْسَهٗ ؕ وَلَا تَتَّخِذُوْٓا اٰيٰتِ اللّٰهِ
هُزُوًا ؗ وَّاذْكُرُوْا نِعْمَتَ اللّٰهِ عَلَيْكُمْ وَمَآ اَنْزَلَ عَلَيْكُمْ مِّنَ الْكِتٰبِ وَ
الْحِكْمَةِ يَعِظُكُمْ بِهٖ ؕ وَاتَّقُوا اللّٰهَ وَاعْلَمُوْٓا اَنَّ اللّٰهَ بِكُلِّ شَىْءٍ عَلِيْمٌ ۝
وَاِذَا طَلَّقْتُمُ النِّسَآءَ فَبَلَغْنَ اَجَلَهُنَّ فَلَا تَعْضُلُوْهُنَّ اَنْ يَّنْكِحْنَ
اَزْوَاجَهُنَّ اِذَا تَرَاضَوْا بَيْنَهُمْ بِالْمَعْرُوْفِ ؕ ذٰلِكَ يُوْعَظُ بِهٖ مَنْ كَانَ مِنْكُمْ
يُؤْمِنُ بِاللّٰهِ وَالْيَوْمِ الْاٰخِرِ ؕ ذٰلِكُمْ اَزْكٰى لَكُمْ وَاَطْهَرُ ؕ وَاللّٰهُ يَعْلَمُ وَ
اَنْتُمْ لَا تَعْلَمُوْنَ ۝

"Divorced women shall wait concerning themselves for three monthly periods. Nor is it lawful for them to hide what Allah hath created in their wombs, if they have faith in Allah and the Last Day. And their husbands have the better right to take them back in that period, if they wish for reconciliation. And women shall have rights similar to the rights against them, according to what is equitable; but men have a degree (of advantage) over them. And Allah is Exalted, Wise.

"A divorce is only permissible twice: After that, the parties should either hold together on equitable terms, or separate with kindness. It is not lawful for you (men) to take back any of your gifts (from your wives), except when both parties fear that they would be unable to keep the limits ordained by Allah. If ye (judges) do indeed fear that they would be unable to keep the limits ordained by Allah, there is no blame on either of them if she gives something for her freedom. These are the limits ordained by Allah; so do not transgress them. If any do transgress the limits ordained by Allah, such persons wrong (themselves as well as others).

"So if a husband divorce his wife (irrevocably), he cannot, after that, re-marry her until after she has married another husband and he has divorced her. In that case there is no blame on either of them if they re-unite, provided they feel that they can keep the limits ordained by Allah. Such are the limits ordained by Allah, which He makes plain to those who understand.

"When ye divorce women, and they fulfil their term, either take them back on equitable terms or set them free with kindness; but do not take them back to injure them, or to take undue advantage; if anyone does that, he wrongs his own soul. Do not treat Allah's Signs as a jest, but solemnly rehearse Allah's favours on you, and the fact that He sent down to you the Book and the Wisdom for your instruction. And fear Allah, and know that Allah is well acquainted with all things.

"When ye divorce women, and they fulfil their term, do not prevent them from marrying their (former) husbands, if they mutually agree on equitable terms. This instruction is for all amongst you, who believe in Allah and the Last Day. That is (the course making for) most virtue and purity amongst you. And Allah knows, and ye know not."
(II:228-232).

وَلِلْمُطَلَّقٰتِ مَتَاعٌۢ بِالْمَعْرُوْفِ ۭ حَقًّا عَلَي الْمُتَّقِيْنَ ○

"For divorced women maintenance (should be provided) on a reasonable (scale). This is a duty on the righteous." (II:241).

لَا جُنَاحَ عَلَيْكُمْ اِنْ طَلَّقْتُمُ النِّسَاۗءَ مَا لَمْ تَمَسُّوْھُنَّ اَوْ تَفْرِضُوْا لَهُنَّ فَرِيْضَةً ښ
وَّمَتِّعُوْھُنَّ ۚ عَلَي الْمُوْسِعِ قَدَرُهٗ وَعَلَي الْمُقْتِرِ قَدَرُهٗ ۚ مَتَاعًۢا بِالْمَعْرُوْفِ ۚ
حَقًّا عَلَي الْمُحْسِنِيْنَ ○ وَاِنْ طَلَّقْتُمُوْھُنَّ مِنْ قَبْلِ اَنْ تَمَسُّوْھُنَّ وَقَدْ
فَرَضْتُمْ لَهُنَّ فَرِيْضَةً فَنِصْفُ مَا فَرَضْتُمْ اِلَّآ اَنْ يَّعْفُوْنَ اَوْ يَعْفُوَا
الَّذِيْ بِيَدِهٖ عُقْدَةُ النِّكَاحِ ۭ وَاَنْ تَعْفُوْٓا اَقْرَبُ لِلتَّقْوٰى ۭ وَلَا
تَنْسَوُا الْفَضْلَ بَيْنَكُمْ ۭ اِنَّ اللّٰهَ بِمَا تَعْمَلُوْنَ بَصِيْرٌ ○

"There is no blame on you if ye divorce women before consummation or the fixation of their dower; but bestow on them (a suitable gift), the wealthy according to his means, and the poor according to his means;—a gift of a reasonable amount is due from those who wish to do the right thing.

"And if ye divorce them before consummation, but after the fixation of a dower for them, then the half of the dower (is due to them), unless they remit it or the man's half is remitted by him in whose hands is the marriage tie; and the remission (of the man's half) is nearest to righteousness. And do not forget liberality between yourselves. For Allah sees well all that ye do." (II:236, 237).

وَإِنْ أَرَدتُّمُ اسْتِبْدَالَ زَوْجٍ مَّكَانَ زَوْجٍ وَآتَيْتُمْ إِحْدَاهُنَّ قِنطَارًا
فَلَا تَأْخُذُوا مِنْهُ شَيْئًا ۚ أَتَأْخُذُونَهُ بُهْتَانًا وَإِثْمًا مُّبِينًا ○ وَكَيْفَ
تَأْخُذُونَهُ وَقَدْ أَفْضَىٰ بَعْضُكُمْ إِلَىٰ بَعْضٍ وَأَخَذْنَ مِنكُم مِّيثَاقًا غَلِيظًا ○

"But if ye decide to take one wife in place of another, even if ye had given the latter a whole treasure for dower, take not the least bit back: would ye take it by slander and a manifest wrong?

"And how could ye take it when ye have gone in unto each other, and they have taken (from you) a solemn covenant?" (IV:20-21).

وَإِنِ امْرَأَةٌ خَافَتْ مِن بَعْلِهَا نُشُوزًا أَوْ إِعْرَاضًا فَلَا جُنَاحَ عَلَيْهِمَا
أَن يُصْلِحَا بَيْنَهُمَا صُلْحًا ۚ وَالصُّلْحُ خَيْرٌ ۗ وَأُحْضِرَتِ الْأَنفُسُ الشُّحَّ ۚ وَإِن
تُحْسِنُوا وَتَتَّقُوا فَإِنَّ اللَّهَ كَانَ بِمَا تَعْمَلُونَ خَبِيرًا ○ وَلَن تَسْتَطِيعُوا أَن
تَعْدِلُوا بَيْنَ النِّسَاءِ وَلَوْ حَرَصْتُمْ ۖ فَلَا تَمِيلُوا كُلَّ الْمَيْلِ فَتَذَرُوهَا
كَالْمُعَلَّقَةِ ۚ وَإِن تُصْلِحُوا وَتَتَّقُوا فَإِنَّ اللَّهَ كَانَ غَفُورًا رَّحِيمًا ○ وَ
إِن يَتَفَرَّقَا يُغْنِ اللَّهُ كُلًّا مِّن سَعَتِهِ ۚ وَكَانَ اللَّهُ وَاسِعًا حَكِيمًا ○

"If a wife fears cruelty or desertion on her husband's part, there is no blame on them if they arrange an amicable settlement between themselves; and such settlement is best; even though men's souls are swayed by greed. And if ye do good and practise self-restraint, Allah is well acquainted with all that ye do.

"Ye are never able to be fair and just as between women even if it is your ardent desire: But turn not away (from a woman) altogether, so as to leave her (as it were) hanging (in the air).[33] If ye come to a friendly understanding and practise self-restraint, Allah is Oft-Forgiving, Most Merciful.

"If they disagree (and must part), Allah will provide abundance for all from His all-reaching bounty: For Allah careth for all and is Wise." (IV:128-130).

(4) Duties Towards Relatives in General

(*i*) Duties of Commission :

The Holy Qur'ãn has enjoined looking after the well-being of one's relatives—sisters, brothers, aunts, uncles, cousins, nieces, nephews, grandparents, grandsons, grand daughters, etc.,—and rendering to them all possible assistance with the purest of motives. In that connection:

(a) It emphasises through conscientiousness in respect of the ties of kinship:

وَاتَّقُوا اللَّهَ الَّذِي تَسَاءَلُونَ بِهِ وَالْأَرْحَامَ

"....and reverence Allah in Whom ye claim (your rights) and (reverence) the wombs (i.e., the ties of kinship)...." (IV:1)

(b) It places the duty of doing good to one's kith and kin immediately next to the duty of doing good to parents—which stands at the highest in the category of social duties—, thus highlighting the great importance of the duty of kith and kin.

---

33. We may refer here also to the customs of *'Ilã* and *Zihãr*, mentioned in the Holy Qur'ãn in II:226 and in XXXIII:4; LVIII:2-4 respectively. They were practised by the pagan Arabs and were repudiated by Islam.

'Ilã is the 'vow of abstinence from one's wife'. "It was a recognised pre-Islamic form of repudiating one's wife and a denial of her rights for a period, definite or indefinite. In Islam the legal effect of such conduct amounts to a single irrevocable divorce". (Abdul Majid Daryabadi, *op.cit.*, p. 71).

Zihãr "was ane evil Arab custom, by which the husband selfishly deprived his wife of her conjugal rights and yet kept her tied to himself like a slave without freeing her to remarry. He pronounced words importing that she was like his mother. After that she could not demand conjugal rights but was not free from his control and could not contract another marriage. See also LVIII:1-5, where this is condemned in the strongest terms and punishment is provided for it. A man sometimes said such words in a fit of anger: they did not affect him, but they degraded her position." (A. Yusuf Ali, *op.cit.*, p. 1103).

وَبِالْوَالِدَيْنِ إِحْسَانًا وَبِذِي الْقُرْبَى

".....and do good to parents and to the kinsfolk...." (IV:36).

(c) It makes economic assistance to the kinsfolk, with the noblest motive, one of the basic ingredients of practical piety:

وَآتَى الْمَالَ عَلَى حُبِّهِ ذَوِي الْقُرْبَى

"....(it is true righteousness) to spend of your substance, out of love for Him (i.e., God), for your kith and kin....." (II:177).

(d) And not only that. Doing good to one's relatives and assisting them in their needs, is not just an optional act of goodness but an unavoidable duty; because the relatives have a definite *right* whose fulfilment a Muslim owes to them:

فَآتِ ذَا الْقُرْبَى حَقَّهُ

"So give what is due to kindred[34]...." (XXX:38).

Again:

إِنَّ اللَّهَ يَأْمُرُ بِالْعَدْلِ وَالْإِحْسَانِ وَإِيتَاءِ ذِي الْقُرْبَى

"Verily Allah enjoineth justice, the doing of good (to others in general), and giving to kinsfolk (their due)....." (XVI:90).

Thus: *Duties of Commission* towards the kinsfolk may be broadly classified into:

(a) Maintaining cordial relations with them, and cultivating love for them;

(b) Rendering economic assistance to them, whenever necessary;

(c) Doing good to them in every other way.

(*ii*) *Duty of Omission:*

The Holy Qur'ān condemns in strong terms the damaging of the ties of relationship with one's kith and kin; hence to abstain from it is duty:

34. Cf. Similar command in XVII:26.

الْفَاسِقِينَ ۝ الَّذِينَ يَنْقُضُونَ عَهْدَ اللَّهِ مِنْ بَعْدِ مِيثَاقِهِ وَيَقْطَعُونَ مَا أَمَرَ اللَّهُ
بِهِ أَنْ يُوصَلَ وَيُفْسِدُونَ فِي الْأَرْضِ أُولَٰئِكَ هُمُ الْخَاسِرُونَ ۝

"....The transgressors, who break the Covenant of Allah after ratifying it, and sever that which Allah ordered to be joined (i.e., damage the relationship with, the violate the duties they owe to, among others, the kinsfolk), and act corruptly on the earth, these are they who are the losers."[35] (II:26, 27).

(5) Duties Towards Domestic Servants

The Qur'ãnic doctrine of love for God and man is so thorough and comprehensive in its scope that it transforms the formal, and often temporary, relationship of "give and take" between the employer and the servant into a relationship of liberality and love, giving to the domestic servant virtually the role of a part and parcel of the family.[36] In any case the Holy Qur'ãn has made it a duty for every Muslim to do good to all those who are under his control and in subjection to him, including the domestic servants,—and to treat it as one of his basic duties:

وَبِالْوَالِدَيْنِ إِحْسَانًا . . . وَمَا مَلَكَتْ أَيْمَانُكُمْ

"....and do good to parents....and to those whom your right hands possess (i.e., those who are subject to your authority)...." (IV:36).

---

35. Ref. also: XIII:25.

36. This aspect of relationship has been explicitly propounded by the Holy Prophet (Peace be upon him). He says in connection with the prisoners of war, who, so long as they do not obtain their freedom, are to be distributed in Muslim families to serve them and who stand below the ordinary free domestic servants and, as enemies, hardly deserve any privilege according to the canons of pre-Qur'ãnic laws and, for all practical purposes, of the post-Qur'ãic laws:

"....Whoever has his brother (human being) under him, he should feed him with the food that he himself eats, and clothe him with such clothing as he himself wears. And do not impose upon him a duty which is beyond his power to perform; if, however, you command them to do what they are unable to do, assist them in that affair." (Bukhãrî: *Sahîh*, vol. II, *Kitãb al-Adãb*).

Chapter II

DUTIES IN RESPECT OF AGE AND RANK

The Holy Qur'ãn says:

وَهُوَ الَّذِىْ جَعَلَكُمْ خَلٰٓئِفَ الْاَرْضِ وَرَفَعَ بَعْضَكُمْ فَوْقَ بَعْضٍ دَرَجٰتٍ لِّيَبْلُوَكُمْ فِىْ مَآ اٰتٰكُمْ ۭ اِنَّ رَبَّكَ سَرِيْعُ الْعِقَابِ ڮ وَاِنَّهٗ لَغَفُوْرٌ رَّحِيْمٌ ۝

"He it is Who hath placed you as vicegerents on the earth and hath raised some of you above others in degrees that He may try you by (the test of) that (position and rank) which He hath given you. Lo! thy Lord is swift in prosecution: yet He is Oft-Forgiving, Most Merciful." (VI:165).

This verse refers to the fact that there have always existed and will always exist gradations in human society in respect of seniority and superiority, giving rise to:

(i) Seniors in age, on the one hand, and juniors in age, on the other;

(ii) Superiors in talents and accomplishments (with respect to piety, knowledge, etc.,), on the one hand, and those inferior to them, on the other;

(iii) Employers and officers, on the one hand, and the employees and the subordinates, on the other.

This social phenomenon has, however, a moral implication according to this verse, as is clearly affirmed by the words: "that He may try you by (the test of) that (position and rank) which He hath given you". This trial consists in the proper and improper moral behaviour in the situations contained in this phenomenon.

There are two attitudes which seem to be ingrained in every healthy and balanced human personality—as is evident from a study of classical morally elevated human personalities in history, to whom the Holy Qur'ãn refers—the attitudes, namely, of:

(i) Respect for everyone who excels in anything of life as compared to one's self; and

(ii) compassionate kindness towards everyone who is deficient in anything of life.

In this respect, the Holy Qur'ãn has commanded its followers to behave in requisite goodness and beauty towards fellow-beings (XVI:90). Moreover, it has enjoined respect for one's parents (XVII:23), on the one hand, and compassionate kindness as a general rule of life, on the other. (XC:17).

Thus, the duty towards those who are one's senior in age, or superior in talents or accomplishments, or one's employers or officers, would be that of showing respect to them; while the duty to those who are one's juniors in age, or inferior to him in talents or accomplishments, or they are one's employees of subordinates, would be that of compassionate kindness.

We find these duties specified in the following words in the Holy Prophet's exposition of the Qur'ãnic Teaching:

ليس منّا من لم يرحم صغيرنا ولم يوقّر كبيرنا

"Whoever does not show compassionate kindness to him who is small (as compared to him in age or rank), or does not observe respect towards him who is big (as compared to him in age or rank), is not one of us (i.e., is not a Muslim)." (Tirmizi: *Jãme*', vol. II, p. 14).

Chapter III

DUTIES TO PARTICULAR CATEGORIES OF NON-RELATIVES

---

(1) Duty towards Neighbours.

(2) Duty towards Friends and Associates.

(3) Duties towards Orphans.

(4) Duties towards Widows.

(5) Duties towards the Needy and the Destitute.

(6) Duties towards Guests and Wayfarers.

(7) Duties towards Slaves.

---

(1) Duty Towards Neighbours

Concerning one's neighbours, the Holy Qur'ãn has classified them into two categories, namely:

(a) *Neighbours who are near*. Nearness includes here nearness in residence as well as nearness in relationship,—the relationship may be of any sort: family ties, religion, etc. Those who enjoy nearness in both ways have a double right on a Muslim.

(b) *Neighbours who are strangers*, i.e., those with whom we have no relationship, and those who reside at some distance from us, and those who belong to a different religion. Their rights would be naturally less than the rights of category (a).

For all of them, *the comprehensive duty of doing good has been enjoined*, as the following verse says:

وَاعْبُدُوا اللّٰهَ وَلَا تُشْرِكُوْا بِهٖ شَيْئًا وَّبِالْوَالِدَيْنِ إِحْسَانًا وَّبِذِي الْقُرْبٰى
وَالْيَتٰمٰى وَالْمَسٰكِيْنِ وَالْجَارِ ذِي الْقُرْبٰى وَالْجَارِ الْجُنُبِ وَالصَّاحِبِ
بِالْجَنْبِ وَابْنِ السَّبِيْلِ وَمَا مَلَكَتْ أَيْمَانُكُمْ إِنَّ اللّٰهَ لَا يُحِبُّ مَنْ
كَانَ مُخْتَالًا فَخُوْرًا ۝

"Serve Allah, and join not equals with Him; and do good—to parents, kinsfolk, orphans, those in need, *neighbours who are near, neighbours who are strangers,* the companion by your side, the wayfarer (ye meet), and what your right hands possess: for Allah loveth not the arrogant, the vainglorious;...." (IV:36)[1]

(2) Duty Towards Friends and Associates

Doing good to friends and associates enjoined:

The verse quoted in connection with 'duty to neighbours' (IV:36) speaks of the 'companion by your side' and *enjoins the duty of doing good to him.*

The words 'companion by your side' mean:

(a) a close friend, and

(b) he with whom one may be associated in any sphere of activity, *e.g.*, a fellow-worker.

(3) Duties Towards Orphans

The Holy Qur'ãn assigns an important place in its system of duties to the doing of good to orphans, so much so that caring for the orphans has assumed the form of a sacred institution in Islam—and that for the first time in the known history of mankind.

The holy book divides the orphans into two categories, namely, (1) those who are destitute; and (2) those who inherit means of subsistence and are under one's care; and it condemns the malpractices of the people in respect of both, and lays down duties of omission and commission with regard to both.

I. Duties Relating to those Orphans who are Destitute and to Orphans in General:

---

1. In respect of this duty, the Holy Prophet (Peace be on him) has given the following stern warning:-

لا يؤمن عبد حتى يحب لجاره ما يحب لنفسه

"None of you will be (counted) a Believer unless he loves for his neighbour what he loves for himself." (Tirmizi: *Jãme*', vol. II, p. 16).

(a) *Duty of Omission:*

Treating the orphan with harshness prohibited:

فَأَمَّا الْيَتِيمَ فَلَا تَقْهَرْ ۝

"Therefore, treat not the orphan with harshness." (XCIII:9).

Because, treating the orphans with harshness should be possible only for him who belies religion and not for a believer in Divine Guidance:

أَرَأَيْتَ الَّذِي يُكَذِّبُ بِالدِّينِ ۝ فَذَٰلِكَ الَّذِي يَدُعُّ الْيَتِيمَ ۝

"Hast thou observed him who belieth religion? That is he who repelleth the orphan (with harshness)." (CVII:1, 2).

(b) *Duties of Commission:*

(i) Doing good to the orphan in every way, enjoined:

وَاعْبُدُوا اللَّهَ وَلَا تُشْرِكُوا بِهِ شَيْئًا وَبِالْوَالِدَيْنِ إِحْسَانًا وَبِذِي الْقُرْبَىٰ
وَالْيَتَامَىٰ

"Serve Allah, and join not equals with Him; and do good—to parents, kinsfolk, *orphans....*" (IV:36).[2]

(ii) Spending one's wealth with the highest motive for the welfare of the orphans emphasised as an act of true righteousness and as one of the acid tests of one's Faith; hence its observance is duty:

لَيْسَ الْبِرَّ أَنْ تُوَلُّوا وُجُوهَكُمْ قِبَلَ الْمَشْرِقِ وَالْمَغْرِبِ وَلَٰكِنَّ الْبِرَّ مَنْ
آمَنَ بِاللَّهِ وَالْيَوْمِ الْآخِرِ وَالْمَلَائِكَةِ وَالْكِتَابِ وَالنَّبِيِّينَ وَآتَى الْمَالَ عَلَىٰ
حُبِّهِ ذَوِي الْقُرْبَىٰ وَالْيَتَامَىٰ

"It is not righteousness that ye turn your faces towards East or West; But it is righteousness—to believe in Allah and the Last Day, and the Angels, and the Book, and the Messengers; to spend of your substance, out of love for Him, for your kin, *for orphans....*" (II:177).

2. Cf. II:83; II:215.

(iii) *The difficult path of duty which brings the highest rewards from God emphasised, among other things, in terms of feeding the orphans in times of distress:*

وَمَآ أَدْرَىٰكَ مَا ٱلْعَقَبَةُ ۝ فَكُّ رَقَبَةٍ ۝ أَوْ إِطْعَٰمٌ فِى يَوْمٍ ذِى
مَسْغَبَةٍ ۝ يَتِيمًا ذَا مَقْرَبَةٍ ۝ أَوْ مِسْكِينًا ذَا مَتْرَبَةٍ ۝

"Ah, what will convey unto thee what the Ascent is: —(it is) to free a slave, and *to feed in a day of privation an orphan near of kin*, or some poor wretch in misery." (XC:12-16).[3]

It may be noted here that, besides the 'orphan near of kin' who has naturally a special claim, orphans in general are included in the category of 'some poor wretch in misery'

(iv) *To set aside a portion of one's wealth for the benefit of orphans when inheritance is divided, enjoined:*

وَإِذَا حَضَرَ ٱلْقِسْمَةَ أُولُوا ٱلْقُرْبَىٰ وَٱلْيَتَٰمَىٰ وَٱلْمَسَٰكِينُ فَٱرْزُقُوهُم مِّنْهُ
وَقُولُوا لَهُمْ قَوْلًا مَّعْرُوفًا ۝

"But if, at the time of division, other relatives, or orphans, or the poor are present, give them something also, and speak to them words of kindness and justice." (IV:8).

(v) *Besides voluntary help from the Muslims, making the orphans beneficiaries in the spoils of war and in enemy property acquired otherwise by the Islamic State, enjoined:*

وَٱعْلَمُوٓا أَنَّمَا غَنِمْتُم مِّن شَىْءٍ فَأَنَّ لِلَّهِ خُمُسَهُۥ وَلِلرَّسُولِ وَلِذِى ٱلْقُرْبَىٰ وَٱلْيَتَٰمَىٰ
وَٱلْمَسَٰكِينِ وَٱبْنِ ٱلسَّبِيلِ إِن كُنتُمْ ءَامَنتُم بِٱللَّهِ وَمَآ أَنزَلْنَا عَلَىٰ عَبْدِنَا يَوْمَ
ٱلْفُرْقَانِ يَوْمَ ٱلْتَقَى ٱلْجَمْعَانِ ۗ وَٱللَّهُ عَلَىٰ كُلِّ شَىْءٍ قَدِيرٌ ۝

"And know that of all the booty that ye may acquire (in war), a fifth share is assigned to Allah,—and to the Messenger, and to near relatives, (and to) the orphans, the needy, and the wayfarer,—if ye do

3. Cf. LXXVI:8.

believe in Allah and in the revelation We sent down to Our Servant on the Day of Testing,—the Day of the meeting of the two forces; for Allah hath power over all things." (VIII:41).

مَآ أَفَآءَ اللّٰهُ عَلٰى رَسُوْلِهٖ مِنْ أَهْلِ الْقُرٰى فَلِلّٰهِ وَلِلرَّسُوْلِ وَلِذِى الْقُرْبٰى وَ
الْيَتٰمٰى وَالْمَسٰكِيْنِ وَابْنِ السَّبِيْلِ كَيْ لَا يَكُوْنَ دُوْلَةً بَيْنَ الْأَغْنِيَآءِ مِنْكُمْ ۚ
وَمَآ اٰتٰكُمُ الرَّسُوْلُ فَخُذُوْهُ ۚ وَمَا نَهٰكُمْ عَنْهُ فَانْتَهُوْا ۚ وَاتَّقُوا اللّٰهَ ۚ إِنَّ
اللّٰهَ شَدِيْدُ الْعِقَابِ ۝

"What Allah has bestowed on His Messenger (and taken away) from the people of the townships,—belongs to Allah,—to His Messenger and to kindred and orphans, the needy and the wayfarer; in order that it may not (merely) make a circuit between the wealthy among you. So take what the Messenger assigns to you, and deny yourselves that which he withholds from you. And fear Allah; for Allah is strict in Punishment." (LIX:7).

2. Duties Relating to those Orphans who Inherit Means of Subsistence and are under one's Care:

(a) Duties of Omission:

To start with: the Holy Qur'ãn condemns very strongly the practice of the pagan Arabs who used to misappropriate the helpless orphan's inheritance.

Taking up the problem of the orphans who may come under a Muslim's care, and for whose property he may be the custodian, *the holy book prohibits all such acts whereby even the slightest injustice may accrue to an orphan—and that in the following terms*:

(i) *It enjoins abstinence from interfering with—nay, even coming near—the orphan's property except when it becomes necessary in the interest of the latter's welfare*:

وَلَا تَقْرَبُوْا مَالَ الْيَتِيْمِ إِلَّا بِالَّتِيْ هِيَ أَحْسَنُ حَتّٰى يَبْلُغَ أَشُدَّهٗ ۖ وَأَوْفُوْا بِالْعَهْدِ ۚ إِنَّ
الْعَهْدَ كَانَ مَسْئُوْلًا ۝

"Come not nigh to the orphan's property except to improve it, until he attains the age of full strength; and fulfil (every) engagement, for (every) engagement will be enquired into (on the Day of Reckoning)." (XVII:34).

إِنَّ الَّذِينَ يَأْكُلُونَ أَمْوَالَ الْيَتٰمٰى ظُلْمًا إِنَّمَا يَأْكُلُونَ فِي بُطُونِهِمْ نَارًا ۖ
وَسَيَصْلَوْنَ سَعِيرًا ۝

"Those who unjustly eat up the property of orphans, eat up a Fire into their own bellies: they will soon be enduring a blazing Fire!" (IV:10).

(ii) *It enjoins abstinence from employing deceptive measures for misappropriating the orphans's property*:

وَآتُوا الْيَتٰمٰى أَمْوَالَهُمْ وَلَا تَتَبَدَّلُوا الْخَبِيثَ بِالطَّيِّبِ ۖ وَلَا تَأْكُلُوا أَمْوَالَهُمْ
إِلَىٰ أَمْوَالِكُمْ ۚ إِنَّهُ كَانَ حُوبًا كَبِيرًا ۝

"To orphans restore their property (when they reach their age), and do not substitute (your) worthless things for (their) good ones; and devour not their substance (by mixing it up) with your own. For this is indeed a great sin." (IV:2).

(iii) *It enjoins abstinence from marrying the orphan-girls with the motive of exploiting their wealth thereby*:

وَإِنْ خِفْتُمْ أَلَّا تُقْسِطُوا فِي الْيَتٰمٰى فَانْكِحُوا مَا طَابَ لَكُمْ مِنَ النِّسَاءِ مَثْنٰى
وَثُلٰثَ وَرُبٰعَ ۚ فَإِنْ خِفْتُمْ أَلَّا تَعْدِلُوا فَوَاحِدَةً أَوْ مَا مَلَكَتْ أَيْمَانُكُمْ ۚ ذٰلِكَ
أَدْنٰى أَلَّا تَعُولُوا ۝

And if ye apprehend that ye may not deal justly with the orphan-girls, then marry such as please you, of other women, by twos and threes or fours, but if ye apprehend that ye shall not act justly, then marry one only, or that which your right hands own, that will be more suitable that ye may swerve not." (IV:3)[4]

(iv) *It enjoins abstinence from wasteful spending of the orphan's property out of dishonest selfish consideration*:

4. This verse embraces two implications. One of them has been mentioned in connection with "polygamy". The other one has been given here.

وَلَا تَأْكُلُوهَا إِسْرَافًا وَبِدَارًا أَنْ يَكْبَرُوا ۚ

".....And consume it not wastefully, not in haste against their growing up...." (IV:6).

(v) *It enjoins abstinence from carelessness in safeguarding the interests of the orphans in respect of restoration of the orphan's property to them*:

وَلَا تُؤْتُوا السُّفَهَاءَ أَمْوَالَكُمُ الَّتِي جَعَلَ اللَّهُ لَكُمْ قِيَامًا وَارْزُقُوهُمْ فِيهَا
وَاكْسُوهُمْ وَقُولُوا لَهُمْ قَوْلًا مَعْرُوفًا ۝

"And give not unto the weak of understanding (what is in) your (keeping of their) wealth, which Allah hath given you to maintain, but feed and clothe them out of it, and speak to them words of kindness and justice." (IV:5).

(vi) *Finally, it makes a touching appeal and registers a stern warning in these words*:

وَلْيَخْشَ الَّذِينَ لَوْ تَرَكُوا مِنْ خَلْفِهِمْ ذُرِّيَّةً ضِعَافًا خَافُوا عَلَيْهِمْ فَلْيَتَّقُوا اللَّهَ
وَلْيَقُولُوا قَوْلًا سَدِيدًا ۝ إِنَّ الَّذِينَ يَأْكُلُونَ أَمْوَالَ الْيَتَامَىٰ ظُلْمًا إِنَّمَا
يَأْكُلُونَ فِي بُطُونِهِمْ نَارًا ۖ وَسَيَصْلَوْنَ سَعِيرًا ۝

"Let those (disposing of an estate) have the same fear in their minds as they would have for their own if they had left a helpless family behind: Let them fear Allah, and speak words of appropriate (comfort). Those who unjustly eat up the property of orphans, eat up a Fire into their bellies; they will soon be enduring a blazing Fire!" (IV.9, 10).

(b) Duties of Commission:

(i) Loving care for, and conscientious service to, the orphans living under one's guardianship, and honest protection of their property, with permission for reasonable remuneration to the manager of orphan's property, in case of his poverty, enjoined:

وَابْتَلُوا الْيَتٰمٰى حَتّٰى إِذَا بَلَغُوا النِّكَاحَ ۚ فَإِنْ آنَسْتُمْ مِّنْهُمْ رُشْدًا فَادْفَعُوا إِلَيْهِمْ
أَمْوَالَهُمْ ۚ وَلَا تَأْكُلُوهَا إِسْرَافًا وَّبِدَارًا أَنْ يَّكْبَرُوا ۚ وَمَنْ كَانَ غَنِيًّا
فَلْيَسْتَعْفِفْ ۚ وَمَنْ كَانَ فَقِيرًا فَلْيَأْكُلْ بِالْمَعْرُوفِ ۚ فَإِذَا دَفَعْتُمْ إِلَيْهِمْ
أَمْوَالَهُمْ فَأَشْهِدُوا عَلَيْهِمْ ۚ وَكَفٰى بِاللّٰهِ حَسِيبًا ○

"And test the orphans (in respect of their capacity to handle their affairs independently) until they reach the marriageable age (i.e., age of majority)[5]; then if ye find them of sound judgment, hand over unto them their property; and consume it not wastefully, nor in haste against their growing up. If the guardian is well off, let him claim no remuneration (for service to an orphan). But if he is poor, let him have for himself (as remuneration) what is just and equitable. When ye release their property to them, take witness in their presence. But all-sufficient is Allah in taking account." (IV:6).

(ii) *Co-partnership with the orphans, for better management of their property and their affairs, permitted:*

وَيَسْأَلُونَكَ عَنِ الْيَتٰمٰى ۚ قُلْ إِصْلَاحٌ لَّهُمْ خَيْرٌ ۚ وَإِنْ تُخَالِطُوهُمْ فَإِخْوَانُكُمْ ۚ وَ
اللّٰهُ يَعْلَمُ الْمُفْسِدَ مِنَ الْمُصْلِحِ ۚ وَلَوْ شَاءَ اللّٰهُ لَأَعْنَتَكُمْ ۚ إِنَّ اللّٰهَ عَزِيزٌ
حَكِيمٌ ○

"They ask thee concerning the orphans. Say: The best thing to do is what is for their good: if ye mix their (financial) affairs with yours (as co-partners), they are your brethren (and as such entitled to all generosity and love). But Allah knoweth the man who means mischief from the man who means good. An if Allah had wished, He could have put you into difficulties: He is indeed Exalted, Wise." (II:220).

(iii) *The principle of the Court of Wards for protecting people of "weak understanding", including minor orphans, through the institution of guardianship, laid*

5. According to the Hanafi school of Islamic Law, the age of majority is 18 years for boys and 17 years for girls. (See: Mustafã Ahmad al-Zarqã: *al-Madkhal al-Fiqhî al-'Ãm*, vol. II, p. 779).

down. Also, permission given to invest the capital of the orphans in trade with a view to benefit them:

وَلَا تُؤْتُوا السُّفَهَاءَ أَمْوَالَكُمُ الَّتِي جَعَلَ اللَّهُ لَكُمْ قِيَامًا وَارْزُقُوهُمْ فِيهَا
وَاكْسُوهُمْ وَقُولُوا لَهُمْ قَوْلًا مَعْرُوفًا ○

"Give not unto the weak of understanding (what is in) your (keeping of their) wealth[6], which Allah hath given you to maintain; but feed and clothe them out of (the profits of) it[7], and speak to them words of kindness and justice". (IV:5).

(iv) Finally, the Holy Qur'ãn enjoins absolute justice in all respects towards the orphans:

وَيَسْتَفْتُونَكَ فِي النِّسَاءِ ۖ قُلِ اللَّهُ يُفْتِيكُمْ فِيهِنَّ ۙ وَمَا يُتْلَىٰ عَلَيْكُمْ فِي
الْكِتَابِ فِي يَتَامَى النِّسَاءِ اللَّاتِي لَا تُؤْتُونَهُنَّ مَا كُتِبَ لَهُنَّ وَتَرْغَبُونَ أَنْ
تَنْكِحُوهُنَّ وَالْمُسْتَضْعَفِينَ مِنَ الْوِلْدَانِ ۙ وَأَنْ تَقُومُوا لِلْيَتَامَىٰ بِالْقِسْطِ ۚ
وَمَا تَفْعَلُوا مِنْ خَيْرٍ فَإِنَّ اللَّهَ كَانَ بِهِ عَلِيمًا ○

"They ask thee concerning the Women. Say: Allah doth instruct you about them: and (remember) what hath been rehearsed unto you in the Book, concerning (justice to) the orphans of women to whom ye give not the portions prescribed, and yet whom ye desire to marry, as also concerning the children who are weak and oppressed: that ye shall stand firm for justice to orphans. There is not a good deed which ye do, but Allah is well acquainted therewith." (IV:127).

(4) Duties Towards Widows

<u>*Basic Observations*</u>:

The position of the widows had been miserable even in certain advanced and civilised communities of the world before the advent of the

---

6. Here the verse lays down the rule of guardianship for all those owners of property who are weak of understanding, thereby establishing the institution of Court of Wards.

7. According to the Qur'ãnic commentary, *Bahr al-Muhît*, it means: "Make it a means of maintaining them so that you invest it in trade and earn profit, and so that you may be able to meet their expenses from the profit and not from the capital". (Vol. III, p. 179).

Holy Qur'ãn. Among the Jews and Christians, they enjoyed no prerogatives, because of the Biblical dogma which affirms woman's responsibility for the Oriential Sin[8], so much so that she could not even benefit from her husband's wealth as an inheritor[9]. Among the Hindus, it was not considered appropriate for her even to remain alive,—it being a virtue for the widow to burn herself alive in the funeral pyre of the husband; and, even when she chose to abstain from suicide, it was her most sacred duty to regard all her remaining life as a period of mourning and to pass it, therefore, in wretchedness and misery—as a mark of devotion to her deceased husband: remarriage being considered a heinous crime. This was so, because "widowhood, according to Hindu doctrine is the penalty incurred for the sins committed in a previous incarnation, entailing hopeless drudgery for the rest of life."[10] In the Greco-Roman culture, "the dying husband could leave her by will to a friend, with his goods and by the same title."[11]

As regards the pagan Arabs themselves, who were the first addressees of the Holy Qur'ãn: "The widows....were regarded as part of the estate, and as such passed ordinarily into the hands of their husband's heirs."[12]

Of course, the widow's right to property was unthinkable in any community of the world, because "women appear to have been *universally and in every respect* regarded as minors so far as rights of property went....Only sons, not daughters, still less wives, can inherit."[13]

It was in this background that the Holy Qur'ãn introduced the following thoroughgoing reforms in respect of the widows, and made it an obligation on the Muslims to practise them:

(i) *The period of mourning has been restricted to four mounts and ten days.* It has been actually called 'period

---

8. According to Lecky, the havoc that this dogma created for a woman among the Jews and Christians was that "woman was represented as the door of hell, as the mother of all human ills. She should be ashamed at the very thought that she is a woman." (*History of European Morals*, II, p. 142).

9. Letourneau: *Evolution of Marriage*, p. 261.

10. Hammerton's *Encyclopaedia of Modern Knowledge*, IV, p. 1927.

11. Letourneau: *Evolution of Marriage*, p. 261.

12. Roberts: *Social Laws of the Qur'ãn*, pp. 62, 63.

13. Cheyne and Black's *Encyclopaedia Biblica*, cc. 2724, 2728.

of waiting', and, as such, it is not a period for imposing wretchedness and misery on the widow but a period prescribed in the interest of her biological preparation for re-marriage and in the interest of finding out if she is with an unborn child by her deceased husband,—all this being for the promotion of human welfare.

The Holy Qur'ãn says:

وَالَّذِينَ يُتَوَفَّوْنَ مِنْكُمْ وَيَذَرُونَ أَزْوَاجًا يَتَرَبَّصْنَ بِأَنْفُسِهِنَّ
أَرْبَعَةَ أَشْهُرٍ وَعَشْرًا ۚ فَإِذَا بَلَغْنَ أَجَلَهُنَّ فَلَا جُنَاحَ عَلَيْكُمْ فِيمَا فَعَلْنَ
فِي أَنْفُسِهِنَّ بِالْمَعْرُوفِ ۗ وَاللَّهُ بِمَا تَعْمَلُونَ خَبِيرٌ ○

"If any of you die and leave widows behind, they (the widows) shall wait, keeping themselves apart (i.e., in restricted social intercourse), four months and ten days. Then when they have fulfilled their (prescribed) terms, there is no blame on you if they (as independent dispensers of their future) dispose of themselves in a just and reasonable manner (in the enjoyment of social life and in connection with their re-marriage)[14]. And Allah is well acquainted with what ye do." (II:234).

(ii) *In case the dower-money has not been already paid by the husband, or has not been written off by the wife, it shall be treated as debt and shall be paid to the wife after the death of her husband before any share is delivered to any inheritor,—this, according to the Qur'ãnic law:*

مِنْ بَعْدِ وَصِيَّةٍ يُوصِي بِهَا أَوْ دَيْنٍ ۗ

"....(The distribution of inheritance in all cases is) after the payment of legacies and debts...." (IV:11).

---

14. In case it is proved that there is unborn issue, a widow will not re-marry until it is born and for a reasonable time thereafter—in which case, the terms may be more or less than four months and ten days; and during the entire period her maintenance is the liability of her late husband and shall be chargeable to whatever assets he leaves behind. (See: *al-Hedãya*, Vol. II, pp. 33, 34., Egyptian edition).

(iii) The widow shall receive her fixed share in inheritance from her husband's estate, according to circumstances:

وَلَهُنَّ الرُّبُعُ مِمَّا تَرَكْتُمْ إِنْ لَمْ يَكُنْ لَكُمْ وَلَدٌ ۚ فَإِنْ كَانَ لَكُمْ وَلَدٌ
فَلَهُنَّ الثُّمُنُ مِمَّا تَرَكْتُمْ ۚ مِنْ بَعْدِ وَصِيَّةٍ تُوصُونَ بِهَا أَوْ دَيْنٍ ۗ

"....In what ye leave, their (i.e., the wives') share is a fourth, if ye leave no child; but if ye leave a child, they get an eighth; after payment of legacies and debts...." (IV:12).

(iv) Re-marriage of widows has been strongly advocated for providing them enjoyment of fullness of life:

The Holy Qur'ãn says:

وَأَنْكِحُوا الْأَيَامَىٰ مِنْكُمْ

"(O Muslims!) Wed those among you who are single (i.e., those who are not already in the bond of wedlock, whether they are unmarried, or lawfully divorced, or widowed)[15]." (XXIV:32).

(v) Abstinence from treating the widow as a chattel, enjoined:

يَا أَيُّهَا الَّذِينَ آمَنُوا لَا يَحِلُّ لَكُمْ أَنْ تَرِثُوا النِّسَاءَ كَرْهًا ۖ

"O ye who believe! It is not lawful for you forcibly to inherit the women (of your deceased kinsmen)...." (IV:19).

(a) Duties of Commission:

Among the above injunctions, numbers (i), (ii), (iii) and (iv) relate serially to the following *three duties of commission:*

(1) *Duty of permitting a period of consolation and readjustment to the widow:*

(2) *Duty of strengthening the widow financially;*

(3) *Duty of encouraging the widow to re-enjoy fullness of life through suitable re-marriage, in case she desires it and consider it conducive to her over-all welfare.*

15. See for this denotation of the Arabic word for 'single': Rãghib Isfahânî *Mufradãt al-Qur'ãn*, p. 31; and '*Alûsî's Rûh al-Ma'ãnî*. Vol. VI, p. 147.

(b) *Duty of Omission:*

Injunction (v), on the other hand, relates to the *duty of omission—the duty, namely, of abstaining from damaging her personality and her human dignity.*

Indeed, according to the Qur'ãnic teaching, a widow possesses a free and independent personality, and anyone who subjects her to humiliation or loss is a sinner.

(5) Duties Towards the Destitute and the Needy

As we have already noticed in the sections on "duties to self" and "duties to others—I (general)", the Holy Qur'ãn lays great emphasis on the cultivation of fellow-felling and maximum assistance to fellow-beings for ensuring their welfare and happiness in all respects, and it regards the economic welfare of the people as a thing of vital import. Here we may take note of such Qur'ãnic statements and injunctions as deal with the service of fellow-beings with specific reference to the destitute and the needy,—statements and injunctions which relate not only to economic assistance but to help in all possible respects.

(a) *Duties of Commission:*

(i) *Food being the most primary and most basic physical need of a human being, feeding the indigent has been classed as one of the outstanding virtues; hence it is duty:*

وَيُطْعِمُونَ الطَّعَامَ عَلَىٰ حُبِّهِ مِسْكِينًا وَيَتِيمًا وَأَسِيرًا ۝ إِنَّمَا نُطْعِمُكُمْ لِوَجْهِ
اللَّهِ لَا نُرِيدُ مِنكُمْ جَزَاءً وَلَا شُكُورًا ۝

"(As to the righteous)....they feed, for the love of Allah, *the indigent*, the orphan, and the captive,—(saying), 'We feed you for the sake of Allah alone: no reward do we desire from you, nor thanks'."
(LXXVI:8-9).

وَمَا أَدْرَاكَ مَا الْعَقَبَةُ ۝ فَكُّ رَقَبَةٍ ۝ أَوْ إِطْعَامٌ فِي يَوْمٍ ذِي
مَسْغَبَةٍ ۝ يَتِيمًا ذَا مَقْرَبَةٍ ۝ أَوْ مِسْكِينًا ذَا مَتْرَبَةٍ ۝

"And what will explain to thee the path that is steep?—(It is) freeing the bondman; or the giving of food in a day of privation to the orphan with claims of relationship, or *to the indigent* (*down*) *in the dust.*" (XC:12-16).

(2)(i) Again, not only feeding those who need it, but all economic assistance to the economically distressed people has been enjoined as the duty of a Muslim, emphasising that it is the fulfilment of a right:

فَاٰتِ ذَا الْقُرْبٰى حَقَّهٗ وَالْمِسْكِيْنَ وَابْنَ السَّبِيْلِ ؕ ذٰلِكَ خَيْرٌ لِّلَّذِيْنَ
يُرِيْدُوْنَ وَجْهَ اللّٰهِ ۫ وَاُولٰٓئِكَ هُمُ الْمُفْلِحُوْنَ ○

"So give what is due to kindred, the *needy*, and the wayfarer. That is best for those who seek the Countenance of Allah, and it is they who will prosper." (XXX:38).

وَفِيْٓ اَمْوَالِهِمْ حَقٌّ لِّلسَّآئِلِ وَالْمَحْرُوْمِ ○

"And in their wealth and possessions (was remembered) the right of the (*needy*), him who asked, and him who (for some reason) was prevented (from asking)." (LI:19).[16]

(ii) Continuing economic assistance to a needy person, even though he gives cause for personal anger through some misbehaviour, enjoined:

وَلَا يَاْتَلِ اُولُوا الْفَضْلِ مِنْكُمْ وَالسَّعَةِ اَنْ يُّؤْتُوْٓا اُولِي الْقُرْبٰى وَالْمَسٰكِيْنَ
وَالْمُهٰجِرِيْنَ فِيْ سَبِيْلِ اللّٰهِ ۪ۖ وَلْيَعْفُوْا وَلْيَصْفَحُوْا ؕ اَلَا تُحِبُّوْنَ اَنْ يَّغْفِرَ
اللّٰهُ لَكُمْ ؕ وَاللّٰهُ غَفُوْرٌ رَّحِيْمٌ ○

"Let not those among you who are endued with grace and amplitude of means resolve by oath against helping their kinsmen, *those in want*, and those who have left their homes in Allah's cause: let them forgive and overlook; do you not wish that Allah should forgive you? For Allah is Oft-Forgiving, Most Merciful." (XXIV:22).

(iii) Kind treatment of the needy person, in case of one's inability in rendering economic assistance, enjoined:

وَاِمَّا تُعْرِضَنَّ عَنْهُمُ ابْتِغَآءَ رَحْمَةٍ مِّنْ رَّبِّكَ تَرْجُوْهَا فَقُلْ لَّهُمْ قَوْلًا مَّيْسُوْرًا ○

---

16. Cf. XVII:26; II:177; II:215; IV:8.

"And even if thou hast to turn away from them in pursuit of the Mercy of thy Lord which thou dost expect, yet speak to them a word of easy kindness." (XVII:28).

(3) The above refers to economic assistance by individuals. The Holy Qur'ãn takes care, however, to make it also *a collective obligation of the Muslims to provide for the economic needs of the economically distressed people out of compulsory charitable taxes:*

وَالَّذِينَ فِيٓ أَمْوَالِهِمْ حَقٌّ مَّعْلُومٌ ۝ لِّلسَّآئِلِ وَالْمَحْرُومِ ۝

"...and those in whose wealth is a *recognized right for the* (*needy*) who asks and him who is prevented (for some reason from asking)...." (LXX:24, 25).

الصَّدَقَٰتُ لِلْفُقَرَآءِ وَالْمَسَٰكِينِ

"Alms are for *the poor and the needy....*" (IX:60)[17].

(4) The Holy Qur'ãn then goes beyond mere economic assistance and enjoins the comprehensive duty of *doing good to the needy in all respects*:

وَبِالْوَٰلِدَيْنِ إِحْسَٰنًا . . . وَالْمَسَٰكِينِ

"....and do good to the parents....and to *those in need....*" (IV:36).

(5) In case a Muslim is not in a position to help someone in need, the Holy Qur'ãn has advocated indirect assistance through recommending and pleading the needy person's case with those who may be capable of solving his difficulty. *Such indirect assistance also is meritorious in the sight of God and to render it, therefore, is duty.*[18]

مَّن يَشْفَعْ شَفَٰعَةً حَسَنَةً يَكُن لَّهُۥ نَصِيبٌ مِّنْهَا ۖ وَمَن يَشْفَعْ شَفَٰعَةً
سَيِّئَةً يَكُن لَّهُۥ كِفْلٌ مِّنْهَا ۗ وَكَانَ اللَّهُ عَلَىٰ كُلِّ شَىْءٍ مُّقِيتًا ۝

---

17. Cf. VIII:41; LIX:7. It may be noted that in these verses the duty of helping the destitute and the needy has been placed on the Islamic State.

18. It becomes duty under the general duty of "doing good" referred to in the foregoing.

"Whoever recommends and helps a good cause becomes a partner therein: and whoever recommends and helps an evil cause, shares in its burden: and Allah hath power over all things." (IV:85).

(b) *Duties of Omission:*

(i) *Not feeding the poverty-stricken people, if one possesses the means to do so, is a grave sin according to the Holy Qur'ān, to avoid which is a duty for all those who wish to escape the terrible punishment mentioned therein:*

Condemning the evils of the pagan Arabs, the holy book says:

كَلَّا بَل لَّا تُكْرِمُونَ الْيَتِيمَ ۝ وَلَا تَحَاضُّونَ عَلَىٰ طَعَامِ الْمِسْكِينِ ۝

"Nay, nay! But ye honour not the orphans! Nor do ye urge upon one another to feed the poor!—" (LXXXIX:17, 18).

أَرَأَيْتَ الَّذِي يُكَذِّبُ بِالدِّينِ ۝ فَذَٰلِكَ الَّذِي يَدُعُّ الْيَتِيمَ ۝ وَلَا يَحُضُّ عَلَىٰ
طَعَامِ الْمِسْكِينِ ۝

"Hast thou observed him who belieth religion (or, Requital)? That is he who repelleth the orphan, and urgeth not the feeding of the needy." (CVII:1-3).

إِنَّهُ كَانَ لَا يُؤْمِنُ بِاللَّهِ الْعَظِيمِ ۝ وَلَا يَحُضُّ عَلَىٰ طَعَامِ الْمِسْكِينِ ۝
فَلَيْسَ لَهُ الْيَوْمَ هَاهُنَا حَمِيمٌ ۝

"Lo! he (i.e., the one condemned to Hell) used not to believe in Allah the Mighty, and urged not on the feeding of the indigent; wherefore hath he no friend here this day...." (LXIX:33-35).

قَالُوا لَمْ نَكُ مِنَ الْمُصَلِّينَ ۝ وَلَمْ نَكُ نُطْعِمُ الْمِسْكِينَ ۝

"They (i.e., those condemned to Hell) will say, 'We were not of those who prayed, nor were we of those who fed the indigent'." (LXXIV:43-44).

(ii) *Abstinence from ill-treating anyone who asks for help, enjoined:*

وَأَمَّا السَّائِلَ فَلَا تَنْهَرْ ۝

"And as to him who solicits help (of any type), scold him not." (XCIII:10).

(6) Duties of Hospitality

I. Duties relating to:

(a) the Guest: and (b) the Host.

II. Duties relating to the Stranded Stranger (Wayfarer).

(I) Duties Relating to the Guest and The Host:

The basic duties towards others which the Holy Qur'ãn has taught and which we have expounded in the foregoing are fully exhaustive for guidance in respect of the highest principles concerning the duties of the guest and the host. These duties have, however, been given explicitly and specifically by the Holy Prophet (Peace be on him) in his Sayings; and because those Sayings form an exposition and explanation of the Qur'ãnic code of life itself, it is necessary to trace them in the Holy Qur'ãn. In doing so we find the problem of guest-host duties contained in the stories of two Prophets, Abraham and Lot (Peace be on them), whose conduct is the standard for a Muslim, and to follow whom is a duty.

Speaking of the guests of Prophet Abraham (Peace be on him), the Holy Qur'ãn says:

هَلْ اَتٰىكَ حَدِيْثُ ضَيْفِ اِبْرٰهِيْمَ الْمُكْرَمِيْنَ ○ اِذْ دَخَلُوْا عَلَيْهِ فَقَالُوْا سَلٰمًا ؕ
قَالَ سَلٰمٌ ۚ قَوْمٌ مُّنْكَرُوْنَ ○ فَرَاغَ اِلٰٓى اَهْلِهٖ فَجَآءَ بِعِجْلٍ سَمِيْنٍ ○ فَقَرَّبَهٗٓ
اِلَيْهِمْ قَالَ اَلَا تَاْكُلُوْنَ ○ فَاَوْجَسَ مِنْهُمْ خِيْفَةً ؕ قَالُوْا لَا تَخَفْ ؕ
وَبَشَّرُوْهُ بِغُلٰمٍ عَلِيْمٍ ○

"Hast the story reached thee, of the honoured guests of Abraham (who were angels). Behold, they entered His presence, and said: 'Peace!' He said: 'Peace!' (and thought, 'These seem) unusual people'. Then he (remarked nothing at their being unusual strangers and) turned quickly to his household (to arrange for hospitality), and brought out a calf fatted (and roasted) (to honour them with the best food). And he set it before them and (seeing that they touched it not) said: 'Will ye not eat?' (When they did not eat and thus appeared to refuse his hospitality,) he conceived a fear of them. They said: 'Fear not', and they gave him glad tidings of a son endowed with knowledge." (LI:24-28).

Again, the holy book says in respect of the guests of Prophet Lot (Peace be on him):

وَجَآءَ أَهْلُ الْمَدِينَةِ يَسْتَبْشِرُونَ ۝ قَالَ إِنَّ هَٰٓؤُلَآءِ ضَيْفِى فَلَا
تَفْضَحُونِ ۝ وَاتَّقُوا اللَّهَ وَلَا تُخْزُونِ ۝

"The inhabitants of the City (who were addicted to unnatural crime) came in (mad) joy (at the news of the arrival of handsome young guests, who were actually angels). Lot said (to them): 'These are my guests: disgrace me not: fear Allah, and shame me not'." (XV:67-69).

(a) *Duties of the host deducible from the above are:*

(*i*) He should wish Peace to his guests, even though they are strangers.

(*ii*) He should make haste with a generous and loving heart to provide comfort for them.

(*iii*) He should defend and protect them against all wrongs.

(b) *Duties of the guest deducible from the above are:*

(*i*) He should wish Peace to the host.

(*ii*) He should demonstrate his goodwill towards the host.

(*iii*) He should behave considerately towards the host.

(II) Duties Towards the Stranded Stranger (Wayfarer).

The stranded strangers constitute actually a category of guests,—of course, guests of the community or the country as a whole.

The general attitude of the human beings is that they regard their relatives and friends only as deserving their altruistic courtesy and hospitality. For, it is innate in man to bestow courtesy without effort on those for whom he cultivates love. But very few are those who may have the same feelings and attitude towards strangers that may be in need of their help and hospitality, although moral goodness manifest itself more positively and more strongly in their case.

The Holy Qur'ãn has taken up their cause, affirming service to them as their right, and has prescribed duties whereby their welfare and comfort has been genuinely and comprehensively ensured.

(i) Concerning economic assistance to them, it has preserved duties on the individual as well as on the collective level:

(a) *Individual level:*

The Holy Qur'ãn says:

فَآتِ ذَا الْقُرْبَىٰ حَقَّهُ وَالْمِسْكِينَ وَابْنَ السَّبِيلِ ۚ ذَٰلِكَ خَيْرٌ لِلَّذِينَ
يُرِيدُونَ وَجْهَ اللَّهِ ۖ وَأُولَٰئِكَ هُمُ الْمُفْلِحُونَ ○

"So give what is due to kindred, the needy, and *the wayfarer*. That is best for those who seek the Countenance of Allah, and it is they who will prosper." (XXX:38).

يَسْأَلُونَكَ مَاذَا يُنْفِقُونَ ۖ قُلْ مَا أَنْفَقْتُمْ مِنْ خَيْرٍ فَلِلْوَالِدَيْنِ وَالْأَقْرَبِينَ
وَالْيَتَامَىٰ وَالْمَسَاكِينِ وَابْنِ السَّبِيلِ ۗ وَمَا تَفْعَلُوا مِنْ خَيْرٍ فَإِنَّ اللَّهَ بِهِ
عَلِيمٌ ○

"They ask thee what they should spend (in charity). Say: 'Whatever ye spend that is good, is for parents and kindred and orphans and those in want and for *wayfarers.* And whatever ye do that is good,—Allah knoweth it well." (II:215).[19]

(b) *Collective level, namely, on the basis of charitable taxes:*

One of the fixed items on which the Compulsory Welfare Tax (*Zakãt*) it to be spent is the welfare of the stranded stranger:

الصَّدَقَاتُ لِلْفُقَرَاءِ وَالْمَسَاكِينِ . . . وَابْنِ السَّبِيلِ ۖ

"Alms are only for the poor and the needy....and (for) *the wayfarers....*" (IX:60).

Also, one of the items on which a fixed portion of war booty and of enemy property acquired otherwise by the Islamic state, is the welfare of the stranded stranger. (Ref: VIII:41 and LIX:7).

In this connection the Muslim jurists have made it clear that besides personal help to the stranded stranger, or the wayfarer, in respect

19. Cf. XVII:26; II:177.

of his needs, the Islamic state may also, if need arises, spend a part of the amount meant for the welfare of the wayfarers on the construction and repairs of roads and highways, bridges and rest-houses.[20]

(ii) Then, going beyond economic assistance and physical comfort, the Holy Qur'ãn has enjoined doing of good to the stranded strangers in all respects. It says:

وَبِالْوَالِدَيْنِ إِحْسَانًا وَّبِذِي الْقُرْبَىٰ ....وَ ابْنِ السَّبِيلِ

"....and do good—to parents, the kinsfolk....and (to) *the wayfarer*...." (IV:36).

(7) Duties Towards Slaves

(A) The Qur'ãnic Stand Concerning Slavery and Prisonership of War:

We have seen in the section on basic duties towards others that the Holy Qur'ãn promulgates and upholds most ardently and without reserve the ideals of human equality, liberty and fraternity, and bestows a most comprehensive system of rights and duties based not only on absolute justice but, beyond that, on liberality, graciousness and compassion.

All rights are, however, always subject to curtailment if the interests of human society or even of the individual so demand, because of the unhealthy and injurious attitude or action on the part of anyone. This is a principle which has been universally accepted by mankind, and its validity is ingrained in the very concept of social justice. As such, it has received sanction in the Qur'ãnic moral code also.

Viewing this principle in the perspective of human freedom, we find that the mission of the Holy Qur'ãn is to establish and promote conditions in which the ideal of human freedom thrives and prospers and all forms of cruel subjection and exploitation of man by man and all types of misery which a human being may be capable of bringing about for any of his fellow-beings, are eliminated.

Thus the Holy Qur'ãn refuses to endorse the different forms of genuine slavery and serfdom practised unblushingly by the ancient primitive communities as well as by such civilised communities as the

20. See: Qãdi Abû Yûsuf's *Kitãb al-Kharãj, Bãb al-Sadqãt.*

Greeks, the Romans, the Christians and the Hindus[21], rcognising *only* prisonership of war, and that too under unavoidable circumstances.

It is essential for every student of the Qur'ãnic teaching to remember that the Holy Qur'ãn came into a world wherein slavery had been practised as a normal pursuit of the powerful since times immemorial; and consequently it had taken deep roots in the socio-economic life of numerous human communities spread all over the world, including the Arabs.

The Holy Qur'ãn had, therefore, to tackle not only time-honoured evil custom but also a deep-rooted economic institution. As such, it adopted a gradual programme for its total abolition, in the meantime laying down moral principles and statutory laws whereby the evils connected with slavery were totally eliminated from the Muslim society during the period of its revelation itself.

We may now examine the Qur'ãnic teachings concerning male and female slaves and the problem of prisonership of war and evaluate them:—

(*i*) The first great truth that reveals itself to a student of the Holy Qur'ãn is that making slaves of human beings has not been *enjoined* anywhere even indirectly. And not only is there no command, even an indirect recommendation does not exist.

(*ii*) Taking prisoners of war as a war-strategy has been, of course, permitted in conformity with the practice of all the nations of the world. The Holy Qur'ãn says:

فَإِذَا لَقِيتُمُ الَّذِينَ كَفَرُوا فَضَرْبَ الرِّقَابِ حَتَّىٰ إِذَا أَثْخَنتُمُوهُمْ فَشُدُّوا الْوَثَاقَ

"Therefore, when ye meet in battle the Unbelievers (*i.e.,* non-Muslim enemies), then it is smiting of the necks; at length when ye have thoroughly routed them, bind a bond firmly (*i.e.*, make them prisoners of war):...."

(XLVII).:4).

---

21. For details of the cruel principles and practices of these communities concerning slavery refer, among other scholarly works, to *Encyclopaedia of Religion and Ethics*, vol. II, Art. "Slavery", pp. 595-631.

Again:

مَا كَانَ لِنَبِيٍّ أَنْ يَكُونَ لَهُ أَسْرَىٰ حَتَّىٰ يُثْخِنَ فِي الْأَرْضِ ۚ

"It is not for a Prophet (and similarly for any of his followers) to have captives unless he has fought and triumphed in the land." (VIII:67).

This verse goes on further, however, to condemn worldly motives in respect of prisoners of war—the motive of benefiting for their services, or the motive of acquiring money in case they are ransomed,—a Muslim's motive for fighting in a war being only the triumph of the Divine Order of Truth and Justice: thus discouraging even retaining prisoners of war:

تُرِيدُونَ عَرَضَ الدُّنْيَا ۖ وَاللَّهُ يُرِيدُ الْآخِرَةَ ۗ وَاللَّهُ عَزِيزٌ حَكِيمٌ ۝

"Ye (O Muslims) desire the temporal goods of this world,[22] while Allah desireth (for you) the (blessings of the) Hereafter (which are attainable only through rising above wordly passions): and Allah is Mighty, Wise." (VIII:67).

(*iii*) As to slavery proper, namely, acquiring men and women in bondage without a just war, there is not even a permission. Rather, the above quoted verse (VIII:67) makes it positively illegal.

(*iv*) As we have already noted, the institution of slavery formed a vital part of Arab life, with all its economic implications, at the time of the advent of the Holy Qur'ãn. The Qur'ãnic method of reform in respect of such complicated evil institutions being their gradual elimination[23], the Holy Qur'ãn began with emphasising the evil nature of that institution through exhortations to Muslims to emancipate the slaves, placing that act in the list of the highest virtues and announcing for it the highest reward to which a Muslim can and should aspire, namely, earning the Divine Pleasure. In the very earliest revelations belonging to the first year of the Call, we find the following historic declaration:—

وَمَا أَدْرَاكَ مَا الْعَقَبَةُ ۝ فَكُّ رَقَبَةٍ ۝

22. This reference is not to Muslims as such but to some of the Muslims of the time when the Qur'ãnic guidance had not yet been completely revealed.

23. Cf. the gradual Qur'ãnic respect of intoxicants.

"Ah, what will convey to thee what the Ascent (i.e., the high and difficult path of Duty) is? (It is) to free a slave." (XC:12, 13).

The exhortation was repeated at Madinah in the following words:—

وَلَٰكِنَّ الْبِرَّ مَنْ . . . اٰتَى الْمَالَ عَلٰى حُبِّهٖ . . . فِي الرِّقَابِ ۚ

"....but righteous is he who.... giveth his wealth for love of Him (i.e., God)...." to set free slaves....." (II:177)[24].

(*v*) When the Holy Prophet (Peace be on him) had established the Islamic state at Madinah, the problem of the prisoners of war arose in consequence of the battles waged by the enemies of Islam, giving birth to another category of bondmen and bondwomen,—the only category permitted by the Holy Qur'ãn, as we have seen above.

Prisonership of war is, like war, a necessary evil, and humanity has never been and can never be immune from it. The Holy Qur'ãn has, however, tried to mitigate this evil to the utmost rational limit.

We have seen above that it has condemned coveting prisoners of war. It being, however, unavoidable to have prisoners of war, the holy book has laid down most humane laws in that respect, giving due weight at the same time to avoidance of positive harm to the Muslims through any politically unrealistic approach—specially in the case when the enemy has also acquired Muslim prisoners of war, takes up an unjust stand concerning them and closes doors on the Islamic state in respect of awarding freedom to the prisoners of war in its hands. For, the Holy Qur'ãn, while preaching forgiveness and compassion, has also permitted the Muslims to retaliate if the enemy continues to stick to mischief and injustice:—

---

24. This clarion call did not go unheeded. Rather, the response was most enthusiastic. According to a conservative estimate, the number of slaves who received their freedom at the hands of the Companions of the Holy Prophet (Peace be on him) reached a total of thirty-nine thousand, two hundred and fifty-nine. (*Fath al-'Allãm*, commentary on *Bulûgh al-Marãm*, p. 332). It may also be pointed out that this estimate does not include many more whose references are found in other books.

As regards the Holy Prophet himself, it has been recorded that he emancipated sixty-three slaves. (*Ibid*).

وَإِنْ عَاقَبْتُمْ فَعَاقِبُوا بِمِثْلِ مَا عُوقِبْتُمْ بِهِ ۖ وَلَئِن صَبَرْتُمْ لَهُوَ
خَيْرٌ لِّلصَّابِرِينَ ۝

"If you punish, then punish with the like of that wherefore ye were afflicted (by the enemies of Islam). But if you endure patiently, verily it is better for the patient." (XVI:126).

Thus, the Qur'ãnic teaching is fundamentally aimed at the elimination of this form of bondage also, and the Islamic state has been exhorted by the Holy Qur'ãn to adopt, according to the exigencies of the situation, either of the following courses for setting free the prisoners of war:—

(*a*) setting free as a favour and out of sheer grace;

(*b*) setting free in return for ransom.

The injunction reads:—

فَإِذَا لَقِيتُمُ الَّذِينَ كَفَرُوا فَضَرْبَ الرِّقَابِ حَتَّىٰ إِذَا أَثْخَنتُمُوهُمْ
فَشُدُّوا الْوَثَاقَ فَإِمَّا مَنًّا بَعْدُ وَإِمَّا فِدَاءً حَتَّىٰ تَضَعَ الْحَرْبُ
أَوْزَارَهَا ۚ ذَٰلِكَ ۛ

"Therefore, when ye meet in battle the Unbelievers (i.e., the non-Muslim enemies), then it is smiting of necks; at length when ye have thoroughly routed them, bind a bond firmly (i.e., make them prisoners of war); thereafter either (setting them free as a matter of) grace[25] or (freeing

25. It is worthy of being remembered that in most cases when the Muslim army captured prisoners of war in the battle fought during the regime of the Holy Prophet (Peace be on him), those captives were awarded their freedom as a mark of sheer grace, in conformity with the alternative permitted in this verse. Thus, several of those who had been taken prisoners after the first battle of Islam, namely, the battle of Badr, were granted freedom without ransom. Similarly, the six thousand prisoners connected with the Banû Mustãlaq expedition, the inveterate enemies of Islam captured after the fall of Makkah, the captives obtained after the siege of Ta'if, and the prisoners captured on some other occasions of warfare, were set free by the Holy Prophet (Peace be on him) by way of grace. (See: Muslim: *Sahîh*, Vol. II, p. 93; Bukhãri: *Sahîh*, Vol. II, pp. 376, 593; Ibn Athîr: *al-Tãrikh*, vol. II, p. 92.

them in return for) ransom; until the war lays down its burdens (i.e., peace returns, after which no one can be made captive). That (is the ordinance)...." (XLVII:4).

In case, however, the Islamic state does not find itself strategically in a position where it may adopt the first alternative with justice to the Cause of Truth, nor are the prisoners in a position to take benefit of the permission to ransom themselves, they must naturally remain captives.

But, then, the Holy Qur'ãn lays down the third ordinance whereby the captives can obtain their freedom in due course. It says:—

وَالَّذِيْنَ يَبْتَغُوْنَ الْكِتٰبَ مِمَّا مَلَكَتْ اَيْمَانُكُمْ فَكَاتِبُوْهُمْ اِنْ عَلِمْتُمْ فِيْهِمْ خَيْرًا ۖ وَّاٰتُوْهُمْ مِّنْ مَّالِ اللّٰهِ الَّذِيْٓ اٰتٰىكُمْ ؕ

"....And if any of those whom your right hands possess ask for a deed in writing (to enable them to earn their freedom for a certain sum) gave them (as your bounden duty) such a deed if ye know in them any good (i.e., fitness for earning their livelihood through some work and thus bettering their position), and (for helping them to freedom) bestow upon them of the wealth of Allah which He hath bestowed upon you....." (XXIV:33).

This actually terminates, from the side of the Holy Qur'ãn, that form of bondage which is incidental to prisonership of war and which concerns Islam's bloodthirsty enemies. Of course, the very creation of every other form of bondage is out of the question, as we have already seen. Thus, there should be no bondsmen and bondswomen of any category in an Islamic state.

Indeed the Holy Qur'ãn is so vehemently opposed to slavery in all its forms that it has ordained redemption of prisoners of war and emancipation of slaves as a collective duty of the Muslims in respect of the definite and permanent functions of the perpetual compulsory Welfare Tax, i.e., *Zakãt* which every Muslim of means has been ordered to pay yearly for planned spending on welfare projects. The holy book says:

اِنَّمَا الصَّدَقٰتُ لِلْفُقَرَآءِ وَالْمَسٰكِيْنِ ...... وَفِي الرِّقَابِ

"Alms (i.e., compulsory Welfare Tax meant to be collected and spent by the communal treasury or by the Islamic state) are for the poor, and the needy.... (and) *for those in bondage....*" (IX:60).

Thus: (*a*) prisoners of war should be redeemed, and (*b*) slaves should be helped to freedom. This injunction forms, indeed, a charter for the Muslims to eradicate slavery from the world on an organized scale.

Here we may refer also to another channel adopted by the Holy Qur'ãn for the emancipation of slaves. That is the channel of recommending to, or commanding, the Muslims to expiate for certain sins through setting slaves free or purchasing for their freedom.

Thus:

(*i*) if a Muslim killed another Muslim by mistake, it was made obligatory for him to emancipate a slave:

وَمَنْ قَتَلَ مُؤْمِنًا خَطَـًٔا فَتَحْرِيْرُ رَقَبَةٍ مُّؤْمِنَةٍ

"He who killeth a Believer by mistake must set free a believing slave....." (IV:92).

(*ii*) It was, however, not only in case the person killed was a Muslim, but also when he was a non-Muslim and belonged to a community with whom Muslims had a treaty of mutual alliance:—

وَ إِنْ كَانَ مِنْ قَوْمٍ بَيْنَكُمْ وَ بَيْنَهُمْ مِّيْثَاقٌ فَدِيَةٌ مُّسَلَّمَةٌ إِلَى
أَهْلِهٖ وَ تَحْرِيْرُ رَقَبَةٍ مُّؤْمِنَةٍ ج

"...If he belonged to a people with whom you have a treaty of mutual alliance, compensation should be paid to his family, and a believing slave be freed...." (IV:92).

(*iii*) For those who had separated from their wive through *Zihãr*, to which a reference has already been made[26], and desired re-union, the first alternative given to them in respect of expiation was that of setting free a slave:—

وَ الَّذِيْنَ يُظٰهِرُوْنَ مِنْ نِّسَآئِهِمْ ثُمَّ يَعُوْدُوْنَ لِمَا قَالُوْا فَتَحْرِيْرُ رَقَبَةٍ مِّنْ
قَبْلِ أَنْ يَّتَمَآسَّا ط ذٰلِكُمْ تُوْعَظُوْنَ بِهٖ ط وَاللّٰهُ بِمَا تَعْمَلُوْنَ خَبِيْرٌ ۝

"As to those who divorce their wives by *Zihãr*, then wish to go back on the words uttered,—(it is ordained that such a one) should free a

26. See page 199.

slave before they touch each other. This are ye admonished to perform and Allah is well acquainted with (all) that ye do". (LVIII:3).

(*iv*) Failure in keeping to one's solemn oath was ordained to be expiated, among other alternatives, by freeing a slave:—

لَا يُؤَاخِذُكُمُ اللّٰهُ بِاللَّغْوِ فِيْٓ اَيْمَانِكُمْ وَلٰكِنْ يُّؤَاخِذُكُمْ بِمَا عَقَّدْتُّمُ الْاَيْمَانَ ۚ فَكَفَّارَتُهٗٓ اِطْعَامُ عَشَرَةِ مَسٰكِيْنَ مِنْ اَوْسَطِ مَا تُطْعِمُوْنَ اَهْلِيْكُمْ اَوْ كِسْوَتُهُمْ اَوْ تَحْرِيْرُ رَقَبَةٍ ؕ

"Allah will not take you to task for that which is unintentional in your oaths, but He will take you to task for the oaths which ye swear in earnest. The expiation thereof is the feeding of ten of the needy with the average of that wherewith ye feed your own folk, or the clothing of them, or the emancipation of a slave....[27]" (V:92)[28].

We should now take note of those verses of the Holy Qur'ãn which speak of the relations of Muslims with slaves and prisoners of war. The question may be asked: If the Holy Qur'ãn stands firmly for the abolition of bondage and slavery in all its forms, why those injunctions? The plain reply is: The Holy Qur'ãn, as we have already noted, came into a world wherein slavery was so deep-rooted that to uproot it at a stroke was to bring into existence some other intolerable evils. Hence, while giving that ethical teaching and laying down those laws whereby this institution was to completely wither away in due course, it tolerated the presence of the pre-existing slaves and of the prisoners of war who could not tread the paths of freedom opened out for them by it and chose to stay in the Muslim community,—laying down, however, definite laws for the eradication of the tortures of slavery. In fact, there have been prisoners of

---

27. In the *Hadîth* we find that if any Muslim terminates his fast deliberately before time, one of the alternatives laid down for him by the Holy Prophet (Peace be on him) for expiating his sin is to free a slave. (Bukhãri: *Sahîh*; vol. I, p. 259). Similarly, if a person slaps or beats his slave, the expiation of that sin is to free the slave. (Abû Dã'ûd: *Sunan*, vol. I., p. 466).

28. Besides the channel of expiation of sins, another channel, which has been mentioned in the *Hadîth*, has also been fixed. The Holy Prophet (Peace be on him) enjoined at Madinah that, on the occasion of the solar eclipse, Muslims of means should not only engage in extra devotions like other Muslims, but should also emancipate slaves. (Muslim: *Sahîh*; vol. I, p. 291).

war even afterwards who did not avail of the opportunity for freedom offered by the Holy Qur'ãn. And the same situation can repeat itself in the future. That, however, has been and would be, not because the Holy Qur'ãn enjoins it or desires it but because of the failure on the side of Islam's enemies.

We may now consider this part of the Qur'ãnic teaching.

(B) Duties:

(a) <u>*Duties of Commission:*</u>

(i) *Doing good to slaves and prisoners of war enjoined:*

The first and foremost teaching of the Holy Qur'ãn in this connection is the promulgation of *the duty of doing good* in all respects to "those whom the right hands possess",—doing good positively as well as negatively; positively, in the sense of doing all positive good possible; and, negatively, in the sense of refraining from all injury:—

وَبِالْوَالِدَيْنِ إِحْسَانًا . . . وَمَا مَلَكَتْ أَيْمَانُكُمْ ۗ إِنَّ اللَّهَ لَا يُحِبُّ
مَنْ كَانَ مُخْتَالًا فَخُورًا ۝

"....and do good to parents.... and to those whom your right hands own[29]. Lo! Allah approveth not the arrogant, the vainglorious". (IV:36).

(ii) Enabling the male and female slaves to enjoy healthy married life, enjoined:

وَأَنْكِحُوا الْأَيَامَىٰ مِنْكُمْ وَالصَّالِحِينَ مِنْ عِبَادِكُمْ وَإِمَائِكُمْ ۚ إِنْ يَكُونُوا
فُقَرَاءَ يُغْنِهِمُ اللَّهُ مِنْ فَضْلِهِ ۗ وَاللَّهُ وَاسِعٌ عَلِيمٌ ۝

"And wed the single among you and the fit ones among your male and female slaves (both of whom to become free by marriage); if they be poor, Allah will give them means out of His grace. For Allah encompasseth all, and He knoweth all things." (XXIV:32).

---

29. "What your right hands own". This includes prisoners of war, slaves, people in one's power and the animals which might belong to a person. (See A. Yusuf Ali, *op.cit.*, p. 191 n. 553).

(iii) Marriage with female slaves advocated and recommended:

فَإِنْ خِفْتُمْ أَلَّا تَعْدِلُوا فَوَاحِدَةً أَوْ مَا مَلَكَتْ أَيْمَانُكُمْ ۚ ذَٰلِكَ أَدْنَىٰ أَلَّا تَعُولُوا ۝

"....But if ye fear that ye shall not be able to deal justly (with wives more than one), then (marry) only one (free woman), or (marry) what your right hands possess (i.e., a prisoner of war or a slave). That will be more suitable, to prevent you from injustice." (IV:3).

(b) <u>*Duties of Omission*</u>*:*

(i) *Compelling slave-girls to prostitution, prohibited:*

وَلَا تُكْرِهُوا فَتَيَاتِكُمْ عَلَى الْبِغَاءِ إِنْ أَرَدْنَ تَحَصُّنًا لِتَبْتَغُوا عَرَضَ الْحَيَاةِ الدُّنْيَا ۚ

"And compel not your slave-girls to prostitution (—a custom practised by the pagan Arabs and certain other pagan communities—), they being desirous of keeping chaste, in order that ye may seek the frail goods of this world's life...." (XXIV:33).

(ii) *Promiscuous relations with female slaves, prohibited:*

وَالْمُحْصَنَاتُ مِنَ النِّسَاءِ إِلَّا مَا مَلَكَتْ أَيْمَانُكُمْ ۖ كِتَابَ اللَّهِ عَلَيْكُمْ ۚ وَأُحِلَّ لَكُمْ مَا وَرَاءَ ذَٰلِكُمْ أَنْ تَبْتَغُوا بِأَمْوَالِكُمْ مُحْصِنِينَ غَيْرَ مُسَافِحِينَ ۚ فَمَا اسْتَمْتَعْتُمْ بِهِ مِنْهُنَّ فَآتُوهُنَّ أُجُورَهُنَّ فَرِيضَةً ۚ وَلَا جُنَاحَ عَلَيْكُمْ فِيمَا تَرَاضَيْتُمْ بِهِ مِنْ بَعْدِ الْفَرِيضَةِ ۚ إِنَّ اللَّهَ كَانَ عَلِيمًا حَكِيمًا ۝ وَمَنْ لَمْ يَسْتَطِعْ مِنْكُمْ طَوْلًا أَنْ يَنْكِحَ الْمُحْصَنَاتِ الْمُؤْمِنَاتِ فَمِنْ مَا مَلَكَتْ أَيْمَانُكُمْ مِنْ فَتَيَاتِكُمُ الْمُؤْمِنَاتِ ۚ وَاللَّهُ أَعْلَمُ بِإِيمَانِكُمْ ۚ بَعْضُكُمْ مِنْ بَعْضٍ ۚ فَانْكِحُوهُنَّ بِإِذْنِ أَهْلِهِنَّ وَآتُوهُنَّ أُجُورَهُنَّ بِالْمَعْرُوفِ مُحْصَنَاتٍ غَيْرَ مُسَافِحَاتٍ وَلَا مُتَّخِذَاتِ أَخْدَانٍ ۚ فَإِذَا أُحْصِنَّ فَإِنْ أَتَيْنَ بِفَاحِشَةٍ فَعَلَيْهِنَّ نِصْفُ مَا عَلَى الْمُحْصَنَاتِ مِنَ الْعَذَابِ ۚ ذَٰلِكَ لِمَنْ خَشِيَ الْعَنَتَ مِنْكُمْ ۚ وَأَنْ تَصْبِرُوا خَيْرٌ لَكُمْ ۗ وَاللَّهُ غَفُورٌ رَحِيمٌ ۝

"Also (forbidden unto you for marriage are) women already in wedlock, except[30] those whom your right hands possess. Thus hath Allah ordained (prohibitions) against you. Except for these, all others (including those whom your right hands possess) are lawful (for marriage), *so that ye seek them with your wealth in honest wedlock, not debauchery.* Seeing that ye derive benefit from them, give them their dowers (at least) as prescribed; but if, after a dower is prescribed, ye agree mutually on aught. Lo! Allah is ever Knower, Wise.

"And whoso is not able to afford to marry free, believing women, let them marry from the believing maids whom your right hands possess. Allah knoweth best (concerning) your faith. Ye (i.e., the free and those in bondage) are one from another (i.e., equals in human status). So (without entertaining the false notion of loss of dignity) wed them by permission of their folk, and give unto them their dowers in kindness (as properly) wedded women, *not (as) fornicatresses, nor as those taking to themselves secret paramours.* When they are taken into wedlock, if they fall into lewdness, their punishment is half that for free women. *This (permission to marry female captives and slaves) is for those among you who fear sin. But is better for you that you practise self-restraint.* And Allah is Oft-Forgiving, Most Merciful." (IV:24, 25).

The above discussion shows that prisonership of war, as also the "slavery" of those whom the early converts to Islam possessed as a pre-Islamic legacy and whom they retained thereafter, is actually "controlled freedom",—the basic human rights, i.e., rights to proper food, clothing, shelter, health, marriage, education, etc., having been ensured with the exception of what falls under the proprietary rights of the guardian in the services of the prisoner of war of his so-called slave. And these proprietary rights in services have been retained, in respect of the prisoner of war, as atonement for his or her crime in engaging in war against the Cause of God, and the restrictions on freedom that have been prescribed are solely with reference to the protection of the Islamic state and of the Muslim community from the harm that he may likely inflict otherwise as an active enemy. It is, thus, not slavery in the sense in which, for instance, the Greeks, the Romans, the Hindus and the Christians have practised it by

---

30. The reason for this exception is that the Holy Qur'ãn places a married female prisoner of war whose husband has not been captured along with her, and who is therefore alone, in the category of a divorced woman. Marriage with her in case her husband has also been captured, is illegal. (See Abdul Majid Daryabadi, *op.cit.*, p. 154, n. 3).

treating their slaves as something sub-human or even non-human. The Holy Qur'ãn, and its exposition: the *Hadîth*, have commanded the Muslims to treat them just like servants and that too with affection and full regard for their welfare.

(C) The Problem of Concubinage:

Concubinage may be defined as the establishment and maintenance of sexual relations between a man and a woman outside the marriage bond. As such, it has been widely practised by human communities, which include not only primitive tribal groups[31] but also civilised peoples like the Japanese, the Chinese, the Hindus, the Greeks, the Romans, the Jews and the Christians[32]. As for the Arabs, they lagged behind none in that respect when the Holy Qur'ãn came.

We have already noted that the Qur'ãnic reform in respect of slavery was of a gradual nature. But the question is: Does the Holy Qur'ãn sanction concubinage?

The reply to this question necessitates certain observations:—

(i) We have already noted that the Holy Qur'ãn prohibits promiscuity and debauchery in relations with those "whom the right hands possess."

(ii) We have also noted that the holy book upholds, advocates and enjoins marriage with them.

(iii) If it is said that marriage with polytheists has been forbidden by the Holy Qur'ãn (II:221), and most of the female captives of war obtained during the period of Qur'ãnic revelation were polytheists, and that, therefore, the Qur'ãn injunction concerning marriage with female captives does not include them; and if the inference is made that the Holy Qur'ãn sets aside that category for being used as concubines, it would be, in the first instance, a fallacious inference, and, secondly, it would go against

---

31. *Encyclopaedia of Religion and Ethics,* vol. 3, pp. 809-811, 813.

32. *Ibid.*, pp. 812-814, 817-820.

We might note here the verdict of a modern English Sociologist also: "Wherever possible, the man should, of course, have a concubine of some sort." (Ludovici: *Woman*, p. 172.

the explicit Qur'ãn injunction which forbids extra-marital relations in an unqualified manner (XVII:32)[33].

Moreover, as we have already noted[34], the Holy Qur'ãn forbids Muslims from employing their female captives for prostitution. Can it be conceivable that a Muslim would be free to establish extra-marital relations with her himself?

(*iv*) There are certain verses in the Holy Qur'ãn wherein those with whom a Muslim can have legitimate sexual relations have been classed separately as 'spouses' and 'those whom their right hands possess'[35]. But this distinction does not imply, even according to the most anti-modernistic, conservative and literatlistic exponents of the Holy Qur'ãn[36], that the expression "those whom their right hands possess" refers to concubines. Rather, the word "spouses" denotes "free women joined to them by regular marriage bond"[37] and the expression: "those whom their right hands possess" stands for "women taken as captives in war and raised to the status of wives"[38].

(v) There is no doubt that, although "those whom the right hands posses" enjoy all the rights as wives, they are distinguishable from those wives who are from among the free women, and hence their separate mention as wives. This distinction of the 'free' and the 'captive' is there even when they are not wives of anyone but merely servants in the household. And this distinction has a natural and rational basis. For, the captive belongs originally to the enemy camp where her original mission was to destroy Islam and Muslims, while the free woman belongs solely to the fold of Islam. The loyalty to Islam and to the Islamic state of the latter cannot be normally doubtful; while in respect of the former's loyalty great precautions are necessary; because even when a captive embraces Islam, it is possible that he or she may have

---

33. Also note IV:24, 25, quoted on p. 251.

34. See p. 250.

35. XXIII:5, 6; XXXIII:50; XXXIII:52; LXX:30.

36. See Abdul Majid Daryabadi, *op.cit.*, vol. 4, p. 477.

37, 38. See: *Ibid.*, Commentary notes on verses 5 and 6 of Chap. XXIII.

> done so to be able to do greater injury to the Muslim community under the mask of conversion. Of course, if he or she is sincere, the devotion from the Muslim community is bound to come to him or her gradually but definitely, to which Muslim history bears ample testimony.

That distinction is there not only with regard to their position in society but also in respect of punishment for crimes, wherein they have been placed at an advantage out of regard for their lesser infusion into Islamic culture. Their punishment is half of that of a free person:[39]—

فَاِذَآ اُحْصِنَّ فَاِنْ اَتَيْنَ بِفَاحِشَةٍ فَعَلَيْهِنَّ نِصْفُ مَا عَلَى الْمُحْصَنٰتِ مِنَ الْعَذَابِ ط

".....When they (i.e., "those whom the right hands possess") are taken in wedlock, if they fall into shame, their punishment is half that of free women...." (IV:25).

To sum up: a critical study of the relevant verses proves that the Holy Qur'ãn does not sanction the institution of Concubinage.

---

39. Contrast it with the outlook of non-Qur'ãnic ideologies where the punishment of those in bondage was higher, often to a most cruel extent, than that of the free persons. (See: *Encyclopaedia of Religion and Ethics*. Art., Slavery").

Chapter IV

DUTIES TOWARDS MUSLIMS AS MUSLIMS

(1) Duties of Commission;

(2) Duties of Omission

(1) *Duties of Commission*

END:

Promotion of the Happiness and Moral Perfection of the Muslims.

(i) *Respecting the sanctity of life, honour and property of other Muslims enjoined:*

This duty is contained in the following directives:—

(*a*) Cultivation and maintenance of genuine brotherly relations have been enjoined:

إِنَّمَا الْمُؤْمِنُونَ إِخْوَةٌ فَأَصْلِحُوا بَيْنَ أَخَوَيْكُمْ وَاتَّقُوا اللَّهَ لَعَلَّكُمْ
تُرْحَمُونَ ۝

"The Believers are but a single Brotherhood[1]: So make peace and reconciliation between your two (contending) brothers; and be careful

---

1. It is a Brotherhood in which:

(*a*) the odious distinctions of caste and colour, and of tribe and race, have been totally eliminated. (See XLIX:13, quoted on p. 165).

(*b*) even the worst enemy of Islam is accepted as a full brother, if he chooses genuinely to be a Muslim:

لَا يَرْقُبُونَ فِي مُؤْمِنٍ إِلًّا وَلَا ذِمَّةً ۚ وَأُولَٰئِكَ هُمُ الْمُعْتَدُونَ ۝
فَإِنْ تَابُوا وَأَقَامُوا الصَّلَوٰةَ وَآتَوُا الزَّكَوٰةَ فَإِخْوَانُكُمْ فِي الدِّينِ ۗ
وَنُفَصِّلُ الْآيَاتِ لِقَوْمٍ يَعْلَمُونَ ۝

"In a Believer they (*i.e.,* the enemies of Islam respect not either the ties of kinship or of covenant! It is they who have transgressed all bounds. But (even so), if they repent, establish regular prayers, and practise regular charity,—they are your brethren in Faith: Thus do We explain the Sings in detail for those who understand."

(IX:10, 11).

of your duty towards Allah (in respect of safeguarding these brotherly relations), that ye may receive Mercy." (XLIX:10).

To maintain the integrity of this world Brotherhood[2] forms one of the highest duties of a Muslim, as we shall note elsewhere.

That cannot be possible, however, without constantly maintaining the attitude of respecting the sanctity of the life, honour and property of individual Muslims. Hence the same is duty.

(*b*) Mercifulness towards Muslims has been proclaimed as one of the basic virtues of Islamic life:

مُحَمَّدٌ رَّسُولُ اللَّهِ ۚ وَالَّذِينَ مَعَهُ أَشِدَّاءُ عَلَى الْكُفَّارِ رُحَمَاءُ بَيْنَهُمْ

"Muhammad is the Messenger of Allah; and those who are with him are strong against (hostile) Disbelievers, and merciful amongst each other...." (XLVIII:29).

(*c*) Observing respectfulness towards other Muslims has been proclaimed as one of the basic virtues which should be possessed by every Muslim:

أَذِلَّةٍ عَلَى الْمُؤْمِنِينَ

"....humble (or, respectful) toward Believers...." (V:57).

(*d*) Absolute honesty in respect of other Muslims' trusts has been enjoined:

فَإِنْ أَمِنَ بَعْضُكُم بَعْضًا فَلْيُؤَدِّ الَّذِي اؤْتُمِنَ أَمَانَتَهُ
وَلْيَتَّقِ اللَّهَ رَبَّهُ ۗ

(*c*) even a human being with practically no social standing, including the humblest slave, who may belong to any race or colour or country, can enter as a full brother by mere acceptance of Islam:

فَإِن لَّمْ تَعْلَمُوا آبَاءَهُمْ فَإِخْوَانُكُمْ فِي الدِّينِ وَمَوَالِيكُمْ ۚ

"....But if ye know not their fathers, they are your Brothers in Faith and your friends...." (XXXIII:5).

2. Having a membership today of seven hundred million souls.

"....And if one of you deposits a thing on trust with another, let the trustee (faithfully) discharge his trust, and let him fear his Lord...."
(II:283).

(*e*) Finally: keeping straight the relations with other Muslims, has been enjoined:

فَاتَّقُوا اللَّهَ وَأَصْلِحُوا ذَاتَ بَيْنِكُمْ

"....so fear Allah, and keep straight the relations between yourselves (i.e., preserve the sanctity of life, honour and property between yourselves)...." (VIII:1).

(ii) Endeavour to ensure peace and justice among Muslims, whether the moral agent is involved in it or not, enjoined:

This duty is contained in the following directives:

(*a*) In case quarrel or fight takes place between two Muslim parties, all possible effort for bringing about just peace between them, and, in case of failure, assisting the wronged party, has been commanded:

وَإِن طَائِفَتَانِ مِنَ الْمُؤْمِنِينَ اقْتَتَلُوا فَأَصْلِحُوا بَيْنَهُمَا ۖ فَإِن
بَغَتْ إِحْدَاهُمَا عَلَى الْأُخْرَىٰ فَقَاتِلُوا الَّتِي تَبْغِي حَتَّىٰ تَفِيءَ
إِلَىٰ أَمْرِ اللَّهِ ۚ فَإِن فَاءَتْ فَأَصْلِحُوا بَيْنَهُمَا بِالْعَدْلِ وَأَقْسِطُوا ۖ
إِنَّ اللَّهَ يُحِبُّ الْمُقْسِطِينَ ۝

"If two parties among the Believers fall into a quarrel, make ye peace between them: But if one of them transgreses beyond bounds against the other, then fight ye against the one that transgresses until it complies with the command of Allah; but if it complies, then make peace between them with justice, and be fair. For Allah loves those who are just."
(XLIX:9).

(*b*) In case of one's personal dispute, rising above self and settling all differences with brother Muslims on the basis of Divine Guidance given in the Holy Qur'ãn and in the *Sunnah* (Way of the Prophet), has been enjoined:

فَإِنْ تَنَازَعْتُمْ فِي شَيْءٍ فَرُدُّوهُ إِلَى اللَّهِ وَالرَّسُولِ إِنْ كُنْتُمْ تُؤْمِنُونَ بِاللَّهِ وَالْيَوْمِ الْآخِرِ ذَٰلِكَ خَيْرٌ وَأَحْسَنُ تَأْوِيلًا ○

"....and if ye dispute in aught (do not try to settle your dispute on the basis of any subjective considerations but purely on the objective grounds of justice, and for that) refer to Allah and His Messenger (Muhammad), if ye (indeed) believe in Allah and the Last Day. That is the best and fairest (course) for final determination." (IV:59).

(*c*) Such an attitude being impossible without the spirit of absolute selflessness, sacrificing personal interests and comforts for other Muslims has been commanded and emphasised as one of the virtues of true Muslims:

وَيُؤْثِرُونَ عَلَىٰ أَنْفُسِهِمْ وَلَوْ كَانَ بِهِمْ خَصَاصَةٌ

"....and they give preference to (the interests and the needs of others) above themselves, though poverty become their lot...." (LIX:9).

(*d*) The spirit of selflessness cannot be maintained without the constant cultivation of the attitude of goodwill towards all Muslims. This has been taught in the following prayer:

رَبَّنَا اغْفِرْ لَنَا وَلِإِخْوَانِنَا الَّذِينَ سَبَقُونَا بِالْإِيمَانِ وَلَا تَجْعَلْ فِي قُلُوبِنَا غِلًّا لِلَّذِينَ آمَنُوا رَبَّنَا إِنَّكَ رَءُوفٌ رَحِيمٌ ○

"....Our Lord! forgive us and our brethren who have preceded us in the Faith, and permit not in our hearts rancour towards the Believers. Our Lord! verily Thou art Kind, Merciful." (LIX:10).

(iii) Ensuring and promoting the moral and spiritual welfare of Muslims, enjoined:

Enjoining right conduct and forbidding all evil ways has been proclaimed as the mission of every Muslim:

Also: constantly exhorting one another to truth, perseverance in the way of truth, and the practice of compassion, have been declared as the basic conditions for the spiritual and moral progress of the Muslims:

Hence to strive for the moral and spiritual perfection of other Muslims in the above ways, is duty.

The Holy Qur'ãn says:

كُنتُمْ خَيْرَ أُمَّةٍ أُخْرِجَتْ لِلنَّاسِ تَأْمُرُونَ بِالْمَعْرُوفِ وَتَنْهَوْنَ عَنِ الْمُنكَرِ وَتُؤْمِنُونَ بِاللَّهِ

"Ye are the best community that hath been raised up for mankind. Ye enjoin right conduct and forbid what is wrong: and ye believe in Allah...." (III:110).

وَتَوَاصَوْا بِالْحَقِّ وَتَوَاصَوْا بِالصَّبْرِ

"....and (those who) exhort one another to truth and exhort one another to perseverance (in the cause of truth)." (CIII:3).

وَتَوَاصَوْا بِالْمَرْحَمَةِ

"....and (those who) exhort one another to compassion...." (XC:17).

(2) <u>*Duties of Omission*</u>:

<u>END</u>:

Preservation of the Happiness and the Moral Health of the Muslims.

(i) *Killing a Muslim most severely condemned and prohibited:*

وَمَا كَانَ لِمُؤْمِنٍ أَن يَقْتُلَ مُؤْمِنًا إِلَّا خَطَـًٔا . . . . . وَمَن يَقْتُلْ مُؤْمِنًا مُّتَعَمِّدًا فَجَزَآؤُهُ جَهَنَّمُ خَالِدًا فِيهَا وَغَضِبَ اللَّهُ عَلَيْهِ وَلَعَنَهُ وَأَعَدَّ لَهُ عَذَابًا عَظِيمًا

"It is not for a Believer to kill a Believer unless (it be) by mistake...."

"Whoso slayeth a Believer of set purpose, his reward is Hell for ever. Allah is worth against him and He hath cursed him and prepared for him an awful doom." (IV:92, 93).

(ii) *Damaging the honour of other Muslims in any form, prohibited:*

(*a*) Insulting in any manner, defaming and backbiting has been ruled out:

يَٰٓأَيُّهَا الَّذِينَ اٰمَنُوْا لَا يَسْخَرْ قَوْمٌ مِّنْ قَوْمٍ عَسٰٓى اَنْ يَّكُوْنُوْا خَيْرًا
مِّنْهُمْ وَلَا نِسَآءٌ مِّنْ نِّسَآءٍ عَسٰٓى اَنْ يَّكُنَّ خَيْرًا مِّنْهُنَّ ۚ وَلَا تَلْمِزُوْٓا
اَنْفُسَكُمْ وَلَا تَنَابَزُوْا بِالْاَلْقَابِ ۭ بِئْسَ الِاسْمُ الْفُسُوْقُ بَعْدَ الْاِيْمَانِ ۚ
وَمَنْ لَّمْ يَتُبْ فَاُولٰٓئِكَ هُمُ الظّٰلِمُوْنَ ۝ . . . .
وَلَا يَغْتَبْ بَّعْضُكُمْ بَعْضًا ۭ اَيُحِبُّ اَحَدُكُمْ اَنْ يَّاْكُلَ لَحْمَ
اَخِيْهِ مَيْتًا فَكَرِهْتُمُوْهُ ۭ وَاتَّقُوا اللّٰهَ ۭ اِنَّ اللّٰهَ تَوَّابٌ رَّحِيْمٌ ۝

"O ye who believe! Let not a folk deride a folk, belike they may be better than they are, not let (some) women (deride) (other) women, belike they may be better than they are; neither defame one another, nor insult one another by nicknames. Ill is the name of sin after belief. And whoso turneth not in repentance, such are evil-doers.

".....nor backbite one another. Would anyone of you love to eat the flesh of his dead brother? Ye abhor that (so abhor the other)! And keep your duty to Allah. Lo! Allah is Relenting, Merciful."

(XLIX:11, 12).

(*b*) Slandering the Muslims has been very severely condemned:

وَالَّذِيْنَ يُؤْذُوْنَ الْمُؤْمِنِيْنَ وَالْمُؤْمِنٰتِ بِغَيْرِ مَا اكْتَسَبُوْا فَقَدِ احْتَمَلُوْا بُهْتَانًا
وَّاِثْمًا مُّبِيْنًا ۝

"And those who hurt (through slander) the believing men and the believing women undeservedly, they bear the guilt of slander and manifest sin." (XXXIII:58).

(iii) *Raking up disputes with other Muslims prohibited, with warning of very serious consequences:*

وَلَا تَنَازَعُوْا فَتَفْشَلُوْا وَتَذْهَبَ رِيْحُكُمْ

"(O ye who believe!)....rake up no disputes (with one another), lest ye lose heart and your power depart...." (VIII:46).

One of the factors which lends ugliness to disputes is rancour. The Holy Qur'ãn deprecates rancour also, and teaches the following prayer:

وَلَا تَجْعَلْ فِي قُلُوبِنَا غِلًّا لِّلَّذِينَ آمَنُوا رَبَّنَا إِنَّكَ رَءُوفٌ رَّحِيمٌ ○

"(The true Muslims pray[3]: Our Lord)....permit not our hearts to suffer from rancour against the Believers. Our Lord! Thou art indeed Kind, Merciful." (LIX:10).

(iv) *Damaging the just interest of other Muslims, prohibited:*

(*a*) In respect of defrauding them in matters pertaining to wealth:

يَا أَيُّهَا الَّذِينَ آمَنُوا لَا تَأْكُلُوا أَمْوَالَكُمْ بَيْنَكُمْ بِالْبَاطِلِ

"O ye who believe! Eat up not your wealth among yourselves (i.e., do not consume one another's wealth) unlawfully...." (IV:29).

(*b*) In respect of concealing evidence:

وَلَا تَكْتُمُوا الشَّهَادَةَ ۚ وَمَن يَكْتُمْهَا فَإِنَّهُ آثِمٌ قَلْبُهُ ۗ وَاللَّهُ بِمَا تَعْمَلُونَ عَلِيمٌ ○

"Conceal not evidence; for whoever conceals it,—his heart is tainted with sin. And Allah knoweth all that ye do." (II:283).

(v) *Damaging the moral tone of the social environment of Muslims prohibited:*

Propagating indencecies, including scandalous gossip, among the Muslims has been condemned very severely; hence, abstinence from the same is duty.

The Holy Qur'ãn says:

إِنَّ الَّذِينَ يُحِبُّونَ أَن تَشِيعَ الْفَاحِشَةُ فِي الَّذِينَ آمَنُوا لَهُمْ عَذَابٌ أَلِيمٌ فِي الدُّنْيَا وَالْآخِرَةِ ۚ وَاللَّهُ يَعْلَمُ وَأَنتُمْ لَا تَعْلَمُونَ ○

---

3. "They pray", says A. Yusuf Ali, "not only for themselves, but for all their brethren, and above all, they pray that their hearts may be purified of any desire or tendency to disparage the work or virtues of other Muslims or to feel any jealousy on account of their success or good fortune." (*Op.cit.*, p. 1524).

"Verily those who love that indecency (and scandalous gossip) should be propagated among, and regarding, those who believe, for them shall be a torment afflictive in the (present) world and the Hereafter. And Allah knoweth (what terrible harm accrues to human society through such acts), and ye know not." (XXIV:19).

Chapter V

DUTIES TOWARDS NON-MUSLIMS[1] AS NON-MUSLIMS

---

(1) Duties towards all non-Muslims irrespective of their being friendly or inimical.

(2) Particular attitude towards those non-Muslims who are either friendly or neutral.

(3) Particular attitude towards those non-Muslims who are active enemies of Islam and Muslims.

---

(1) Duties Towards all Non-Muslims Irrespective of their being Friendly or Inimical

END:

(1) Ensuring justice to, and co-operation in goodness with, the non-Muslims;

(2) Active sympathy with non-Muslims in rescuing them from spiritual and moral evils.

(1) Ensuring justice to, and co-operation in Goodness with, the Non-Muslims:

(a) Duties of Commission:

(i) *Absolute justice under all circumstances enjoined:*

يَٰٓأَيُّهَا ٱلَّذِينَ ءَامَنُوا۟ كُونُوا۟ قَوَّٰمِينَ لِلَّهِ شُهَدَآءَ بِٱلْقِسْطِ ۖ وَلَا يَجْرِمَنَّكُمْ
شَنَـَٔانُ قَوْمٍ عَلَىٰٓ أَلَّا تَعْدِلُوا۟ ۚ ٱعْدِلُوا۟ هُوَ أَقْرَبُ لِلتَّقْوَىٰ ۖ وَٱتَّقُوا۟ ٱللَّهَ ۚ
إِنَّ ٱللَّهَ خَبِيرٌۢ بِمَا تَعْمَلُونَ ۝

"O ye who believe! be ye maintainers of your pact with Allah (stand out firmly for Allah), as witnesses to fair dealing, and let not the hatred of others to you make you swerve to wrong and depart from justice. Be just: that is nearer to Duty: and fear Allah. For Allah is well acquainted

---

1. Refer also to Duties to Human Beings in general, from page 199 onwards.

with all that ye do." (V:9).

(ii) *Fulfilment of pacts, contracts and treaties enjoined:*

يٰۤاَيُّهَا الَّذِيْنَ اٰمَنُوْۤا اَوْفُوْا بِالْعُقُوْدِ

"O ye who believe! fulfil the compacts (with whomsoever you may make them)...." (V:1).

(iii) *Forgiveness, in case of personal injuries from non-Muslims, enjoined:*

قُلْ لِّلَّذِيْنَ اٰمَنُوْا يَغْفِرُوْا لِلَّذِيْنَ لَا يَرْجُوْنَ اَيَّامَ اللّٰهِ لِيَجْزِيَ
قَوْمًا بِمَا كَانُوْا يَكْسِبُوْنَ ۝

"Tell those who believe, to forgive those who do not look forward to the Days of Allah (i.e., the non-Muslims); it is for Him to recompense (for good or ill) each People according to what they have earned." (XLV:14).

(iv) *Granting protection to non-Muslims, even from amongst enemies, if they so desire, enjoined:*

وَاِنْ اَحَدٌ مِّنَ الْمُشْرِكِيْنَ اسْتَجَارَكَ فَاَجِرْهُ حَتّٰى يَسْمَعَ كَلٰمَ اللّٰهِ
ثُمَّ اَبْلِغْهُ مَاْمَنَهٗ ۭ ذٰلِكَ بِاَنَّهُمْ قَوْمٌ لَّا يَعْلَمُوْنَ ۝

"If one amongst the Pagans asks thee for asylum, grant it to him, so that he may hear the Word of Allah; and then escort him to where he can be secure. That is because they are men without knowledge." (IX:6).

(b) Duties of Omission:

(i) *Transgressing the limits of justice in respect of non-Muslims and persecuting even the enemies of Islam among them, prohibited:*

وَلَا يَجْرِمَنَّكُمْ شَنَاٰنُ قَوْمٍ اَنْ صَدُّوْكُمْ عَنِ الْمَسْجِدِ الْحَرَامِ اَنْ تَعْتَدُوْا ۘ

".....And let not the hatred of some people—because they shut you out from the Sacred Mosque—incite you to transgress (the limits of justice and humanity in respect of them)...." (V:3).

(ii) *Co-operation in sin and transgression prohibited:*

وَلَا تَعَاوَنُوْا عَلَى الْاِثْمِ وَالْعُدْوَانِ ۠ وَاتَّقُوا اللّٰهَ ۭ اِنَّ اللّٰهَ شَدِيْدُ الْعِقَابِ ۝

"....and co-operate not in sin and transgression, but keep your duty to Allah. Lo! Allah is strict in punishment." (V:3).

(2) ***Active Sympathy with non-Muslims in Rescuing them from Spiritual and Moral Evils, Enjoined:***

(a) *Duties of Commission:*

(i) *Duty of reaching out the Message of Islam to non-Muslims enjoined:*

Inviting fellow-beings to Truth, and, for that purpose, the dissemination and propagation of the eternal Message of Islam, constitutes one of the noblest tasks, as the Holy Qur'ãn says:

وَمَنْ اَحْسَنُ قَوْلًا مِّمَّنْ دَعَآ اِلَى اللّٰهِ وَ عَمِلَ صَالِحًا وَّقَالَ اِنَّنِيْ مِنَ الْمُسْلِمِيْنَ ○

"Who is better in speech than one who calls (men) to Allah, works righteousness, and says: 'I am of those who bow in Islam'?" (XLI:33).

This task has been made the obligation of every Muslim, because it has devolved on the Muslim community as a whole:

كُنْتُمْ خَيْرَ اُمَّةٍ اُخْرِجَتْ لِلنَّاسِ تَاْمُرُوْنَ بِالْمَعْرُوْفِ وَ تَنْهَوْنَ عَنِ الْمُنْكَرِ وَ تُؤْمِنُوْنَ بِاللّٰهِ ؕ

"Ye are the best of Peoples, evolved for (the service of) mankind, enjoining what is right, forbidding what is wrong, and believing in Allah...." (III:110).

Reaching out the Message of Islam successfully is, however, a difficult and highly specialised task—a task for which God raised the Prophets. It, therefore, necessitates high-class organization and highly qualified and superbly trained missionaries. The Holy Qur'ãn is fully alive to it and mikes it a duty of the Muslims to provide both:

وَلْتَكُنْ مِّنْكُمْ اُمَّةٌ يَّدْعُوْنَ اِلَى الْخَيْرِ وَيَاْمُرُوْنَ بِالْمَعْرُوْفِ وَيَنْهَوْنَ عَنِ الْمُنْكَرِ ؕ وَاُولٰٓئِكَ هُمُ الْمُفْلِحُوْنَ ○

"Let there arise out of you (O Muslims!) a band (of missionaries) inviting to all that is good, enjoining what is right, and forbidding what is wrong: They are the ones to attain felicity." (III:104).

The necessity of the creation of a high-class missionary organization as well as of superb accomplishments of those who might undertake to serve as missionaries of Islam, have both been emphasised in the following verse—the former in the word "wisdom", the latter in the verse as a whole:

ادْعُ إِلَىٰ سَبِيلِ رَبِّكَ بِالْحِكْمَةِ وَالْمَوْعِظَةِ الْحَسَنَةِ وَجَادِلْهُم بِالَّتِي
هِيَ أَحْسَنُ ۚ إِنَّ رَبَّكَ هُوَ أَعْلَمُ بِمَن ضَلَّ عَن سَبِيلِهِ وَهُوَ أَعْلَمُ
بِالْمُهْتَدِينَ

"Invite (all) to the Way of thy Lord with wisdom and beautiful preaching; and argue with them in ways that are best and most gracious: For thy Lord knoweth best, who have strayed from His Path, and who receive guidance."[2] (XVI:125).

All in all, reaching out the Message of the Holy Qur'ān—the message of Islam—to every human being, and to exert to the utmost in that way, is the bounden duty of the Muslims towards God, towards themselves and towards the non-Muslims.

The Holy Qur'ān enjoins:

وَجَاهِدُوا فِي اللَّهِ حَقَّ جِهَادِهِ ۚ هُوَ اجْتَبَاكُمْ وَمَا جَعَلَ عَلَيْكُمْ فِي
الدِّينِ مِنْ حَرَجٍ ۚ مِّلَّةَ أَبِيكُمْ إِبْرَاهِيمَ ۚ هُوَ سَمَّاكُمُ الْمُسْلِمِينَ
مِن قَبْلُ وَفِي هَٰذَا لِيَكُونَ الرَّسُولُ شَهِيدًا عَلَيْكُمْ وَتَكُونُوا
شُهَدَاءَ عَلَى النَّاسِ

"And strive hard for (the Cause of) Allah (i.e., reaching out to

---

2. The comments of Abdullah Yusuf Ali on this verse are very edifying. He says:

"In this wonderful passage are laid down principles of religious teaching, which are good for all time. But where are the Teachers with such qualifications? We must invite all to the Way of God, and expound His Universal Will; we must do it with wisdom and discretion, meeting people on their own knowledge and experience, which may be very narrow, or very wide. Our preaching must be, not dogmatic, not self-guarding, not offensive, but gentle, considerate, and such as would attract their attention. Our manner and arguments should not be acrimonious, but modelled on the most courteous and the most gracious example, so that the hearer may say to himself; 'This man is not dealing merely with dialectics; he is not trying to get a rise out of me; he is sincerely expounding the faith that is in him, and his motive is the love of man and love of God." (*Op.cit.*, p. 689, n. 2161).

all mankind the Religion of Allah and consolidating it all over the earth[3]) with the (sincere, disciplined and hard) striving which is His right.

"He hath chosen you (for this), and hath not laid upon you in Religion any hardship (but only blessing); it is the Faith of your father Abraham. It is He Who hath named you Muslims (lit. 'those who have surrendered to God'), both (in the Revelation that came) before (since the time of Adam) and in this (Revelation), that the Messenger (Muhammad) may be a witness for you, and ye be (by word and deed) witnesses (of the truth of Islam) for (all) mankind." (XXII:78).

(ii) *Co-operation in deeds of righteousness enjoined:*

وَتَعَاوَنُوا عَلَى الْبِرِّ وَالتَّقْوَىٰ

"....and co-operate in righteousness and pious duty". (V:3).

(*b*) Duties of Omission:

(i) *Forced conversion of non-Muslims prohibited:*

The Holy Qur'ãn says:

لَا إِكْرَاهَ فِي الدِّينِ قَد تَّبَيَّنَ الرُّشْدُ مِنَ الْغَيِّ

"Let there be no compulsion in (respect of adoption of the) religion (of Islam): Truth stands out clear from error[4]...." (II:256).

Note: This verse also rules out persectuion of non-Muslims on religious basis.

---

3. Ref:

هُوَ الَّذِي أَرْسَلَ رَسُولَهُ بِالْهُدَىٰ وَدِينِ الْحَقِّ لِيُظْهِرَهُ عَلَى الدِّينِ كُلِّهِ وَلَوْ كَرِهَ الْمُشْرِكُونَ ○

"It is He Who has sent His Messenger with Guidance and the Religion of Truth, that He may proclaim it (make it triumph) (as the supreme spiritual force) over all religion (i.e., overall systems of belief and action), even though the Pagans may detest (it)." (LXI:9).

4. Cf. VIII:42:-

لِيَهْلِكَ مَنْ هَلَكَ عَنْ بَيِّنَةٍ وَيَحْيَىٰ مَنْ حَيَّ عَنْ بَيِّنَةٍ

"....so that he who was to perish (spiritually), should perish by a clear proof (of the Truth of Islam); and he who was to remain alive (spiritually) may remain alive by a clear proof...."

(ii) *Hurting the religious feelings through hurtful language, even when it relates to pure and simple superstitions, prohibited:*

وَلَا تَسُبُّوا الَّذِينَ يَدْعُونَ مِنْ دُونِ اللَّهِ

"Revile not ye (O Muslims!) those (false deities) whom they call upon besides Allah...." (VI:108).

It may, however, be noted that, in controversies with the non-Muslims, if they attack Islam maliciously, a Muslim has been permitted to retort but with the condition of sticking to strictest equity. At the same time, however, the Holy Qur'ãn wants the Muslim debater and controversialist to restrain himself, not losing temper and not forgetting his religion's sublime principles of conduct. We are told:

وَإِنْ عَاقَبْتُمْ فَعَاقِبُوا بِمِثْلِ مَا عُوقِبْتُمْ بِهِ ۖ وَلَئِنْ صَبَرْتُمْ لَهُوَ
خَيْرٌ لِلصَّابِرِينَ ○

"And if ye catch them out (in a controversy), catch them out no worse than they catch you out: But if ye show forbearance, that is indeed the best (i.e., the most appropriate course) of those who are forbearing." (XVI:126).

(2) Particular Attitude Towards those Non-Muslims who are either Friendly or Neutral

(*a*) *Duty of Commission:*

Social Intercourse and Benevolence permitted:

(*i*) The Holy Qur'ãn says:

لَا يَنْهَاكُمُ اللَّهُ عَنِ الَّذِينَ لَمْ يُقَاتِلُوكُمْ فِي الدِّينِ وَلَمْ يُخْرِجُوكُمْ
مِنْ دِيَارِكُمْ أَنْ تَبَرُّوهُمْ وَتُقْسِطُوا إِلَيْهِمْ ۚ إِنَّ اللَّهَ يُحِبُّ الْمُقْسِطِينَ ○

"Allah forbiddeth you not that ye should deal benevolently and equitably with those who fought not against you on account of religion nor drove you out from your homes; verily Allah loveth those who are just." (LX:8).

(*ii*) The Holy Qur'ãn permits the extension of social relations with non-Muslims in proportion to the affinity which they may have with the Qur'ãnic moral and spiritual values. Thus, it permits marriage with the women who follow some revealed religion and have thus affinity with Islam. It also allows partaking of their lawful food:

الْيَوْمَ أُحِلَّ لَكُمُ الطَّيِّبٰتُ ۖ وَطَعَامُ الَّذِينَ أُوتُوا الْكِتٰبَ حِلٌّ لَّكُمْ
وَطَعَامُكُمْ حِلٌّ لَّهُمْ ۖ وَالْمُحْصَنٰتُ مِنَ الْمُؤْمِنٰتِ وَالْمُحْصَنٰتُ مِنَ الَّذِينَ
أُوتُوا الْكِتٰبَ مِن قَبْلِكُمْ إِذَآ آتَيْتُمُوهُنَّ أُجُورَهُنَّ مُحْصِنِينَ غَيْرَ مُسٰفِحِينَ
وَلَا مُتَّخِذِيٓ أَخْدَانٍ ۗ وَمَن يَكْفُرْ بِالْإِيمٰنِ فَقَدْ حَبِطَ عَمَلُهُۥ وَهُوَ فِي
الْآخِرَةِ مِنَ الْخٰسِرِينَ ۝

"This day are (all) good things made lawful for you. The food of those who have received the Scripture is lawful for you (provided it consists of lawful things), and your food is lawful for them And so are the virtuous women of the believers and the virtuous women of those who received the Scripture before you (lawful for you) when ye give them their marriage portions and live with them in honour, not in fornication, nor taking them as secret concubines. Whoso denieth the faith, his work is vain and he will be among the losers in the Hereafter." (V:6)[5].

---

5. "The question is for food generally, such as is ordinarily 'good and pure': in the matter of meat it should be killed with some sort of solemnity analogous to that of the *Kalima*. The rules of Islam in this respect being analogous to those of the People of the Book, there is no objections to mutual recognition, as opposed to meat killed by Pagans with superstitious rites. In this respect the Christian rule is the same: 'That ye abstain from meats offered to idols, and from blood, and from things strangled, and from fornication.' (*Acts*, XV:29). Notice the bracketing of fornication with things unlawful to eat.

"Islam is not exclusive. Social intercourse, including intermarriage, is permitted with the People of the Book. A Muslim man may marry a woman from their ranks on the same terms as he would marry a Muslim woman, i.e., he must give her an economic and moral status, and must not be actuated merely by motives of lust or physical desire. A Muslim woman may not marry a non-Muslim man, because her Muslim status would be affected: the wife ordinarily takes the nationality and status given by her husband's law. A non-Muslim woman marrying a Muslim husband would be expected eventually to accept Islam. Any man or woman, of any race or faith, may, on accepting Islam, freely marry any Muslim woman or man, provided it be from motives of purity and chastity and not of lewdness." (A. Yusuf Ali, *op.cit.*, p. 241).

(*b*) Duty of Omission:

Marriages with : (a) polytheistic and idolatrous women or men, or (b) men belonging to the 'People of the Book', even when they are friendly or neutral, prohibited:

As to (a):

وَلَا تَنْكِحُوا الْمُشْرِكٰتِ حَتّٰى يُؤْمِنَّ ؕ وَلَاَمَةٌ مُّؤْمِنَةٌ خَيْرٌ مِّنْ مُّشْرِكَةٍ
وَّلَوْ اَعْجَبَتْكُمْ ۚ وَلَا تُنْكِحُوا الْمُشْرِكِيْنَ حَتّٰى يُؤْمِنُوْا ؕ وَلَعَبْدٌ مُّؤْمِنٌ
خَيْرٌ مِّنْ مُّشْرِكٍ وَّلَوْ اَعْجَبَكُمْ ؕ اُولٰٓئِكَ يَدْعُوْنَ اِلَى النَّارِ ۖۚ وَاللّٰهُ يَدْعُوْٓا اِلَى
الْجَنَّةِ وَالْمَغْفِرَةِ بِاِذْنِهٖ ۚ وَيُبَيِّنُ اٰيٰتِهٖ لِلنَّاسِ لَعَلَّهُمْ
يَتَذَكَّرُوْنَ ۝

"And do not marry the idolatresses until they believe, and certainly a believing slave woman is better than an idolatress woman, even though she should please you; and do not give (believing women) in marriage to idolaters until they believe, and certainly a believing male slave is better than an idolater even though he should please you; these invite to the Fire, and Allah invites to the Garden (of Bliss) and forgiveness by His will, and makes clear His Signs to human beings, that they might be mindful." (II:221).

As to (b):

Verse 6 of Chapter V, quoted above, confines the permission of marriage with the 'People of the Book' to their women only, thus definitely excluding their males whom, therefore, a Muslim woman is not allowed to marry.

(3) Particular Attitude towards those Non-Muslims who are active enemies of Islam and Muslims:

(*a*) Duties of Omission:

END:

Preservation of Islam and Muslims.

(*i*) *Befriending active enemies, who are devoted to the destruction of Islam and Muslims, and establishing with them intimate relations, even though they are near relatives, prohibited:*

There are several verses in the Holy Qur'ãn which bear reference to this problem. We quote all the important ones herein below: Every such verse relates, without exception, only to those non-Muslims of the days of Qur'ãnic Revelation—Pagans, Jews and Christians—who were sworn enemies of Islam and whose active hostility towards Muslims had reached the highest limits[6]. They had it as their permanent mission to do all in their power for destroying and annihilating Islam and Muslims. It was, thus, for protecting Islam and Muslims against their enemies and not out of spite for non-Muslims as such, that the following verses were revealed, and they hold good wherever and whenever similar situation arises. The rationality and justice of laying down this duty is obvious and must be accepted by every reasonable human being.

The Holy Qur'ãn says:

لا يتخذ المؤمنون الكافرين أولياء من دون المؤمنين ۖ ومن
يفعل ذلك فليس من الله في شيء إلا أن تتقوا منهم تقاة ۗ

"Let not the Believers take for friends or helpers infidels[7] rather than believers: if ye do that, in nothing will there be help from Allah: except (entering into some no-war pact with them) by way of precaution, that ye may guard yourselves from them...." (III:28).

يا أيها الذين آمنوا لا تتخذوا بطانة من دونكم لا يألونكم خبالا
ودوا ما عنتم قد بدت البغضاء من أفواههم وما تخفي صدورهم
أكبر ۚ قد بينا لكم الآيات ۖ إن كنتم تعقلون ○ ها أنتم أولاء تحبونهم
ولا يحبونكم وتؤمنون بالكتاب كله وإذا لقوكم قالوا آمنا وإذا
خلوا عضوا عليكم الأنامل من الغيظ ۚ قل موتوا بغيظكم ۗ إن الله
عليم بذات الصدور ○ إن تمسسكم حسنة تسؤهم وإن تصبكم
سيئة يفرحوا بها ۖ وإن تصبروا وتتقوا لا يضركم كيدهم شيئا ۗ
إن الله بما يعملون محيط ○

---

6. This can be verified from the historical records, for which any detailed and proper book on Islamic history will suffice.

7. (actively hostile to Islam).

"Oh ye who believe! take not into your intimacy those outside your ranks. They will not fail to corrupt you. *They only desire your ruin: Rank hatred has already appeared from their mouths: Something far worse is hidden in their hearts*. We have made plain to you to the Signs, if ye have wisdom. Ah! ye are those who love them, but they love you not,—though ye believe in the whole of the Book. When they meet you, they say, 'We believe'; but when they are alone, they bite off the very tips of their fingers at you in their rage. Say: 'Perish in your rage; Allah knoweth well all the secrets of the heart'. If aught that is good befalls you, it grieves them; but if some misfortune overtakes you, they rejoice at it. But if ye are constant and do right, not the least harm will their cunning do to you; for Allah compasseth round about all that they do." (III:118-120).

وَدُّوا لَوْ تَكْفُرُونَ كَمَا كَفَرُوا فَتَكُونُونَ سَوَآءً فَلَا تَتَّخِذُوا مِنْهُمْ أَوْلِيَآءَ حَتّٰى
يُهَاجِرُوا فِي سَبِيلِ اللّٰهِ ۚ فَإِنْ تَوَلَّوْا فَخُذُوهُمْ وَاقْتُلُوهُمْ حَيْثُ وَجَدْتُمُوهُمْ ۪
وَلَا تَتَّخِذُوا مِنْهُمْ وَلِيًّا وَّلَا نَصِيرًا ۝

"*They but wish that ye should reject Faith, as they do, and be on the same footing* (*as they*): but take not friends from their ranks until they flee in the Way of Allah (from what is forbidden). But if they turn renegades seize them and slay them; and (in any case) take no friends or helpers from their ranks:...." (IV:89).

وَقَدْ نَزَّلَ عَلَيْكُمْ فِي الْكِتٰبِ أَنْ إِذَا سَمِعْتُمْ اٰيٰتِ اللّٰهِ يُكْفَرُ بِهَا وَ
يُسْتَهْزَاُ بِهَا فَلَا تَقْعُدُوا مَعَهُمْ حَتّٰى يَخُوضُوا فِي حَدِيثٍ غَيْرِهٖٓ ۖ إِنَّكُمْ
إِذًا مِّثْلُهُمْ ۗ إِنَّ اللّٰهَ جَامِعُ الْمُنٰفِقِينَ وَالْكٰفِرِينَ فِي جَهَنَّمَ جَمِيعًا ۝

"Already have We sent you word in the Book, that when ye hear *the Signs of Allah held in defiance and ridicule*, ye are not to sit with them unless they turn to a different theme; if ye did, ye would be like them. For Allah will collect the Hypocrites and those who defy Faith—all in Hell;...." (IV:140).

يٰٓأَيُّهَا الَّذِينَ اٰمَنُوا لَا تَتَّخِذُوا الْيَهُودَ وَالنَّصٰرٰٓى أَوْلِيَآءَ ۘ بَعْضُهُمْ أَوْلِيَآءُ
بَعْضٍ ۚ وَمَنْ يَّتَوَلَّهُمْ مِّنْكُمْ فَإِنَّهُ مِنْهُمْ ۚ إِنَّ اللّٰهَ لَا يَهْدِي الْقَوْمَ
الظّٰلِمِينَ ۝

"Oh ye who believe! take not the Jews and the Christians for your friends and protectors: They are but friends and protectors to each other[8]. And he amongst you that turn to them (for friendship) is of them. Verily Allah guideth not a people unjust." (V:54).

يَا أَيُّهَا الَّذِينَ آمَنُوا لَا تَتَّخِذُوا الَّذِينَ اتَّخَذُوا دِينَكُمْ هُزُوًا وَلَعِبًا
مِنَ الَّذِينَ أُوتُوا الْكِتَابَ مِنْ قَبْلِكُمْ وَالْكُفَّارَ أَوْلِيَاءَ ۚ وَاتَّقُوا اللَّهَ
إِنْ كُنْتُمْ مُؤْمِنِينَ ○

"Oh ye who believe! take not for friends and protectors those who take your religion for a mockery or sport,—whether amongst those who received the Scripture before you, or among those who reject Faith; But fear ye Allah, if ye have Faith (indeed)." (V:60).

وَإِذَا رَأَيْتَ الَّذِينَ يَخُوضُونَ فِي آيَاتِنَا فَأَعْرِضْ عَنْهُمْ حَتَّىٰ يَخُوضُوا فِي
حَدِيثٍ غَيْرِهِ ۚ وَإِمَّا يُنْسِيَنَّكَ الشَّيْطَانُ فَلَا تَقْعُدْ بَعْدَ الذِّكْرَىٰ مَعَ
الْقَوْمِ الظَّالِمِينَ ○

"When thou seest men engaged in vain discourse about Our Signs, turn away from them unless they turn to a different theme. If Satan even makes thee forget, then after recollection, sit not thou in the company of the ungoldly." (VI:68).

فَإِذَا انْسَلَخَ الْأَشْهُرُ الْحُرُمُ فَاقْتُلُوا الْمُشْرِكِينَ حَيْثُ وَجَدْتُمُوهُمْ
وَخُذُوهُمْ وَاحْصُرُوهُمْ وَاقْعُدُوا لَهُمْ كُلَّ مَرْصَدٍ ۚ فَإِنْ تَابُوا وَ
أَقَامُوا الصَّلَاةَ وَآتَوُا الزَّكَاةَ فَخَلُّوا سَبِيلَهُمْ ۚ إِنَّ اللَّهَ غَفُورٌ رَحِيمٌ ○

"But when the forbidden months are past, then fight and slay the Pagans[9] wherever ye find them, or seize them, beleaguer them, and lie in wait for them in every stratagem (of war); but if they repent, and establish regular prayers and practise regular charity, then open the way for them; for Allah is Oft-Forgiving, Most Merciful." (IX:5).

---

8. The Holy Qur'ãn refers to a well attested historical fact.

9. (of Arabia, who were in a state of pitched war with Islam and Muslims).

يٰٓاَيُّهَا الَّذِيْنَ اٰمَنُوْا لَا تَتَّخِذُوْٓا اٰبَآءَكُمْ وَاِخْوَانَكُمْ اَوْلِيَآءَ اِنِ اسْتَحَبُّوا
الْكُفْرَ عَلَى الْاِيْمَانِ ۭ وَمَنْ يَّتَوَلَّهُمْ مِّنْكُمْ فَاُولٰٓئِكَ هُمُ الظّٰلِمُوْنَ ۝

"Oh ye who believe! Take not for protectors your fathers and your brothers if they love infidelity above Faith: If any of you do so, they do wrong." (IX:23).

يٰٓاَيُّهَا النَّبِيُّ جَاهِدِ الْكُفَّارَ وَالْمُنٰفِقِيْنَ وَاغْلُظْ عَلَيْهِمْ ۭ وَمَاْوٰىهُمْ
جَهَنَّمُ ۭ وَبِئْسَ الْمَصِيْرُ ۝

"Oh Prophet! Strive hard against the Rejecters and the Hypocrites (to combat the evils of their hostility). And be firm against them. Their abode is Hell,—an evil refuge indeed." (IX:73).

يَحْلِفُوْنَ بِاللّٰهِ مَا قَالُوْا ۭ وَلَقَدْ قَالُوْا كَلِمَةَ الْكُفْرِ وَكَفَرُوْا بَعْدَ
اِسْلَامِهِمْ وَهَمُّوْا بِمَا لَمْ يَنَالُوْا ۚ وَمَا نَقَمُوْٓا اِلَّآ اَنْ اَغْنٰىهُمُ اللّٰهُ وَرَسُوْلُهٗ
مِنْ فَضْلِهٖ ۚ فَاِنْ يَّتُوْبُوْا يَكُ خَيْرًا لَّهُمْ ۚ وَاِنْ يَّتَوَلَّوْا يُعَذِّبْهُمُ اللّٰهُ عَذَابًا
اَلِيْمًا ۙ فِي الدُّنْيَا وَالْاٰخِرَةِ ۚ وَمَا لَهُمْ فِي الْاَرْضِ مِنْ وَّلِيٍّ وَّلَا نَصِيْرٍ ۝

"They (i.e., the Hypocrites) swear by Allah that they said nothing (evil), but indeed they uttered blasphemy, and they did it after accepting Islam; and they meditated a plot which they were unable to carry out: this revenge of theirs was (their) only return for the bounty with which Allah and His Messenger had enriched them! If they repent, it will be best for them. But if they turn back (to their evil ways), Allah will punish them with a grievous penalty in this life and in the Hereafter: they shall have none on earth to protect or help them." (IX:74).

يٰٓاَيُّهَا الَّذِيْنَ اٰمَنُوْا قَاتِلُوا الَّذِيْنَ يَلُوْنَكُمْ مِّنَ الْكُفَّارِ وَلْيَجِدُوْا فِيْكُمْ
غِلْظَةً ۭ وَاعْلَمُوْٓا اَنَّ اللّٰهَ مَعَ الْمُتَّقِيْنَ ۝

"O ye who believe! Fight the (hostile) infidels who gird you about, and let them find firmness in you: and know that Allah is with those who fear Him". (IX:123).

لا تجد قوما يؤمنون بالله واليوم الآخر يوادون من حاد الله ورسوله
ولو كانوا آباءهم أو أبناءهم أو إخوانهم أو عشيرتهم ،

"Thou wilt not find any people who believe in Allah and the Last Day, befriending those who oppose Allah and His Messenger, even though they were their fathers or their sons, or their brothers, or their kindred...." (LVIII:22).

يا أيها الذين آمنوا لا تتخذوا عدوي وعدوكم أولياء تلقون إليهم
بالمودة وقد كفروا بما جاءكم من الحق يخرجون الرسول وإياكم
أن تؤمنوا بالله ربكم ، إن كنتم خرجتم جهادا في سبيلي وابتغاء
مرضاتي تسرون إليهم بالمودة وأنا أعلم بما أخفيتم وما أعلنتم ، و
من يفعله منكم فقد ضل سواء السبيل ○ إن يثقفوكم يكونوا لكم
أعداء ويبسطوا إليكم أيديهم وألسنتهم بالسوء وودوا لو
تكفرون ○ لن تنفعكم أرحامكم ولا أولادكم يوم القيامة يفصل بينكم ،
والله بما تعملون بصير ○

"O ye who believe! take not My enemies and yours as friends (or protectors),—offering them (your) love, even though they have rejected the Truth that has come to you, and *have driven out the Prophet and yourselves* (*from your homes*), (*simply*) *because ye believe in Allah your Lord!* If ye have come out to strive in My Way and to seek My Good Pleasure (take them not as friends), holding secret converse of love (and friendship) with them: for I know full well all that ye reveal. And any of you that does this has strayed from the Straight Path. *If they were to get the better of you, they would behave to you as enemies, and stretch forth their hands and their tongues against you for evil; and they desire that ye should reject the Truth.* Of no profit to you will be your relatives and your children on the Day of Judgment: He will judge between you: For Allah sees well all that ye do." (LX:1-3).

إنما ينهاكم الله عن الذين قاتلوكم في الدين وأخرجوكم من
دياركم وظاهروا على إخراجكم أن تولوهم ، ومن يتولهم فأولئك
هم الظالمون ○

"*Allah only forbids you with regard to those who fight you for* (*your*) *Faith, and drive you out of your homes, and support* (*others*) *in driving you out, from turning to them* (*for friendship and protection*). It is such as turn to them (in the circumstances), that do wrong." (LX:9).

(ii) *Firmness against the enemies of Islam enjoined:*

مُحَمَّدٌ رَّسُولُ اللَّهِ ۚ وَالَّذِينَ مَعَهُ أَشِدَّاءُ عَلَى الْكُفَّارِ

"Muhammad is the Messenger of Allah; and those who are with him are strong against (the evils of) the Rejectors...." (XLVIII:29).

(iii) *Mightiness against the enemies of Islam enjoined:*

أَعِزَّةٍ عَلَى الْكَافِرِينَ

"....(The quality of true Muslims should be that they should be) mighty against the (hostile) Rejectors...." (V:57).

(iv) *Building up military strength in the highest possible measure, as a safeguard against dangers from the side of the enemies of Islam, enjoined:*

وَأَعِدُّوا لَهُم مَّا اسْتَطَعْتُم مِّن قُوَّةٍ وَمِن رِّبَاطِ الْخَيْلِ تُرْهِبُونَ بِهِ
عَدُوَّ اللَّهِ وَعَدُوَّكُمْ وَآخَرِينَ مِن دُونِهِمْ لَا تَعْلَمُونَهُمُ اللَّهُ
يَعْلَمُهُمْ ۚ وَمَا تُنفِقُوا مِن شَيْءٍ فِي سَبِيلِ اللَّهِ يُوَفَّ إِلَيْكُمْ وَأَنتُمْ
لَا تُظْلَمُونَ ○

"Against them (i.e., your enemies) make ready your Power to the utmost of your strength, including steeds of war, to strike terror into (the hearts of) the enemies of Allah and your enemies, and others besides, whom ye know not, but whom Allah doth know. Whatever ye shall spend in the Cause of Allah, shall be repaid unto you, and ye shall not be treated unjustly." (VIII:60).

(v) *Fighting against the enemies with the fullest enthusiasm and to the finish, in order to defend Islam and Muslims and make them safe, in case the non-Muslims create a state of war, enjoined:*

يَا أَيُّهَا النَّبِيُّ حَرِّضِ الْمُؤْمِنِينَ عَلَى الْقِتَالِ ۚ إِن يَكُن مِّنكُمْ
عِشْرُونَ صَابِرُونَ يَغْلِبُوا مِائَتَيْنِ ۚ وَإِن يَكُن مِّنكُم مِّائَةٌ يَغْلِبُوا
أَلْفًا مِّنَ الَّذِينَ كَفَرُوا بِأَنَّهُمْ قَوْمٌ لَّا يَفْقَهُونَ ۝

"Oh Messenger! rouse the Believers to the fight. If there are twenty among you, patient and persevering, they will conquer two hundred: if a hundred, they will conquer a thousand of the Rejectors: for these are a people without understanding." (VIII:65).

أُذِنَ لِلَّذِينَ يُقَاتَلُونَ بِأَنَّهُمْ ظُلِمُوا ۚ وَإِنَّ اللَّهَ عَلَىٰ نَصْرِهِمْ
لَقَدِيرٌ ۝ الَّذِينَ أُخْرِجُوا مِن دِيَارِهِم بِغَيْرِ حَقٍّ إِلَّا أَن يَقُولُوا
رَبُّنَا اللَّهُ ۗ وَلَوْلَا دَفْعُ اللَّهِ النَّاسَ بَعْضَهُم بِبَعْضٍ لَّهُدِّمَتْ صَوَامِعُ وَبِيَعٌ
وَصَلَوَاتٌ وَمَسَاجِدُ يُذْكَرُ فِيهَا اسْمُ اللَّهِ كَثِيرًا ۗ

"*To those against whom war is made, permission is given (to fight), because they are wronged;—and verily Allah is Most Powerful for their aid;—(they are) those who have been expelled from their homes in defiance of right,—(for no cause) except that they say, 'Our Lord is Allah'*, Did not Allah check one set of people by means of another, there would surely have been pulled down monasteries, churches, synagogues, and mosques, in which the name of Allah is commemorated in abundant measure...." (XXII:39, 40)[10].

(*b*) <u>Duties of Commission</u>:

<u>END</u>:

Promotion of Peace, Justice and Goodwill among mankind.

(i) Maintaining the attitude of readiness for making peace with the

---

10. "Several translators have failed to notice the *yuqãtalûna* (in the best approved texts) is in the passive voice, 'against whom war is made'....not 'who take arms against the unbelievers' as Sale translates it. The cause 'and verily....their aid' is parenthetical. Verse 40 connects on with 'they are wronged'. The wrong is indicated: 'driven by persecution from their home, for no other reason than that they worshipped the One True God'. This was the first occasion on which fighting—in self defence—was permitted. This passage therefore undoubtedly dates from Madinah." (Abdullah Yusuf Ali, *op.cit.*, p. 86).

enemies of Islam in the interest of human welfare, enjoined:

وَإِنْ جَنَحُوا لِلسَّلْمِ فَاجْنَحْ لَهَا وَتَوَكَّلْ عَلَى اللَّهِ ۚ إِنَّهُ هُوَ السَّمِيعُ الْعَلِيمُ ○ وَإِنْ يُرِيدُوا أَنْ يَخْدَعُوكَ فَإِنَّ حَسْبَكَ اللَّهُ ۚ

"But if the enemy incline towards peace, do thou (also) incline towards peace, and trust in Allah: for He is the One who heareth and knoweth (all things). Should they intend to deceive thee,—verily Allah sufficeth thee...." (VIII:61, 62).

(ii) *Finally, observing absolute justice in all respects and in all dealings with the enemies of Islam enjoined as bounden duty:*

يَا أَيُّهَا الَّذِينَ آمَنُوا كُونُوا قَوَّامِينَ لِلَّهِ شُهَدَاءَ بِالْقِسْطِ ۖ وَلَا يَجْرِمَنَّكُمْ شَنَآنُ قَوْمٍ عَلَىٰ أَلَّا تَعْدِلُوا ۚ اعْدِلُوا هُوَ أَقْرَبُ لِلتَّقْوَىٰ ۖ وَاتَّقُوا اللَّهَ ۚ إِنَّ اللَّهَ خَبِيرٌ بِمَا تَعْمَلُونَ ○

"Oh ye who believe! be maintainers of your pact with Allah (i.e., stand out firmly for Allah) as witnesses to fair dealing, and let not the hatred of others to you make you swerve to wrong and depart from justice. Be just: that is nearer to Duty: and fear Allah. For Allah is well acquainted with all that ye do." (V:9).

(iii) *In the case of non-Muslim parents, continued service to them enjoined, even when they exert to turn a Muslim away from Islam:*

وَإِنْ جَاهَدَاكَ عَلَىٰ أَنْ تُشْرِكَ بِي مَا لَيْسَ لَكَ بِهِ عِلْمٌ فَلَا تُطِعْهُمَا ۖ وَصَاحِبْهُمَا فِي الدُّنْيَا مَعْرُوفًا ۖ وَاتَّبِعْ سَبِيلَ مَنْ أَنَابَ إِلَيَّ ۚ ثُمَّ إِلَيَّ مَرْجِعُكُمْ فَأُنَبِّئُكُمْ بِمَا كُنْتُمْ تَعْمَلُونَ ○

"But if they (i.e., the non-Muslim parents) strive to make thee join in worship with Me things of which thou hast no knowledge, obey them not; yet bear them company in this life with justice (and consideration) and follow the way of those who turn to Me (in love). In the end the return of you all is to Me, and I will tell you the truth (and meaning) of all that ye did." (XXXI:15).

Part III

DUTIES IN RESPECT OF MANNERS

END:

Practical demonstration, in terms of etiquette, of the Qur'ãnic spiritual, moral and social ideals in life, with a view to refinement of culture.

I. Religious Manners. II. Personal and Social Manners.

Chapter I

RELIGIOUS MANNERS

(1) **In respect of beginning an act: To say at the beginning of every act**:

بِسْمِ اللهِ الرَّحْمٰنِ الرَّحِيْمِ ○

(Bismillãhir-Rahmãnir-Rahîm)

"In the name of Allah, Most Gracious, Most Merciful."[1]

This 'manner' is contained in the following Qur'ãnic references:

(*i*) *In respect of seeking knowledge and guidance:*

اِقْرَاْ بِاسْمِ رَبِّكَ الَّذِىْ خَلَقَ ○

"Read in the name of thy Lord and Cherisher Who created." (XCVI:1).

(*ii*) *In respect of beginning a communication or discourse:*

اِنَّهٗ مِنْ سُلَيْمٰنَ وَاِنَّهٗ بِسْمِ اللهِ الرَّحْمٰنِ الرَّحِيْمِ ○

1. All the chapters of the Holy Qur'ãn, except one, begin with this spiritual formula, which fact highlights its importance in Muslim life.

"It (i.e., this communication) is from Solomon, and is (as follows): 'In the name of Allah, Most Gracious, Most Merciful."

(XXVII:30).

(*iii*) *In respect of riding a vehicle and beginning a journey:*

وَقَالَ ارْكَبُوا فِيهَا بِسْمِ اللَّهِ مَجْرٰىهَا وَمُرْسٰىهَا

"So he (Noah) said: 'Embark ye thereon (i.e., on the Ark)!' 'In the name of Allah be its course and its mooring'." (XI:41).

(*iv*) *In respect of slaughtering animals:*

وَلِكُلِّ أُمَّةٍ جَعَلْنَا مَنسَكًا لِّيَذْكُرُوا اسْمَ اللَّهِ عَلٰى مَا رَزَقَهُم مِّن بَهِيمَةِ الْأَنْعَامِ

"To every people did We appoint rites (of sacrifice), that they might celebrate the name of Allah[2] over the sustenance He gave them from animals (fit for food.)..." (XXII:34).

(2) **<u>In respect of Praise to God: the Holy Qur'ān's first chapter opens with the words</u>**:

اَلْحَمْدُ لِلّٰهِ

(Alhamdo-lillāh)

"Praise be to Allah." (I:2).

Muslim writings and speeches may begin with these words.

Also, a Muslim should utter them whenever he is delivered from evil (XXIII:28) or sorrow (XXXV:34), or he is blessed with God's Grace in any way (XXVII:19).

Indeed, the accomplishment of every good and beneficial act should be followed by these words as expression of thankfulness, as it has been commanded:

قُلِ الْحَمْدُ لِلّٰهِ

"Say: 'Praise be to Allah'...." (XVII:111).

---

2. A Muslim should say: "*Bismillāhe Allāho-Akbar*" ("In the name of Allah: Allah is Possessor of all Greatness").

Thus, these words should be uttered after enjoying food or drink and when putting on new clothes.

(3) **In respect of affirming the Glory of God**:

The Holy Qur'ãn says:

سَبِّحِ اسْمَ رَبِّكَ الْأَعْلَى

"Glorify the name of thy Lord, Most High." (LXXXVII:1).

Hence, on all occasions when God's Glory is to be proclaimed, a Muslim should say:

سُبْحٰنَ اللّٰهِ

(Subhãn-Allah)

"Glory to Allah". (XII:108).

Or,

سُبْحَانَ رَبِّيْ

(Subhãna-Rabbî)

"Glory to my Lord!" (XVII:93)

(4) **In respect of affirming the Greatness of God**:

A Muslim derives all his strength from faith in God. Hence, he has been commanded to affirm constantly, through his attitude, and through words, whenever occasion arises, the greatness of God, as the Holy Qur'ãn says:

وَكَبِّرْهُ تَكْبِيْرًا

"Yea, magnify Him for His Greatness and Glory."

(XVII:111).

The standard expression in this respect is:

اَللّٰهُ اَكْبَرُ

(Allãho-Akbar)

"Allah is Possessor of all Greatness."

(5) **<u>In respect of affirming God's excellence as Creator</u>**:

Admiring anything in God's creation, a Muslim should say:

فَتَبٰرَكَ اللّٰهُ اَحْسَنُ الْخٰلِقِيْنَ

(Fa tabãrak-Allaho ahsan-ul-Khãliqin)

"So blessed be Allah, the Best to create!" (XXIII:14).

(6) **<u>In respect of God's Forgiving and Mercy</u>**:

On occasions of consciousness of one's error or guilt, a Muslim should say:

اَسْتَغْفِرُ اللّٰهَ

(Astaghfirullãh)

"I ask the forgiveness of Allah."

Because, the Holy Qur'ãn says:

وَالَّذِيْنَ اِذَا فَعَلُوْا فَاحِشَةً اَوْ ظَلَمُوْٓا اَنْفُسَهُمْ ذَكَرُوا اللّٰهَ فَاسْتَغْفَرُوْا لِذُنُوْبِهِمْ وَمَنْ يَّغْفِرُ الذُّنُوْبَ اِلَّا اللّٰهُ

"And those who, having done something to be ashamed of, or having wronged their own souls, earnestly bring Allah to mind, and ask for forgiveness for their sins,—and who can forgive sins except Allah?...." (III:135).

He may also say, when the consciousness of the violation of Divine Law deepens:

لَآ اِلٰهَ اِلَّآ اَنْتَ سُبْحٰنَكَ اِنِّيْ كُنْتُ مِنَ الظّٰلِمِيْنَ

(Lã ilãha illã anta Subhãnaka innî kuntu min-az-Zãlimîn)

".....There is no God but Thou: Glory to Thee: I was indeed wrong!" (XXI:87)[3]

---

3. He should pray to God in these words:

رَّبِّ اغْفِرْ وَارْحَمْ وَاَنْتَ خَيْرُ الرّٰحِمِيْنَ

(Rabbighfîr warham wa anta khair-ur-Rahîmin)

"O my Lord! Grant Thou forgiveness and mercy! For Thou art the best of those who show mercy!" (XXIII:118).

(7) **In respect of guarding against evil in general**:

When an evil is imputed to a Muslim, or he is invited to evil, he should say:

مَعَاذَ اللّٰهِ

(Ma'âz-Allah)

"I seek refuge in Allah." (XII:23).

(8) **In respect of guiding against Satan**:

For keeping evil thoughts away, or for casting them off, a Muslim has been commanded:

وَإِمَّا يَنْزَغَنَّكَ مِنَ الشَّيْطٰنِ نَزْغٌ فَاسْتَعِذْ بِاللّٰهِ ۚ إِنَّهُ سَمِيعٌ عَلِيمٌ ۝

"If a suggestion from Satan assail thy (mind), seek refuge with Allah; for He heareth and knoweth all things." (VII:200).

Its usual form, based on this verse, is:

اعوذ بالله من الشيطٰن الرجيم

(A'ûzo billâhi min-ash-Shaitân-ir-Rajîm)

"I seek refuge in Allah from the accursed Devil."

Its other form, mentioned in the Holy Qur'ân, is:

وَقُلْ رَّبِّ أَعُوذُ بِكَ مِنْ هَمَزٰتِ الشَّيٰطِينِ ۝ وَأَعُوذُ بِكَ رَبِّ أَنْ يَحْضُرُونِ ۝

(Rabbe a-'ûzo bika min hamazât-ish Shayâtine wa a'ûzo bika Rabbe anyyahdurûn)

"O my Lord! I seek refuge with Thee from the suggestions of the Evil Ones. And I seek refuge with Thee O my Lord! lest they should come near me." (XXIII:97, 98).[4]

(9) **In respect of guarding serenity in afflictions**:

When confronted with any calamity or saddening news, a Muslim has been guided thus:

إِذَآ أَصَابَتْهُمْ مُّصِيبَةٌ ۙ قَالُوٓا إِنَّا لِلّٰهِ وَإِنَّآ إِلَيْهِ رٰجِعُونَ ۝

---

4. Prayers contained in chapters CXIII and CXIV are also recited on such occasions.

"They say, when afflicted with calamity: 'To Allah we belong, and to Him is our return'[5]". (II:156).

(10) **<u>In respect of thoughts of elation and pride</u>**:

When there is occasion for elation and pride, in respect of oneself or someone else, a Muslim, suppressing pride and attributing all achievements to the Power of God, should say:

مَا شَآءَ اللّٰهُ ۙ لَا قُوَّةَ اِلَّا بِاللّٰهِ ۚ

(Mãshã-Allah Lã quwwata illã billãh)

".....'Allah's Will (be done)! There is no power but with Allah!'....." (XVIII:39).

(11) **<u>In respect of making a promise</u>**:

When a Muslim makes a promise, he should on the one hand make a firm resolve to carry out his promise at all cost, and on the other hand say, seeking the help of God:

اِنْ شَآءَ اللّٰهُ

(Inshã-Allah)

"If Allah wills." (XLVIII:27)[6].

Similarly, he should say these words when he anticipates something. Because the Holy Qur'ãn has commanded the Muslims to do so:

وَلَا تَقُوْلَنَّ لِشَایْءٍ اِنِّیْ فَاعِلٌ ذٰلِكَ غَدًا ۙ اِلَّآ اَنْ يَّشَآءَ اللّٰهُ ۫

"Nor say of anything, I shall be sure to do so and so tomorrow without adding, 'So please Allah!'....." (XVIII:23, 24).

(12) **<u>In respect of recalling something forgotten</u>**:

The Holy Qur'ãn says:

وَاذْكُرْ رَّبَّكَ اِذَا نَسِيْتَ وَقُلْ عَسٰٓى اَنْ يَّهْدِيَنِ رَبِّيْ لِاَقْرَبَ مِنْ هٰذَا رَشَدًا ۝

5. (Innã lillãhi wa innã ilaihi rãje'ûn).

6. These words have been used not only by the Holy Prophet Muhammad (Peace be on him), as in this verse, but by other Prophets also. Ref: XII:99; XVIII:69; XXVIII:27; XXXVIII:102.

".....and call thy Lord to mind when thou forgettest, and say, 'I hope that my Lord will guide me ever closer (even) than this to the right road"[7]." (XVIII:24).

(13) **<u>In respect of safeguarding devotion to the Holy Prophet (Peace be on him)</u>**:

Affirming, and invoking increase in, Divine Blessings and Peace on the Holy Prophet Muhammad (Divinely Blessed is he and in eternal Peace) whenever his name is mentioned,—doing this with all respect and as a mark of gratitude for his suffering in the cause of the service of mankind, and in obedience to the command of God given in the Holy Qur'ãn:

إِنَّ اللَّهَ وَمَلَٰٓئِكَتَهُۥ يُصَلُّونَ عَلَى النَّبِيِّ ۚ يَٰٓأَيُّهَا الَّذِينَ ءَامَنُوا۟ صَلُّوا۟ عَلَيْهِ وَسَلِّمُوا۟ تَسْلِيمًا

"Lo! Allah and His angels shower Blessings (always) on the Prophet. O ye who believe! Ask blessings on him and salute him with a worthy salutation (i.e., with all respect)." (XXXIII:56)[8].

The shortest and the most generally used expression for affirming Divine Blessings and Peace on him is:

صلى الله عليه وسلم

(Sallallãho 'alaihe wa sallam)

i.e., "Allah has bestowed upon him His Blessings and Peace."[9]

---

7. ('Asa anyyahdiyane Rabbî li aqraba min hãzã rashadã).

8. This verse has a profound spiritual implication. We are, however, concerned here only with its implication in respect of manners.

9. It is necessary to point out here the grave mischief of those non-Muslim scholars who translate the expression in question as: "God bless him and grant him salvation." (*A Dictionary of Modern Written Arabic*, edited by J. Milton Cowan, p. 425). As regards salvation, every Prophet of God was born with his salvation ensured, because he was the Messenger of God and, as such, remained all his life, under Divine Protection, immune from sins. And this is perfectly logical, because he came to lead others into salvation. With reference to Muhammad, this fact has been clearly affirmed by the Qur'ãn in several contexts, e.g., in XLVIII:2. My rendering is according to the classical commentators of the Qur'ãn. (See *Tafsir al-Jalãlain*, p. 357).

The shortest comprehensive expression for invoking increase[10]—infinite increase—in God's Blessings and Peace for him, is:

اللّٰهمّ صلّ على محمّد وبارك وسلّم

(Allãhumma Salle'alã Muhammadin wa bãrik wa sallim)

"O Allah! shower Thine Mercy, Thine Benediction and Thine Peace on Muhammad."

In English, the words "Peace be on him" have been used by Muslim writers. These words form the translation of:

عليه السّلام

('Alaihis-Salãm)

That expression, however, also means:

"He is blessed with Peace."

(14) **<u>In respect of revering the Holy Prophet's memory, and hence, his grave at Madinah</u>:**

The Holy Qur'ãn says:

لِتُؤْمِنُوْا بِاللّٰهِ وَ رَسُوْلِهٖ وَ تُعَزِّرُوْهُ وَ تُوَقِّرُوْهُ ؕ

"....in order that ye (O mankind) may believe in Allah and His Messenger (Muhammad) and may assist and *honour* him....." (XLVIII:9).

Moreover, the Holy Qur'ãn lays down:

اِنَّ اَكْرَمَكُمْ عِنْدَ اللّٰهِ اَتْقٰكُمْ ؕ

"Verily the most honourable among you is he who excels in Piety." (XLIX:13).

---

10. The Holy Prophet's entire life, since the very first day of his existence, has been, and is, and will be, under Divine Blessings and Peace. It is, therefore, increase which is invoked, and not mere bestowal. And this invoking for increase, again, is actually for getting blessings ourselves and not because the Holy Prophet needs it from us,—the continuous and abiding evolution of his personality in Beauty, Grace and Perfection having been already ensured by God (XCIII:4, 5).

And the Holy Prophet, according to Islamic theology, excels all human beings is Piety. He is, therefore, not only honourable but the most honourable in entire creation.

Besides that, he is the first Muslim among God's creatures (VI:163); hence he deserves honour foremost in God's creation.[11]

Thus, when a Muslim visits Madinah, he should treat the Holy Prophet's Mausoleum with deep and unstinted reverence, stand before his grave most respectfully while paying hcmage to him and seeking God's Blessings for himself.

(15) **<u>In respect of revering the Holy Ka'bah at Makkah</u>**:

The Holy *Ka'bah* is one of the 'Symbols of God'; and the Holy Qur'ãn teaches:

وَمَنْ يُعَظِّمْ شَعَآئِرَ اللّٰهِ فَاِنَّهَا مِنْ تَقْوَى الْقُلُوْبِ ۝

".....whoever holds in honour the Symbols of Allah, it surely is from piety of the hearts." (XXII:32).

Hence, when a Muslim visits the Holy *Ka'bah* and looks at it, he should do so with a deep reverential attitude and even his formal behaviour there should be such as to be entirely based on its sacredness.

(16) **<u>In respect of revering the Holy Qur'ãn</u>**:

(*a*) The Holy Qur'ãn says about itself:

لَا يَمَسُّهٗٓ اِلَّا الْمُطَهَّرُوْنَ ۝

"which none shall touch but those who are clean." (LVI:79).

Hence, a Muslim should handle it only when he is in a state of formal purity with *wudû* and his total personality is in a state of communion with God.

(*b*) We are also told:

وَاِذَا قُرِئَ الْقُرْاٰنُ فَاسْتَمِعُوْا لَهٗ وَاَنْصِتُوْا لَعَلَّكُمْ تُرْحَمُوْنَ ۝

---

11. He is the first in Creation. This is borne out by the facts that:-

(1) everything in the universe is Muslim (III:83); and (2) the Holy Prophet is the first Muslim (VI:163).

"When the Qur'ãn is read, listen to it with attention, and hold your peace: that ye may receive Mercy." (VII:204).

Hence, when the Holy Qur'ãn is read loudly, a Muslim should not only concentrate his mind on it but should also adopt the attitude of reverence.

(17) **In respect of venerating the mosque**:

The Holy Qur'ãn says:

يَٰبَنِيٓ ءَادَمَ خُذُواْ زِينَتَكُمْ عِندَ كُلِّ مَسْجِدٍ

"O Children of Adam! Wear your beautiful apparel (adornment) at every (time and) place of prayer:....." (VII:31).

Hence, when a Muslim visits the mosque, he should go there properly dressed and with respectful attitude.

And as long as he stays there, he should observe the most dignified manners, in accordance with the advice given in XXII:32, quoted in the text of "manner 15"

Chapter II

PERSONAL AND SOCIAL MANNERS

(1) **In respect of employing the concept of "Rightism"**:

The Holy Qur'ãn designates the Muslims as "the Companions of the Right Hand", and "those on the right hand" (LVI:8). From here emerges the concept of "Rightism" which projects itself in the domain of manners and is employed in all acts involving cleanliness, beneficiality, sanctity, and the like.

The *Hadîth* supplies the details in this respect, which have been incorporated in the book of *Fiqh* (Islamic Law).[1]

(2) **In respect of greeting one another**:

The Holy Qur'ãn says:

وَإِذَا حُيِّيتُم بِتَحِيَّةٍ فَحَيُّوا بِأَحْسَنَ مِنْهَا أَوْ رُدُّوهَا إِنَّ اللَّهَ كَانَ عَلَىٰ كُلِّ شَيْءٍ حَسِيبًا ○

"When a (courteous) greeting is offered to you, meet it with a greeting still more courteous, or (at least) of equal courtesy. Allah takes

---

1. Such laws relating to manners are:

The right hand should be used for: (*a*) eating and drinking, (*b*) putting on clothes on the upper part of the body, and (*c*) giving and receiving gifts and washing hands.

The left hand should be used for: (*a*) cleansing the nose and (*b*) washing soiled part of the body after the call of nature.

The right foot should be: (*a*) placed first in entering the mosque, (*b*) used in putting on trousers, pants, socks and shoes, (*c*) employed in coming out of the toilet; and (*d*) handled first when washing the feet.

The left foot should be: (*a*) employed in coming out of the mosque, (*b*) entered first into the toilet, and (*c*) used in putting off clothes, etc., from the lower part of the body.

When a person lies down to take rest, he should rest on his right side first.

These manners are not based on any superstition, but are meant to form the symbolic reminders of the fact that a Muslim has to build up his life as one of the "Companions of the Right Hand." The other end is the creation of the sense of discipline and of uniformity of behaviour among Muslims. (For references, see: *Kitãb al-Adãb* in the Compendiums of *Hadîth* and the relevant sections in the books on Islamic Law.

careful account of all things." (IV:86).

The basic form of greeting has been given in the Holy Qur'ān at several places, as for instance in the following verse:

وَإِذَا جَاءَكَ الَّذِينَ يُؤْمِنُونَ بِآيَاتِنَا فَقُلْ سَلَامٌ عَلَيْكُمْ كَتَبَ رَبُّكُمْ عَلَى نَفْسِهِ الرَّحْمَةَ

"When those come to thee who believe in Our Sings, say: 'Peace be on you: your Lord hath prescribed for Himself (the rule of) Mercy....."
(VI:54).

سَلَامٌ عَلَيْكُم بِمَا صَبَرْتُمْ فَنِعْمَ عُقْبَى الدَّارِ ۝

"Peace unto you for that ye persevered in patience! Now how excellent is the final Home!" (XIII:24).

وَالسَّلَامُ عَلَى مَنِ اتَّبَعَ الْهُدَى ۝

".....and peace to all who follow the Guidance." (XX:47).

The Islamic *Sharī'ah* has prescribed the following standard form:

السلام عليكم

(Assalāmo 'alaikum)

"Peace be on (or, with) you",

which, as a reply, take the form:

وعليكم السلام

(Wa 'alaikum-us-Salām)

"and on you (also) be Peace."

To it can be added:

ورحمة الله

(Wa Rahmatullāh)

"and the Mercy of Allah."

And after that, also:

وبركاته

(Wa Barakãtuhû)

"and His Blessings."

These additions are meant to raise the standard of greeting in the expression of love.

(3) **In respect of dignified bearing in life**:

A Muslim should keep aloof from all unedifying things in word and deed, not to speak of indulging in them. (XXIII:3). In spite of that, however, if he is ever confronted with an unedifying situation or thing, it is his duty to withdraw in an honourable and dignified manner. The Holy Qur'ãn says:

وَإِذَا مَرُّوا بِاللَّغْوِ مَرُّوا كِرَامًا ○

"....and when they pass by any senseless thing, they pass by it with dignified (avoidance)." (XXV:72).

(4) **In respect of dealing with unreasonable people**:

With aggressive, unreasonable people who dispute merely for the sake of disputing, a Muslim should deal in a dignified manner, courteously withdrawing from their wranglings. The Holy Qur'ãn says:

وَإِذَا خَاطَبَهُمُ الْجَاهِلُونَ قَالُوا سَلَامًا ○

"....and when the ignorant address them, they say, 'Peace'." (XXV:63).

(5) **In respect of talking to people**:

A Muslim's manner of talk should contain the elements of courtesy, serenity and dignity.

The Holy Qur'ãn says:

وَقُولُوا لِلنَّاسِ حُسْنًا

".....and speak in goodly (i.e., courteous and dignified) manner to mankind...." (II:83).

وَاغْضُضْ مِنْ صَوْتِكَ ۚ

".....and lower thy voice (i.e., speak to people with serenity)...." (XXXI:19).

(6) **In respect of avoidance of ostentation and haughtiness and observance of humility**:

A Muslim's manners should always reflect the above virtues. The Holy Qur'ãn says:

وَلَا تَمْشِ فِي الْأَرْضِ مَرَحًا ۖ إِنَّكَ لَن تَخْرِقَ الْأَرْضَ وَلَن تَبْلُغَ الْجِبَالَ طُولًا ۝

"Nor walk on the earth with insolence: For thou canst not rend the earth asunder, nor reach the mountains in height." (XVII:37).

وَاقْصِدْ فِي مَشْيِكَ وَاغْضُضْ مِن صَوْتِكَ ۚ إِنَّ أَنكَرَ الْأَصْوَاتِ لَصَوْتُ الْحَمِيرِ ۝

"And be moderate in thy pace, and lower thy voice; for the harshest of sounds without doubt is the braying of the ass." (XXXI:19).

وَعِبَادُ الرَّحْمَٰنِ الَّذِينَ يَمْشُونَ عَلَى الْأَرْضِ هَوْنًا

"And the servants of (Allah) Most-Gracious are those who walk on the earth in humility....." (XXV:63).

(7) **In respect of avoidance of light-heartedness**:

A Muslim's manner's should always be based on avoidance of light-heartedness and vainglory and should reflect dignified bearing, because, according to the Holy Qur'ãn.

إِنَّ اللَّهَ لَا يُحِبُّ الْفَرِحِينَ ۝

"Verily Allah approveth not those who exult in vanity." (XXVIII:76).

(8) **In respect of being thankful**:

The Holy Qur'ãn has repeatedly emphasised thankfulness as one of the basic qualities of Islamic character and has condemned ungratefulness[2],—thankfulness benefiting not only the personality of the moral agent in respect of its harmonious build-up but also bringing reward from God in the Hereafter:

وَسَنَجۡزِى الشّٰكِرِيۡنَ ۝

"....and Allah will reward those who give thanks (to God and man)." (III:145).

Hence, a Muslim should always thank in suitable word everyone who does any good to him.

(9) **In regard to demonstration of respect towards the elders**:

A Muslim should always maintain a respectful attitude towards his elders and demonstrate this attitude even in his manners, as it has been commanded in the case of one's parents:

وَاخۡفِضۡ لَهُمَا جَنَاحَ الذُّلِّ مِنَ الرَّحۡمَةِ

"And, out of kindness, lower unto them the wing of humility—" (XVII:24).

(10) **In respect of compassion**:

A Muslim should not only maintain in his heart but also demonstrate through his manners compassionate kindness for all those who are weaker than him in any way or junior to him in age or rank, because the Holy Qur'ãn has laid down this virtue as one of the qualities of Muslim character. It says:—

ثُمَّ كَانَ مِنَ الَّذِيۡنَ اٰمَنُوۡا وَتَوَاصَوۡا بِالصَّبۡرِ وَتَوَاصَوۡا بِالۡمَرۡحَمَةِ ۝

"...and to be of those who believe and exhort one another to perseverance and exhort one another to compassionate kindness." (XC:17).

(11) **In respect of treating those who seek help**:

A Muslim should treat politely and nor rudely everyone who ask for his help, because the Holy Qur'ãn says:

وَاَمَّا السَّآئِلَ فَلَا تَنۡهَرۡ ۝

2. As recorded in the foregoing.

"And as to one who asks (for thine help) scold (him) not".
(XCIII:10).

(12) **In respect of visiting the people**:

(i) Respect for each other's privacy with a view to maintain personal and family privacy and to avoid social scandal to which its non-observance is likely to give rise, enjoined:

يَٰٓأَيُّهَا ٱلَّذِينَ ءَامَنُواْ لِيَسۡتَـٔۡذِنكُمُ ٱلَّذِينَ مَلَكَتۡ أَيۡمَٰنُكُمۡ وَٱلَّذِينَ لَمۡ يَبۡلُغُواْ ٱلۡحُلُمَ
مِنكُمۡ ثَلَٰثَ مَرَّٰتٍ مِّن قَبۡلِ صَلَوٰةِ ٱلۡفَجۡرِ وَحِينَ تَضَعُونَ ثِيَابَكُم مِّنَ ٱلظَّهِيرَةِ
وَمِنۢ بَعۡدِ صَلَوٰةِ ٱلۡعِشَآءِ ثَلَٰثُ عَوۡرَٰتٍ لَّكُمۡ لَيۡسَ عَلَيۡكُمۡ وَلَا عَلَيۡهِمۡ
جُنَاحُۢ بَعۡدَهُنَّ طَوَّٰفُونَ عَلَيۡكُم بَعۡضُكُمۡ عَلَىٰ بَعۡضٍ كَذَٰلِكَ يُبَيِّنُ ٱللَّهُ
لَكُمُ ٱلۡأٓيَٰتِ وَٱللَّهُ عَلِيمٌ حَكِيمٌ ۝ وَإِذَا بَلَغَ ٱلۡأَطۡفَٰلُ مِنكُمُ ٱلۡحُلُمَ فَلۡيَسۡتَـٔۡذِنُواْ
كَمَا ٱسۡتَـٔۡذَنَ ٱلَّذِينَ مِن قَبۡلِهِمۡ كَذَٰلِكَ يُبَيِّنُ ٱللَّهُ لَكُمۡ ءَايَٰتِهِۦ وَٱللَّهُ
عَلِيمٌ حَكِيمٌ ۝ وَٱلۡقَوَٰعِدُ مِنَ ٱلنِّسَآءِ ٱلَّٰتِي لَا يَرۡجُونَ نِكَاحًا فَلَيۡسَ عَلَيۡهِنَّ
جُنَاحٌ أَن يَضَعۡنَ ثِيَابَهُنَّ غَيۡرَ مُتَبَرِّجَٰتِۭ بِزِينَةٍ وَأَن يَسۡتَعۡفِفۡنَ خَيۡرٌ
لَّهُنَّ وَٱللَّهُ سَمِيعٌ عَلِيمٌ ۝

"O ye who believe! let those whom your right hands own and those of you who have not attained puberty ask leave of you three times, before the dawn-prayer, and when ye lay aside your garments at noonday, and after the night-prayer: three times of privacy for you. No fault there is upon them beyond these times going round upon you, some of you upon some other. In this wise Allah expoundeth unto you the commandments: and Allah is Knowing, Wise.

"And when the children among you attain puberty, then let them ask leave even as those befor them asked leave. In this wise Allah expoundeth unto you His commandments; and Allah is Knowing, Wise.

"And past child-bearing women who have no hope of wedlock—upon them it is no fault that they lay aside their outer garments, not flaunting their adornment. And that they should restrain themselves is better for them; Allah is Hearing, Knowing." (XXIV:58-60).

(ii) *Soliciting permission before entering another person's house, enjoined:*

(iii) *Respect for the inmate's decision in refusing permission, enjoined:*

In connection with these two manners, the Holy Qur'ãn says:—

يَٰٓأَيُّهَا ٱلَّذِينَ ءَامَنُوا۟ لَا تَدْخُلُوا۟ بُيُوتًا غَيْرَ بُيُوتِكُمْ حَتَّىٰ تَسْتَأْنِسُوا۟ وَتُسَلِّمُوا۟
عَلَىٰٓ أَهْلِهَا ۚ ذَٰلِكُمْ خَيْرٌ لَّكُمْ لَعَلَّكُمْ تَذَكَّرُونَ ۝ فَإِن لَّمْ تَجِدُوا۟ فِيهَآ أَحَدًا
فَلَا تَدْخُلُوهَا حَتَّىٰ يُؤْذَنَ لَكُمْ ۖ وَإِن قِيلَ لَكُمُ ٱرْجِعُوا۟ فَٱرْجِعُوا۟ ۖ هُوَ أَزْكَىٰ لَكُمْ ۚ
وَٱللَّهُ بِمَا تَعْمَلُونَ عَلِيمٌ ۝ لَّيْسَ عَلَيْكُمْ جُنَاحٌ أَن تَدْخُلُوا۟ بُيُوتًا غَيْرَ
مَسْكُونَةٍ فِيهَا مَتَٰعٌ لَّكُمْ ۚ وَٱللَّهُ يَعْلَمُ مَا تُبْدُونَ وَمَا تَكْتُمُونَ ۝

"O ye who believe enter not houses other than your own until ye have asked leave and invoked peace on the inmates thereof. That is better for you, haply ye may take heed.

"Then if ye find no one therein, enter not until leave hath been given you. And if it is said unto you, go back, then go back. It is cleaner for you, and Allah is of that which ye work Knower.

"No fault it is upon you that ye enter houses uninhabited wherein there is some property for you, and Allah knoweth that what ye disclose and that which ye hide." (XXIV:27-29).

(iv) *Greeting the inmates on entering a house, enjoined:*

فَإِذَا دَخَلْتُم بُيُوتًا فَسَلِّمُوا۟ عَلَىٰٓ أَنفُسِكُمْ تَحِيَّةً مِّنْ عِندِ ٱللَّهِ مُبَٰرَكَةً طَيِّبَةً ۚ

"....Then when ye enter houses, salute one another with a greeting from Allah, blessed and sweet." (XXIV:61).

(v) *Obtaining permission from the host before leaving him, enjoined:*

The Holy Qur'ãn says:—

إِنَّمَا ٱلْمُؤْمِنُونَ ٱلَّذِينَ ءَامَنُوا۟ بِٱللَّهِ وَرَسُولِهِۦ وَإِذَا كَانُوا۟ مَعَهُۥ عَلَىٰٓ أَمْرٍ
جَامِعٍ لَّمْ يَذْهَبُوا۟ حَتَّىٰ يَسْتَـْٔذِنُوهُ ۚ

"The Believers are those alone who have believed in Allah and His Messenger, and when they are with him on (some) affair collecting (people together) they depart not until they have asked his leave...."

(XXIV:62).

This verse, although particular in its reference, contains the general principle of Muslim conduct and manners.

(13) **<u>In respect of dining at other persons' homes</u>**:

(i) Coming to dine without invitation deprecated.

(ii) Coming to dine before the appointed time deprecated.

(iii) Seeking to stay after dining for indulging in idle talk deprecated

All these there injunctions are contained in the following verse, in its general application:—

يَٰٓأَيُّهَا ٱلَّذِينَ ءَامَنُوا۟ لَا تَدْخُلُوا۟ بُيُوتَ ٱلنَّبِىِّ إِلَّآ أَن يُؤْذَنَ لَكُمْ إِلَىٰ طَعَامٍ
غَيْرَ نَٰظِرِينَ إِنَىٰهُ وَلَٰكِنْ إِذَا دُعِيتُمْ فَٱدْخُلُوا۟ فَإِذَا طَعِمْتُمْ فَٱنتَشِرُوا۟
وَلَا مُسْتَـْٔنِسِينَ لِحَدِيثٍ

"O ye who believe! enter not the Prophet's houses,—until leave is given you,—for a meal, (and then) not (so early as) to wait for its preparation; but when ye are invited, enter; and when ye have taken your meal, disperse without seeking familiar talk......." (XXXIII:53).

(14) **<u>In respect of assemblies</u>**:

(i) Considerateness for others in accommodating them, enjoined:

يَٰٓأَيُّهَا ٱلَّذِينَ ءَامَنُوٓا۟ إِذَا قِيلَ لَكُمْ تَفَسَّحُوا۟ فِى ٱلْمَجَٰلِسِ فَٱفْسَحُوا۟ يَفْسَحِ ٱللَّهُ
لَكُمْ وَإِذَا قِيلَ ٱنشُزُوا۟ فَٱنشُزُوا۟

"O ye who believe! When it is said, make room! in assemblies, then make room. Allah will make way for you (hereafter). And when it is said, Come up higher! go up higher." (LVIII:11).

(ii) Engaging in whispers with someone to the annoyance of others while participating in an assembly, deprecated:

إِنَّمَا ٱلنَّجْوَىٰ مِنَ ٱلشَّيْطَٰنِ لِيَحْزُنَ ٱلَّذِينَ ءَامَنُوا۟

"Secret counsels are from Satan that he may cause grief to the Believers". (LVIII:10).

(15) **<u>In respect of modesty in relation with members of the opposite sex</u>:**

Note.— Injunctions under this head, together with those relating to privacy (quoted in the foregoing), lay down the basis of domestic peace and happiness and form a preventive measure against sexual vices and slander. They are meant to promote purity of the heart and chastity.

These injunctions may be divided into two categories, namely:—

(*a*) those relating to men; and

(*b*) those relating to women.

(*a*) *Relating to men*:

When meeting those women who are categorised as strangers by Islam:—

(i) *Lowering the gaze out of respect for modesty, enjoined:*

(ii) *Guarding modesty through proper covering of the body,*[3] *enjoined:*

The Holy Qur'ãn says:

قُلْ لِّلْمُؤْمِنِيْنَ يَغُضُّوْا مِنْ اَبْصَارِهِمْ وَ يَحْفَظُوْا فُرُوْجَهُمْ ؕ ذٰلِكَ اَزْكٰى
لَهُمْ ؕ اِنَّ اللّٰهَ خَبِيْرٌۢ بِمَا يَصْنَعُوْنَ ۝

"Say to the believing men that they should lower their gaze and guard their modesty: that will make for greater purity for them: and Allah is well acquainted with all that they do." (XXIV:30).

(*b*) *Relating to women*:

When meeting those men who are categorised as strangers by Islam:—

(*i*) *Lowering the gaze out of modesty, enjoined:*

(*ii*) *Guarding modesty through proper covering of the body, enjoined:*

(*iii*) *Use, in public appearance, of long gowns covering the whole body, enjoined:*

---

3. This rules out nudism, and even semi-nudism.

(*iv*) *Display of beauty and ornaments, except what must appear thereof, prohibited:*

(*v*) *Thinking the ankle ornaments, thereby attracting the attention of male passers-by,*[4] *prohibited:*

All these injunctions are covered by the following two verses:—

وَقُل لِّلْمُؤْمِنَٰتِ يَغْضُضْنَ مِنْ أَبْصَٰرِهِنَّ وَيَحْفَظْنَ فُرُوجَهُنَّ وَلَا يُبْدِينَ
زِينَتَهُنَّ إِلَّا مَا ظَهَرَ مِنْهَا وَلْيَضْرِبْنَ بِخُمُرِهِنَّ عَلَىٰ جُيُوبِهِنَّ

"And say to the believing women that they should lower their gaze and guard their modesty; that they should not display their beauty and ornaments except what (must ordinarily) appear thereof; that they should draw their scarves over their bosoms—" (XXIV:31).

يَٰٓأَيُّهَا ٱلنَّبِىُّ قُل لِّأَزْوَٰجِكَ وَبَنَاتِكَ وَنِسَآءِ ٱلْمُؤْمِنِينَ يُدْنِينَ عَلَيْهِنَّ
مِن جَلَٰبِيبِهِنَّ ذَٰلِكَ أَدْنَىٰٓ أَن يُعْرَفْنَ فَلَا يُؤْذَيْنَ وَكَانَ ٱللَّهُ غَفُورًا رَّحِيمًا

"O Prophet! Tell thy wives and daughters, and the believing women, that they should cast their outer garments over their persons (when abroad); that is better, that they should be known (as such) and not molested. And Allah is Oft-Forgiving, Most Merciful". (XXXIII:59).

---

4. Such actions are possible only for those who are inclined to unchastity.

Book III

DUTIES RELATING TO THE SOCIETAL WHOLE

Part I

DUTIES OF THE INDIVIDUAL TOWARDS THE MUSLIM SOCIETY

Part II

DUTIES OF THE MUSLIM SOCIETY TOWARDS THE INDIVIDUAL

Part III

PENAL ETHICS

Part I

DUTIES OF THE INDIVIDUAL TOWARDS THE MUSLIM SOCIETY

END: Creation, Preservation and Promotion of Collective Life in a manner which ensures the Spiritual, Moral and Social Progress of the Individual in a healthy manner and eliminates the contrary.

I.— Preamble:

Society *vis-a-vis* the Individual.

II.— Duties:

1. Duty relating to active struggle for the Spiritual and Moral Perfection of the Muslim society.

2. Duties relating to active struggle for ensuring and promoting the economic soundness of the Muslim society.

3. Duties relating to active struggle for ensuring and promoting the political stability of the Muslim society.

Chapter I

PREAMBLE

Society vis-a-vis the Individual:

(i) The organic nature of human society:

يٰٓاَيُّهَا النَّاسُ اتَّقُوْا رَبَّكُمُ الَّذِىْ خَلَقَكُمْ مِّنْ نَّفْسٍ وَّاحِدَةٍ وَّخَلَقَ
مِنْهَا زَوْجَهَا وَبَثَّ مِنْهُمَا رِجَالًا كَثِيْرًا وَّنِسَآءً ۚ وَاتَّقُوا اللّٰهَ الَّذِىْ تَسَآءَلُوْنَ
بِهٖ وَالْاَرْحَامَ ۭ اِنَّ اللّٰهَ كَانَ عَلَيْكُمْ رَقِيْبًا ۝

"O mankind! reverence your Guardian-Lord, Who created you from a single soul, created, of like nature, his mate, and from them twain scattered (like seeds) countless men and women;—Reverence Allah through Whom ye demand your mutual (rights), and (reverence) the wombs (that bore you): for Allah ever watches over you." (IV:1).

يٰٓاَيُّهَا النَّاسُ اِنَّا خَلَقْنٰكُمْ مِّنْ ذَكَرٍ وَّ اُنْثٰى وَجَعَلْنٰكُمْ شُعُوْبًا وَّقَبَآئِلَ
لِتَعَارَفُوْا ۭ اِنَّ اَكْرَمَكُمْ عِنْدَ اللّٰهِ اَتْقٰكُمْ ۭ اِنَّ اللّٰهَ عَلِيْمٌ خَبِيْرٌ ۝

"O mankind! We created you from a single (pair) of a male and a female, and made you into nations and tribes, that ye may known each other (not that ye may despise each other). Verily the most honoured of you in the sight of Allah is (he who is) the most righteous of you. And Allah has full knowledge and is well acquainted (with all things)." (XLIX:13).

مَا خَلْقُكُمْ وَلَا بَعْثُكُمْ اِلَّا كَنَفْسٍ وَّاحِدَةٍ ۭ اِنَّ اللّٰهَ سَمِيْعٌۢ بَصِيْرٌ ۝

"And your creation and your resurrection is in no wise but as an individual soul: for Allah is He Who hears and sees (all things)." (XXXI:28).

(ii) The organic nature of Muslim society as coming into existence by a "Contract":

اِنَّ اللّٰهَ اشْتَرٰى مِنَ الْمُؤْمِنِيْنَ اَنْفُسَهُمْ وَاَمْوَالَهُمْ بِاَنَّ لَهُمُ الْجَنَّةَ ۭ يُقَاتِلُوْنَ
فِىْ سَبِيْلِ اللّٰهِ فَيَقْتُلُوْنَ وَيُقْتَلُوْنَ ۣ وَعْدًا عَلَيْهِ حَقًّا فِى التَّوْرٰىةِ وَالْاِنْجِيْلِ

وَالْقُرْآنِ ۚ وَمَنْ أَوْفَىٰ بِعَهْدِهِ مِنَ اللَّهِ فَاسْتَبْشِرُوا بِبَيْعِكُمُ الَّذِي بَايَعْتُمْ
بِهِ ۚ وَذَٰلِكَ هُوَ الْفَوْزُ الْعَظِيمُ ۝

"Allah hath purchased of the Believers their persons and their goods; for theirs (in return) is the Garden (of Paradise): They fight in His Cause, and slay and are slain: a promise binding on Him in Truth, through the *Taurāt*, the *Injīl*, and the Qur'ān: and who is more faithful to his Covenant than Allah? Then rejoice in the bargain which ye have concluded: That is the achievement supreme." (IX:111).

(iii) *The manifoldness of social life as the natural condition of the progress of human civilisation:*

وَاللَّيْلِ إِذَا يَغْشَىٰ ۝ وَالنَّهَارِ إِذَا تَجَلَّىٰ ۝ وَمَا خَلَقَ الذَّكَرَ وَالْأُنْثَىٰ ۝
إِنَّ سَعْيَكُمْ لَشَتَّىٰ ۝

"By the Night as it conceals (the light); by the Day as it appears in glory; by (the mystery of) the creation of male and female;—verily (the ends) ye strive for are diverse." (XCII:1-4).

(iv) *The importance of social environment for the development of the individual:*

وَاتَّقُوا فِتْنَةً لَا تُصِيبَنَّ الَّذِينَ ظَلَمُوا مِنْكُمْ خَاصَّةً ۚ وَاعْلَمُوا
أَنَّ اللَّهَ شَدِيدُ الْعِقَابِ ۝

"And fear tumult (or oppression), which affecteth not in particular (only) those of you who do wrong: and know that Allah is strict in punishment." (VIII:25).

(v) *Treating the demands of society above the demands of self, i.e., subordinating personal interests to the interests of the Social Whole created by Islam, enjoined:*

قُلْ إِنْ كَانَ آبَاؤُكُمْ وَأَبْنَاؤُكُمْ وَإِخْوَانُكُمْ وَأَزْوَاجُكُمْ وَعَشِيرَتُكُمْ وَ
أَمْوَالٌ اقْتَرَفْتُمُوهَا وَتِجَارَةٌ تَخْشَوْنَ كَسَادَهَا وَمَسَاكِنُ تَرْضَوْنَهَا
أَحَبَّ إِلَيْكُمْ مِنَ اللَّهِ وَرَسُولِهِ وَجِهَادٍ فِي سَبِيلِهِ فَتَرَبَّصُوا حَتَّىٰ
يَأْتِيَ اللَّهُ بِأَمْرِهِ ۗ وَاللَّهُ لَا يَهْدِي الْقَوْمَ الْفَاسِقِينَ ۝

"Say: if it be that your fathers, your sons, your brothers, your mates, or your kindred; the wealth that ye have gained; the commerce in which ye fear a decline; or the dwellings in which ye delight—are dearer to you than Allah, or His Messenger, or the striving in His cause;— then wait until Allah brings about His decision: and Allah guides not the rebellious."

(IX:24).

Chapter II

DUTIES

I. Duty Relating to Active Struggle for the Spiritual and Moral Perfection of the Muslim Society

Active struggle for the spiritual and moral perfection of humanity in general, and of their own community in particular, is the very mission of the Muslims:

كُنْتُمْ خَيْرَ أُمَّةٍ أُخْرِجَتْ لِلنَّاسِ تَأْمُرُونَ بِالْمَعْرُوفِ وَتَنْهَوْنَ عَنِ
الْمُنْكَرِ وَتُؤْمِنُونَ بِاللّٰهِ

"Ye are the best of People, evolved for (the service of) mankind, enjoining what is right, forbidding what is wrong, and believing in Allah....." (III:110).

Indeed, it is the inseparable quality of Muslim character:

الْآمِرُونَ بِالْمَعْرُوفِ وَالنَّاهُونَ عَنِ الْمُنْكَرِ

"....(it is their character that) they (always) enjoin good and (always) forbid evil....." (IX:112).

Hence, Muslims have been commanded to set aright their affairs:

فَاتَّقُوا اللّٰهَ وَأَصْلِحُوا ذَاتَ بَيْنِكُمْ

".....So be careful of your duty to Allah and set aright matters among you (in respect of your mutual duties)....." (VÍII:1).

Nay, the Holy Qur'ãn goes beyond that. It orders *all* Muslims to engage in an unceasing struggle for the promotion of the Cause of spiritual and moral perfection of Muslim society in particular and of humanity in general. It says:

يَا أَيُّهَا الَّذِينَ آمَنُوا كُونُوا أَنْصَارَ اللّٰهِ

"O ye who believe! Be ye helpers (in the Cause) of Allah (—the Cause of helping human beings to spiritual and moral perfection)....." (LXI:14).

While laying down that duty, however, the Holy Qur'ãn also guarantees success, if the struggle is pursued with the fulfilment of all the prescribed conditions:

وَلَيَنْصُرَنَّ اللهُ مَنْ يَّنْصُرُهٗ ؕ اِنَّ اللهَ لَقَوِیٌّ عَزِیْزٌ ۝

".....Allah will certainly aid those who aid His (Cause);—for verily Allah is Full of Strength, Exalted in Might, (able to enforce His Will)." (XXII:40).

يٰۤاَيُّهَا الَّذِيْنَ اٰمَنُوْۤا اِنْ تَنْصُرُوا اللهَ يَنْصُرْكُمْ وَ يُثَبِّتْ اَقْدَامَكُمْ ۝

"O ye who believe! if ye will aid (the Cause of) Allah, He will aid you and will make your foothold firm." (XLVII:7).

One of those conditions is that the struggle has to be pursued not only as an individual responsibility but also co-operatively and collectively:

تَعَاوَنُوْا عَلَى الْبِرِّ وَالتَّقْوٰى ۖ وَلَا تَعَاوَنُوْا عَلَى الْاِثْمِ وَالْعُدْوَانِ ۖ

"....Help ye one another in righteousness and piety, but help not one another in sin and enmity....." (V:3).

2. Duties[1] Relating to Active Struggle for Ensuring and Promoting the Economic Soundness of the Muslim Society

I. <u>The Principle of 'Wealth for Welfare'</u>:

The Holy Qur'ãn denounces inordinate love of wealth as an anti-Islamic quality of character, which leads to hell:

وَيْلٌ لِّكُلِّ هُمَزَةٍ لُّمَزَةِۣ ۝ الَّذِیْ جَمَعَ مَالًا وَّعَدَّدَهٗ ۝ يَحْسَبُ اَنَّ مَالَهٗۤ اَخْلَدَهٗ ۝
كَلَّا لَيُنْۢبَذَنَّ فِی الْحُطَمَةِ ۝

"Woe to every (kind of) scandalmonger and back-biter, who pileth up wealth and layeth it by, thinking that his wealth would make him last for ever! By no means! he will be surely thrown into 'That which Breaks to Pieces'." (CIV:1-4).

---

1. All those duties which relate to economic matters and which have been listed in the previous sections, are also directly related here.

Similarly, it condemns those who amass wealth, make it idle, and do not spend freely for the good of their fellow-beings:

وَالَّذِينَ يَكْنِزُونَ الذَّهَبَ وَالْفِضَّةَ وَلَا يُنْفِقُونَهَا فِي سَبِيلِ اللَّهِ
فَبَشِّرْهُمْ بِعَذَابٍ أَلِيمٍ ۝ يَوْمَ يُحْمَىٰ عَلَيْهَا فِي نَارِ جَهَنَّمَ فَتُكْوَىٰ بِهَا
جِبَاهُهُمْ وَجُنُوبُهُمْ وَظُهُورُهُمْ ۖ هَٰذَا مَا كَنَزْتُمْ لِأَنْفُسِكُمْ فَذُوقُوا
مَا كُنْتُمْ تَكْنِزُونَ ۝

"....And there are those who bury gold and silver and spend it not in the Way of Allah: announce unto them a most grievous penalty— On the Day when heat will be produced out of that (wealth) in the fire of Hell, and with it will be branded their foreheads, their flanks, and their backs.—'This is the (treasure) which ye buried for yourselves: taste ye, then, the (treasure) ye buried!' " (IX:34-35).

Abstaining from spending for the promotion of truth and righteousness and the welfare of fellow-beings leads to the ruin (moral, spiritual and economic) of the individual and the cummunity:

وَأَنْفِقُوا فِي سَبِيلِ اللَّهِ وَلَا تُلْقُوا بِأَيْدِيكُمْ إِلَى التَّهْلُكَةِ ۛ وَأَحْسِنُوا ۛ
إِنَّ اللَّهَ يُحِبُّ الْمُحْسِنِينَ ۝

"And spend of your substance in the cause of Allah, and make not your own hands contribute to your destruction; but do good; for Allah loveth those who do good." (II:195).

Its consequences are, indeed, grave, as exemplified in the story of Qãrûn (or, Korah):

إِنَّ قَارُونَ كَانَ مِنْ قَوْمِ مُوسَىٰ فَبَغَىٰ عَلَيْهِمْ ۖ وَآتَيْنَاهُ مِنَ الْكُنُوزِ
مَا إِنَّ مَفَاتِحَهُ لَتَنُوءُ بِالْعُصْبَةِ أُولِي الْقُوَّةِ إِذْ قَالَ لَهُ قَوْمُهُ لَا تَفْرَحْ ۖ
إِنَّ اللَّهَ لَا يُحِبُّ الْفَرِحِينَ ۝ وَابْتَغِ فِيمَا آتَاكَ اللَّهُ الدَّارَ الْآخِرَةَ ۖ
وَلَا تَنْسَ نَصِيبَكَ مِنَ الدُّنْيَا ۖ وَأَحْسِنْ كَمَا أَحْسَنَ اللَّهُ إِلَيْكَ ۖ
وَلَا تَبْغِ الْفَسَادَ فِي الْأَرْضِ ۖ إِنَّ اللَّهَ لَا يُحِبُّ الْمُفْسِدِينَ ۝ قَالَ
إِنَّمَا أُوتِيتُهُ عَلَىٰ عِلْمٍ عِنْدِي ۚ أَوَلَمْ يَعْلَمْ أَنَّ اللَّهَ قَدْ أَهْلَكَ مِنْ قَبْلِهِ

مِنَ الْقُرُونِ مَنْ هُوَ أَشَدُّ مِنْهُ قُوَّةً وَأَكْثَرُ جَمْعًا ۚ وَلَا يُسْأَلُ عَنْ
ذُنُوبِهِمُ الْمُجْرِمُونَ ۝ فَخَرَجَ عَلَىٰ قَوْمِهِ فِي زِينَتِهِ ۖ قَالَ الَّذِينَ
يُرِيدُونَ الْحَيَاةَ الدُّنْيَا يَا لَيْتَ لَنَا مِثْلَ مَا أُوتِيَ قَارُونُ إِنَّهُ لَذُو حَظٍّ
عَظِيمٍ ۝ وَقَالَ الَّذِينَ أُوتُوا الْعِلْمَ وَيْلَكُمْ ثَوَابُ اللَّهِ خَيْرٌ لِمَنْ آمَنَ وَ
عَمِلَ صَالِحًا ۚ وَلَا يُلَقَّاهَا إِلَّا الصَّابِرُونَ ۝ فَخَسَفْنَا بِهِ وَبِدَارِهِ الْأَرْضَ فَمَا كَانَ
لَهُ مِنْ فِئَةٍ يَنْصُرُونَهُ مِنْ دُونِ اللَّهِ وَمَا كَانَ مِنَ الْمُنْتَصِرِينَ ۝

"Qãrûn was, doubtless, of the people of Moses; but he acted insolently towards them: Such were the treasures We had bestowed on him, that their very keys would have been a burden to a body of strong men. Behold, his people said to him: 'Exult not, for Allah loveth not those who exult (in riches). But seek, with the (wealth) which Allah has bestowed on thee, the Home of the Hereafter, nor forget thy portion in this world: but do thou good, as Allah has been good to thee, and seek not (occasions for) mischief in the land: for Allah loves not those who do mischief.' He said: 'This has been given to me because of a certain knowledge which I have.' Did he not know that Allah had destroyed before him (whole) generations,—which were superior to him in strength and greater in the amount (of riches) they had collected? But the wicked are not called (immediately) to account for their sins. So he went forth among his people in the (pride of his worldly) glitter. Said those whose aim is the Life of this World: 'Oh! that we had the like of what Qãrûn has got! for he is truly a lord of mighty good fortune!' But those who had been granted (true) knowledge said: 'Alas for you! The reward of Allah (in the Hereafter) is best for those who believe and work righteousness: but this none shall attain, save those who steadfastly persevere (in good). Then, We caused the earth to swallow up him and his house; and he had not (the least little) party to help him against Allah, nor could he defend himself." (XXVIII:76-81).

Viewing the problem from the other side, we find that, according to the Holy Qur'ãn, spending freely in the service of fellow-beings[2] forms

2. Exhortations to this effect have been repeatedly and emphatically made in the Holy Qur'ãn, both in the form of injunctions and otherwise, and have been quoted in detail on pp. 217-220.

a sure guarantee for the prosperity of the individual as well as of the community. We are told:

مَثَلُ الَّذِيْنَ يُنْفِقُوْنَ اَمْوَالَهُمْ فِيْ سَبِيْلِ اللّٰهِ كَمَثَلِ حَبَّةٍ اَنْۢبَتَتْ سَبْعَ سَنَابِلَ فِيْ كُلِّ سُنْۢبُلَةٍ مِّائَةُ حَبَّةٍ ؕ وَاللّٰهُ يُضٰعِفُ لِمَنْ يَّشَآءُ ؕ وَاللّٰهُ وَاسِعٌ عَلِيْمٌ ۝

"The parable of those who spend their substance in the Way of Allah is that of a grain of corn: it groweth seven ears, and each ear hath a hundred grains. Allah giveth manifold increase to whom He pleaseth: for Allah careth for all, and He knoweth all things." (II:261).

اِنَّ الَّذِيْنَ اٰمَنُوْا وَعَمِلُوا الصّٰلِحٰتِ وَاَقَامُوا الصَّلٰوةَ وَاٰتَوُا الزَّكٰوةَ لَهُمْ اَجْرُهُمْ عِنْدَ رَبِّهِمْ ۚ وَلَا خَوْفٌ عَلَيْهِمْ وَلَا هُمْ يَحْزَنُوْنَ ۝

"Lo! those who believe and do good works and establish worship and pay the poor-due, their reward is with their Lord and there shall no fear come upon them, neither shall they grieve." (II:277).

II. Duties:

The Holy Qur'ãn does not, however, confine itself to mere exhortation, but lays down economic duties of the individual towards the Muslim society in concrete terms.

In this respect, there are:

(*a*) Duties of Commission; and

(*b*) Duties of Omission;

We may now take up these duties.

(*a*) Duties of Commission:

(i) *An annual Welfare Tax, called al-Zakãh*[3], *enjoined:*

3. According to Islamic Law, *al-Zakãh* is leviable annually on all Muslims of means, at the rate of 2 1/2%, on all uninvested wealth like silver, gold, jewellery (in the view of Hanafi Law), cash, commercial goods and debts receivable. It is not imposed on the value of built-up houses, tools of the artisan—including industrial machinery, and agricultural implements. (For detailed laws concerning this tax, reference may be made to *Fath al-Bãrî*, the Commentary on Bukhãrî's

The Holy Qur'ãn says:

وَأَقِيمُوا الصَّلَوٰةَ وَآتُوا الزَّكَوٰةَ ۚ وَمَا تُقَدِّمُوا لِأَنفُسِكُم مِّنْ خَيْرٍ تَجِدُوهُ عِندَ اللَّهِ ۗ إِنَّ اللَّهَ بِمَا تَعْمَلُونَ بَصِيرٌ ۝

"And establish (regular) Prayer and pay *al-Zakãh* (i.e., the obligatory annual poor-rate, or, welfare tax)[4]. And whatever good ye send forth for your souls before you, ye will find it with Allah. Lo! Allah is the Seer of all that ye do." (II:110)[5].

Note 1:— There is another annual welfare tax also, which is very much like *al-Zakãh*, i.e., the *Sadaqah al-Fitr*. It becomes due every year at the end of the fasting month, i.e., *Ramadãn*, and is to be compulsorily paid, for the benefit of the poor, by every Muslim of means, on his behalf as well as on behalf of everyone of his dependants. Its rate has been fixed in terms of four pounds of wheat flour per head, and payment can be made according to its market-price. It has been prescribed

---

Sahih, vol. IV, in *Hadīth* literature, and to *Hedâya* in Hanafi law: chapters on *al-Zakãh*).

It may be noted here that the institution of *al-Zakãh*, as it exists today, is in urgent need of recasting and re-evaluation.

4. That *al-Zakãh* is a welfare-tax is borne out explicitly by verse IX:60, quoted elsewhere.

The Holy Qur'ãn further mentions the aim of this tax in terms of the "eradication of economic fear and sorrow." It says:

إِنَّ الَّذِينَ آمَنُوا وَعَمِلُوا الصَّالِحَاتِ وَأَقَامُوا الصَّلَوٰةَ وَآتَوُا الزَّكَوٰةَ لَهُمْ أَجْرُهُمْ عِندَ رَبِّهِمْ ۚ وَلَا خَوْفٌ عَلَيْهِمْ وَلَا هُمْ يَحْزَنُونَ ۝

"Lo! those who believe and do deeds of righteousness and establish (regular) Prayer and pay *al-Zakãh*, their reward is with their Lord. On them (as a community) shall be no fear, nor shall they grieve (i.e., they shall not suffer from fear and sorrow, either in respect of their Salvation in the Hereafter as individuals, or in respect of their collective economic life on the earth)." (II:277).

5. Other verses on *al-Zakãh*, where the command has been repeated, are: XXII:78; XXIV:56; XXXIII:33; LXXIII:20.

That this has been God's Law since all time, and forms one of the bases of economic welfare, has been affirmed in the following verses: II:43; II:83; XIX:13; XIX:31; XIX:55; XXI:73; XCVIII:5.

by the Holy Prophet (Peace be on him)[6] and not by the Holy Qur'ãn. It is, however, directly covered by the following Qur'ãnic injunction:

وَاٰتِ ذَا الْقُرْبٰى حَقَّهٗ وَالْمِسْكِيْنَ

"And render to the kindred their due rights, as (also) to those in want....." (XVII:26).

Note 2:— There is still another tax prescribed by the Holy Qur'ãn in VI:141. It is called *'Ushr* in Islamic Law, and is levied as 1/20th of the agricultural produce on artificially irrigated land, and 1/10th of the agricultural produce on land benefiting from rain or natural spring only. It gives the appearance of being a tax like *al-Zakãh*[7], but it has been regarded in Islamic Law as land-revenue, pure and simple.

(ii) *Paying honestly and cheerfully any other taxes imposed by the Islamic State on the wealthy—for the welfare of the people and defence of the state, enjoined:*

When we study the scheme of taxation given by the Holy Qur'ãn, it is revealed to us that its outlook in that respect is rational and aimed at taxing the common man as lightly as possible. Indeed, that cruel type of heavy taxation which sucks the blood out of the common man is absolutely foreign to the spirit and the letter of the holy book.

The economic ideal of the Holy Qur'ãn being, however, the eradication of poverty and of the multifaced evils to which the possession of excessive wealth by individuals leads, spending of wealth by the wealthy freely[8] and at the highest level[9] for the benefit of their unfortunate fellow-

---

6. See: *Fath al-Bãrî*, vol. IV, p. 117.

7. See: Bukhãrî's *Sahîh*, *Bãb al-Zakãh*.

8. Cf:

الَّذِيْنَ يُنْفِقُوْنَ فِى السَّرَّآءِ وَالضَّرَّآءِ

"Those who spend (freely), whether in prosperity, or in adversity." (III:134).

9. Cf:

لَنْ تَنَالُوا الْبِرَّ حَتّٰى تُنْفِقُوْا مِمَّا تُحِبُّوْنَ

"By no means shall ye attain righteousness unless ye give (freely) of that which ye love;...." (III:92).

beings has been proclaimed as the characteristic and unavoidable virtue of every wealthy Muslim[10]. Indeed, the holy book regards it as the duty of a Muslim to spend all that he can save from his basic needs for the welfare of others:

وَيَسْأَلُونَكَ مَاذَا يُنفِقُونَ ۖ قُلِ الْعَفْوَ ۗ كَذَٰلِكَ يُبَيِّنُ اللَّهُ لَكُمُ الْآيَاتِ
لَعَلَّكُمْ تَتَفَكَّرُونَ

"They ask thee how much they are to spend (for the welfare of others). Say: 'What is beyond your needs'. Thus doth Allah make clear to you His Signs: in order that ye may consider....." (II:219).

This is so, because a Muslim is only a *trustee* of the wealth that he possesses, and not its "owner" in the sense of having the right to do with it whatever he likes:

إِنَّ اللَّهَ اشْتَرَىٰ مِنَ الْمُؤْمِنِينَ أَنفُسَهُمْ وَأَمْوَالَهُم بِأَنَّ لَهُمُ الْجَنَّةَ ۚ

"Allah hath purchased of the Believers their persons and their goods; for theirs (in return) is the Garden (of Paradise):...." (IX:111).

Moreover, the Holy Qur'ãn has emphasised that the have-nots have an inalienable *right* in the wealth of those who possess beyond their needs:

وَآتِ ذَا الْقُرْبَىٰ حَقَّهُ وَالْمِسْكِينَ وَابْنَ السَّبِيلِ

"And render to the kindred their due *rights* as (also) to *those in want*, and to the wayfarer:...." (XVII:26).

This Qur'ãnic right of the economically distressed has led eminent exponents of Islam, like Caliph 'Ali, 'Abdullah ibn 'Umar, Mujahid, Taoos, Ibn Hazm, etc., to lay down the rule that there are

10.

وَلَٰكِنَّ الْبِرَّ مَنْ . . . آتَى الْمَالَ عَلَىٰ حُبِّهِ . . . أُولَٰئِكَ الَّذِينَ صَدَقُوا ۖ
وَأُولَٰئِكَ هُمُ الْمُتَّقُونَ

"....but it is (true) righteousness....to spend of your wealth, out of love for Him.... Such are they who are sincere (in their Faith); such are the God-fearing." (II:177).

economic *duties* on the wealthy Muslims, in respect of those who may be in economic distress, beyond the payment of the welfare taxes prescribed by the Holy Qur'ãn[11], and that the Islamic state[12] has the right—nay, it is its duty, to impose further taxes on the wealthy, if it finds that with its normal scheme of taxation it is unable to meet the challenge of expenditure on the welfare of the people and the state.[13]

(iii) *Voluntary economic assistance to others, subject to one's ability, enjoined:*

The Holy Qur'ãn has exhorted the Muslims at numerous places and in different ways and contexts to render voluntary economic assistance to their fellow-beings.[14] The following verse, however, proclaims that virtue in the form of command:

وَأَقِيمُوا الصَّلَوٰةَ وَءَاتُوا الزَّكَوٰةَ وَأَقْرِضُوا اللَّهَ قَرْضًا حَسَنًا ۚ وَمَا تُقَدِّمُوا
لِأَنفُسِكُم مِّنْ خَيْرٍ تَجِدُوهُ عِندَ اللَّهِ هُوَ خَيْرًا وَأَعْظَمَ أَجْرًا ۚ وَ
اسْتَغْفِرُوا اللَّهَ ۖ إِنَّ اللَّهَ غَفُورٌ رَّحِيمٌ ۝

".....And establish regular Prayer and give regular Charity; and loan to Allah a Beautiful Loan. And whatever good ye send forth for your souls, ye shall find it in Allah's Presence,—yea, better and greater in Reward. And seek ye the Grace of Allah: for Allah is Oft-forgiving, Most Merciful." (LXXIII:20).

Now, voluntary economic assistance to others can assume the following forms:

(1) Casual assistance:

(a) *Casual Gifts and Donations:*

(b) *Repayable interest-free monetary loans;*

(c) *Returnable rent-free loans of things.*

---

11. For reference see: Ibn Hazm's *al-Mohallã*, vol. VI, p. 156.

12. It should be clearly noted that an 'Islamic State' is only that state which is dedicated to the mission of Islam and is governed solely and comprehensively by the Islamic norms, principles and laws.

13. Ibn Hazm: *al-Mohallã*, vol. VI, p. 158.

14. Such verses have been already quoted. See pp. 234-236; etc.

(2) Permanent assistance:

(a) *Bequests for individuals or for welfare projects (orphanages, homes of the destitute, hospitals, hostels, educational institutions, etc.).*

(b) *Donating funds and creating charitable Trusts for the above purposes in one's own lifetime.*

All the above forms are comprehended by the above verse and have found their due place in their Holy Prophet's exposition of the Qur'ãnic teaching. They have been included in the Islamic Law under the names, respectively, of: *Hibah; Qard al-Hasanah*, *'Ãriyah* and *Waqf*; and rules and regulations relating to them have been laid down in full-fledged form[15].

(iv) *Research in agricultural production and cattle-breeding with a view to proper utilization and advancement in those fields and for promoting the welfare of mankind, advocated; hence a duty:*

The Holy Qur'ãn says:

إِنَّ فِي خَلْقِ السَّمٰوٰتِ وَالْأَرْضِ وَاخْتِلَافِ الَّيْلِ وَالنَّهَارِ وَالْفُلْكِ
الَّتِي تَجْرِي فِي الْبَحْرِ بِمَا يَنْفَعُ النَّاسَ وَمَا أَنْزَلَ اللّٰهُ مِنَ السَّمَاءِ
مِنْ مَّاءٍ فَأَحْيَا بِهِ الْأَرْضَ بَعْدَ مَوْتِهَا وَبَثَّ فِيهَا مِنْ كُلِّ دَابَّةٍ وَّ
تَصْرِيفِ الرِّيٰحِ وَ السَّحَابِ الْمُسَخَّرِ بَيْنَ السَّمَاءِ وَ الْأَرْضِ لَاٰيٰتٍ
لِّقَوْمٍ يَّعْقِلُوْنَ ○

"Behold! In the constitution of the heavens and the earth; in the alternation of the Day and the Night; in the sailing of the ships through the Ocean for the profit of mankind; in the rain which Allah sends down from the skies, and *the life which it gives to an earth that is dead: in the beasts of all kinds that He scatters through the earth*; in the change of the winds, and the clouds which they trail like their slaves between the sky and the earth;—here indeed are Signs for (study, observation and research by) those who employ reason." (II:164).

---

15. For the *Hadîth*, refer to: Tirmizi, *Sunan*, vol. II., p. 345; Bukhãrî: *Sahîh*, vol. II, pp. 243, 541; Abu Dã'ûd: *Sunan*, vol. II., p. 501. For Islamic Law, refer to such books as *al-Hedãyã*, vol. II., p. 289, etc.

وَالْأَنْعَامَ خَلَقَهَا ۚ لَكُمْ فِيهَا دِفْءٌ وَّمَنَافِعُ وَمِنْهَا تَأْكُلُونَ ۝ وَلَكُمْ فِيهَا
جَمَالٌ حِينَ تُرِيحُونَ وَحِينَ تَسْرَحُونَ ۝ وَتَحْمِلُ أَثْقَالَكُمْ إِلَىٰ بَلَدٍ لَّمْ
تَكُونُوا بَالِغِيهِ إِلَّا بِشِقِّ الْأَنفُسِ ۚ إِنَّ رَبَّكُمْ لَرَءُوفٌ رَّحِيمٌ ۝ وَّ
الْخَيْلَ وَالْبِغَالَ وَالْحَمِيرَ لِتَرْكَبُوهَا وَزِينَةً ۚ وَيَخْلُقُ مَا لَا تَعْلَمُونَ ۝

"And callte He has created for you (O mankind): from them ye derive warmth, and numerous benefits, and of their meat ye eat. And ye have a sense of pride and beauty in them as ye drive them home in the evening, and as ye lead them forth to pasture in the morning. And they carry your heavy loads to lands that ye could not otherwise reach except with souls distressed: for your Lord is indeed Most Kind, Most Merciful. And (He has created) horses, mules, and donkeys, for you to ride and as an adornment; and He will create (in future, other vehicles, through the ingenuity of Man) of which ye have no knowledge." (XVI:5-8).

هُوَ الَّذِي أَنزَلَ مِنَ السَّمَاءِ مَاءً لَّكُم مِّنْهُ شَرَابٌ وَّمِنْهُ شَجَرٌ فِيهِ
تُسِيمُونَ ۝ يُنبِتُ لَكُم بِهِ الزَّرْعَ وَالزَّيْتُونَ وَالنَّخِيلَ وَالْأَعْنَابَ وَ
مِن كُلِّ الثَّمَرَاتِ ۚ إِنَّ فِي ذَٰلِكَ لَآيَةً لِّقَوْمٍ يَتَفَكَّرُونَ ۝

"It is He Who sends down rain from the sky: from it ye drink, and out of it grows the vegetation on which ye feed your cattle. With it He produces for you corn, olives, date-palms, grapes, and every kind of fruit: verily in this is a Sign for (observation, study and research by) those who reflect (on the nature, constitution and functions of things)."
(XVI:10-11).

وَإِنَّ لَكُمْ فِي الْأَنْعَامِ لَعِبْرَةً ۚ نُّسْقِيكُم مِّمَّا فِي بُطُونِهِ مِن بَيْنِ
فَرْثٍ وَّدَمٍ لَّبَنًا خَالِصًا سَائِغًا لِّلشَّارِبِينَ ۝ وَمِن ثَمَرَاتِ النَّخِيلِ وَ
الْأَعْنَابِ تَتَّخِذُونَ مِنْهُ سَكَرًا وَّرِزْقًا حَسَنًا ۚ إِنَّ فِي ذَٰلِكَ لَآيَةً لِّقَوْمٍ
يَّعْقِلُونَ ۝ وَأَوْحَىٰ رَبُّكَ إِلَى النَّحْلِ أَنِ اتَّخِذِي مِنَ الْجِبَالِ بُيُوتًا وَّمِنَ
الشَّجَرِ وَمِمَّا يَعْرِشُونَ ۝ ثُمَّ كُلِي مِن كُلِّ الثَّمَرَاتِ فَاسْلُكِي سُبُلَ
رَبِّكِ ذُلُلًا ۚ يَخْرُجُ مِن بُطُونِهَا شَرَابٌ مُّخْتَلِفٌ أَلْوَانُهُ فِيهِ شِفَاءٌ
لِّلنَّاسِ ۚ إِنَّ فِي ذَٰلِكَ لَآيَةً لِّقَوْمٍ يَتَفَكَّرُونَ ۝

"And verily in the cattle will ye find an instructive Sign. From what is within their bodies, between excretions and blood, We produce, for your drink, milk, pure and agreeable to those who drink it. And from the fruit of the date-palm and the vine, ye get out wholesome drink and food: behold! in this also is a Sign for those who employ reason. And thy Lord taught the Bee to build its cells in the hills, on trees and in (Men's) habitations; then to eat of all the produce (of the earth), and find with skill the specious Paths of its Lord: there issues from within their bodies a drink of varying colours, wherein is healing for men: verily in this is a Sign for (observation, study and research by) those who reflect (on the nature, constitution and function of things)." (XVI:66-69).

الَّذِي جَعَلَ لَكُمُ الْأَرْضَ مَهْدًا وَسَلَكَ لَكُمْ فِيهَا سُبُلًا وَأَنْزَلَ مِنَ السَّمَاءِ
مَاءً فَأَخْرَجْنَا بِهِ أَزْوَاجًا مِنْ نَبَاتٍ شَتَّىٰ ۝ كُلُوا وَارْعَوْا أَنْعَامَكُمْ إِنَّ
فِي ذَٰلِكَ لَآيَاتٍ لِأُولِي النُّهَىٰ ۝

"(he said)....'He Who has made for you the earth as a bed, and has enabled you to go about therein by roads (and channels); and has sent down water from the sky'. With it have We produced divers pairs of plants, each separate from the others. Eat (for yourselves) and pasture your cattle; verily in this are Signs for (observation, study and research by) the intellectuals." (XX:53, 54).

(v) *Pursuit and promotion of commerce in general, and international commerce in particular, advocated: here a duty:*

The Holy Qur'ãn says:

(a) *legalising commerce:*

وَأَحَلَّ اللَّهُ الْبَيْعَ

"....and Allah hath permitted (i.e., hath made lawful) trade...." (II:275).

(b) *defining the basis of commercial morality:*[16]

أَنْ تَكُونَ تِجَارَةً عَنْ تَرَاضٍ مِنْكُمْ

16. It may also be noted that the Holy Qur'ãn lays down the law of commercial morality in II:282.

".....let there be amongst you traffic and trade by mutual goodwill...." (IV:29).

(c) *referring to the benefits of inland commerce:*

وَلَكُمْ فِيهَا مَنَافِعُ وَلِتَبْلُغُوا عَلَيْهَا حَاجَةً فِي صُدُورِكُمْ وَعَلَيْهَا وَعَلَى
الْفُلْكِ تُحْمَلُونَ ۝

"And there are other advantages in them (i.e., the cattle) for you; that you may through them attain to any need in your hearts (in respect of the provision of transport for human necessities); and on them and in the boats ye are carried (to distant places for the fulfilment of your needs)." (XL:80).

(d) *advocating advancement in commerce through technological advance based on the pursuit of physical sciences, and referring to international trade in terms of Divine Bounty:*

اللّٰهُ الَّذِي سَخَّرَ لَكُمُ الْبَحْرَ لِتَجْرِيَ الْفُلْكُ فِيهِ بِأَمْرِهِ وَلِتَبْتَغُوا مِنْ فَضْلِهِ
وَلَعَلَّكُمْ تَشْكُرُونَ ۝ وَسَخَّرَ لَكُمْ مَّا فِي السَّمٰوٰتِ وَمَا فِي الْأَرْضِ
جَمِيعًا مِّنْهُ ۚ إِنَّ فِي ذٰلِكَ لَاٰيٰتٍ لِّقَوْمٍ يَّتَفَكَّرُونَ ۝

"It is Allah Who has subjected the sea to you, that ships may sail through it by His Command, that ye may seek of His Bounty, and that ye may show gratefulness (to God by developing those bounties further through the conquest of Nature spoken of in the following verse).

"And He hath subjected to you, as from Him, all that is in the heavens and on the earth: behold! in that indeed are Signs for those who reflect (on the nature, constitution and utility of things)." (XLV:12, 13).

(vi) *Pursuit and promotion of industrial technology based on steel industry prescribed as the basic material means of maintaining and advancing the mission of the Holy Qur'ãn, hence a duty:*

The Holy Qur'ãn refers to shipbuilding by the Holy Prophet Noah (Peace be on him)[17] and the steel industry pursued by the Holy Prophet David (Peace be on him),[18] thus placing industrial technology

17. XI:38.

18. XXI:80; XXXIV:10.

among holy pursuits and making its acquisition and cultivation one of the sacred duties of a Muslim.

The holy book does not stop at that, however. It emphasises the importance of iron and steel industry directly—an industry whose development led to the Industrial Revolution and which forms the foundation of power and prosperity of the advanced nations of today—and projects it as the deciding factor in respect of the dominance of Islam in the industrial age as a world-force. The Qur'ãnic statement has already proved prophetic to the core. The verse reads:

لَقَدْ أَرْسَلْنَا رُسُلَنَا بِالْبَيِّنٰتِ وَأَنْزَلْنَا مَعَهُمُ الْكِتٰبَ وَالْمِيزَانَ
لِيَقُومَ النَّاسُ بِالْقِسْطِ ۚ وَأَنْزَلْنَا الْحَدِيدَ فِيهِ بَأْسٌ شَدِيدٌ وَمَنَافِعُ
لِلنَّاسِ وَلِيَعْلَمَ اللّٰهُ مَنْ يَنْصُرُهُ وَرُسُلَهُ بِالْغَيْبِ ۚ إِنَّ اللّٰهَ قَوِيٌّ
عَزِيزٌ ۝

"We verily sent Our messengers (to different communities of the world) with clear proofs, and revealed with them the Scripture and the Balance that mankind may observe right measure (in all their affairs); and We sent down Iron[19], wherein is (material for) mighty war, as well as many (industrial) benefits for mankind, that Allah may test who it is that will help (the Religion of) Him and His Messengers though unseen:[20] Lo!

---

19. "Sending down" of iron have reference to the meteoric origin of this metal in ages gone by.

20. God is unseen. But the Messengers of God also having been referred to as "unseen", the verse seems to refer to the present industrial age which began after the last Messenger (Muhammad) had departed and had become "unseen", and which saw the enemies of Islam in such power through industrialisation that industrialisation and technological advancement on a higher scale alone could have saved the Muslims from the defeat and decline which they suffered during to nineteenth and the early twentieth centuries and which has been the source of the ruin of Islam and Muslims up to this day. Indeed, if the Muslims had maintained their lead in physical sciences and technology as wise followers of the Holy Qur'ãn, they would never have fallen on evil days and would have continued to maintain their international supremacy. Their failure, however, spelled their destruction as a world-power and led ultimately to those servile conditions which have progressively assisted in the de-Islamisation of the rising generation of Muslim, until non-Islamic and even anti-Islamic ideologies are now being foisted on free Muslim countries.

Allah is full of Strength, Exalted in Might (and able to make Muslims triumphant against all odds; and promise to do so if they follow His Guidance honestly)." (LVII:25).

It may be emphasised with regard to (iv), (v), (vi) above that a categorical command is explicitly contained in the following verse in respect thereof:

وَأَعِدُّوا لَهُم مَّا اسْتَطَعْتُم مِّن قُوَّةٍ وَمِن رِّبَاطِ الْخَيْلِ تُرْهِبُونَ بِهِ عَدُوَّ اللَّهِ وَعَدُوَّكُمْ وَآخَرِينَ مِن دُونِهِمْ لَا تَعْلَمُونَهُمُ اللَّهُ يَعْلَمُهُمْ

"Against them (i.e., your enemies) make ready your Power to the utmost of your capacity, including steeds of war, to strike terror into (the hearts of) the enemies of Allah and your enemies, and others (i.e., enemies of the future) besides, whom ye know not, but whom Allah doth know." (VIII:60).

Mark how clearly God had warned the followers of Islam of those formidable enemies who rose against them after the Industrial Revolution and whose might the Muslims were, and have been so far, unable to counteract mainly because of their backwardness in respect of physical science and technology.

(*b*) <u>*Duties of Omission*</u>:

(i) *Wasting money in luxuries and unproductive pursuits, prohibited:*

The Holy Qur'ãn says:

وَلَا تُسْرِفُوا إِنَّهُ لَا يُحِبُّ الْمُسْرِفِينَ

"And act not wastefully (i.e., unproductively). Lo! He approveth not the wasters." (VI:141).

وَلَا تُبَذِّرْ تَبْذِيرًا إِنَّ الْمُبَذِّرِينَ كَانُوا إِخْوَانَ الشَّيَاطِينِ وَكَانَ الشَّيْطَانُ لِرَبِّهِ كَفُورًا

".....and squander not (thy wealth) in wantonness. Lo! the squanderers were ever brothers of the devil, and the devil was ever an ingrate to his Lord." (XVII:26-27).

(ii) *Withholding money from expenditure in doing good to others and in productive pursuits, prohibited:*

وَلَا تَجْعَلْ يَدَكَ مَغْلُولَةً إِلَىٰ عُنُقِكَ

"And let not thy hand be chained to the neck (in respect of wealth)...." (XVII:29).

(iii) *Hoarding wealth and withholding it from circulation and expenditure in good causes, most vehemently condemned: hence abstinence from the same is duty:*

The Holy Qur'ãn says:

وَالَّذِينَ يَكْنِزُونَ الذَّهَبَ وَالْفِضَّةَ وَلَا يُنفِقُونَهَا فِي سَبِيلِ اللَّهِ فَبَشِّرْهُم بِعَذَابٍ أَلِيمٍ ۝

"....And there are those who bury gold and silver and spend it not in the Way of Allah: announce unto them a most grievous penalty—" (IX:34).

(iv) *Economic exploitation of others condemned; hence abstinence from it is duty:*

The Holy Qur'ãn says, condemning the Jews of those days:

وَتَرَىٰ كَثِيرًا مِّنْهُمْ يُسَارِعُونَ فِي الْإِثْمِ وَالْعُدْوَانِ وَأَكْلِهِمُ السُّحْتَ ۚ لَبِئْسَ مَا كَانُوا يَعْمَلُونَ ۝

"And thou shalt see many of them hastening toward sin and transgression and their devouring of ill-gotten wealth (obtained through the exploitation of others). Vile indeed is that which they have been doing." (V:65).

(v) *All types and forms of interest totally banned and abstinence from interest-bearing transactions enjoined:*

الَّذِينَ يَأْكُلُونَ الرِّبَوٰا لَا يَقُومُونَ إِلَّا كَمَا يَقُومُ الَّذِي يَتَخَبَّطُهُ الشَّيْطَٰنُ مِنَ الْمَسِّ ۚ ذَٰلِكَ بِأَنَّهُمْ قَالُوٓا إِنَّمَا الْبَيْعُ مِثْلُ الرِّبَوٰا ۗ وَأَحَلَّ اللَّهُ الْبَيْعَ وَحَرَّمَ الرِّبَوٰا ۚ

"Those who devour *ribã* (usury and interest) will not stand except as standeth one whom the satan hath confounded with his touch. That is because they say: 'Trade is like *ribã*'. But Allah hath permitted trade and hath forbidden *ribã*....." (II:275).

يَا أَيُّهَا الَّذِينَ آمَنُوا لَا تَأْكُلُوا الرِّبَوٰا أَضْعَافًا مُّضَاعَفَةً وَاتَّقُوا اللَّهَ
لَعَلَّكُمْ تُفْلِحُونَ ۝

"O ye who believe! Devour not usury, doublign and quadrupling (the sum lent). Observe your duty to Allah that ye may be successful." (III:130).

Two important points are worthy of being noted here:

(*a*) While banning *ribã*, the Holy Qur'ãn has forbidden not only usury but also interest in other forms. Because according to the best authorities[21], the word *ribã*, which means literally 'an excess or addition', denotes as a term of economics 'any addition, however slight, over and above the principal sum lent'; and, as such, *ribã* includes both 'usury' and 'interest'.

(*b*) Because *ribã* is generally translated as usury, and because in modern parlance 'usury' signifies only an 'exorbitant rate of interest', some people have fallen into the error that what the Holy Qur'ãn has really forbidden is an excessive rate of interest. In truth, it is only a misinterpretation of the term *ribã* and a perversion of the Qur'ãnic teaching. That the holy book does not distinguish between 'exorbitant' and 'reasonable' rates of interest is clear from the following:

يَا أَيُّهَا الَّذِينَ آمَنُوا اتَّقُوا اللَّهَ وَذَرُوا مَا بَقِيَ مِنَ الرِّبَوٰا إِنْ كُنْتُمْ
مُّؤْمِنِينَ ۝ فَإِنْ لَّمْ تَفْعَلُوا فَأْذَنُوا بِحَرْبٍ مِّنَ اللَّهِ وَرَسُولِهِ ۚ وَإِنْ
تُبْتُمْ فَلَكُمْ رُءُوسُ أَمْوَالِكُمْ ۚ لَا تَظْلِمُونَ وَلَا تُظْلَمُونَ ۝ وَإِنْ كَانَ ذُو
عُسْرَةٍ فَنَظِرَةٌ إِلَىٰ مَيْسَرَةٍ ۚ وَأَنْ تَصَدَّقُوا خَيْرٌ لَّكُمْ إِنْ كُنْتُمْ
تَعْلَمُونَ ۝

---

21. *Mufradãt al-Qur'ãn* by Imãm Rãghib; *Tãj al-'Ãrus;* Lane's *Arabic-English Lexicon.*

"O ye who believe! Fear Allah, and give up what remains of your demand for *ribã*, if ye are indeed believers. If ye do it not, take notice of war from Allah and His Messenger: But if ye turn back (from charging interest), ye shall have your capital sums: deal not unjustly, and ye shall not be dealt with unjustly. If the debtor is in a difficulty, grant him time till it is easy for him to repay (the capital sum). But if ye remit it by way of charity, that is best for you if ye only know." (II:278-280).

Mark the words in verse 279. "ye shall have your capital sums". The Holy Qur'ãn does not say: "ye shall have your capital sums plus interest at a reasonable rate."

(vi) *Creation of monopolies in trade and industry prohibited:*

When the Holy Qur'ãn lays down the basic principle concerning wealth that "it may not (merely) make a circuit between the wealthy among you"[22] (LIX:7), it negates the legality of all those means and methods whereby wealth becomes concentrated in the hands of a few, making the rich richer. The aim of the creation of monopoly being nothing else than the concentration of wealth in the hands of the bigger business magnates and industrial barons, who either buy out the lesser fry or create mergers and trusts or enter into private agreements—all with a view to charging higher prices for their goods and thus exploiting and fleecing the consumers, its prohibition is directly contained in that verse.

Islam stands for the common man and not for the privileged few. It is thus that the Holy Prophet (Peace be on him) condemned the monopolist trader and forbade the hoarding of grain and its withholding from sale in times of scarcity[23]; and, in Islamic Law, the Hanafi jurists have explicitly ruled against monopoly in food-stuffs.[24]

(vii) *Speculative deals classed as gambling and prohibited:*

Speculative deals in trade are actually a form of gambling, and about gambling the Holy Qur'ãn says:

---

22. كَيْ لَا يَكُونَ دُولَةً بَيْنَ الْأَغْنِيَاءِ مِنْكُمْ

23. Muslim: *Sahîh*, vol. II., p. 31.

24. *Hedãya*, vol. IV, p. 47.

يٰٓاَيُّهَا الَّذِيْنَ اٰمَنُوْٓا اِنَّمَا الْخَمْرُ وَالْمَيْسِرُ . . . . رِجْسٌ
مِّنْ عَمَلِ الشَّيْطٰنِ فَاجْتَنِبُوْهُ لَعَلَّكُمْ تُفْلِحُوْنَ ○

"O ye who believe! Intoxicants and gambling....are an abomination,—of Satan's handiwork: eschew such (abomination), that ye may prosper." (V:93).

Expounding this detail of the Qur'ãnic teaching, the Holy Prophet (Peace be on him) has laid down positive injunctions. For instance:

"It is related by Ibn 'Umar that the Messenger of Allah (Peace be on him) prohibited the sale of commodity not in stock with another commodity also not in stock."[25]

"It is related on the authority of Hakim ibn Hizam, who said: 'The Messenger of Allah (Peace be on him) prohibited me bargaining about anything which I did not possess'. In another account, he (is reported to have) said, 'I said, O Messenger of Allah, a person comes to me and wishes me to bargain about a thing which I do not possess. May I purchase for him from the market?' The Prophet replied, 'Bargain not about that which is not with you'."[26]

"It is related on the authority of Anas (may Allah be pleased with him!) that the Prophet (Peace be on him) prohibited dealings in fruits, as long as they were not ripe. It was asked: 'How to know their ripeness?' He said, 'Until they grow red'. Then he said, 'Do you think that anyone of you would be able to take the property of his brother if Allah were to stop fruit from ripening?' In the account given by Ibn 'Umar, it is stated that the Prophet (Peace be on him) prohibited the purchase and sale of date trees until the dates ripened, and from dealings in ears of corn until they grew (ripe and) white, or they were safe from calamities. He prohibited both the seller and the purchaser from such transactions."[27]

The speculation market has unfortunately become a part and parcel of the present-day commerce. It is, however, nothing better than a gambling den. An economist says:

---

25. *Mishkãt al-Masãbih*, Vol. I., pp. 247, 248.

26. *Ibid*., Vol. I., p. 248.

27. *Ibid*., Vol. I., p. 247.

"In the speculation market, the person who gains most is the broker. His role is that of the managing committee of a racecourse or the keeper of a gambling den. The operator buy and sell through him and he goes on charging his brokerage on each purchase and sale, just as the punters or the card players gain or lose among themselves and the race-committee or the den-keeper go on deducting their commission at a finish of each event. Money that ought to have been invested in industry or commerce finds its way into the speculative market, where it is feeding disguised and parasitical works like brokers and shrewd operators. In a world clamouring for capital formation in, and capital diversion into, the under developed countries, a futures market is a regressive step."

(viii) *Betting in races prohibited:*

In the Qur'ãnic verse quoted above in respect of speculative deals, the word used for 'gambling' is *maisir*, which means 'getting something too easily': hence getting a profit without proper labour. In its wider acceptance, it means 'any game of hazard, or play or stakes, or wagers'.[28]

As 'game of hazard', it refers to speculative deals.

As 'play of stakes or wagers', it refers to froms of gambling like betting in races—an evil which is quite old but which has assumed devastating proportions in the present age in the form of the Derby horse-race in England and of the Preakness and the Kentucky Derby races in the United States.

(ix) *Lottery or Raffle, prohibited:*

Let us refer to verse V:93 again. Commenting on this verse Abdullah Yusuf Ali says:

"The form most familiar to the Arabs was gambling by casting lots by means of arrows, on the principle of a lottery: the arrows were marked, and served the same purpose as a modern lottery ticket. Something, e.g., the car case of a slaughtered animal, was divided into unequal parts. The marked arrows were drawn from a bag. Some were blank and those who drew them got nothing. Others indicated prizes, which were big or small. Whether you got a big share or a small share, or nothing depended on pure luck, unless there was fraud also on the part of

28. Lane's *Arabic-English Lexicon.*

some persons concerned. The principle on which the objection is based is: that, even if there is no fraud, you gain what you have not earned, or lose on a mere chance. Dice and wagering are rightly held to be within the definition of gambling...." (*op.cit.*, p. 86).

3. Duties Relating to Active Struggle for Ensuring and Promoting the Political Stability of the Muslim Society

(a) *Duties of Commission:*

(i) *Collective discipline enjoined:*

The Holy Qur'ãn says:

وَرَابِطُوا

"....and strengthen ye one another...." (III:200).

وَأَطِيعُوا اللَّهَ وَرَسُولَهُ وَلَا تَنَازَعُوا فَتَفْشَلُوا وَتَذْهَبَ رِيحُكُمْ وَ
اصْبِرُوا إِنَّ اللَّهَ مَعَ الصَّابِرِينَ ○

"And obey Allah and His Messenger; and dispute not one with another, lest ye lose heart and your power depart; and be patient and persevering: for Allah is with those who patiently persevere." (VIII:46).

(ii) *Disciplined obedience to the Leader, in so far as he leads according to, and in the best interests of Islam, enjoined:*

فَاتَّقُوا اللَّهَ مَا اسْتَطَعْتُمْ وَاسْمَعُوا وَأَطِيعُوا وَأَنْفِقُوا خَيْرًا
لِأَنْفُسِكُمْ ۗ وَمَنْ يُوقَ شُحَّ نَفْسِهِ فَأُولَٰئِكَ هُمُ الْمُفْلِحُونَ ○

"So keep your duty to Allah as best as ye can, and listen (obediently to the Divine Call that comes through the Leader), and spend (in the Way of Allah) for the benefit of your own souls. And those saved from the covetousness of their own souls (i.e., those who rise above personal interests)—they are the ones that attain felicity." (LXIV:16).

يَا أَيُّهَا الَّذِينَ آمَنُوا أَطِيعُوا اللَّهَ وَأَطِيعُوا الرَّسُولَ وَأُولِي الْأَمْرِ مِنْكُمْ ۖ فَإِنْ
تَنَازَعْتُمْ فِي شَيْءٍ فَرُدُّوهُ إِلَى اللَّهِ وَالرَّسُولِ إِنْ كُنْتُمْ تُؤْمِنُونَ
بِاللَّهِ وَالْيَوْمِ الْآخِرِ ۚ ذَٰلِكَ خَيْرٌ وَأَحْسَنُ تَأْوِيلًا ○

"O ye who believe! obey Allah and obey the Messenger (Muhammad) and owners of authority from amongst you (as leaders and administrators or as leaders only)[29]; then if ye differ in aught, refer it to Allah and His Messenger, if ye do believe in Allah and the Last Day. That is best, and most suitable for final determination." (IV:59).

(iii) *Constant effort for the consolidation of Muslim Brotherhood, enjoined:*

وَاعْتَصِمُوا بِحَبْلِ اللَّهِ جَمِيعًا

"And hold fast, all together, by the Rope which Allah (stretches out for you)....." (III:103).

(iv) Active, profound, ceaseless and balanced struggle for making the Muslim community immune from all internal and external evils in order to promote piety, progress and peace, enjoined:

مَنْ قَتَلَ نَفْسًا بِغَيْرِ نَفْسٍ أَوْ فَسَادٍ فِي الْأَرْضِ فَكَأَنَّمَا قَتَلَ النَّاسَ
جَمِيعًا وَمَنْ أَحْيَاهَا فَكَأَنَّمَا أَحْيَا النَّاسَ جَمِيعًا

".....If any one slew a person—unless it be for murder or for spreading mischief in the land—it would be as if he slew the whole people: and if any one saved a life, it would be as if he saved the life of the whole people....." (V:35).

وَجَاهِدُوا فِي اللَّهِ حَقَّ جِهَادِهِ هُوَ اجْتَبَاكُمْ وَمَا جَعَلَ عَلَيْكُمْ فِي
الدِّينِ مِنْ حَرَجٍ مِلَّةَ أَبِيكُمْ إِبْرَاهِيمَ هُوَ سَمَّاكُمُ الْمُسْلِمِينَ
مِنْ قَبْلُ وَفِي هَٰذَا لِيَكُونَ الرَّسُولُ شَهِيدًا عَلَيْكُمْ وَتَكُونُوا
شُهَدَاءَ عَلَى النَّاسِ فَأَقِيمُوا الصَّلَاةَ وَآتُوا الزَّكَاةَ وَ
اعْتَصِمُوا بِاللَّهِ هُوَ مَوْلَاكُمْ فَنِعْمَ الْمَوْلَىٰ وَنِعْمَ النَّصِيرُ

"And strive in His cause as ye ought to strive (with sincerity and under discipline). He has chosen you, and has imposed no difficulties on

---

29. According to Lane's *Lexicon*:

"In general, those who are termed *Ulu al-Amr* of the Muslims, are those who superinted the affairs of such with respect of religion, and everything conducing to the right disposal of their affairs."

you in religion; it is the Faith of your father Abraham. It is He Who has named you Muslims, both before and in this (Revelation); that the Messenger may be a witness for you, and ye be witnesses for mankind! So establish regular Prayer, give regular charity, and hold fast to Allah! He is your Protector—the best to protect and the best to help!" (XXII:78).

يايها الذين امنوا هل ادلكم على تجارة تنجيكم من عذاب اليم ○
تؤمنون بالله ورسوله وتجاهدون في سبيل الله باموالكم و
انفسكم ذلكم خير لكم ان كنتم تعلمون ○ يغفر لكم ذنوبكم
ويدخلكم جنت تجري من تحتها الانهر ومسكن طيبة في
جنت عدن ذلك الفوز العظيم ○ واخرى تحبونها
نصر من الله وفتح قريب وبشر المؤمنين ○

"O ye who believe! shall I lead you to a bargain that will save you from a grievous penalty?—that ye believe in Allah and His Messenger, and that ye strive (your utmost) in the Cause of Allah with your property and your persons: that will be best for you, if ye but knew! He will forgive you your sins, and admit you to a Garden beneath which rivers flow, and to beautiful Mansions in Gardens of Eternity: that is indeed the supreme Achievement. And another (favour will He bestow), which ye do love,—help from Allah and a speedy victory. So give the Glad Tidings to the Believers". (LXI:10-13).

(v) *Fighting against the enemies of Islam in defence of truth, justice and righteousness and for making Islam and Muslims safe against all aggression, enjoined:*

وقاتلوا في سبيل الله الذين يقاتلونكم ولا تعتدوا ان الله لا يحب
المعتدين ○

"Fight in the Cause of Allah those who fight you, but do not transgress limits; for Allah loveth not transgressors." (II:190).

وقتلوهم حتى لا تكون فتنة ويكون الدين لله فان انتهوا فلا
عدوان الا على الظلمين ○

"And fight them on until there is no more tumult or oppression, and there prevail justice and faith in Allah; but if they cease, let there be no hostility except to those who practice oppression." (II:193).

أُذِنَ لِلَّذِينَ يُقَاتَلُونَ بِأَنَّهُمْ ظُلِمُوا ۚ وَإِنَّ اللَّهَ عَلَىٰ نَصْرِهِمْ لَقَدِيرٌ ۝

"To those against whom war is made, permission is given (to fight), because they are wronged:—and verily Allah is Most Powerful for their aid:....." (XXII:39).

(vi) *Migrating from such places where Islam is persecuted and suppressed, thus saving one's own faith and strengthening the Cause of Islam and the Muslim community elsewhere, even though it involves losses from the material point of view, enjoined:*

إِنَّ الَّذِينَ تَوَفَّاهُمُ الْمَلَائِكَةُ ظَالِمِي أَنفُسِهِمْ قَالُوا فِيمَ كُنتُمْ ۖ قَالُوا كُنَّا مُسْتَضْعَفِينَ فِي الْأَرْضِ ۚ قَالُوا أَلَمْ تَكُنْ أَرْضُ اللَّهِ وَاسِعَةً فَتُهَاجِرُوا فِيهَا ۚ فَأُولَٰئِكَ مَأْوَاهُمْ جَهَنَّمُ ۖ وَسَاءَتْ مَصِيرًا ۝ إِلَّا الْمُسْتَضْعَفِينَ مِنَ الرِّجَالِ وَالنِّسَاءِ وَالْوِلْدَانِ لَا يَسْتَطِيعُونَ حِيلَةً وَلَا يَهْتَدُونَ سَبِيلًا ۝ فَأُولَٰئِكَ عَسَى اللَّهُ أَن يَعْفُوَ عَنْهُمْ ۚ وَكَانَ اللَّهُ عَفُوًّا غَفُورًا ۝ وَمَن يُهَاجِرْ فِي سَبِيلِ اللَّهِ يَجِدْ فِي الْأَرْضِ مُرَاغَمًا كَثِيرًا وَسَعَةً ۚ وَمَن يَخْرُجْ مِن بَيْتِهِ مُهَاجِرًا إِلَى اللَّهِ وَرَسُولِهِ ثُمَّ يُدْرِكْهُ الْمَوْتُ فَقَدْ وَقَعَ أَجْرُهُ عَلَى اللَّهِ ۗ وَكَانَ اللَّهُ غَفُورًا رَّحِيمًا ۝

"When angels take the souls of those who die in sin against their souls, they say: 'In what (fight) were ye?' They reply: 'Weak and oppressed were we in the earth.' They say: 'Was not the earth of Allah spacious enough for you to move yourselves away (from evil)?' Such men will find their abode in Hell,—what an evil refuge!—Except those who are (really) weak and oppressed— men, women, and children—who have no means in their power, nor a guide-post to direct their way. For these, there is hope that Allah will forgive: for Allah doth blot out (sins) and forgive again and again. He who forsakes his home in the Cause of Allah, finds in the earth many a refuge, wide and spacious: should he die as a refugee from home for Allah and His Messenger, his reward becomes due and sure with Allah: and Allah is Oft-Forgiving, Most Merciful."

(IV:97-100).

(*b*) <u>*Duties of Omission*</u>:

(i) *Doing anything which might create disruption and disunity among the Muslim community, prohibited*:

وَلَا تَفَرَّقُوا ۚ وَاذْكُرُوا نِعْمَتَ اللّٰهِ عَلَيْكُمْ إِذْ كُنْتُمْ أَعْدَاءً فَأَلَّفَ بَيْنَ
قُلُوبِكُمْ فَأَصْبَحْتُمْ بِنِعْمَتِهِ إِخْوَانًا ۚ وَكُنْتُمْ عَلَىٰ شَفَا حُفْرَةٍ مِنَ النَّارِ فَأَنْقَذَكُمْ
مِنْهَا ۗ كَذَٰلِكَ يُبَيِّنُ اللّٰهُ لَكُمْ آيَاتِهِ لَعَلَّكُمْ تَهْتَدُونَ ○

".....and be not divided among yourselves; and remember with gratitude Allah's favour on you; for ye were enemies and He joined your hearts in love, so that by His Grace by became brethren; and yet ye were on the brink of the Pit of Fire, and He saved you from it. Thus doth He make His Signs clear to you: that ye may be guided" (III:103).

وَلَا تَنَازَعُوا

".....and dispute not one with another...." (VIII:46).

(ii) *Creating religious sects and thus dividing the Muslim community into hostile sections, prohibited*:

وَلَا تَكُونُوا كَالَّذِينَ تَفَرَّقُوا وَاخْتَلَفُوا مِنْ بَعْدِ مَا جَاءَهُمُ الْبَيِّنَاتُ ۚ
وَأُولَٰئِكَ لَهُمْ عَذَابٌ عَظِيمٌ ○

"Be not like those who are divided among themselves and fall into disputations after receiving Clear Sings: for them is a dreadful Penalty...." (III:105).

مُنِيبِينَ إِلَيْهِ وَاتَّقُوهُ وَأَقِيمُوا الصَّلَاةَ وَلَا تَكُونُوا مِنَ الْمُشْرِكِينَ ○ مِنَ الَّذِينَ
فَرَّقُوا دِينَهُمْ وَكَانُوا شِيَعًا ۖ كُلُّ حِزْبٍ بِمَا لَدَيْهِمْ فَرِحُونَ ○

"Turn ye back in repentance to Him, and fear Him; establish regular prayers, and be not ye among those who join gods with Allah,—those who split up their Religion, and become (mere) Sects,—each party rejoicing in that which is with itself!" (XXX:31, 32).

(iii) *Tyrannising over other Muslims prohibited:*

قُلْ اِنَّمَا حَرَّمَ رَبِّيَ الْفَوَاحِشَ مَا ظَهَرَ مِنْهَا وَمَا بَطَنَ وَالْاِثْمَ وَالْبَغْيَ بِغَيْرِ الْحَقِّ وَاَنْ تُشْرِكُوْا بِاللّٰهِ مَا لَمْ يُنَزِّلْ بِهٖ سُلْطٰنًا وَّاَنْ تَقُوْلُوْا عَلَى اللّٰهِ مَا لَا تَعْلَمُوْنَ ○

"Say: 'My Lord forbiddeth only indecencies, such of them as are apparent and such as are within, and sin and *wrongful oppression*, and that ye associate with Allah that for which no warrant hath been revealed, and that ye tell concerning Allah that which ye know not." (VII:33).

(iv) *Creation of and participation in secret societies whose object is destruction of truth and justice, prohibited:*

يٰۤاَيُّهَا الَّذِيْنَ اٰمَنُوْۤا اِذَا تَنَاجَيْتُمْ فَلَا تَتَنَاجَوْا بِالْاِثْمِ وَالْعُدْوَانِ وَمَعْصِيَتِ الرَّسُوْلِ

"O ye who believe! When ye conspire together, conspire not together for crime and wrongdoing and disobedience toward the Messenger....." (LVIII:9).

Part II

DUTIES OF MUSLIM SOCIETY TOWARDS THE INDIVIDUAL

END:

Collective effort by the Muslim society (*Millat*) for:

(*a*) Moral perfection of the individual;

(*b*) Happiness of the individual.

I.— Fundamental Principles governing the Muslim Society and the Islamic State.

II.— Duties:

(1) Duty of ensuring the spiritual welfare of the people.

(2) Duty of ensuring the moral welfare of the people.

(3) Duty relating to the intellectual development of the people.

(4) Duties relating to the political and social welfare of the people.

(5) Duties relating to the economic welfare of the people.

Chapter I

FUNDAMENTAL PRINCIPLES GOVERNING THE MUSLIM SOCIETY AND THE ISLAMIC STATE

I. Individual vis-a-vis Society

(*i*) As we have already seen in the foregoing,[1] the Holy Qur'ãn has emphasised the importance of social life and its demands. Here we may emphasise that simultaneously *it recognises the worth of the individual and the development of individual personality.* The holy book says:

مَنْ قَتَلَ نَفْسًا بِغَيْرِ نَفْسٍ أَوْ فَسَادٍ فِي الْأَرْضِ فَكَأَنَّمَا قَتَلَ النَّاسَ جَمِيعًا

"....whosoever killeth a human being for other than manslaughter or corruption in the earth, it shall be as if he had killed all mankind...."
(V:35).

Again, it says:

وَأَمْرُهُمْ شُورَىٰ بَيْنَهُمْ

".....Their affairs are by mutual Consultation". (XLII:38).

Mark that in this verse the principle of consultation is founded on the concept of the importance of the individual.

(*ii*) *The Holy Qur'ãn makes it the obligation of the Millat to look after and promote the spiritual, moral and general welfare of the individual.* Collective effort for establishing what is right and eradicating what is wrong for the individual, and the creation of conditions wherein truth, perseverance in truth and mutual compassion and well-doing prevail for the benefit of the individual, has been directly affirmed and emphasised. The holy book says:

تَأْمُرُونَ بِالْمَعْرُوفِ وَتَنْهَوْنَ عَنِ الْمُنْكَرِ

"....ye enjoin what is right and forbid what is wrong...." (III:110).

---

1. See pages 285-287.

وَتَوَاصَوْا بِالْمَرْحَمَةِ ۝

".....and exhort one another to compassion." (XC:17).

إِلَّا الَّذِينَ آمَنُوا وَعَمِلُوا الصَّالِحَاتِ وَتَوَاصَوْا بِالْحَقِّ وَتَوَاصَوْا بِالصَّبْرِ ۝

".....Save those who believe and do good works, and exhort one another to truth and exhort one another to endurance (in the cause of truth)....." (CIII:3).

(*iii*) Side by side with that, *the concept of collectivism is the very warp and woof of Islam*, and it has to be cultivated in Muslim society to the extent that even in his prescribed prayers a Muslim has to pray using the plural "we"[1]

2. Obligation of organising collective welfare of Muslims even where they are a Small Group only

This necessitates the establishment of the Islamic state. That does not mean, however, that Muslim minorities living in non-Muslim state have no obligation with respect to their collective life. Because *Islam insists on collective duties to such an extent as to make it imperative for the Muslims, even when they do not possess a state of their own, to organise themselves into a well-knit community which should function under one leader*. That leader should be elected by the Muslims on the basis of his piety, knowledge and other merits of leadership; and, united under him, they should employ every means and strive in every way to build up their lives, individually as well as collectively, in a manner whereby they may be able to imbibe and assimilate the spiritual, moral and social blessings of Islam in as wide a range and on as high a level as possible.

All this is borne out by the organisation of the Muslim community under the direction of, and according to the instructions given in, the Holy Qur'ãn, during the Makkan period of the Holy Prophet's career. In addition to that, the following among several verses, have a direct bearing on the above-mentioned obligation:

يَا أَيُّهَا الَّذِينَ آمَنُوا ادْخُلُوا فِي السِّلْمِ كَافَّةً

---

1. See *Sura al-Fãtihah* (Chapter I) and other prayers taught by the Holy Qur'ãn.

"O ye who believe! Enter into Islam (i.e., its comprehensive discipline) all ye together....." (II:208).

وَاعْتَصِمُوا بِحَبْلِ اللّٰهِ جَمِيعًا وَّلَا تَفَرَّقُوا

"And hold fast, all together, by the Rope which Allah (stretches out for you) and be not divided among yourselves...." (III:103).

يَاۤاَيُّهَا الَّذِيْنَ اٰمَنُوۤا اَطِيْعُوا اللّٰهَ وَاَطِيْعُوا الرَّسُوْلَ وَاُولِى الْاَمْرِ مِنْكُمْ

"O ye who believe! obey Allah, and obey the Messenger, and those charged with authority among you....." (IV:59).

3. Obligation of Establishing the Islamic State

The collective effort of the *Millat* for the moral perfection and happiness of the individual cannot, however, gain its ends truly and comprehensively unless it transforms itself into a free theo-democratic state, whose function should be to enforce the Islamic Way of Life in its totality and to act as a condition for the natural flowering of the ideals of Islam. Hence *the establishment of the Islamic State, whenever and wherever possible, forms, according to the Holy Qur'ãn, the duty of the Millat, not only towards Islam but also towards the individual.*

That it is an unavoidable duty, in case of ability, is borne out by the fact that the Holy Prophet (Peace be on him) established the state at Madinah at the very first opportunity.

Further, this duty is contained and emphasised in the following verse:

هُوَ الَّذِىۤ اَرْسَلَ رَسُوْلَهٗ بِالْهُدٰى وَدِيْنِ الْحَقِّ لِيُظْهِرَهٗ عَلَى الدِّيْنِ كُلِّهٖ
وَلَوْ كَرِهَ الْمُشْرِكُوْنَ ○

"He it is Who hath sent His Messenger with the Guidance and the Religion of Truth, that He may cause it to prevail over all religion, however much the idolaters may be averse." (IX:33).

It should be noted that the domination of Islam as a Way of Life is not possible without the establishment of the Islamic State. Hence it is the collective duty of the Muslims to strive for it with might and main.

Again, the Muslims have been commanded:

وَ أَعِدُّوا لَهُمْ مَّا اسْتَطَعْتُمْ مِّنْ قُوَّةٍ

"Against them (i.e., your enemies) make ready your Power to the utmost...." (VIII:60).

This injunction makes it an obligation to establish the Islamic State, because without that it is impossible to carry it out truly and comprehensively.

4. The Constitution of the Islamic State

The Qur'ānic Constitution of the State rests on the following principles:

(*i*) Sovereignty:

Sovereignty belongs to God:

إِنِ الْحُكْمُ إِلَّا لِلَّهِ ۚ أَمَرَ أَلَّا تَعْبُدُوا إِلَّا إِيَّاهُ ۚ ذَٰلِكَ الدِّينُ الْقَيِّمُ وَلَٰكِنَّ أَكْثَرَ النَّاسِ لَا يَعْلَمُونَ ○

"....Authority and control belong to Allah only.[2] He hath commanded that ye serve none save Him: that is the right religion, but most human beings understand not." (XII:40).

أَلَا لَهُ الْحُكْمُ وَهُوَ أَسْرَعُ الْحَاسِبِينَ ○

"Is not His the Command? And He is the Swiftest in taking account." (VI:62).

لَهُ مُلْكُ السَّمٰوٰتِ وَ الْأَرْضِ

"To Him belongeth the kingdom of the heavens and the earth." (XLIII:85).

وَلَا يُشْرِكُ فِي حُكْمِهِ أَحَدًا ○

"He does not share His Command with any person whatsoever." (XVIII:26).

2. Cf. VI:57. XII:67; etc.

Besides the above verses, the following Excellent Names also bear reference to Divine Sovereignty:

رَبِّ الْعٰلَمِيْنَ	:	Lord of the worlds	(I:2);
رَبُّ الْعَرْشِ الْعَظِيْمِ	:	Lord of the Throne (of Glory) Supreme	(IX:129);
مٰلِكَ الْمُلْكِ	:	(Lord of Power and Rule	(III:26);
اَحْكَمُ الْحٰكِمِيْنَ	:	Ruler of rulers, or, Greatest of rulers	(XI:45).
اَلْمَلِكُ	:	the Sovereign	(LIX:23);
مَلِكِ النَّاسِ	:	the King (i.e., Ruler and Legislator) of mankind	(CXIV:2).

(*ii*) <u>*The right to legislate*</u>:

(a) The right to legislate belongs basically to God:

In the Holy Qur'ãn we read:

اِنَّآ اَنْزَلْنَآ اِلَيْكَ الْكِتٰبَ بِالْحَقِّ لِتَحْكُمَ بَيْنَ النَّاسِ بِمَآ اَرٰىكَ اللّٰهُ ط

"Lo! We (God) have revealed unto thee (O Muhammad) the Scripture with truth, that thou mayest judge between mankind by that (Law) which Allah hath shown (i.e., hath revealed unto thee)." (IV:105).

لَقَدْ اَرْسَلْنَا رُسُلَنَا بِالْبَيِّنٰتِ وَ اَنْزَلْنَا مَعَهُمُ الْكِتٰبَ
وَالْمِيْزَانَ لِيَقُوْمَ النَّاسُ بِالْقِسْطِ ج

"We (God) sent aforetime Our Messengers with clear Signs and sent down with them the Book and the Balance, that human beings may conduct themselves with equity" (LVII: 25).

These verses affirm direct Divine legislation.

(b) However, *the laws given by the Holy Prophet Muhammad (Peace be on him), in addition to the Qur'ãnic Laws, also fall under the category*

of what "Allah hath revealed" because:

وَمَا يَنْطِقُ عَنِ الْهَوٰىؕ ۝ اِنْ هُوَ اِلَّا وَحْیٌ يُّوْحٰىۙ ۝

"Nor does he (i.e., Muhammad) say (aught) of (his own) Desire. It is not less than inspiration sent down to him." (LIII:3, 4).

Hence: it has been commanded:

وَمَآ اٰتٰكُمُ الرَّسُوْلُ فَخُذُوْهُ ۚ وَمَا نَهٰكُمْ عَنْهُ فَانْتَهُوْا ۚ

"And whatever the Messenger (Muhammad) gives you, accept it, and from whatever he forbids you, keep back." (LIX:7).

(c) Having been given the Divine Law *it is not permitted to the Muslims to adopt, when they have their own State, any law which is repugnant to it.* The following verses emphasise this fact very vehemently:

وَمَنْ لَّمْ يَحْكُمْ بِمَآ اَنْزَلَ اللّٰهُ فَاُولٰٓئِكَ هُمُ الْكٰفِرُوْنَ ۝

"If any do fail to judge and command by (the light of) what Allah hath revealed, they are Unbelievers." (V:47).

وَمَنْ لَّمْ يَحْكُمْ بِمَآ اَنْزَلَ اللّٰهُ فَاُولٰٓئِكَ هُمُ الظّٰلِمُوْنَ ۝

"If any do fail to judge and command by (the light of) what Allah hath revealed, they are committers of severe wrong." (V:48).

وَمَنْ لَّمْ يَحْكُمْ بِمَآ اَنْزَلَ اللّٰهُ فَاُولٰٓئِكَ هُمُ الْفٰسِقُوْنَ ۝

"If any do fail to judge and command by (the light of) what Allah hath revealed, they are the transgressors." (V:50).

(*d*) It should be noted that the Holy Qur'ãn prohibits only the violation of "what Allah hath revealed". But, it does not lay down, either in the verses just quoted or anywhere else, that Muslims are forbidden from following any laws which Allah has not revealed, thus leaving it open to frame new Laws for meeting the exigencies of new situations. Of course, all such laws should be in conformity with the Divine Guidance, as the holy book says:

أَفَحُكْمَ الْجَاهِلِيَّةِ يَبْغُونَ ۚ وَمَنْ أَحْسَنُ مِنَ اللَّهِ حُكْمًا لِقَوْمٍ يُوقِنُونَ ۝

"Seek they then the judgment of Paganism? And who is better in judgment than Allah unto a people whose faith is assured?" (V:53).

Thus, a *controlled and limited, but positive, freedom has been given to the Muslims in respect of legislation.*

(*iii*) *Status of Governmental Authority:*

Human beings are vicegerents of God: Hence, governmental authority can be held by them only as a delegated function and as a trust under the sovereignty of God:

The Holy Qur'ãn says:

وَإِذْ قَالَ رَبُّكَ لِلْمَلَائِكَةِ إِنِّي جَاعِلٌ فِي الْأَرْضِ خَلِيفَةً ۖ

"Behold, thy Lord said to the angels: 'Verily I am going to place a vicegerent on the earth." (II:30).

(*iv*) *Objectives of the Islamic State:*

The objectives of the Islamic State are:

(a) *To maintain internal order and ward off external aggression:*

In respect of maintenance of internal order, the Holy Qur'ãn says:

وَلَوْلَا دَفْعُ اللَّهِ النَّاسَ بَعْضَهُمْ بِبَعْضٍ لَفَسَدَتِ الْأَرْضُ

".....And if Allah had not repelled some men by others, the earth would have been filled with mischief." (II:251).

Commenting on this verse, a learned commentator of the Holy Qur'ãn remarks: "This verse emphasises the importance of the State and establishes the fact that but for the existence of organised government, human society would have been destroyed. On truth is based the maxim that Religion and State are twins." (*Rûh al-Ma'ãnî*, vol. II, p. 173).

As regards warding off external aggression, we are told:

أذن للذين يقاتلون بأنهم ظلموا ۚ وإن الله على نصرهم
لقدير ○

"To those against whom war is made, permission is given (to fight), because they are wronged;—and verily, Allah is Most Powerful for their aid." (XXII:39).

(b) *To establish absolute justice for all citizens:*

The Holy Qur'ãn says:

إن الله يأمركم أن تؤدوا الأمانات إلى أهلها وإذا حكمتم بين الناس أن
تحكموا بالعدل ۚ إن الله نعما يعظكم به ۗ إن الله كان سميعا
بصيرا ○

"Allah doth command you to render back your Trusts to those to whom they are due; and when ye judge between man and man (whether Muslims or non-Muslims), that ye judge with justice: Lo! comely is the teaching which He giveth you! Lo! Allah is He Who heareth and seeth all things." (IV:58).

يا أيها الذين آمنوا كونوا قوامين بالقسط شهداء لله ولو على أنفسكم
أو الوالدين والأقربين ۚ إن يكن غنيا أو فقيرا فالله أولى بهما ۖ فلا
تتبعوا الهوى أن تعدلوا ۚ وإن تلووا أو تعرضوا فإن الله كان بما
تعملون خبيرا ○

"O ye who believe! stand out firmly for justice, as witnesses to Allah, even as against yourselves, or your parents, or your kin, and whether it be (against) rich or poor: For Allah can best protect both. Follow not the lusts of your hearts, lest ye swerve, and if ye distort (justice) or decline to do justice, verily Allah is well acquainted with all that ye do." (IV:135).

(c) *To do all that lies in its power and to employ all means and media, including tableegh,*[3] *for the establishment of "all that is right"* (al-ma'rûf) *and the elimination of "all that is wrong"* (al-munkar);

3. *i.e.,* dissemination and propagation of the teachings of Islam from the pulpit and the platform and through the press, the radio and the television, with a view to persuading and inspiring the people in respect of the Islamic Way of Life.

(d) *To organise institutions for spiritual and social welfare:*

In respect of (c) and (d) above, the Holy Qur'ãn says:

ٱلَّذِينَ إِن مَّكَّنَّٰهُمْ فِى ٱلْأَرْضِ أَقَامُوا ٱلصَّلَوٰةَ وَءَاتَوُا ٱلزَّكَوٰةَ وَأَمَرُوا
بِٱلْمَعْرُوفِ وَنَهَوْا عَنِ ٱلْمُنكَرِ ۗ وَلِلَّهِ عَٰقِبَةُ ٱلْأُمُورِ ۝

"(Muslims are) those who, if we bestow on them (authority) in the land, establish regular prayer (—pursue spiritual welfare) and give regular charity (—pursue economic welfare), enjoin (all) that which is right and forbid (all) that which is wrong (—pursue moral and political welfare). And unto Allah is the end of (all) affairs." (XXII:41).

Again:

لَّا خَيْرَ فِى كَثِيرٍ مِّن نَّجْوَىٰهُمْ إِلَّا مَنْ أَمَرَ بِصَدَقَةٍ أَوْ مَعْرُوفٍ أَوْ
إِصْلَٰحٍۭ بَيْنَ ٱلنَّاسِ ۚ وَمَن يَفْعَلْ ذَٰلِكَ ٱبْتِغَآءَ مَرْضَاتِ ٱللَّهِ فَسَوْفَ نُؤْتِيهِ
أَجْرًا عَظِيمًا ۝

"In most of their secret conferences there is no good: but if one commandeth a deed of economic well-doing or justice or *'islãh* (i.e., establishment of peace, happiness and order) among human beings: to him who does this, seeking the good pleasure of Allah, We shall soon give a reward of the highest value." (IV:114).

Moreover, from the social and economic point of view, the function of the Islamic State is to transform the Muslim community into a community of middle-roaders—or of the middle-class standard—with the elimination of the evils of poverty, on the one hand, and the evils of riches, on the other, as the Holy Qur'ãn proclaims:

وَكَذَٰلِكَ جَعَلْنَٰكُمْ أُمَّةً وَسَطًا لِّتَكُونُوا شُهَدَآءَ عَلَى ٱلنَّاسِ وَيَكُونَ
ٱلرَّسُولُ عَلَيْكُمْ شَهِيدًا ۗ

"Thus We have appointed you (O Muslims) a middle nation (or, a nation conforming to the just mean[4]), that ye may be witnesses against mankind, and that the Messenger (Muhammad) may be in regard to you a witness." (II:143).

---

4. Lane's *Lexicon*.

Islam steers the middle course between Capitalism and Communism and bears witness to the evil of their extremism—an evil from which they themselves are trying to recede gradually, thus proving the truth of Islam. The famous philosopher of history, Prof. Arnold Toynbee admits: "If Russia has moved to 'the right' her neighbours have moved to 'the left'.....the apparently irresistible encroachment of planning on the once unregimented economies of the democratic countries suggests that the social structure of all countries in the near future is likely to be both national and socialist. Not only do the Capitalist and Communist regimes seem likely to continue side by side; it may well be that Capitalism and Communism....are becoming different names for very much the same things."[5]

(e) *To actively endeavour for making Islam the supreme ideological force on the world-front:*

هُوَ الَّذِيْٓ اَرْسَلَ رَسُوْلَهٗ بِالْهُدٰى وَدِيْنِ الْحَقِّ لِيُظْهِرَهٗ عَلَى الدِّيْنِ
كُلِّهٖ وَلَوْ كَرِهَ الْمُشْرِكُوْنَ ۝

"It is He Who has sent His Messenger with Guidance and the Religion of Truth, that he may proclaim it (as the supreme ideological force) over all religion (namely, over all systems of belief and action), even though the Pagans may detest (it)." (LXI:9).

Again:

وَاَعِدُّوْا لَهُمْ مَّا اسْتَطَعْتُمْ مِّنْ قُوَّةٍ

"Against them (i.e., your enemies) make ready your Power to the utmost...." (VIII:60).

(v) Democratic Rights of the People:

People are to be free and in possession of democratic rights:

People in the Islamic State are to be free subjection to any human being, because their government is the government of Law and they are subjects of God alone.

We have been told:

---

5. Arnold Toynbee: *A Study of History.* Abridgement of Volumes I—VI by D.C. Somervell, *ed.*, 1946, p. 400.

إِنِ الْحُكْمُ إِلَّا لِلَّهِ ۚ أَمَرَ أَلَّا تَعْبُدُوا إِلَّا إِيَّاهُ ۚ ذَٰلِكَ الدِّينُ الْقَيِّمُ وَلَٰكِنَّ
أَكْثَرَ النَّاسِ لَا يَعْلَمُونَ ○

"The authority and control belong to Allah *only*. He hath commanded that ye serve none save Him. That is the right religion but most human beings understand not." (XII:40).

Then, the Holy Qur'ãn lays down the following principle in respect of the collective life of Muslims:

وَأَمْرُهُمْ شُورَىٰ بَيْنَهُمْ

".....Who (conduct) their affairs (or, government) by mutual consultation...." (XLII:38).

It is evident that the administration of the State on the basis of mutual consultation is impossible and unthinkable without the citizens enjoying freedom and full democratic rights.

Moreover, it is the essential condition and consequence of the establishment of absolute justice enjoined vehemently by the Holy Qur'ãn[6] that the people should be in possession of freedom and equality of opportunity—in other words, full democratic rights: and this actually has been realised in the Islamic State.

(vi) *Qualifications, status and functions of the Head of the Islamic State (Amîr al-Mo'minîn)*:

1. *He must be a Muslim, endowed with a high standard of piety, knowledge, wisdom and physical qualities, including bravery:*

That he must be a Muslim is borne out by the words "from amongst you" in the following Qur'ãnic verse:

يَا أَيُّهَا الَّذِينَ آمَنُوا أَطِيعُوا اللَّهَ وَأَطِيعُوا الرَّسُولَ وَأُولِي الْأَمْرِ مِنْكُمْ ۖ

"O ye who believe! obey Allah and obey the Messenger and those who wield authority from amongst you...." (IV:59).

Even from the purely rational point of view, the head of an ideological state can reasonably be only he who believes in and represents that ideology.

---

6. See (iv) (b), as also other reference on this topic.

As regards the high standard of piety, the Holy Qur'ãn lays down the law:

إِنَّ أَكْرَمَكُمْ عِندَ اللَّهِ أَتْقَاكُمْ

"....Verily, the most honoured of you with Allah is (he who is) the most pious of you....." (XLIX:13).

Knowledge, wisdom and physical merits have been affirmed in the following verses:

وَقَالَ لَهُمْ نَبِيُّهُمْ إِنَّ اللَّهَ قَدْ بَعَثَ لَكُمْ طَالُوتَ مَلِكًا ۚ قَالُوا أَنَّىٰ
يَكُونُ لَهُ الْمُلْكُ عَلَيْنَا وَنَحْنُ أَحَقُّ بِالْمُلْكِ مِنْهُ وَلَمْ يُؤْتَ سَعَةً مِّنَ
الْمَالِ ۚ قَالَ إِنَّ اللَّهَ اصْطَفَاهُ عَلَيْكُمْ وَزَادَهُ بَسْطَةً فِي الْعِلْمِ وَ
الْجِسْمِ ۖ وَاللَّهُ يُؤْتِي مُلْكَهُ مَن يَشَاءُ ۚ وَاللَّهُ وَاسِعٌ عَلِيمٌ ۝

"Their Prophet said to them, 'Allah hath appointed Talut as king over you'. They said: 'How can he exercise authority over us when we are better fitted than he to exercise authority, and he is not even gifted with wealth in abundance?' He said: 'Allah hath chosen him above you, and hath gifted him abundantly with knowledge and physique (i.e., physical merits): Allah bestoweth His power on whom He pleaseth. Allah careth for all, and He knoweth all things." (II:247).

وَقَتَلَ دَاوُودُ جَالُوتَ وَآتَاهُ اللَّهُ الْمُلْكَ وَالْحِكْمَةَ وَعَلَّمَهُ مِمَّا يَشَاءُ ۗ

"And David slew Goliath; and Allah gave him power and wisdom and taught him whatever (else) He willed." (II:251).

2. *His status is that of: (a) the Vicegerent of God; (b) the Successor to the Holy Prophet Muhammad (Peace be on him) (c) the Representative of the People who delegate their Authority to him:*

(a) He is the vicegerent of God: as it has been said about David (Peace be on him):

يَا دَاوُودُ إِنَّا جَعَلْنَاكَ خَلِيفَةً فِي الْأَرْضِ

"O David We did indeed make thee a vicegerent on earth...." (XXXVIII:26).

(This is his cosmic status, or status in relation to God).

(b) *He is the successor to the Holy Prophet Muhammad (Peace be on him):*

The Holy Prophet being the founder and the first head of the Islamic State, every other head of the Islamic State who comes after him is naturally his successor.

(This is his historical status, or status in relation to the Holy Prophet, Peace be on him).

(c) *He is the representative of the people, who, as vicegerents of God, delegate their authority, out of organisational and administrative necessity, to him.*

The administration of the Islamic State being based on "mutual consultation" , as seen in the foregoing[7], no one can impose himself as a despotic ruler on the Muslims. Rather, he is to be elected by them; and, as such, he is to be their representative.

(This is his political status, or status in relation to the people).

3. *His functions are:*

(a) As vicegerent of God, his natural function is *to live for God,* to carry out Divine commands and to surrender his ego completely to Divine Pleasure.

(b) As Successor to the Holy Prophet (Peace be on him), his natural function is *to imitate the Holy Prophet* as a Muslim and as head of the state, as best as he can.

(c) As representative of the people, his natural function is *to be the servant of the people* and not their master.

Hence *he should lead a life of austerity and self-negation.* It has been said about good Muslims that they sacrifice their own interests and comforts for the sake of other Muslims.[8] The head of the Islamic State is, therefore, duty-bound, more than any other Muslim, to base his life on self-sacrifice.

---

7. See p. 327.

8. LIX:9.

Thus, *his life must be exemplary for the people in respect of the Islamic Way of Life.*

4. *His relationship with his people:*

(a) *Parliament:*

He should rule the State in consultation with the people. Thus, there should be a *parliament.*

According to the Holy Qur'ān, the Holy Prophet (Peace be on him) was commanded by God, in spite of his unique position as God's Messenger, to administer the State in consultation with the people, who were his followers. The command reads:

وَشَاوِرْهُمْ فِى الْاَمْرِ

".....And consult with them upon the conduct of affairs." (III:159).

Thus, as Successor to the Holy Prophet (Peace be on him), the head of the Islamic State cannot assume the position of an autocrat or a dictator and cannot disturb the democratic rights of the people.

(b) *People's Right to differ:*

The citizens of the Islamic State have the right to differ with the head of the State; and when such a situation arises, the dispute is to be referred to the Holy Qur'ān and the Prophetic Guidance (*Sunnah*) for arbitration.

The right to differ is directly contained in the right to give opinion[9], while the principle for settlement of differences has been given in the following verse:

فَاِنْ تَنَازَعْتُمْ فِىْ شَىْءٍ فَرُدُّوْهُ اِلَى اللّٰهِ وَالرَّسُوْلِ اِنْ كُنْتُمْ تُؤْمِنُوْنَ
بِاللّٰهِ وَالْيَوْمِ الْاٰخِرِ ۚ ذٰلِكَ خَيْرٌ وَّاَحْسَنُ تَاْوِيْلًا ۝

"If ye differ in anything among yourselves, refer it to Allah and His Messenger, if ye do believe in Allah and the Last Day: That is best, and most suitable for final determination." (IV:59).

(c) *Supremacy of the Law:*

The above brings out that the head of the Islamic State is not above Law, his function being not to administer the State arbitrarily and

9. XLII:38, quoted on p. 327.

at will but positively on the basis of Truth and Justice as given in the Divine Law, as the following verse establishes:

فَاحْكُمْ بَيْنَ النَّاسِ بِالْحَقِّ وَلَا تَتَّبِعِ الْهَوٰى فَيُضِلَّكَ عَنْ سَبِيْلِ اللّٰهِ

".....So judge between mankind with truth, and follow not caprice and lust of the heart, lest it cause thee to err from the path of Allah (i.e., do not subordinate the welfare of the people to thy personal inclinations and interests, because that would lead thee away from absolute obedience to the Divine Law and upholding it as supreme)." (XXXVIII:26).

However, as long as he administers in conformity with the Guidance given by God and His Messenger Muhammad (Peace be on him), he should be implicitly obeyed by all, as it has been commanded:

يٰٓاَيُّهَا الَّذِيْنَ اٰمَنُوْٓا اَطِيْعُوا اللّٰهَ وَاَطِيْعُوا الرَّسُوْلَ وَاُولِي الْاَمْرِ مِنْكُمْ

"O ye who believe! Obey Allah, and obey the Messenger and those charged with authority among you." (IV:59).

(*vii*) <u>*Separation of the Executive and the Judiciary*</u>:

If as we have noted, the head of the Islamic State is subordinate to the Law given by God and His Messenger (Peace be on him), *the principle of the Supremacy of Law is established. Now, the only way to ensure the Supremacy of Law is the keeping of the judiciary independent of the executive and the total avoidance by the head of the State of tampering with the functioning of the judiciary.*

(*viii*) <u>*Qualifications of State's Functions*</u>:

Functionaries of the State are to be appointed on no other consideration but genuine merits like knowledge, practical wisdom, efficiency, honesty and integrity.

The Holy Qur'ãn says:

اِنَّ اللّٰهَ يَاْمُرُكُمْ اَنْ تُؤَدُّوا الْاَمٰنٰتِ اِلٰٓى اَهْلِهَا

"Verily Allah doth command you to make over Trusts to those to whom they are due (or to those who are worthy of them)". (IV:58).

We have already seen that those in authority hold the State and all that it stands for as a trust from God. All the offices of the State, from the highest to the lowest, are thus trusts; and one of the implications of above command, according to orthodox authoritative thought, is that which relates to the appointments to governmental services only of persons who are worthy of those jobs[10].

(*ix*) *Obedience in People's own interest:*

Obedience to the head of the state has been imposed as a duty upon the citizens for:

(*a*) the co-ordination of their democratic rights;

(*b*) the establishment and maintenance of collective discipline;

(*c*) the establishment and maintenance of a unitary policy for the State.

These three principles are contained in "enjoining what is right", which is one of the functions of the Islamic State, and, among other verses, in the following verse which lays down the command:

وَأَصْلِحُوا ذَاتَ بَيْنِكُمْ

"Establish happiness, peace and order among yourselves."

(VIII:1).

10. "The concept of 'trusts' covers the principle that offices should go only to the really deserving". (*Ruh al-Ma'ãnî*, vol. V, p. 64).

Chapter II

DUTIES

Preliminary

"Enjoining what is right and forbidding what is wrong"[1] assumes, as instrument of the state, the form of:

(*a*) the actual establishment of conditions and requirements which preserve and promote human good;

(*b*) the active obliteration of such conditions as destroy human good.

Now, *Good*, being a comprehensive term, includes all *goods*, namely, spiritual, moral, intellectual, political and economic.

In other words, the function of the Islamic State should be the spiritual, moral, intellectual, physical and social preservation and development of the individuals, with a view to the establishment of a righteous society, i.e., a society which is healthy in all respects.

In this connection, besides those duties which shall be shortly mentioned, *a basic duty of the Islamic State is the education and training of the experts of Islam*[2] *belonging to all the required levels of learning.* The following verses bear reference to this duty:

وَلْتَكُن مِّنكُمْ أُمَّةٌ يَدْعُونَ إِلَى الْخَيْرِ وَيَأْمُرُونَ بِالْمَعْرُوفِ وَيَنْهَوْنَ
عَنِ الْمُنكَرِ ۚ وَأُولَٰئِكَ هُمُ الْمُفْلِحُونَ ○

"Let there arise out of you a band of people inviting to all that is good, enjoining what is right, and forbidding what is wrong: They are the ones to attain felicity." (III:104).

فَلَوْلَا نَفَرَ مِن كُلِّ فِرْقَةٍ مِّنْهُمْ طَائِفَةٌ لِّيَتَفَقَّهُوا فِي الدِّينِ وَلِيُنذِرُوا
قَوْمَهُمْ إِذَا رَجَعُوا إِلَيْهِمْ لَعَلَّهُمْ يَحْذَرُونَ ○

---

1. III:110, XXII:41.

2. Basic education in Islam shall have to be provided to every Muslim citizen of the State, as we shall shortly see.

".....If a contingent from every expedition remained behind, they could devote themselves to studies in religion, and admonish the people when they return to them,—that thus they (may learn) to guard themselves (against evil)". (IX:122).

(1) Duty of Ensuring the Spiritual Welfare of the People

The Holy Qur'ãn proclaims "exhortation to Truth" as one of the essential conditions of human success (CIII:3). Hence, it is the duty of the Islamic State as the vicegerent of God, Successor to the Holy Prophet (God's blessings be on him), and representative of the people, to uphold, propagate and ensure the functioning of Truth, and consequently, the spiritual values—which form the basic content of Truth in the lives of the Muslims.

The Holy Qur'ãn says:

الَّذِينَ إِن مَّكَّنَّاهُمْ فِي الْأَرْضِ أَقَامُوا الصَّلَوٰةَ وَآتَوُا الزَّكَوٰةَ وَأَمَرُوا
بِالْمَعْرُوفِ وَنَهَوْا عَنِ الْمُنكَرِ ۗ وَلِلَّهِ عَاقِبَةُ الْأُمُورِ ○

"(Muslims are) those who, if We establish them (in authority and power) in the land, establish regular prayer and give regular charity, enjoin the right and forbid the wrong: With Allah rests the end (and decision) of (all) affairs". (XXII:41).

As a duty of the Islamic State, "establishment of regular prayer" and "enjoining what is right and forbidding what is wrong" in spiritual affairs, mean:—

(*a*) the construction and maintenance of mosques;

(*b*) appointment and maintenance of the requisite staff for the proper functioning of the mosques;

(*c*) organisation of spiritual education at the highest levels as well as at the level of the general masses, and making it compulsory for every Muslim citizen of the state to acquire that education;

(*d*) enforcement of laws whereby the above is ensured;

(*e*) curbing and eliminating all those forces, customs and institutions which are opposed to, or are capable of hindering, the proper functioning of the Islamic spiritual values.

(2) Duty of Ensuring the Moral Welfare of the People

Taking up the verse just quoted (i.e., XXII:41), it lays down "enjoining what is right and forbidding what is wrong" as one of the functions of the Islamic State. Viewing this function in the perspective of morals, the fact stands out as self-evident that *it is the duty of the Islamic State*:

(i) *to organise and institute the moral education of the people, and to do in that behalf all that is necessary*;

(ii) *to take all positive steps, including the enactment and enforcement of laws, for ensuring the proper practice of Islamic morals* with a view to preserve and promote moral welfare;

(iii) *to adopt all measures necessary, including the enactment and enforcement of laws, for combating all tendencies, acts and forces that are detrimental to the cause of moral welfare, and for punishing the actual offenders.*

In fact, the Holy Qur'ãn demands severe punishments for those who promote what is detrimental to the maintenance of the proper moral tone of society:

إِنَّ الَّذِينَ يُحِبُّونَ أَنْ تَشِيعَ الْفَاحِشَةُ فِي الَّذِينَ آمَنُوا لَهُمْ عَذَابٌ أَلِيمٌ فِي
الدُّنْيَا وَالْآخِرَةِ ۚ وَاللَّهُ يَعْلَمُ وَأَنْتُمْ لَا تَعْلَمُونَ ۝

"Verily those who love that immorality is propagated among the Believers, for them is a grievous penalty *in this life*[3] and in the Hereafter: and Allah knoweth (its far reaching evil effects) and ye know (or discern) not."[4] (XXIV:19).

3. Duty Relating to the Intellectual Development of the People

When we study the attitude of the Holy Qur'ãn regarding the intellectual development of human beings, we find that:

---

3. This refer to the punishment of the offenders by the Islamic State.

4. The punishments prescribed by the Holy Qur'ãn for different offences have been given in Part III.

(i) it classifies humanity distinctly into two groups: the possessors of knowledge and the ignorant, and emphasises clearly the superiority of the former over the latter:

هَلْ يَسْتَوِي الَّذِينَ يَعْلَمُونَ وَالَّذِينَ لَا يَعْلَمُونَ ۗ إِنَّمَا يَتَذَكَّرُ أُولُوا
الْأَلْبَابِ ۝

"Are the possessors of knowledge equal with those who possess not knowledge? It is the possessors of understanding that are mindful." (XXXIX:9).

(ii) Nay, it goes beyond that. Because while emphasising most vehemently the importance of intellectual development in human life, it makes the quest of knowledge a duty of paramount importance for an individual. We have noticed that in detail already in Book I, chapter on "Duties to Self" (section: 'Duties as Rational Beings').

The problem with which we are concerned here is: Has the Islamic State any duty towards the citizens in respect of their intellectual development? The plain answer is: Yes, as the following observations bear out:

(*i*) According to the Holy Qur'ãn, God educated Adam, the progenitor of the human race:

وَعَلَّمَ آدَمَ الْأَسْمَاءَ كُلَّهَا

"And He imparted to Adam the knowledge of the nature of all things[5]." (II:31).

Then, the Holy Qur'ãn lays down the law that Divine Blessings are meant to be transmitted to others:

وَأَحْسِن كَمَا أَحْسَنَ اللَّهُ إِلَيْكَ

---

5. The Arabic word is *asma'*, plural of "*ism*". The commentators of the Holy Qur'ãn explain this word to mean: "the attributes of things and their descriptions and their characteristics, the attributes of a thing being indicative of its nature." (See: Saiyid Qutb's Commentary named *Fi Zilãl-il-Qur'ãn*, p. 126).

".....and do thou good (to others) as Allah has been good to thee...." (XXVIII:77).

Thus, the knowledge imparted by God to Adam was meant to be transmitted to mankind, generation after generation, and to be developed further by them.

Now: who can organise this difficult and great pursuit better than the possessor of the powers of collective vicegerency of God?

Thus, it is the duty of the Islamic State to organise universal education for the intellectual development of its citizens.

(ii) The Holy Qur'ãn has taught the prayer:

رَبِّ زِدْنِي عِلْمًا ۝

".....O my Lord! advance me in knowledge". (XX:114).

This shows that it is God who advances the human beings in knowledge. He does so, however, through human beings, of which the institution of prophethood is the proof.

All the prophets, from Adam to Muhammad (Allah bless them all) were the vicegerents of God par excellence and, as such, the teachers of mankind.

Every State is also the vicegerent of God, the Islamic State being supremely so, because besides its status as "state", it is also the inheritor of the blessings conferred on mankind by God through His Messengers.

This vicegerency makes it incumbent on the Islamic State to undertake the development of knowledge to higher and higher levels and to organise and enforce the education of all its citizens with a view to their intellectual advancement, with all the resources at its command.

(iii) The Holy Qur'ãn refers to the establishment of justice and balanced life among human beings as the objective of Divine Guidance and, consequently, as the objective of the Islamic State:

لَقَدْ أَرْسَلْنَا رُسُلَنَا بِالْبَيِّنٰتِ وَأَنْزَلْنَا مَعَهُمُ الْكِتٰبَ
وَالْمِيزَانَ لِيَقُومَ النَّاسُ بِالْقِسْطِ

"We sent aforetime Our Messengers with Clear Signs and sent down with them the Book and the Balance (of Right and Wrong), that men may stand forth in justice....." (LVII:25).

This objective cannot, however, be achieved without a universal dissemination among the people of the knowledge of Islamic Way of Life, as a compulsory measure.

The Islamic Way of Life is, in its turn, built upon Divine Guidance, which is the highest knowledge, and as such necessitates the acquisition of all knowledge for its proper understanding.

Thus free, compulsory and universal education, based on Divine Guidance, having the promotion of the Islamic Way of Life as its objective, and being widest in its scope, stands out as one of the foremost duties of the Islamic State.

(iv) The Holy Qur'ãn commands the Muslims to build up their *power* to the utmost and in all respects (VIII:60)[6]. That objective is only achievable, among other things[7], through:

(*a*) universal and basic religious and general[8] education of the people, and

(*b*) the highest theological, philosophical, scientific and technological education of those who possess the proper aptitude;

thereby building up a community of intellectuals which should endeavour ceaselessly to attain the highest level in every field of knowledge.

All that education should, of course, be inspired by the ideal of making Truth and Justice reign supreme in the world, whereby alone the mission of Islam is fulfilled.[9]

---

6. Already quoted on p. 351.

7. The eminent *Muhaddith* Daw'oodi has deduced the necessity of the development of agriculture from the verse under reference (*See: 'Ainî: Commentary* on Bukhãrî's *Sahîh*, vol. V, p. 712).

8. It may be emphasised here that Islam being the religion of Unity it does not recognise any distinction between the "religious" and the "secular". The distinction made here is purely nominal, and not functional.

9. It may be remarked here that the present day Islamic theological education is unbalanced, defective and narrow in conception; while the secular education

The crux of the above discussion is that:—

In respect of intellectual development, it is the duty of the Islamic State:

(*a*) *to organise, establish and enforce free compulsory basic universal education;*

(*b*) *to devise ways and means whereby all branches of knowledge are cultivated at the highest level; and*

(*c*) *to harness all intellectual endeavour in the cause of the advancement of Truth and Justice.*

(4) Duties Relating to the Political and Social Welfare of the People

(i) Establishment of happiness, peace and order for ensuring healthy existence and development of the individuals, enjoined:

The Holy Qur'ãn says:

فَاتَّقُوا اللّٰهَ وَاَصْلِحُوْا ذَاتَ بَيْنِكُمْ

".....So fear Allah and pursue *islãh* (i.e., happiness, peace and order) between yourselves......" (VIII:1).

(ii) Administering justice without discrimination and without any extraneous consideration, for the preservation of life, honour and property of the individuals, enjoined:

The Holy Qur'ãn says:

يٰٓاَيُّهَا الَّذِيْنَ اٰمَنُوْا كُوْنُوْا قَوّٰمِيْنَ بِالْقِسْطِ شُهَدَآءَ لِلّٰهِ وَلَوْ عَلٰٓى اَنْفُسِكُمْ
اَوِ الْوَالِدَيْنِ وَالْاَقْرَبِيْنَ ۚ اِنْ يَّكُنْ غَنِيًّا اَوْ فَقِيْرًا فَاللّٰهُ اَوْلٰى بِهِمَا ۫ فَلَا
تَتَّبِعُوا الْهَوٰٓى اَنْ تَعْدِلُوْا ۚ وَاِنْ تَلْوٗٓا اَوْ تُعْرِضُوْا فَاِنَّ اللّٰهَ كَانَ بِمَا
تَعْمَلُوْنَ خَبِيْرًا ۝

---

that is being imparted in the Muslim countries is breeding, because of its wrong orientation, aimlessness and even un-Islamic and anti-Islamic bias. (For a detailed discussion, see the author's: *The Present Crisis in Islam and Our Future Educational Programme*).

"O ye who believe! stand out firmly for justice, as witnesses to Allah, even as against yourselves or your parents, or your kin, and whether it be (against) rich or poor; for Allah can best protect both. Follow not the lusts of your hearts, lest ye swerve, and if ye desert (justice) or decline to do justice, verily Allah is well acquainted with all that ye do." (IV:135).

Again:

يٰٓاَيُّهَا الَّذِيْنَ اٰمَنُوْا كُوْنُوْا قَوّٰمِيْنَ لِلّٰهِ شُهَدَآءَ بِالْقِسْطِ ۖ وَلَا يَجْرِمَنَّكُمْ
شَنَاٰنُ قَوْمٍ عَلٰٓى اَلَّا تَعْدِلُوْا ۚ اِعْدِلُوْا ۗ هُوَ اَقْرَبُ لِلتَّقْوٰى ۖ وَاتَّقُوا اللّٰهَ ۚ اِنَّ
اللّٰهَ خَبِيْرٌۢ بِمَا تَعْمَلُوْنَ ○

"O ye who believe! be maintainers of your pact with Allah, as witnesses to fair dealing, and let not the hatred of others to you make you swerve to wrong and depart from justice. Be just: that is nearest to Piety: and fear Allah. For Allah is well acquainted with all that ye do." (V:9).

(iii) *Ensuring the democratic rights of the people, enjoined*:

اِنَّ اللّٰهَ يَاْمُرُكُمْ اَنْ تُؤَدُّوا الْاَمٰنٰتِ اِلٰٓى اَهْلِهَا ۙ

"Allah doth command you to render back your Trusts (i.e., all obligations towards God and fellow-beings)[10] to those to whom they are due....." (IV:58).

(iv) *Honouring all human beings as human beings: Hence no law, whereby the human dignity of any citizen is jeopardised unjustly, is to be adopted:*

The Holy Qur'ãn says:

وَلَقَدْ كَرَّمْنَا بَنِيْٓ اٰدَمَ

"We have honoured the children of Adam." (XVII:70).

(v) *Punishing the violators of law and those who endanger the security of the State made a function of the State: Hence State's duty:*

---

10. Ref: comments on this verse in *Ruh al-Ma'ãni*, vol. I. It should also be noted that every government which wields authority as a delegated privilege, is, in the very nature of the case, a trustee of the democratic rights of the people.

The Holy Qur'ãn says:

الَّذِينَ إِنْ مَكَّنَّاهُمْ فِي الْأَرْضِ أَقَامُوا الصَّلَاةَ وَآتَوُا الزَّكَاةَ وَأَمَرُوا
بِالْمَعْرُوفِ وَنَهَوْا عَنِ الْمُنْكَرِ ۗ وَلِلَّهِ عَاقِبَةُ الْأُمُورِ ۝

"(Muslims are) those who, if We establish them (in authority and power) in the land, establish regular prayer and give regular charity, enjoin the right and forbid what is wrong....." (XXII:41).

In this verse, "forbidding (or, restraining from) what is wrong" relates to the function of the Islamic State with regard to the punishment of offenders against Law.

Also: punishing the criminals[11] is a positive demand of justice; and the Holy Qur'ãn enjoins:

وَإِذَا حَكَمْتُمْ بَيْنَ النَّاسِ أَنْ تَحْكُمُوا بِالْعَدْلِ ۚ

".....And that when ye judge between human beings (whether Muslims or non-Muslims), ye judge with justice." (IV:58).

(vi) *Defence of Islam and Muslims against internal disruption:*

In this connection, it should be noted that:

(a) *Damaging Islam through the creation of mutually hostile religious groups has been condemned and prohibited by the Holy Qur'ãn*:

وَلَا تَكُونُوا مِنَ الْمُشْرِكِينَ ۝ مِنَ الَّذِينَ فَرَّقُوا دِينَهُمْ وَكَانُوا شِيَعًا ۖ كُلُّ حِزْبٍ
بِمَا لَدَيْهِمْ فَرِحُونَ ۝

"And be not ye among those who join gods with Allah,—those who split up their Religion, and become (mere) Sects, each party rejoicing in that which is with itself". (XXX:31, 32).

It is, therefore, the duty of the Islamic State as the defender of Islam, to foster religious unity among Muslims and to put down all attempts at religious disruption and disputes with an iron hand, leaving no place for religious adventurers.

---

11. Punishments shall be stated shortly. See pp. 352-364.

(b) *Damaging Muslim unity and solidarity socially and politically, through the formation of mutually hostile political, tribal, regional or racial*[12] *groups, has been condemned, and the duty of punishing those who are guilty of such offence, and enforcing unity with justice, has been enjoined by the Holy Qur'ãn:*

وَإِنْ طَآئِفَتَانِ مِنَ الْمُؤْمِنِيْنَ اقْتَتَلُوْا فَأَصْلِحُوْا بَيْنَهُمَا ۚ فَإِنْ
بَغَتْ إِحْدٰىهُمَا عَلَى الْأُخْرٰى فَقَاتِلُوا الَّتِيْ تَبْغِيْ حَتّٰى تَفِيْٓءَ
إِلٰٓى أَمْرِ اللّٰهِ ۚ . . . . . إِنَّمَا الْمُؤْمِنُوْنَ إِخْوَةٌ فَأَصْلِحُوْا بَيْنَ
أَخَوَيْكُمْ وَاتَّقُوا اللّٰهَ لَعَلَّكُمْ تُرْحَمُوْنَ ۝

"If two parties among the Believers fight (against one another), make ye peace between them: but if one of them transgresses beyond bounds against the other, then fight ye (all) against the one that transgresses until it complies with the command of Allah: but if it complies, then make peace between them with justice and be fair: for Allah loves those who are fair (and just). The Believers are but a single Brotherhood: so make peace and reconciliation between your two (contending) brothers; and fear Allah, that ye may receive Mercy". (XLIX:9-10).

It is, therefore, the duty of the Islamic State to combat and eliminate all such tendencies in the community on the basis of truth and justice.

(vii) *Defence of Islam and Muslims against external aggression, enjoined:*

أُذِنَ لِلَّذِيْنَ يُقٰتَلُوْنَ بِأَنَّهُمْ ظُلِمُوْا ۚ

"To those against whom war is made, permission is given (to fight) because they are wronged....." (XXII:39).

Again:

وَأَعِدُّوْا لَهُمْ مَّا اسْتَطَعْتُمْ مِّنْ قُوَّةٍ وَّمِنْ رِّبَاطِ الْخَيْلِ تُرْهِبُوْنَ بِهٖ
عَدُوَّ اللّٰهِ وَعَدُوَّكُمْ وَاٰخَرِيْنَ مِنْ دُوْنِهِمْ ۚ لَا تَعْلَمُوْنَهُمْ ۚ اَللّٰهُ

---

12. The Holy Qur'ãn recognises no tribal, racial, linguistic or regional distinctions as a basis for political divisions. (XLIX:13).

يَعْلَمُهُمْ ۚ وَمَا تُنْفِقُوا مِنْ شَيْءٍ فِي سَبِيلِ اللَّهِ يُوَفَّ إِلَيْكُمْ وَأَنْتُمْ
لَا تُظْلَمُونَ ۝

"Against them (i.e., your enemies) make ready your Power to the utmost of your capacity, including steeds of war, to strike terror into (the hearts of) the enemies of Allah and your enemies, and others besides, whom ye know not, but whom Allah doth know. Whatever ye shall spend in the Cause of Allah, shall be repaid unto you, and ye shall not be treated unjustly." (VIII:60).

(5) Duties Relating to the Economic Welfare of the People

I. *Harmonising different interests to end exploitation and the creation of a classless society, enjoined:*

In this respect:

(i) The Holy Qur'ãn establishes the Brotherhood of Muslims:

إِنَّمَا الْمُؤْمِنُونَ إِخْوَةٌ فَأَصْلِحُوا بَيْنَ أَخَوَيْكُمْ ۚ وَاتَّقُوا اللَّهَ لَعَلَّكُمْ
تُرْحَمُونَ ۝

"The Believers are but a single Brotherhood. Therefore, establish happiness, peace and order among two (contending) members of your Brotherhood, and observe your duty to Allah that haply ye may obtain mercy." (XLIX:10).

It should be noted that:

(a) the concept of the Brotherhood of Believers is outright the concept of a classless society;

(b) the establishment of happiness, peace and order in that Brotherhood refers to the preservation of the Brotherhood as a classless society through the requisite principles and laws: social, political and economic;

(c) the establishment of happiness, peace and order is truly possible only for the state which controls the life of the people comprehensively and with coercive authority. Hence, this verse relates primarily and essentially to the duties of the Islamic State.

(ii) The Holy Qur'ãn lays down the law for ending exploitation at all levels and in all respects:

لَا تَظْلِمُونَ وَلَا تُظْلَمُونَ ○

"Ye shall neither wrong, nor be wronged". (II:279).

Again:

إِنَّمَا السَّبِيلُ عَلَى الَّذِينَ يَظْلِمُونَ النَّاسَ وَيَبْغُونَ فِي الْأَرْضِ بِغَيْرِ
الْحَقِّ ۚ أُولَٰئِكَ لَهُمْ عَذَابٌ أَلِيمٌ ○

"The blame is only against those who oppress men with wrongdoing and insolently transgress beyond bounds through the land, denying right and justice: For such there will be a penalty grievous". (XLII:42).

(iii) The Holy Qur'ãn enjoins active steps, through coercive authority, for ending exploitation:

وَإِن طَائِفَتَانِ مِنَ الْمُؤْمِنِينَ اقْتَتَلُوا فَأَصْلِحُوا بَيْنَهُمَا ۖ فَإِن
بَغَتْ إِحْدَاهُمَا عَلَى الْأُخْرَىٰ فَقَاتِلُوا الَّتِي تَبْغِي حَتَّىٰ تَفِيءَ
إِلَىٰ أَمْرِ اللَّهِ ۚ

"If two parties among the Believers fall into a quarrel, make ye peace between them: but if one of them transgresses beyond bounds against the other then fight ye (all) against the one that transgresses until it complies with the command of Allah....." (XLIX:9).

The first implication of this verse is that which has been given in the previous section.

In its general bearing, it provides also the principle that if a group of Muslims tries to exploit another group, it is the duty of the Islamic State to restrain the exploiters by force.

Prohibition of usury and interest[13], whereby the rich exploit the poor, is a part of Qur'ãnic legislation in this regard.

---

13. See pp. 304-306..

II. Ensuring the economic characteristics of the Muslim society in terms of its being the "balanced community"[14] *by eliminating the evils of poverty as well as the evils of riches*[15] *enjoined:*

The means which the Holy Qur'ãn prescribes, for adoption by the Islamic State, are:

(i) *It propounds the principle that all human beings have equal right to the means of sustenance found on earth,*—and that, consequently, the citizens of the Islamic State have equal right to the means of sustenance found in the State:

هُوَ الَّذِي خَلَقَ لَكُم مَّا فِي الْأَرْضِ جَمِيعًا

"He (Allah) it is Who created for you (i.e., for the benefit of all of you, O mankind!) all that is on the earth." (II:29).

Mark that, according to this verse, no human being has originally any exclusive and absolute right to anything found on the earth.

Again:

وَجَعَلْنَا لَكُمْ فِيهَا مَعَايِشَ وَمَن لَّسْتُمْ لَهُ بِرَازِقِينَ ۝

"And We have provided therein (i.e., in the earth) means of subsistence,—for you and for those for whom ye provide not". (XV:20).

Still again:

وَقَدَّرَ فِيهَا أَقْوَاتَهَا فِي أَرْبَعَةِ أَيَّامٍ سَوَاءً لِّلسَّائِلِينَ ۝

---

14. II: 143, quoted on p. 325.

15. That this is a necessary condition for every social order for being healthy and strong has been referred to in the following verse which emphasises that deviation of the economic order of a community from the "just mean" leads to disaster as regards the very existence of that community. God says:

وَكَمْ أَهْلَكْنَا مِن قَرْيَةٍ بَطِرَتْ مَعِيشَتَهَا

"And how many populations We destroyed, whose way of life and livelihood became reckless (leading to corruption)........." (XXVIII:58).

".....and (Allah) ordained in due proportion therein (i.e., in the earth) the sustenance thereof (for the purpose of fulfilling the requirements of its inhabitants) in four Days: equal for those who seek (to fulfil their needs)". (XLI:10).

(ii) *It lays down the law that value lies in labour*:

أَن لَّيْسَ لِلْإِنسَانِ إِلَّا مَا سَعَىٰ ۝

"That man can have nothing but what he strives for (through labour)". (LIII:39).

(iii) It teaches that God rewards man's labour in full. Hence, *it is the duty of the Islamic State, as the vicegerent of God, to establish an economic order wherein the labour of every citizen is fully rewarded:*

وَأَنَّ سَعْيَهُ سَوْفَ يُرَىٰ ۝ ثُمَّ يُجْزَاهُ الْجَزَاءَ الْأَوْفَىٰ ۝

"And that his (man's) effort will be seen; then he will be repaid for it with fullest payment." (LIII:40, 41).

(iv) *It sets forth the principle that all human beings are equally honourable in respect of their humanity: It has been proclaimed:*

وَلَقَدْ كَرَّمْنَا بَنِي آدَمَ

"Verily We have honoured the children of Adam". (XVII:70).

Hence, it is the duty of the Islamic State, as God's vicegerent, to organise, ensure and promote honourable living and livelihood for all of its citizens.

(v) *It approves*[16] *the right to private property;*

لِلرِّجَالِ نَصِيبٌ مِّمَّا تَرَكَ الْوَالِدَانِ وَالْأَقْرَبُونَ وَلِلنِّسَاءِ نَصِيبٌ مِّمَّا
تَرَكَ الْوَالِدَانِ وَالْأَقْرَبُونَ مِمَّا قَلَّ مِنْهُ أَوْ كَثُرَ ۚ نَصِيبًا مَّفْرُوضًا ۝

16. Let it be noted that the Holy Qur'ān does not make ownership of private property an *obligation*.

"From what is left by parents and those nearest related there is a share for men (to own) and there is a share for women (to own), whether the property be small or large,—a determinate share". (IV:7).

Again:

لِلرِّجَالِ نَصِيبٌ مِّمَّا اكْتَسَبُوا ۖ وَلِلنِّسَاءِ نَصِيبٌ مِّمَّا اكْتَسَبْنَ ۚ

".....To men the benefit of what they earn and to women the benefit of what they earn....." (IV:32).

(vi) *It protects the rights of the owner of private property against violations by others:*

وَلَا تَبْخَسُوا النَّاسَ أَشْيَاءَهُمْ

".....and wrong not mankind in their goods (i.e., possessions)[17]....." (VII:85).

(vii) *It does not, however, permit the institution of private property to promote the evil of concentration of wealth.* Rather, among other measures to which references have been made in the foregoing, it lays down the principle for the division of property among inheritors on a wide scale, by taking into consideration all the male and female categories of near relatives and permitting bequest of one-third property for the welfare of the non-inheritors, so that the Muslim community may remain essentially a community of middle-roaders from the economic point of view.

(See IV:11, 12, etc., where the share of the different beneficiaries in a Muslim's property have been given)[18].

The foregoing makes it evident that the Qur'ãnic point of view steers clear of both: free economy (capitalist) and controlled economy (communist), and prescribes a partially free and partially controlled economy.

---

17. Cf. Prescription of punishments for theft, robbery, etc. (pp. 358-360).

18. Speaking of the Qur'ãnic law of inheritance, Macknaughten observes in the 'Preliminary Remarks' to his *Principles and Presidents of Muhammadan Law";*.......indeed it is difficult to conceive any system containing rules more strictly just and equitable".

In that respect:—

(*a*) it sanctions the right of private ownership;

(*b*) its principle that value lies in labour envisages peasant-proprietorship of agricultural land and forms a condemnation of absentee landlordship;

(*c*) it advocates wages for the labourer commensurate with honourable living;

(*d*) its emphasis on the gifts of nature being meant for all human beings, the right to own mines, water, perennial forests, etc., should belong only to people as a whole, namely, to the State.

(*e*) its emphasis on the principle that wealth should not be permitted to become concentrated in a few hands makes it incumbent that the economic order should be such as to have no room for monopolists of wealth—the industrial barons and the business lords.

Besides these principles, however:

(viii) *It emphasises the Brotherhood of Muslims, as already noted.*

This makes the provision of social security a duty, because a Brotherhood without social security for its members is hardly worth the name.

Provision of social security will have no meaning, however, if the Islamic State does not, side by side with eliminating exploitation in all its forms[19], ensure:

(*a*) the right to work and employment;

(*b*) the right to free choice of profession;

(*c*) the right to decent wages for labour, and the consequent decent living.

These rights are directly traceable in the Holy Prophet's practice in respect of Qur'ãnic Guidance[20].

---

19. Reference has been made to this duty on p. 344.

20. See: Bukhãrî: *Sahîh*, Vol. I., p. 275; *Mishkãt al-Masãbîh*, Vol. I., pp. 242, 290.

(ix) *It:*

(*a*) *ensures economic assistance to those who, for any reason, are incapable of earning their livelihood, through the Welfare Taxes which we have discussed already*[21].

(b) *lays down the principle of spending profusely*[22] *for public good, thereby creating, in the case of the Islamic State, public works,—thus warding off unemployment.*

III. <u>*Provision of basic necessities of life to all the citizens, enjoined*</u>:

This problem has been covered indirectly and in different details in the foregoing. It is a problem of such vital importance, however, that the statement of its positive and direct affirmation by the Holy Qur'ãn is necessary.

In this connection, we have to consider:

(*a*) the Qur'ãnic concept of God;

(*b*) the Qur'ãnic description of the life of Adam and Eve—the parents of humanity—in the Heavenly Garden;

(*c*) the Qur'ãnic promise, given by God, after the Repentance by Adam and Eve, concerning the elimination of fear and sorrow from the lives of human beings, during their sojourn on earth, and the condition thereof.

As to (*a*), the Holy Qur'ãn says:

اَلْحَمْدُ لِلّٰهِ رَبِّ الْعٰلَمِيْنَ ۙ

"Praise be to Allah, the Cherisher and Sustainer of the Worlds." (I:2).

Thus God is the Cherisher and Sustainer of all human beings.

Indeed, He has taken upon Himself the obligation of providing the livelihood, or, basic necessities of life, to all living beings:

وَمَا مِنْ دَآبَّةٍ فِي الْاَرْضِ اِلَّا عَلَى اللّٰهِ رِزْقُهَا

---

21. See: p. 314, *et foll.*

22. See: II:274.

"There is no moving creature on earth but upon Allah is the livelihood thereof." (XI:6).

As to (*b*), the Holy Qur'ãn refers to the basic necessities, provided by God to Adam and Eve in their heavenly Abode, as: food, clothing, health, shelter and education. The holy book says:

وَقُلْنَا يَٰآدَمُ اسْكُنْ اَنْتَ وَزَوْجُكَ الْجَنَّةَ وَكُلَا مِنْهَا رَغَدًا حَيْثُ شِئْتُمَا

"And We said: 'O Adam! dwell thou and thy wife in the Garden (in health and happiness); and eat of the bountiful things therein (in healthy enjoyment) as ye wish." (II:35).

Again:

فَقُلْنَا يَٰآدَمُ اِنَّ هٰذَا عَدُوٌّ لَّكَ وَلِزَوْجِكَ فَلَا يُخْرِجَنَّكُمَا مِنَ الْجَنَّةِ
فَتَشْقٰى ○ اِنَّ لَكَ اَلَّا تَجُوْعَ فِيْهَا وَلَا تَعْرٰى ○ وَاَنَّكَ لَا تَظْمَؤُا
فِيْهَا وَلَا تَضْحٰى ○

"Then We said: 'O Adam! verily, this is an enemy to thee and thy wife: so let him not get you both out of the Garden, so that thou art landed in misery (in many ways, including the problem of suffering in respect of health). There is therein (enough provision) for thee not to go hungry (—food) nor to go naked (—clothing) nor to suffer from thirst (—food nor from the sun's heat (—shelter)." (XX: 117-119).

Still again:

وَعَلَّمَ اٰدَمَ الْاَسْمَآءَ كُلَّهَا

"And He imparted to Adam the knowledge of all things." (II:31).

As to (*c*), God says:

قُلْنَا اهْبِطُوْا مِنْهَا جَمِيْعًا ۚ فَاِمَّا يَاْتِيَنَّكُمْ مِّنِّيْ هُدًى فَمَنْ تَبِعَ هُدَايَ فَلَا خَوْفٌ
عَلَيْهِمْ وَلَا هُمْ يَحْزَنُوْنَ ○

"We said 'Get ye down all together; and if, as is sure, there comes to you Guidance from Me whosoever follows My Guidance, on them shall be no fear, nor shall they grieve!" (II:38).

This verse denotes that proper enforcement of Divine Guidance, which is possible only through State Authority, ensures, to the limit possible under the conditions obtaining on earth, freedom from all fears and sorrows, including the economic fear and sorrow.

This whole discussion brings out that:

The Islamic State, as functioning under the Sovereignty of God, and in the capacity of His vicegerent, and as governed by the Divine Law, is duty-bound to arrange and organise the economics of the state in such a way[23] *that every citizen obtains the basic necessities of life—those necessities being: food, clothing, health, shelter, and education, thereby obtaining all possible immunity from economic fear and sorrow.*

---

23. The provision of basic necessities to every citizen forms such an important part of the Qur'ãnic teaching that even the right of the individual to private ownership of wealth and of private enterprise can be curtailed by the State Authority in case there is no other way to meet that objective, as the eminent jurist Ibn Hazm affirms. (See: *al-Mohallã*, vol. 6, p. 156).

Part III

THE PENAL CODE

There are certain offences against the honour, property and life of the citizens, and against the security of the state, with respect to which the Holy Qur'ãn has ordained punishments[1] that are to be executed by the government of the Islamic State.

The punishments specifically mentioned in the Holy Qur'ãn are:

I. *Punishments pertaining to the interests of the Individuals*:

(i) *Punishments relating to Honour*—in respect of:

(*a*) Slandering of chaste women;

(*b*) Fornication and adultery;

(*c*) Homosexuality.

(ii) *Punishments relating to Property*—in respect of:

(*a*) Theft;

(*b*) Robbery.

(iii) *Punishments relating to Life*—in respect of:

(*a*) Murder:

(*b*) Mutilation.

II. *Punishments pertaining to the interests of the State*:

Treason.

---

1. Punishments for other offences, prescribed by the Islamic Code of Law, are traceable to the *Hadîth* or to the deductions of the Muslim jurists. (See: *al-Tãj al-Jãme 'li al-Usûl*).

Chapter I

PUNISHMENTS PERTAINING TO THE INTERESTS OF THE INDIVIDUAL

1. Punishments Relating to Honour

(a) *In Respect of Slandering of Chaste Women*:

The Holy Qur'ãn says:

والذين يرمون المحصنت ثم لم يأتوا بأربعة شهداء فاجلدوهم
ثمنين جلدة ولا تقبلوا لهم شهادة أبدا وأولئك هم الفسقون ۝ إلا
الذين تابوا من بعد ذلك وأصلحوا فإن الله غفور رحيم ۝

"And those who accuse chaste women (of unchastity), and produce not four witnesses (to support their allegations), flog them with eighty stripes; and reject their evidence ever after; for such men and wicked transgressors;—unless they repent thereafter and mend (their conduct); for Allah is Oft-Forgiving, Most Merciful." (XXIV:4, 5).

Thus, the punishment prescribed is that of:

(i) *flogging the offender with eighty stripes;*

(ii) *deprivation of the civic right of giving evidence—appearing as witness—in a court of law.*

As for the effects of repentance, "Abu Hanifa (the Imam of Hanafi school of Law) considers that neither the stripes nor the incompetence for giving further evidence is cancelled by repentance, but only the spiritual stigma of being 'wicked transgressor'. This of course is the more serious punishment, though it cannot be enforced in the Courts." (A. Yusuf Ali, *op.cit.*, p. 897).

In case the accusation of unchastity is brought by the husband against his wife, the Holy Qur'ãn lays down the following procedure to be observed in a court of law;

والذين يرمون أزواجهم ولم يكن لهم شهداء إلا أنفسهم فشهادة أحدهم
أربع شهدت بالله إنه لمن الصدقين ۝ والخامسة أن لعنت الله عليه إن

كَانَ مِنَ الْكٰذِبِيْنَ ۝ وَيَدْرَؤُا عَنْهَا الْعَذَابَ اَنْ تَشْهَدَ اَرْبَعَ شَهٰدٰتٍۭ بِاللّٰهِ ۙ
اِنَّهٗ لَمِنَ الْكٰذِبِيْنَ ۝ وَالْخَامِسَةَ اَنَّ غَضَبَ اللّٰهِ عَلَيْهَآ اِنْ كَانَ مِنَ
الصّٰدِقِيْنَ ۝

"And for those who launch a charge (of unchastity) against their spouses, and have (in support) no evidence but their own, their solitary evidence (can be received) if they bear witness four times (with an oath) by Allah that they are solemnly telling the truth; and the fifth (oath) should be that they solemnly invoke the curse of Allah on themselves if they tell a lie. But it would avert the punishment from the wife, if she bears witness four times (with an oath) by Allah, that (her husband) is telling a lie; and the fifth (oath) should be that she solemnly invokes the wrath of Allah on herself if (her accuser) is telling the truth." (XXIV:6-9).

Commenting on this Qur'ãnic ordinance, A. Yusuf Ali says: "The case of married persons is different from that of outsiders. If one of them accuses the other of unchastity, the accusation partly reflects on the accuser as well. Moreover, the link which unites married people, even where differences supervene, is sure to act as a steadying influence against the concoction of false charges of unchastity, particularly where divorce is allowed (as in Islam) for reasons other than unchastity. Suppose a husband catches a wife in adultery. In the nature of thing four witnesses—or even one outside witness—would be impossible. Yet after such an experience it is against human nature that he can live a normal married life. The matter is then left to the honour of the two spouses. If the husband can solemnly swear four times to the fact, and in addition invoke a curse on himself if he lies, that is *prima facie* evidence of the wife's guilt. But if the wife swears similarly four times and similarly invokes a curse on herself, she is in law acquitted of the guilt. If she does not take this step, the charge is held proved and the punishment follows. In either case the marriage is dissolved, as it is against human nature that the parties can live together happily after such an incident". (*op.cit*., p. 897).

(b) *__In Respect of Adultery and Fornication__*:

As for illicit sexual relations between man and woman, i.e., adultery and fornication, which are very widespread and devastating evils of the Western civilisation, the Holy Qur'ãn ordains:

اَلزَّانِيَةُ وَالزَّانِيْ فَاجْلِدُوْا كُلَّ وَاحِدٍ مِّنْهُمَا مِائَةَ جَلْدَةٍ ۪ وَّلَا تَاْخُذْكُمْ بِهِمَا
رَاْفَةٌ فِيْ دِيْنِ اللّٰهِ اِنْ كُنْتُمْ تُؤْمِنُوْنَ بِاللّٰهِ وَالْيَوْمِ الْاٰخِرِ ۚ وَلْيَشْهَدْ عَذَابَهُمَا
طَآئِفَةٌ مِّنَ الْمُؤْمِنِيْنَ ○ اَلزَّانِيْ لَا يَنْكِحُ اِلَّا زَانِيَةً اَوْ مُشْرِكَةً ۫ وَّالزَّانِيَةُ
لَا يَنْكِحُهَآ اِلَّا زَانٍ اَوْ مُشْرِكٌ ۚ وَحُرِّمَ ذٰلِكَ عَلَى الْمُؤْمِنِيْنَ ○

"The woman and the man guilty of adultery or fornication, flog each of them with a hundred stripes: Let not compassion move you in their case, in a matter prescribed by Allah, if ye believe in Allah and the Last Day: and let a party of the Believers witness their punishment. Let no man guilty of adultery or fornication marry any but a woman similarly guilty, or an Unbeliever; nor let any but such a man or an Unbeliever marry such a woman; to the Believers such a thing is forbidden."

(XXIV:2, 3).[1]

Thus, the punishment prescribed for adultery and fornication is public flogging of the offenders with a hundred stripes.

Verse 3 speaks of further punishment of debarring those guilty of sexual immorality from establishing the marriage-tie in the circle of the chaste.

(c) *In respect of Homosexuality*[2]:

The Holy Qur'ãn says:

وَالّٰتِيْ يَاْتِيْنَ الْفَاحِشَةَ مِنْ نِّسَآئِكُمْ فَاسْتَشْهِدُوْا عَلَيْهِنَّ اَرْبَعَةً مِّنْكُمْ ۚ فَاِنْ
شَهِدُوْا فَاَمْسِكُوْهُنَّ فِي الْبُيُوْتِ حَتّٰى يَتَوَفّٰىهُنَّ الْمَوْتُ اَوْ يَجْعَلَ اللّٰهُ
لَهُنَّ سَبِيْلًا ○ وَالَّذٰنِ يَاْتِيٰنِهَا مِنْكُمْ فَاٰذُوْهُمَا ۚ فَاِنْ تَابَا وَاَصْلَحَا
فَاَعْرِضُوْا عَنْهُمَا ۗ اِنَّ اللّٰهَ كَانَ تَوَّابًا رَّحِيْمًا ○

"If any of your women are guilty of lewdness, take the evidence of four (reliable) witnesses from amongst you against them; and if they

1. The Holy Qur'ãn takes a very strong view of fornication and adultery, because they seriously damage the social health and because the Qur'ãnic Guidance has already provided such conditions of life as totally nullify the normal incentives to commit such crimes.

2. Mark the severe condemnation of sodomy in VII:81-84, XXIX: 28, etc.

testify, confine them to houses until death do claim them, or Allah ordains for them some (other) way. If two men among you are guilty of lewdness, punish them both. If they repent and amend, leave them alone; for Allah is Oft-Returning, Most Merciful." (IV:15, 16).

Commenting on verse 15, A. Yusuf Ali says: "Most commentators understand this to refer to adultery or fornication; in that case they consider that the punishment was altered to 100 stripes by the later verse XXIV:2. But I think it refers to unnatural crime between women, analogous to unnatural crime between men in verse 16 below; because (1) no punishment is specified here for the man, as would be the case where a man was involved in the crime; (2) the word *al-lãti*, is used for the parties to the crime; (3) the punishment is indefinite.....If we understand the crime to be unnatural crime, we might presume, in the absence of any definite order ("some other way") that the punishment would be similar to that for men in the next verse. That is itself indefinite, and perhaps intentionally so, as the crime is most shameful, and should be unknown in a well regulated society. The maximum punishment would of course be imprisonment for life." (*op.cit.*, pp. 183, 184).

2. Punishments Relating to Property

(a) *In Respect of Theft*:

The Holy Qur'ãn says:

وَالسَّارِقُ وَالسَّارِقَةُ فَاقْطَعُوٓا أَيْدِيَهُمَا جَزَآءًۢ بِمَا كَسَبَا نَكَالًا مِّنَ
اللّٰهِ ۗ وَاللّٰهُ عَزِيزٌ حَكِيمٌ ۝ فَمَنْ تَابَ مِنْۢ بَعْدِ ظُلْمِهٖ وَأَصْلَحَ فَإِنَّ اللّٰهَ
يَتُوبُ عَلَيْهِ ۗ إِنَّ اللّٰهَ غَفُورٌ رَّحِيمٌ ۝

"As to the thief, male or female, cut off (O men of authority) his or her hands[3], a meed for that which they have earned,—an exemplary punishment from Allah; and Allah is Mighty, Wise. Then whosoever

3. "The Canon Law jurists are not unanimous as to the value of the property stolen, which would involve the penalty of the cutting off of the hand. The majority hold that petty thefts are exempt from this punishment. The general opinion is that only one hand should be cut off for the first theft, on the principle that 'if thy hand or thy foot offend thee, cut them off, and cast them from thee' (Matt. XVIII:8). Apparently in the age of Jesus thieves were crucified (Matt. XXVII:38)." (A. Yusuf Ali, *op.cit.*, p. 254).

According to Hanafi school of Islamic Law: a theif's hand shall not be cut off if the value of the thing stolen is less than one dinar, and if two male witnesses

repenteth after his wrongdoing (i.e., returns the stolen goods to, or is forgiven by the owner) and amendeth (his criminal attitude of stealing), verily Allah shall relent towards him. Verily Allah is Forgiving, Merciful."
(V:41, 42,).[4]

(b) *In Respect of Robbery and Bloodshed*:

The Holy Qur'ãn says:

إِنَّمَا جَزَٰٓؤُا الَّذِينَ يُحَارِبُونَ اللّٰهَ وَرَسُولَهُ وَيَسْعَوْنَ فِي الْأَرْضِ
فَسَادًا أَنْ يُقَتَّلُوٓا أَوْ يُصَلَّبُوٓا أَوْ تُقَطَّعَ أَيْدِيهِمْ وَأَرْجُلُهُمْ مِنْ خِلَافٍ
أَوْ يُنْفَوْا مِنَ الْأَرْضِ ۚ ذٰلِكَ لَهُمْ خِزْيٌ فِي الدُّنْيَا وَلَهُمْ فِي
الْاٰخِرَةِ عَذَابٌ عَظِيمٌ ۝ إِلَّا الَّذِينَ تَابُوا مِنْ قَبْلِ أَنْ تَقْدِرُوا
عَلَيْهِمْ ۚ فَاعْلَمُوٓا أَنَّ اللّٰهَ غَفُورٌ رَحِيمٌ ۝

"The punishment of those who wage war against Allah and His Messenger (by violating public security for the establishment of which the Divine law has come) and go about in the land causing corruption (in

---

of good character are not available for testimony. (*Hedaya al-awwalain*, p. 539). Also it "shall not be cut off for the theft of what cannot be guarded, or is not worth guarding, being found in the land in great quantity, such as dry wood, hay grass, reeds, game, fish, lime, etc.; also such articles of food as are quickly perishable, as milk, meat, fresh fruit, etc..... Finally, a thief's hand shall not be cut off if the thing stolen has no conventional value, even though it be otherwise regarded as of great worth." (Roberts: *Social Laws of the Qur'ãn*, p. 93).

4. We might compare this Qur'ãnic ordinance with the Biblical law. There we find that: "If a thief be found breaking up, and be smitten that he die, there shall no blood be shed for him." (*Ex*. 22:2). "If a man be found stealing any of his brethren of the children of Israel, and maketh merchandise of him, or selleth him; then that theif shall die." (*Dt*. 24:7).

In the Hammurabi, the Greek and the Roman codes, as also in the common law of England until recently, theft has been classed as a capital crime of grave nature. (See: *Encyclopaedia Britannica*, XIII, p. 721).

It should be noted that the deterrent effect of this mode of punishment has been very remarkable in all the Muslim lands where it has been enforced, *e.g.*, in Arabia.

It should also be noted that this severe punishment has been prescribed for the members of a society which ensures the provision of the basic human needs to every individual.

terms of robbery and bloodshed) is execution (in case they are guilty of murder), or crucifixion (in case they commit murder and robbery both), or the cutting off of hands and feet from opposite sides (if they commit robbery only), or exile from the land (if the murder or robbery has not yet been committed, but the persons concerned are arrested while on the point of doing so). That is their disgrace in this world, and a heavy punishment awaits them in the Hereafter; except for those who repent before they fall into your power (i.e., prior to their arrest); in that case, know that Allah is Oft-Forgiving, Most Merciful. (He will condone their guilt in respect of the punishment which is to be received in the Hereafter)". (V:36, 37).

Thus, the punishments are:

(*i*) Slaying the offenders, in case murder only has been committed and no robbery has taken place.

(*ii*) Cutting off of the opposite hand and foot of the offender, in case robbery alone has been committed.

(*iii*) Crucifying the offenders, in case both robbery and murder have been committed.

(*iv*) Exiling the offenders, in case they are arrested in the situation of crime before the actual commission.

3. Punishments Relating to Life

(a) *In respect of Murder*:

The Holy Qur'ãn says:

يٰٓاَيُّهَا الَّذِيْنَ اٰمَنُوْا كُتِبَ عَلَيْكُمُ الْقِصَاصُ فِي الْقَتْلٰى ۭ اَلْحُرُّ بِالْحُرِّ
وَالْعَبْدُ بِالْعَبْدِ وَالْاُنْثٰى بِالْاُنْثٰى ۭ فَمَنْ عُفِيَ لَهٗ مِنْ اَخِيْهِ شَيْءٌ
فَاتِّبَاعٌۢ بِالْمَعْرُوْفِ وَاَدَاۗءٌ اِلَيْهِ بِاِحْسَانٍ ۭ ذٰلِكَ تَخْفِيْفٌ مِّنْ رَّبِّكُمْ وَ
رَحْمَةٌ ۭ فَمَنِ اعْتَدٰى بَعْدَ ذٰلِكَ فَلَهٗ عَذَابٌ اَلِيْمٌ ۝ وَلَكُمْ فِي
الْقِصَاصِ حَيٰوةٌ يّٰٓاُولِي الْاَلْبَابِ لَعَلَّكُمْ تَتَّقُوْنَ ۝

"O ye who believe! The Law of Equality is prescribed to you in case of murder: the free for the free, the slave for the slave, the woman for the woman[5]. But if any remission is

---

5. "Our law of equality only takes account of three conditions of civil society: free for free, slave for slave, woman for woman. Among free men or women,

made[6] by the brother (i.e., the heirs of the murdered person), then grant any reasonable demand, and compensate him (in the form of blood-money) with handsome gratitude. This is a concession[7] and a Mercy[8] from your Lord. After this, whoever exceeds the limits shall be in grave penalty. In the Law of Equality there is (saving of) Life to you (as it cuts the roots of endless blood-feuds) o ye men of understanding, that ye may restrain yourselves." (II:178, 179).

---

all are equal: you cannot ask that because a wealthy, or high-born, or influential man is killed, his life is equal to two or three lives among the poor or the lowly. Nor, in cases of murder, can you go into the value or abilities of a slave. A woman is mentioned separately because her position as a mother or an economic worker is different. She does not form a third class but a division of the other two classes. One life having been lost, do not waste many lives in retaliation: at most, let the Law take one life under strictly prescribed conditions, and shut the door to private vengeance or tribal realiation. But if the aggrieved party consents (and this condition of consent is laid down to prevent worse evils), forgiveness and brotherly love is better, and the door of Mercy is kept open." (Abdullah Yusuf Ali, *op.cit.*, p. 70, n. 182).

"According to the Hanafis", says Abdur Rahim, "the life of a slave stands on equal footing with that of a free-man, of woman with that of a man, of a non-Muslim subject with that of a Muslim." (*Muhammadan Jurisprudence*, p. 359).

6. "Islam while recognising retaliation as the basic principle of remedial right, favours compensation as being a principle which is most consistent with the peace and progress of society, and lays down rules for the purpose of confining retaliation within the narrowest possible limit." (Abdur Rahim, *op.cit.*, p. 359).

7. "Retaliation being the right of the person injured or of his heirs, they can compound with the offender for money, or, if they choose, pardon him. Wherever retaliation for murder or hurt is compounded, the money payable as consideration can be realised only from the offender himself. So also when compensation is ordered in cases where there is a doubt as to the wilful nature of the homicide. Similarly when the hurt caused has not resulted in death, the wrongdoer alone can be called upon to pay compensation. But when death has been caused by negligence or mistake, the offender's Akilas, that is his tribe or regiment, or the inhabitants of the town to which he belongs, are to pay the blood-money to the heirs of the deceased. The reason is that it is the duty of a persons' Akilas to watch over his conduct and the law presumes that the wrongdoer would not have acted in the way he did unless they neglected their duty." (Abdur Rahim, *op.cit.*, p. 359).

8. "The law, though it recognises retaliation in theory, discourages this form of remedy in every possible way. For example, if there be the least doubt as to the wilful character of the offence or the proof, retaliation will not be ordered." (Abdur Rahim, *op.cit.*, p. 359).

There are two points contained in these verses:

(*a*) Punishment for murder is the taking of the murderer's life.

(*b*) If, however, the heirs of the murdered person agree without any compulsion, the law of mercy can be allowed to operate on the basis of reasonable monetary compensation to the heirs,—that with a view to ward off worse evils;—and the government will allow it.

(b) *<u>In Respect of Mutilation</u>:*

The Holy Qur'ãn says:

وَكَتَبْنَا عَلَيْهِمْ فِيهَا أَنَّ النَّفْسَ بِالنَّفْسِ وَالْعَيْنَ بِالْعَيْنِ وَالْأَنْفَ
بِالْأَنْفِ وَالْأُذُنَ بِالْأُذُنِ وَالسِّنَّ بِالسِّنِّ وَالْجُرُوحَ قِصَاصٌ
فَمَنْ تَصَدَّقَ بِهِ فَهُوَ كَفَّارَةٌ لَهُ وَمَنْ لَمْ يَحْكُمْ بِمَا أَنْزَلَ اللَّهُ
فَأُولَٰئِكَ هُمُ الظَّالِمُونَ ○

"We ordained therein for them: 'Life for life, eye for eye, nose for nose, ear for ear, tooth for tooth, and wounds equal for equal. But if any one remits the retaliation by way of charity, it is an act of atonement for himself. And if any fail to judge by (the light of) what Allah hath revealed, they are (no better them) wrongdoers." (V: 48)[9]

This verse prescribes the Law of Equality in connection with murder as well as in respect to loss of, or damage to, the limbs of the human body caused by one person to another.

However, as in the case of murder, the permission of foregoing, in the interest of moral excellence, the right of demanding the enforcement of the Law of Equality has been given to the aggrieved party.

---

9. We may note with advantage the comments of A. Yusuf Ali on this verse. He says: "The retaliation is prescribed in three places in the *Pentateuch*, viz., *Exod*: XXI:23-25; *Leviticus* XXIV:8-21, and *Deut*. XIX:21. The wording in the three quotations is different. But in none of them is found the additional rider for mercy, as here. Note that in Matt. v: 38, Jesus quotes the Old Law 'eye for eye', etc., and modifies it in the direction of forgiveness, but the Qur'ãnic injunction is more practical. This appeal for Mercy is as between man and man in the spiritual world. Even where the injured one forgives the State or Ruler is competent to take such action as is necessary for the preservation of law and order in Society. For crime has a bearing that goes beyond the interests of the person injured: the Community is affected (See Q. V: 35)." (*op cit*., p. 25).

Chapter II

PUNISHMENTS PERTAINING TO THE INTERESTS OF THE STATE

Treason

Concerning the crime of treason, the Holy Qur'ãn says:

إِنَّمَا جَزٰٓؤُا الَّذِيْنَ يُحَارِبُوْنَ اللّٰهَ وَ رَسُوْلَهٗ وَ يَسْعَوْنَ فِي الْاَرْضِ
فَسَادًا اَنْ يُّقَتَّلُوْٓا اَوْ يُصَلَّبُوْٓا اَوْ تُقَطَّعَ اَيْدِيْهِمْ وَ اَرْجُلُهُمْ مِّنْ خِلَافٍ
اَوْ يُنْفَوْا مِنَ الْاَرْضِ ؕ ذٰلِكَ لَهُمْ خِزْيٌ فِي الدُّنْيَا وَ لَهُمْ فِي
الْاٰخِرَةِ عَذَابٌ عَظِيْمٌ ۝ اِلَّا الَّذِيْنَ تَابُوْا مِنْ قَبْلِ اَنْ تَقْدِرُوْا
عَلَيْهِمْ ۚ فَاعْلَمُوْٓا اَنَّ اللّٰهَ غَفُوْرٌ رَّحِيْمٌ ۝

"The punishment of those who wage war against Allah and His Messenger (in respect of endangering the security of the State established under the Divine Law) and strive with might and main for mischief through the land, is: execution, or crucifixion, or the cutting off of hands and feet from opposite sides, or exile from the land: that is their disgrace in this world, and a heavy punishment is theirs in the Hereafter; except for those who repent before they fall into your power: in that case, know that Allah is Oft-Forgiving, Most Merciful." (V:36, 37).

A. Yusuf Ali comments on this verse thus: "For the double crime of treason against the State, combined with treason against Allah, as shown by overt crimes, four alternative punishments are mentioned, any one of which is to be applied according to circumstances: viz., execution (cutting off of the head), crucifixion, maiming, or exile. These were features of the Criminal Law then and for centuries afterwards, except that tortures such as 'hanging, drawing, and quartering' in English Law, and piercing of eyes and leaving the unfortunate victim exposed to a tropical sun, which was practised in Arabia, and all such tortures, were abolished. In any case sincere repentance, before it was too late, was recognised as a ground of mercy."[1] (*op.cit.*, p. 252).

---

1. It may be noted that the law of treason must, in the very nature of the case, be of a severe type. As to 'drawing and quartering', prescribed in the English Criminal Code of the past and mentioned by A. Yusuf Ali, such punishment

was "inflicted on those found guilty of high treason touching the king's person or government. The person committed was usually drawn on a sledge to the place of execution: there he was hung by the neck from a scaffold, being cut down and disembowelled, while still alive: his head then was cut from his body and his corpse divided into four quarters. ......In the reign of Henry III and Edward I there is abundant evidence that death was the common punishment for felony; and this continued to be the law of the land as to treason and as to all felonies, except petty larceny, down to the year 1826". (Stephen: *History of the Criminal Law of England*, I, p. 458).